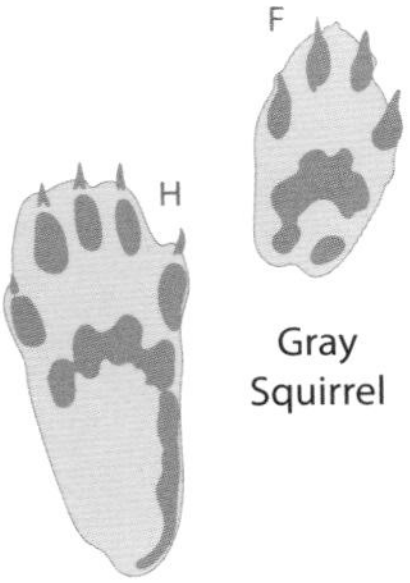
F
H

1 in.

Pg. 302

Gray Squirrel

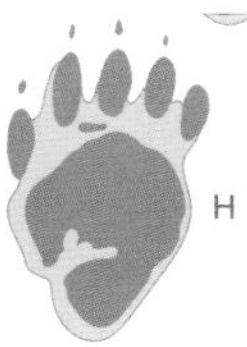
H

Striped Skunk

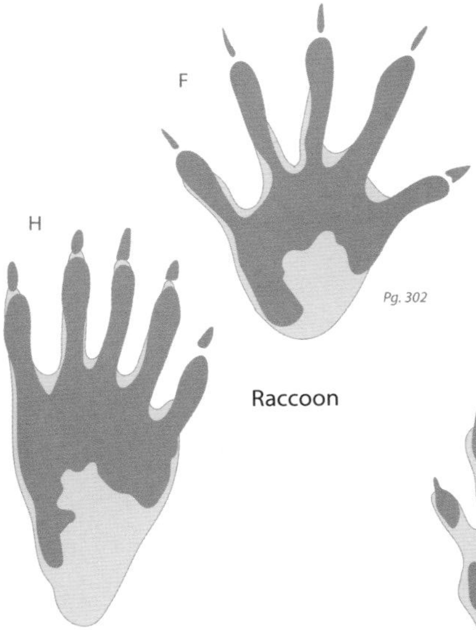
F
H

2.5 in.

Pg. 302

Raccoon

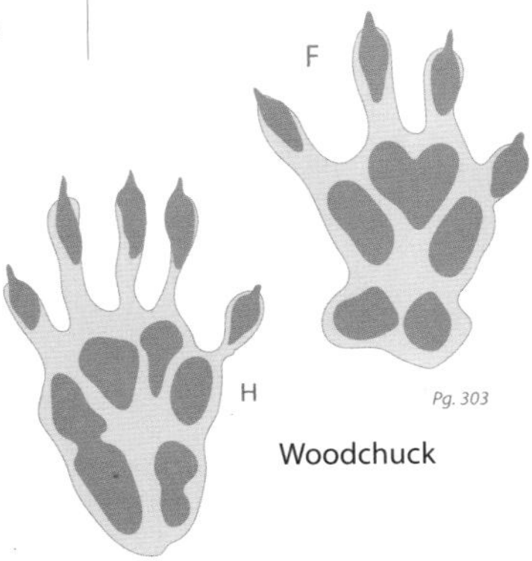
F
H

2.5 in.

Pg. 303

Woodchuck

2 in.

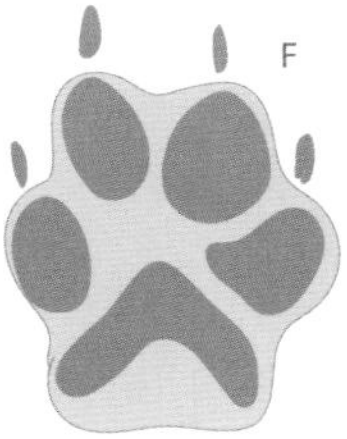
F

Pg. 257, 303

Red Fox

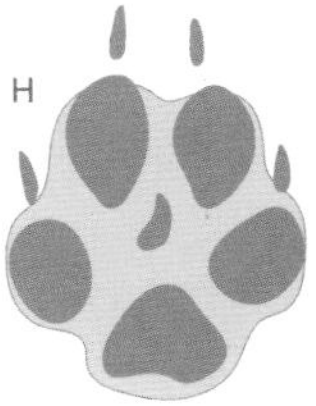
H

3 in.

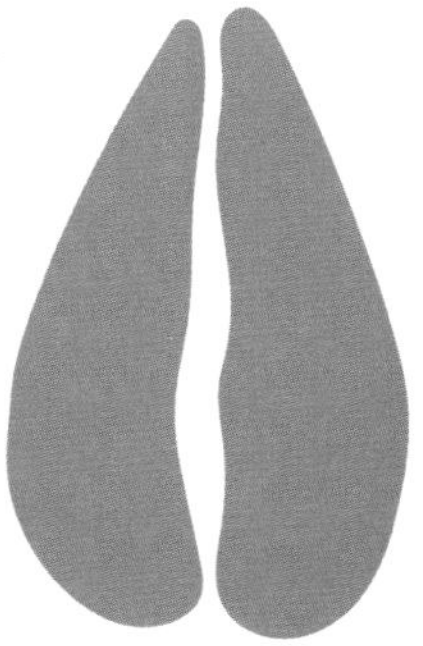

White-tailed Deer

Pg. 302

A Field Guide to the

MID-ATLANTIC COAST

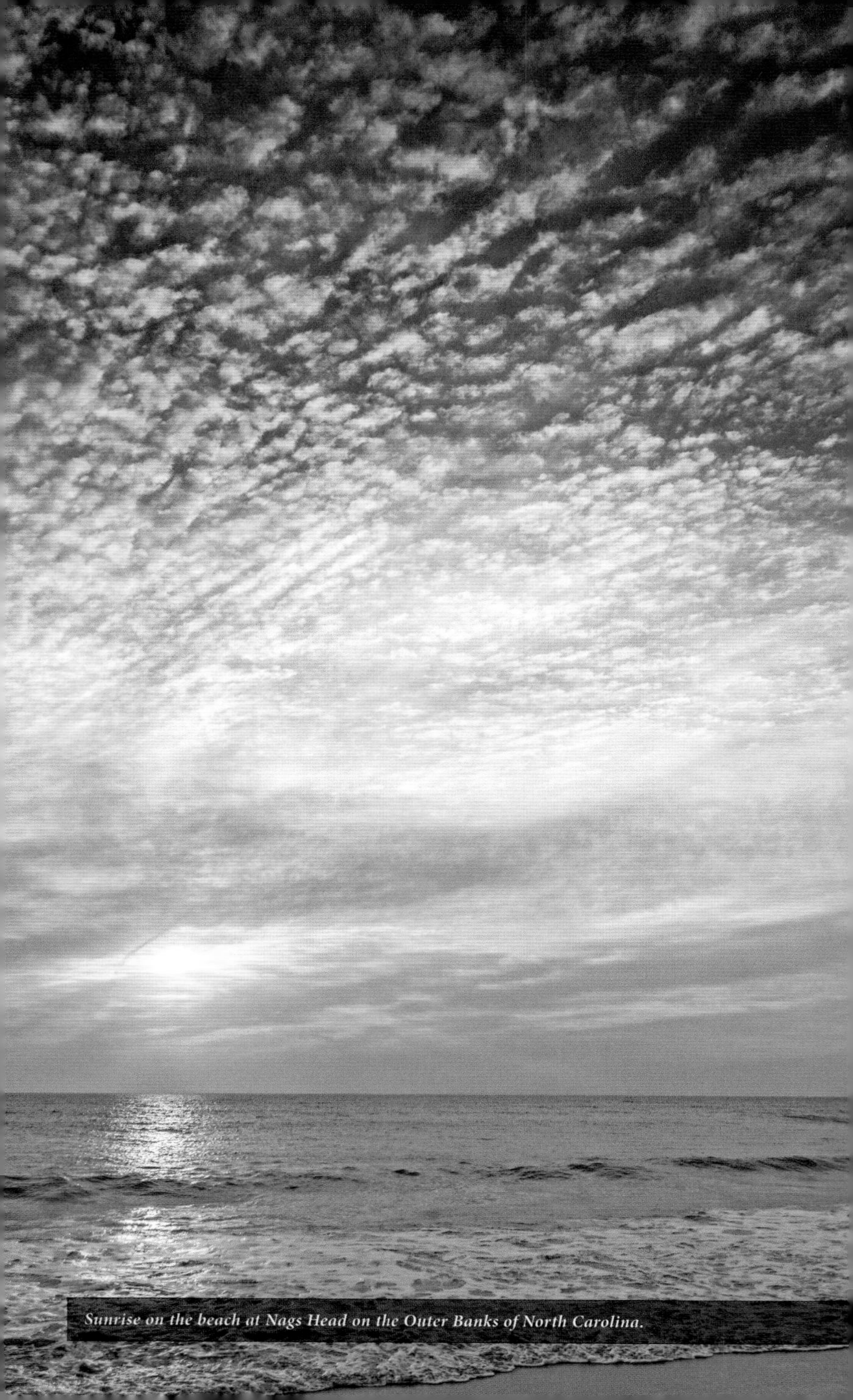

Sunrise on the beach at Nags Head on the Outer Banks of North Carolina.

A Field Guide to the

MID-ATLANTIC COAST

INCLUDING THE JERSEY SHORE, CAPE MAY, DELAWARE BAY, THE DELMARVA PENINSULA, & THE OUTER BANKS

PATRICK J. LYNCH

All illustrations, maps, & photography by the author unless otherwise noted

Yale
UNIVERSITY
PRESS

To Susan, my best friend

coastfieldguides.com

Yale University Press books may be purchased in quantity for educational, business, or promotional use. For information, please e-mail sales.press@yale.edu (US office) or sales@yaleup.co.uk (UK office).

Designed by Patrick J. Lynch.

Printed in China.

ISBN 978-0-300-24646-9

Library of Congress Control Number: 2020941592

This paper meets the requirements of ANSI/NISO Z39.48-1992 (Permanence of Paper).

10 9 8 7 6 5 4 3 2 1

CONTENTS

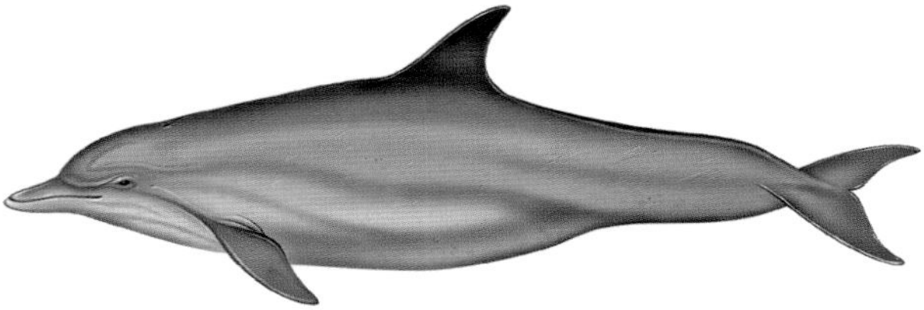

Lighthouse Pond West in Cape May Point State Park, New Jersey. The pond and surrounding woodland paths offer some of the best migration birding on the East Coast.

During many trips to the Atlantic Coast over the past 40 years I have benefited from the good company and deep birding and natural history expertise of Frank Gallo. Thanks, Frank, for all the great times, and for dragging me to those wonderful out-of-the-way birding spots, many of which enrich this book.

I'd like to thank Patrick Comins, executive director of Connecticut Audubon, for his great advice and thorough review on my *Field Guide to Long Island Sound,* much of which also informs this book.

I thank Mark Bertness of Brown University for his detailed review of the manuscript and many helpful suggestions and corrections. I thank Ralph Lewis, professor of geology at the University of Connecticut Avery Point campus and former State Geologist of Connecticut. Ralph went above and beyond in sharing his expertise on the East Coast's complex geologic history, particularly on the Wisconsinan Glaciation.

I offer particular thanks to Jean Thomson Black, senior executive editor for life sciences at Yale University Press, for her faith in my work over the years and for being my constant advocate at the Press. I also thank the manuscript editor on this project, Laura Jones Dooley, for her wisdom, expertise, and guidance on every page here.

I also thank my teacher, mentor, and friend, the late Noble Proctor, for his 43 years of wise counsel, for countless days of great birding and whale watching, and for introducing me to advanced birding and natural history. I know that I and Noble's hundreds of friends throughout the world miss his good humor, sharp eyes, and awesome breadth of knowledge about the natural world. This book would not exist without Noble's decades of wisdom and support.

Most of all I thank my wife, Susan Grajek, my mentor, muse, wise woman, and best friend. I literally could not have done it without you.

Pat Lynch

North Haven, Connecticut

coastfieldguides.com
@patrlynch
https://www.facebook.com/patrick.lynch1
patrlynch1@gmail.com

The salt marsh edge near the Life of the Marsh boardwalk at Assateague Island National Seashore, Maryland. The Black Cherry at the right is losing its battle against saltwater intrusion and the effects of sea level rise.

This book is a general introduction to the natural history of the Mid-Atlantic Coast, from Sandy Hook in New Jersey south to Cape Hatteras on the Outer Banks of North Carolina. I have organized the book around environments, not on particular locations. Although my focus is on the plants, animals, and physical foundations of this region, you cannot write about the natural world these days without constant reference to the effects of environmental history and anthropogenic climate change. We live in the Anthropocene Epoch: human activity and climate change have become the dominant forces that shape our geophysical and biological environments.

The geologic and human history of this region also remind us that we live on shifting ground. Sea level rise and evolving coastlines are nothing new, but the accelerating pace of climate change in the past 50 years has altered both our shorelines and the life around the region. Many places along the ocean and estuary shores are already facing crises of rising seas and the increasing severity of coastal storms. Here my emphasis is on the growing physical effects of climate change on natural environments. Once you know the subtle but already pervasive signs of warming and sea level rise along our coasts, you see the changes everywhere.

This guide cannot be an exhaustive catalog of everything that lives in or near the shores of this region—such a book would be neither practical as a field guide nor very useful to the typical hiker, birder, kayaker, fisher, or boater. Here I have emphasized the most dominant and common plants and animals, plus a few interesting rarities like the Snowy Owl and locally threatened species like the Least Tern and the Piping Plover. My intent is to show you the major plants and animals that populate our coastal environments, so that you can walk into a salt marsh or onto a beach and be able to identify much of what you see, the first step in developing a deeper, more ecological understanding of the unique and beautiful aspects of the Mid-Atlantic Coast.

For recommended field guides to plants, wildflowers, geology, birding, insects, and other natural history topics, please see the works listed in Further Reading.

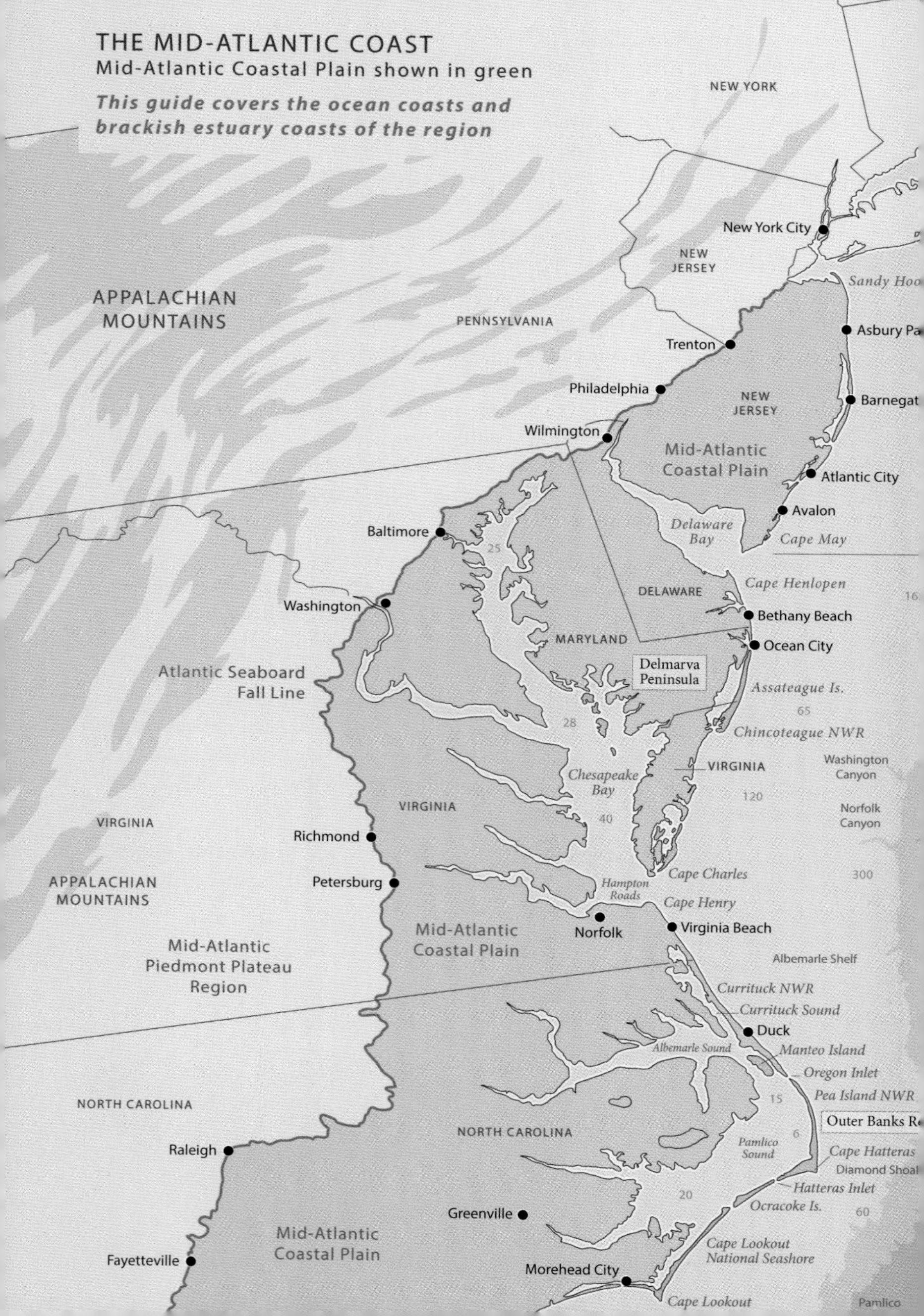
THE MID-ATLANTIC COAST
Mid-Atlantic Coastal Plain shown in green
This guide covers the ocean coasts and brackish estuary coasts of the region
NEW YORK
New York City
NEW JERSEY
Sandy Hoo
APPALACHIAN MOUNTAINS
PENNSYLVANIA
Asbury Pa
Trenton
Philadelphia
NEW JERSEY
Barnegat
Wilmington
Mid-Atlantic Coastal Plain
Atlantic City
Avalon
Baltimore
Delaware Bay
Cape May
25
DELAWARE
Cape Henlopen
16
Washington
Bethany Beach
MARYLAND
Ocean City
Atlantic Seaboard Fall Line
Delmarva Peninsula
Assateague Is.
65
28
Chincoteague NWR
VIRGINIA
Washington Canyon
Chesapeake Bay
VIRGINIA
120
Norfolk Canyon
VIRGINIA
40
Richmond
Cape Charles
300
APPALACHIAN MOUNTAINS
Petersburg
Hampton Roads
Cape Henry
Norfolk
Virginia Beach
Mid-Atlantic Coastal Plain
Mid-Atlantic Piedmont Plateau Region
Albemarle Shelf
Currituck NWR
Currituck Sound
Duck
Albemarle Sound
Manteo Island
Oregon Inlet
NORTH CAROLINA
15
Pea Island NWR
Outer Banks R
NORTH CAROLINA
Pamlico Sound
6
Raleigh
Cape Hatteras
Diamond Shoal
20
Hatteras Inlet
Ocracoke Is.
60
Greenville
Mid-Atlantic Coastal Plain
Cape Lookout National Seashore
Fayetteville
Morehead City
Cape Lookout
Pamlico

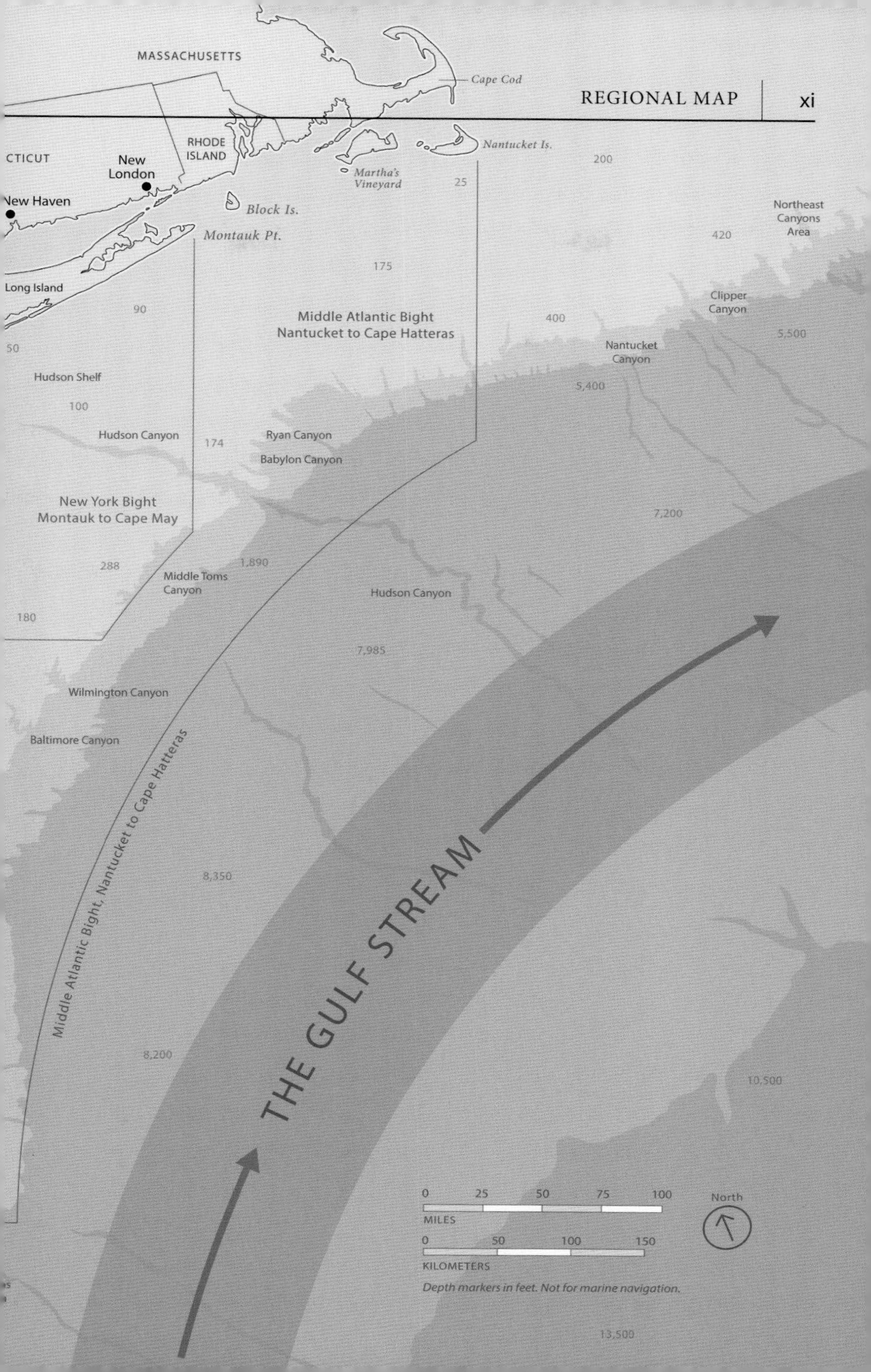
MASSACHUSETTS
Cape Cod
RHODE ISLAND
CTICUT
New London
New Haven
Nantucket Is.
Martha's Vineyard
Block Is.
Montauk Pt.
Long Island
200
25
175
Northeast Canyons Area
420
90
Middle Atlantic Bight
Nantucket to Cape Hatteras
400
Clipper Canyon
5,500
50
Nantucket Canyon
Hudson Shelf
5,400
100
Hudson Canyon
174
Ryan Canyon
Babylon Canyon
New York Bight
Montauk to Cape May
7,200
288
1,890
Middle Toms Canyon
Hudson Canyon
180
7,985
Wilmington Canyon
Baltimore Canyon
Middle Atlantic Bight, Nantucket to Cape Hatteras
8,350
THE GULF STREAM
8,200
10,500
0 25 50 75 100
MILES
0 50 100 150
KILOMETERS
North
Depth markers in feet. Not for marine navigation.
13,500

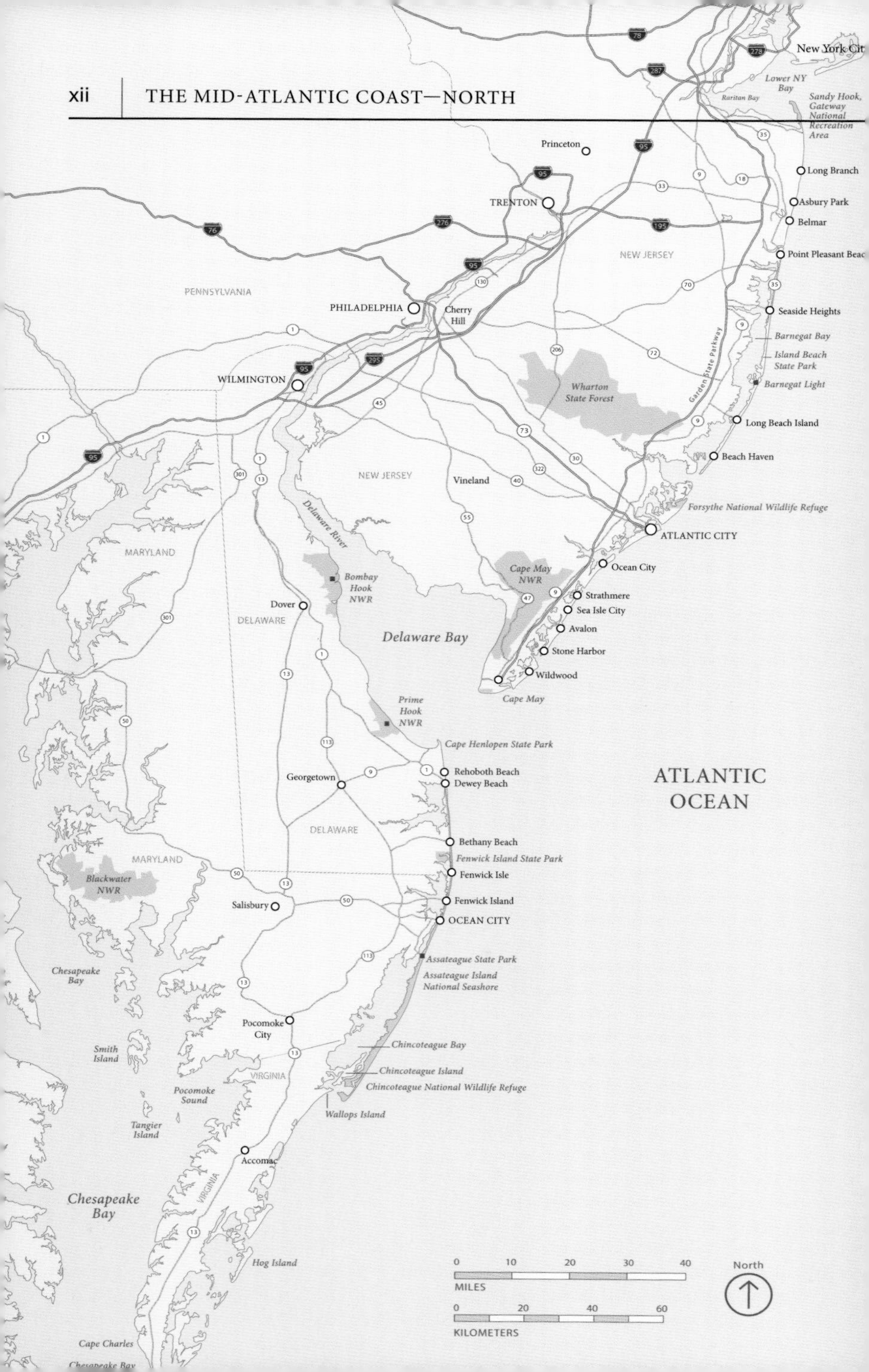
New York City
Lower NY Bay
Raritan Bay
Sandy Hook, Gateway National Recreation Area
Princeton
Long Branch
TRENTON
Asbury Park
Belmar
NEW JERSEY
Point Pleasant Beach
PENNSYLVANIA
PHILADELPHIA
Cherry Hill
Seaside Heights
Barnegat Bay
Island Beach State Park
Barnegat Light
Garden State Parkway
WILMINGTON
Wharton State Forest
Long Beach Island
Beach Haven
NEW JERSEY
Vineland
Forsythe National Wildlife Refuge
ATLANTIC CITY
Delaware River
MARYLAND
Ocean City
Cape May NWR
Bombay Hook NWR
Strathmere
Dover
Sea Isle City
DELAWARE
Delaware Bay
Avalon
Stone Harbor
Wildwood
Cape May
Prime Hook NWR
Cape Henlopen State Park
Georgetown
Rehoboth Beach
Dewey Beach
ATLANTIC OCEAN
DELAWARE
Bethany Beach
MARYLAND
Fenwick Island State Park
Blackwater NWR
Fenwick Isle
Salisbury
Fenwick Island
OCEAN CITY
Assateague State Park
Assateague Island National Seashore
Chesapeake Bay
Pocomoke City
Chincoteague Bay
Smith Island
VIRGINIA
Chincoteague Island
Chincoteague National Wildlife Refuge
Pocomoke Sound
Wallops Island
Tangier Island
Accomac
VIRGINIA
Chesapeake Bay
Hog Island
0 10 20 30 40
MILES
0 20 40 60
KILOMETERS
North
Cape Charles

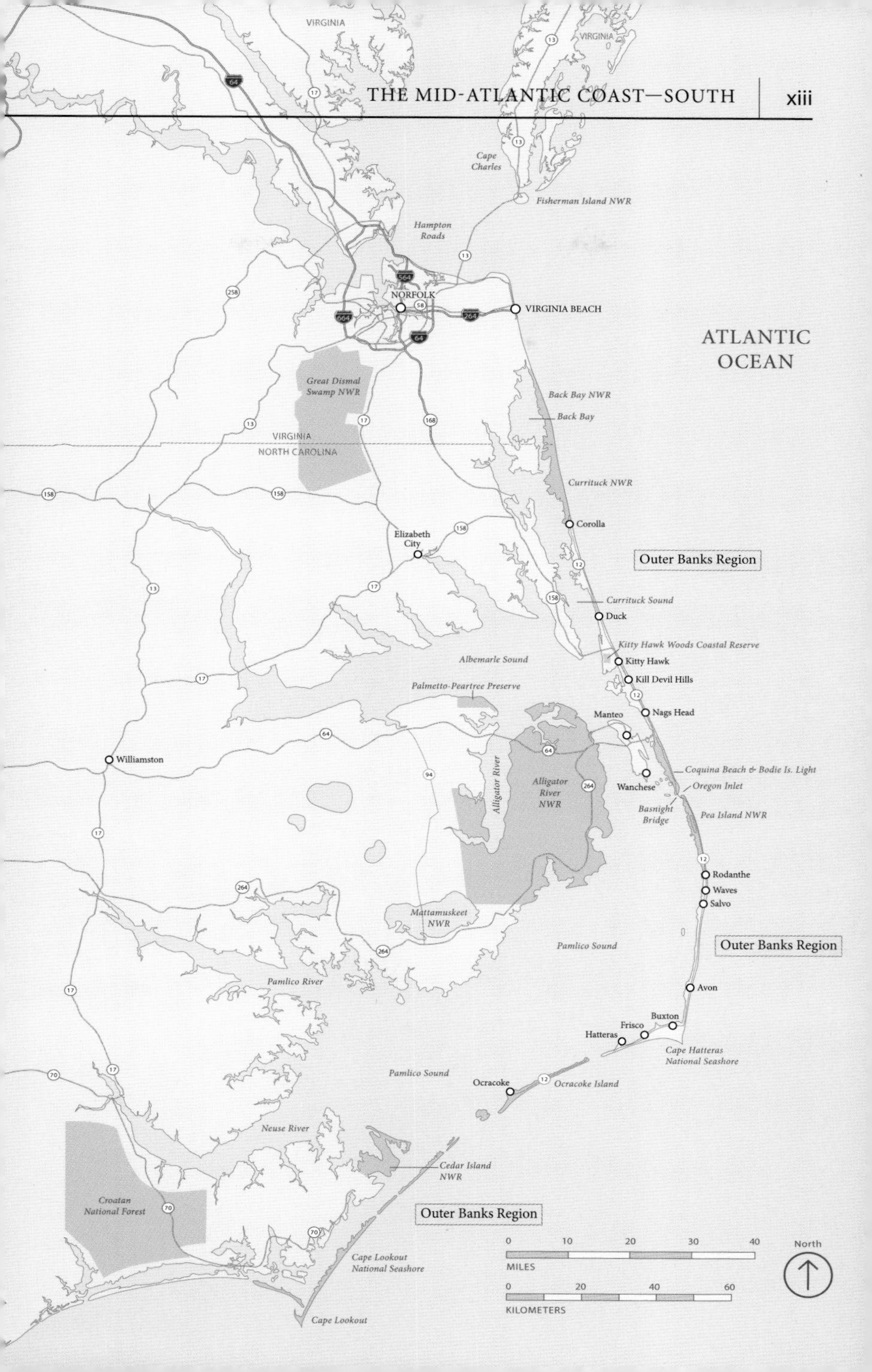
VIRGINIA
Cape Charles
Fisherman Island NWR
Hampton Roads
NORFOLK
VIRGINIA BEACH
ATLANTIC OCEAN
Great Dismal Swamp NWR
Back Bay NWR
Back Bay
VIRGINIA
NORTH CAROLINA
Currituck NWR
Corolla
Elizabeth City
Outer Banks Region
Currituck Sound
Duck
Kitty Hawk Woods Coastal Reserve
Albemarle Sound
Kitty Hawk
Kill Devil Hills
Palmetto-Peartree Preserve
Manteo
Nags Head
Williamston
Alligator River
Alligator River NWR
Wanchese
Coquina Beach & Bodie Is. Light
Oregon Inlet
Basnight Bridge
Pea Island NWR
Rodanthe
Waves
Salvo
Mattamuskeet NWR
Pamlico Sound
Outer Banks Region
Pamlico River
Avon
Buxton
Frisco
Hatteras
Cape Hatteras National Seashore
Pamlico Sound
Ocracoke
Ocracoke Island
Neuse River
Cedar Island NWR
Croatan National Forest
Outer Banks Region
Cape Lookout National Seashore
Cape Lookout
0 10 20 30 40
MILES
0 20 40 60
KILOMETERS
North

Introduction

Salt marsh at Assateague Island National Seashore, Maryland.

This is a guide to the natural history of the Mid-Atlantic Coast—the sandy, ocean-facing islands, peninsulas, and mainland beaches, as well as the more oceanic portions of bays and inlets near the coast. This book describes the principal habitats of the region: barrier islands, beaches, dunes, salt marshes, estuaries, and maritime forests near the shoreline. Ecologists call these coastal environments littoral zones—wild habitats directly under the influence of ocean wind, waves, saltwater tides, and salt aerosols (salt spray).

The plants and animals that make up our wild environments do not live in a dimension separate from human activity. Even the wildest, most remote areas of the Atlantic Coast exist within the Anthropocene Epoch of human domination of earth's ecology. This book presents the predominant environments and organisms, along with reminders that the landscape and animals we see in nature are the survivors of centuries of interactions with humanity. This is a guide to the "how and why" of the coast as it exists today, not just a natural history catalog of the "what."

The Mid-Atlantic Coast is unique in North American geography, both in its ancient and complex geology and in the vast estuarine environments of the Chesapeake Bay, Delaware Bay, and Albemarle and Pamlico Sounds behind North Carolina's Outer Banks. These coasts are low in relief and were formed over the past 100 million years of slow erosion from the ancient Appalachian Mountains. The massive ice sheet of the Wisconsinan Glaciation (our most recent ice age, 25,000 years ago) never reached south of New Jersey's Sandy Hook, but sea levels over the past 2 million years have been 400 feet lower than today, as well as more than 200 feet higher. The Mid-Atlantic Coastal Plain slopes gently from the rocky Piedmont foothills of the Appalachians down to sea level. Beyond the water line, the broad continental shelf slopes gradually 20–30 miles offshore, reaching a depth of about 600 feet before plunging into the Atlantic abyssal plain. Twenty-five thousand years ago, when the ocean was 400 feet lower than now, the continental shelf was dry land and the Mid-Atlantic Coastal Plain was twice as wide as it is today (see map, pp. 20–21).

Our major rivers are ancient as well. When sea levels were much lower, the Delaware, Susquehanna, Potomac, James, Chowan, and Pamlico Rivers cut deep valleys into the Eastern Coastal Plain. As sea levels rose when the earth warmed after the Wisconsinan Glaciation, the ancient river valleys flooded, giving us our significant bays and estuaries. Today, northern rivers such as the Delaware and Susquehanna flow swiftly down bedrock gorges in the Appalachians, car-

The beautiful brackish marshes of the Currituck Banks Reserve on the Outer Banks in Corolla, North Carolina. These marshes are dominated by Black Needlerush, along with Big Cordgrass and Olney's Three-Square Bulrush.

rying little sediment. Southern rivers like the Potomac, James, Pamlico, and Neuse have slower flow rates across the board-flat Mid-Atlantic Coastal Plain and typically carry large sediment loads that settle out into the Chesapeake Bay and Pamlico Sound. The vast sand supplies that lie on the continental shelf derive from past ages. Today's rivers empty into large estuaries or into bays and sounds between barrier islands and the mainland, and very little river sediment reaches the ocean.

The mature flower heads of Big Cordgrass (*Spartina cynosuroides*), which can grow to heights of six to seven feet at the wet edges of brackish creeks and marshes.

The earth's crust beneath the Mid-Atlantic Coast is still subsiding as a consequence of the last glacial period. At the peak of the Wisconsinan Glaciation, much of New England lay under a blanket of ice up to two miles thick. As the enormous weight of the glacial ice pushed the earth's crust downward under New York and New England, the crust of the Mid-Atlantic Coast, like a giant seesaw, rose several feet. When the Wisconsinan glacier melted and eased the load on New England, the crust that was trapped under ice began to rebound upward, and the Mid-Atlantic started to sink. This ancient tilt and rebound have worsened the state of sea level rise all along the Mid-Atlantic Coast: the land is sinking even as the sea level is rising at a faster rate (see illustration, p. 73).

Pitch Pine *(Pinus rigida)*, the dominant maritime forest tree from Cape Cod, Massachusetts, south to Cape May, New Jersey.

The long, narrow barrier islands and peninsulas that make up most of the Mid-Atlantic Coast owe their existence to the relatively moderate tide ranges in the region (see illustration, p. 68). Two other elements combine to produce the world's longest stretch of sandy coastal barriers: the steady rise of sea levels over the past 25,000 years and the enormous supplies of sand that lie on the continental shelf.

A transitional coast

The Mid-Atlantic Coast is a realm of transitions. This region includes several terrestrial ecoregions, from the cool, glacier-created coast of southern Long Island, New York, to the near-tropical Live Oak and Saw Palmetto forests near Cape Hatteras. In winter on the Jersey Shore, you can watch Harlequin Ducks from the Arctic swim in the frigid waters of Barnegat Inlet, a scene reminiscent of the rocky coast of Maine. On the Outer Banks of North Carolina, there are Live Oak forests draped with Spanish Moss, much like you'd see in the Georgia Sea Islands or northern Florida, and the tropical-looking White Ibis becomes common. The roughly 400 miles of coastline from New Jersey's Sandy Hook to Cape Hatteras in North Carolina transitions from Northern Coastal Forest and Atlantic Coast Pine Barrens to the milder realm of the Middle Atlantic Coastal Forest.

This Pitch Pine–dominated maritime forest habitat stretches from the Provincelands of northern Cape Cod and nearby islands through New York's eastern Long Island to the Jersey Shore. These forests have nutrient-poor sandy soils and the constant threat of forest fires. Pitch Pines are particularly resistant to fire damage and thus dominate the habitat. Pine Barrens forests typically have an understory of acid-loving plants like Highbush and Lowbush Blueberry, Northern Bayberry, and Bear Oak. A very similar maritime forest continues south from the Delaware Bay, but along the Delmarva Peninsula and the Outer Banks, Loblolly Pines replace Pitch Pines, and Wax Myrtle gradually replaces Northern Bayberry.

The huge duck and goose flocks of the Chesapeake and Delaware Bays are both an ancient wonder and a modern phenomenon. Before Europeans arrived in the region, the duck and geese flocks of the Chesapeake must have been stunning in the sheer number and variety of birds. Sadly, market gunning in the late 1800s reduced once-common duck species like the gorgeous Canvasback to near extinction in the region. Today's Chesapeake duck population is recovering with protection and habitat management. The huge Mid-Atlantic flocks of Canada Geese and Snow Geese also thrive under protection from indiscriminate hunting. Agricultural practices further benefit the geese. Modern corn harvesting machinery leaves a large amount of grain in the bare fields, providing the geese with almost unlimited supplies of food in winter. Modern farming techniques also use huge amounts of nitrogen and other fertilizers. Wastage from the massive corn crops feeds the geese but pollutes the Chesapeake Bay and other estuaries and kills marine life. The unnaturally large numbers of geese also damage wild environments through their constant grubbing and trampling of the soil, and their huge amounts of fecal matter contaminate local waters.

Canvasback (*Aythya valisineria*), the most regal of all the diving ducks, was once abundant in Mid-Atlantic coastal waters but was indiscriminately hunted almost to local extirpation by market gunners in the late 1800s. Today Canvasback populations have partially recovered.

Harlequin Ducks are marine diving birds that specialize in rocky bottom areas, particularly near fast-flowing inlets. One of the few places you can regularly see Harlequins south of the Gulf of Maine is in winter at Barnegat Inlet on the Jersey Shore. There the birds feed on small fish and bottom invertebrates along the massive rock jetties that flank the inlet channel.

Harlequin Duck
Histrionicus histrionicus

A flooding coast

Low, sandy ocean coasts have always been restless places, evolving with the winds and tides, and constantly subject to ocean storms. Due to anthropogenic climate change (driven by human activity), however, the current rates of global warming are unprecedented in human history. In general, climate zones migrate northward about 35–50 miles for every 1 degree Celsius rise in average temperature. At present, the earth has warmed by a little more than 1 degree Celsius over preindustrial levels. Estimates of climate warming on the distribution of marine fish show populations moving north about 10 miles per decade. The waters of the Mid-Atlantic Coast, because of complex interactions with the Gulf Stream and other ocean currents, are

Sea level rise and the increased flooding of salt marshes has endangered one of our rarest sparrow species, the Saltmarsh Sparrow (*Ammodramus caudacutus*). These sparrows must complete the nesting cycle from egg-laying to mobile chicks in between the twice-monthly spring tides. Higher water shortens the time even further and often results in flooded nests and dead chicks.

Nest photo courtesy of biologist Jeanna Mielcarek.

A vibrant salt marsh creek in Chincoteague National Wildlife Refuge at the southern end of Assateague Island, Virginia.

rising in temperature at twice the global average, about 0.5 degree Celsius per decade from 1982 to 2006.

Changes in climate and sea levels that used to take millennia are now happening in mere decades—far too fast for natural systems to keep up. Our fundamental paradigms about nature healing itself are no longer valid. We are now well past the point where simply "leaving nature alone" would allow the damage we've done to restore itself in the time frame of a human life.

Our most productive and beneficial coastal habitat is already suffering. Salt marshes are among the most fertile and essential environments on earth, but the vast wetlands that make the Mid-Atlantic Coast so distinctive are sustaining damage caused by sea level rise. The higher waters erode the banks of marshes, washing them away. Powerful storms tear away huge chunks of marsh every year, lessening their capacity to buffer our coasts. Marshes are also the nurseries and habitats for most of our commercial seafood and sport fish. This rapid evolution of climate and sea level has wrought havoc on the bird and animal life of marshes as well.

Salt marsh and maritime forest at Assateague Island National Seashore, Maryland.

A ghost forest at the edge of a salt marsh at Chincoteague National Wildlife Refuge, Virginia. Here saltwater infiltration at the edge of the forest has killed a grove of Loblolly Pines (*Pinus taeda*), leaving only their dead trunks at the marsh edge. As the sea level rises, what was once high ground becomes salty, and the marsh extends into what was formerly forest.

Severely endangered birds such as the Saltmarsh Sparrow will likely disappear in the next few decades as their home marshes flood.

We are entering a critical time for both the built environments of the coastline and the wild environments that remain on our shores. The coming decades will be a severe test of our commitments, both to the social costs of retreating from rising seas and to our dedication to preserving a place in our world for natural environments. The current record levels of carbon dioxide in earth's atmosphere are not an ugly legacy of the early industrial age. This is a crisis caused mostly by people who are alive today. Half the carbon dioxide and other emissions that cause global warming were emitted in just the past 30 years. We did this to ourselves and to the wild plants and animals around us.

As we enter a new and more severe phase of climate change, what is the point of a natural history guide? The point is to bear witness to these changes in the natural world knowledgeably—and to help save what we can. Our wild coasts and most of their native inhabitants will not disappear, and both nature and humanity will evolve to meet the challenges ahead. Far better that we enter these times with a clear understanding of the complexity and value of wild environments, not the least of which is because they may help save us. We need a wiser, more rational, more sustainable approach to protecting human habitats from the rising waters, where we use our barrier islands, estuaries, beaches, and salt marshes as storm buffers and natural filters. An ecological approach to sea level rise and climate change will help both wild and human environments to evolve in the complex times ahead.

The beautiful White Ibis is a southeastern and tropical bird that is now common south of Chesapeake Bay. White Ibises have been slowly extending their range northward as average temperatures have climbed in recent decades.

White Ibis
Eudocimus albus

Seaoats (Uniola paniculata) on a foredune. Without the stabilizing effects of beach grasses, barrier islands could not persist over time.

Geology of Beaches and Barrier Islands

Sea level rise and wave erosion on the sound side of the Outer Banks at Nags Head Woods Preserve are gradually claiming the western edges of the maritime forest.

The outstanding feature of the Middle Atlantic Coast is a segment of the world's longest string of barrier islands, with the sounds and bays that separate these islands from the mainland Atlantic coast. The barrier islands of the Mid-Atlantic Coast are part of a series of sand and coral coastal islands that stretch south through the Florida Keys and around the Gulf Coast to the Mexican border. This chapter looks at how these sandy barrier islands of the Mid-Atlantic Coast came to be, concentrating on the geologic processes that created this unique coastline.

Broad, shallow lagoons lie behind the barrier islands, sheltering extensive areas of salt marsh and biologically rich estuaries—places where salt water and freshwater meet—that are the nurseries for most coastal and many marine creatures. This happy combination of protective barrier islands harboring enormously productive marshes and estuaries has made the Mid-Atlantic Coast one of the richest coasts in the world: rich in beautiful beaches, rich in seafood production, and rich in natural sounds, bays, and harbors to support wildlife, fishing, and commerce.

Barrier islands are almost invariably described as fragile ecosystems, always vulnerable to storm waves and ocean and wind currents. But seeing barrier islands as fragile ignores the inherent toughness and flexibility of natural coastal ecosystems, which have withstood the worst of what the Atlantic Ocean could throw at them for more than 5,000 years in their current configuration. Sand islands are almost as fluidly changeable as the seas around them. Only when we build fixed structures on these dynamic, variable strands do the islands begin to seem frail. In reality it is our buildings, roads, and bridges that are fragile when we construct them on shifting sand.

A trailing edge coastline

Although the ancient North American East Coast had a violent early geologic history, for the past 100 million years or so the East Coast and the Appalachian Mountains have been geologically quiet. The Atlantic Ocean continues very gradually to widen as the African plate and North American plates drift apart. The East Coast of North America has become what geologists call a passive or trailing edge coastline, dominated by the slow forces of weathering and erosion. The once-mighty Appalachians have steadily worn down from

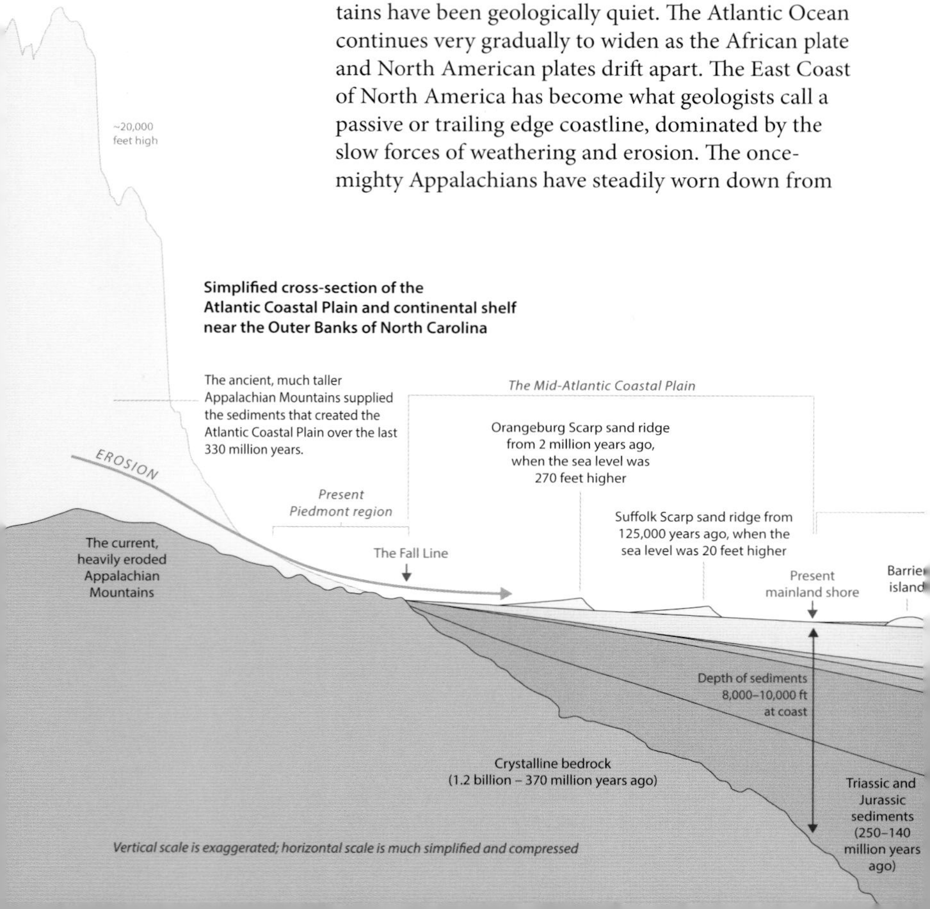
~20,000 feet high
Simplified cross-section of the Atlantic Coastal Plain and continental shelf near the Outer Banks of North Carolina
The ancient, much taller Appalachian Mountains supplied the sediments that created the Atlantic Coastal Plain over the last 330 million years.
The Mid-Atlantic Coastal Plain
Orangeburg Scarp sand ridge from 2 million years ago, when the sea level was 270 feet higher
EROSION
Present Piedmont region
Suffolk Scarp sand ridge from 125,000 years ago, when the sea level was 20 feet higher
The current, heavily eroded Appalachian Mountains
The Fall Line
Present mainland shore
Barrie island
Depth of sediments 8,000–10,000 ft at coast
Crystalline bedrock (1.2 billion – 370 million years ago)
Triassic and Jurassic sediments (250–140 million years ago)
Vertical scale is exaggerated; horizontal scale is much simplified and compressed

high, rugged peaks to low, eroded stumps, remnants of their former selves.

As erosion and weathering attacked the Appalachians, gravel, sand, and mud flowed down their eastern slopes to blanket and bury the bedrock topography of the East Coast, creating a broad apron of deep soils and sediments called the Atlantic Coastal Plain (see map, pp. x–xi). The coastal plain sediments continue below today's sea level as the broad continental shelf off the coastline. Most of the coastal plain sediments were laid down in the Cretaceous Period (140–66 million years ago), late in the age of dinosaurs. So much eroded material has accumulated along the coastal plain that the Appalachian Mountains are now situated more than 100 miles inland, and the blanket of coastal plain sediments is as much as 15,000 feet thick in some areas of the Atlantic Coastal Plain and continental shelf.

The continental shelf offshore of the central Atlantic Coast is a thick wedge of sand, silt, and clay sediments, thinner near the coast and thickening near where the continental shelf drops off sharply into the Atlantic abyssal plain. Heavier sand and gravel sediments were generally deposited near the coastline, while lighter silt and clay sediments drifted farther offshore toward the edge of the continental shelf. Studies on the sediments of the continental shelf show at least seven distinct cycles of sea level rise and fall, each associated with sand deposits from ancient beaches and barrier islands,

Videowokart

Today's low, rounded Appalachian Mountains are the heavily eroded remnants of taller, more rugged peaks that once probably looked like these mountains in the modern Sierra Nevada. Much of today's Atlantic Coastal Plain and the continental shelf off the Mid-Atlantic Coast originated as sediments eroded from those ancient Appalachians.

The Continental Shelf

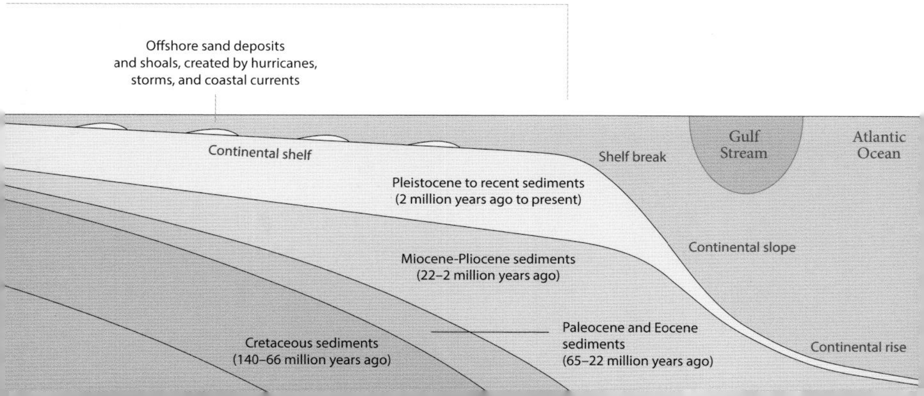
Offshore sand deposits
and shoals, created by hurricanes,
storms, and coastal currents
Continental shelf
Shelf break
Gulf
Stream
Atlantic
Ocean
Pleistocene to recent sediments
(2 million years ago to present)
Continental slope
Miocene-Pliocene sediments
(22–2 million years ago)
Paleocene and Eocene
sediments
(65–22 million years ago)
Cretaceous sediments
(140–66 million years ago)
Continental rise

now all submerged by today's sea level. The continental shelf off the Mid-Atlantic Coast is large, encompassing roughly as much area as the Atlantic Coastal Plain. At its outer margins, the shelf dips sharply downward at the shelf break, and the bottom continues down as the continental slope until it bottoms out at the Atlantic abyssal plain.

The gentle slope of the continental shelf off the Mid-Atlantic Coast and the moderate tidal ranges were critical to the formation and later landward migration of barrier islands. Long barrier islands cannot form on steeply sloping bottoms or in areas where the daily tide range exceeds about 10 feet.

The Pleistocene Ice Ages

The character of the East Coast changes abruptly north of New York Harbor and Long Island, due to the effects of multiple glacial periods that reached their southernmost extent in the area. North of New York Harbor the Pleistocene glaciations scraped the ancient coastal plain sediments off the landscape, depositing much of

The Laurentide Ice Sheet. At its maximum extent, during the Wisconsinan Glacial Episode 25,000 years ago, the Laurentide Ice Sheet, a single, massive glacier, covered most of northeastern, eastern, and north-central North America. It may be easiest to think of the Wisconsinan glacier as a giant extension of the polar ice cap.

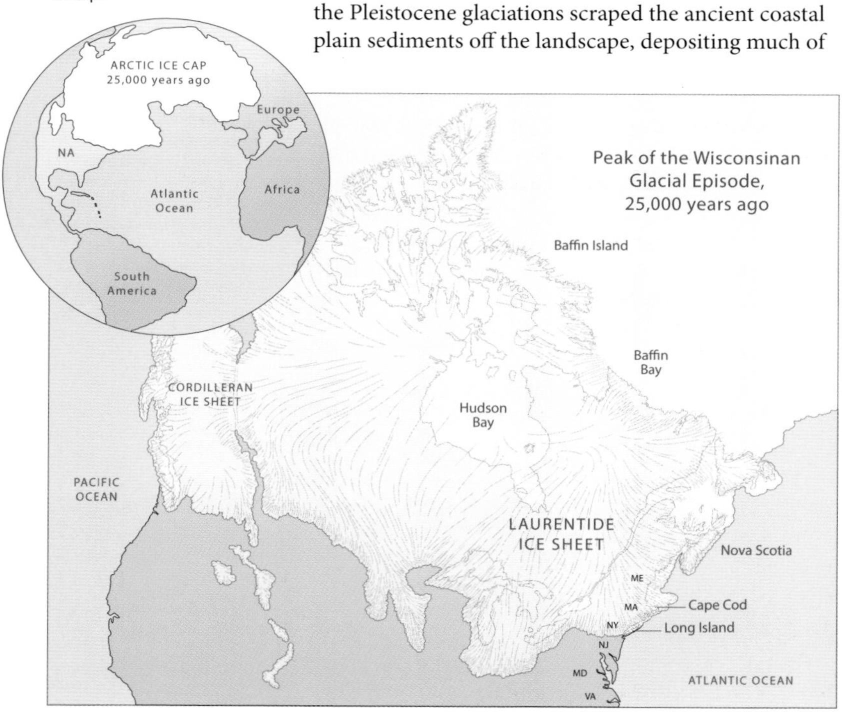
ARCTIC ICE CAP
25,000 years ago
Europe
NA
Atlantic Ocean
Africa
South America
Peak of the Wisconsinan Glacial Episode, 25,000 years ago
Baffin Island
Baffin Bay
CORDILLERAN ICE SHEET
Hudson Bay
PACIFIC OCEAN
LAURENTIDE ICE SHEET
Nova Scotia
ME
MA
Cape Cod
NY
Long Island
NJ
MD
VA
ATLANTIC OCEAN

the sediment as the great regional moraines that created the coastal surface geology of Long Island, Block Island, Martha's Vineyard, Cape Cod, and Nantucket. The northern coastal plain sediments have not entirely disappeared in the glaciated coastline, but in places they are buried well below more recent surface glacial deposits. For example, New York's Long Island is a complex layer cake of ancient coastal plain sediments, topped by a relatively thin veneer of glacial sediments from the Wisconsinan Glacial Episode, which ended about 11,000 years ago. Those ancient, sandy Cretaceous coastal plain sediments under Long Island are very important today, as they supply most of Long Island's drinking water.

PATRICK J. LYNCH
A Field Guide To
LONG ISLAND SOUND

PATRICK J. LYNCH
A Field Guide To
CAPE COD
Including Nantucket, Martha's Vineyard, Block Island, & Eastern Long Island

See *A Field Guide to Long Island Sound* and *A Field Guide to Cape Cod* for more information on the geology of New England's coastline.

South of New York Harbor the coastline and Atlantic Coastal Plain were never covered by glacial ice, but that doesn't mean that the Mid-Atlantic region was unaffected by the glacial periods. The Atlantic Coastal Plain and the continental shelf offshore show evidence of many different shorelines in the Quaternary Period (2.6 million years ago to the present) as sea levels rose and fell in response to climatic and geologic changes.

Ancient changes in sea level

Global sea levels have never been constant, and over the past several million years sea levels along the East Coast have been as much as 200 feet higher and almost 400 feet lower than today. The higher sea levels were probably the result of undersea volcanic activity along geologically active ocean ridges such as the Mid-Atlantic Ridge, where molten magma created lines of new undersea mountains large enough to raise sea levels.

The ice sheets of Antarctica have not always been in today's relatively stable configuration, and geologists think that some past rises in sea level might have been due to large amounts of Antarctic ice suddenly entering the ocean, driving up sea levels for a time. During major glacial periods, the polar ice caps held so much frozen water that sea levels were sometimes lowered hundreds of feet.

Geologists think that there may have been a glacial episode roughly every 100,000 years over the 2.6 million years of the Quaternary Period, and each of those episodes affected global sea levels and left behind ancient shoreline deposits of sand.

The remnants of these ancient shorelines are found in today's landscape. The Orangeburg Scarp is a 2-million-year-old shoreline that runs north-south for 80 miles across the coastal plain of North Carolina. The Orangeburg Scarp formed when the sea level was 270 feet higher than it is today. Much younger and closer to the coast, the Suffolk Scarp is an ancient line of eroded dune and beach sand that crosses the Tidewater Plain of North Carolina and Virginia. The Suffolk Scarp formed about 125,000 years ago during a period of global warming when the sea level was about 20 feet higher than it is today.

We will look at today's issues with sea level rise and its effects on the coast in the next chapter, on weather, water, and climate.

The Mid-Atlantic Coast 25,000 years ago

The most recent glacial episode, the Wisconsinan Glaciation (what most people think of as the Ice Age), started about 85,000 years ago, peaked about 25,000 years ago, and ended in the Atlantic Coast region about 11,000 years ago. At the peak of this glaciation, the sea level was almost 400 feet lower than it is today because so much of the earth's water was bound up in the expanded polar ice caps. At that time most of the continental shelf off the Atlantic Coast was dry land, and the climate was much colder and drier than today.

Analysis of pollen buried in lake-bed sediments shows that the landscape as far south as northern Florida was a mix of spruce-pine forests much like what you would now see in northern New England and southern Canada. Buried layers of old charcoal show that the dry, cool environment was susceptible to forest fires. Extinct species like the Giant Muskox, Mastodon, Dire Wolf, and Saber-Toothed Cat roamed a landscape of boreal forests, great rivers, and coastal heaths and grasslands (see illustration, pp. 20–21).

Paleo-Indians may well have inhabited the continental shelf areas beginning about 11,000–10,000 years ago, but evidence of these ancient peoples has long since vanished under the rising seas. As the planet warmed and the Ice Age waned, the forests began to convert to more temperate oak-hickory hardwoods, and by about 7,200 years ago the plant communities of the Mid-Atlantic Coast began to resemble today's habitats.

Petrov Vadim

25,000 years ago, during the most recent glacial period, the Mid-Atlantic Coast area was not covered with ice, but the climate was much colder than today. Pollen studies show ancient forests much like the spruce-pine forests we see in the Canadian Maritime provinces today.

Ancient beaches build modern beaches

At the peak of glaciation 25,000 years ago, the Mid-Atlantic beaches were out at the margins of the continental shelf, some 20–60 miles east of today's coastline. These ancient beach lines and the sand they contain were critical to the development of today's barrier islands, which formed many miles east of their current locations. As the planet warmed, the glaciers melted, the sea level rose, and many different shorelines marked the steady progress of ancient beaches and barriers as they migrated back from the rising sea. These ancient shoreline deposits of sand that are now submerged on the continental shelf are also the primary source of new sand on today's barrier islands.

You might think that the Mid-Atlantic coastal rivers would be the chief source of beach and barrier island sand, and it's true that millions of years ago the sediments carried by East Coast rivers built the sandy continental shelf deposits off the East Coast. But as barrier islands came to line the Atlantic Coast over the past 5,000 years, river sediments began to settle into the lagoons, bays, and sounds behind the barrier islands, and little river sediment now reaches the beaches.

Most coastal geologists think that the direct ancestors of today's barrier islands came into being about 5,000 years ago. The seas steadily rose with the melting of the Wisconsinan Glaciation, but starting about 5,000 years ago the rate of sea level rise slowed, allowing longer-lived barrier sandspits to grow out from the coastal headlands, eventually forming the long barrier peninsulas and islands we see today.

The coastal sand system

The beaches of the Mid-Atlantic Coast do not begin at the water line. To understand how beaches and barrier islands evolve, you need to look far past the waves breaking on the beach to the offshore sandbars and the continental shelf sand deposits that are both

THE MIDDLE ATLANTIC COAST 25,000 YEARS AGO

At the peak of the Wisconsinan Glacial Episode 25,000 years ago, so much of the earth's water was bound up in the Ice Age glaciers that the sea level was 400 feet lower than today. What is now the broad continental shelf off the Mid-Atlantic Coast was mostly dry land out to the margins of the shelf, where the continental slope drops off into the depths of the Atlantic Ocean.

The ancestors of today's major rivers once crossed the land of the continental shelf, carving the deep, fish-rich marine canyons of the East Coast: the Hudson, Wilmington, Washington, Norfolk, and Hatteras Canyons.

The climate of the ancient Middle Atlantic coastal region was much colder and drier than today, with forests, heaths, and marshes that were much more like what you would find in Maine or the Canadian Maritime regions today. Great forests of spruce, pine, and northern birches covered what is now the submerged continental shelf. We know the approximate composition of the forests from studies of fossil pollen in lake-bed sediments, and we also know that the ancient forests were prone to fires because of buried layers of charcoal.

The bright green area shows the modern coastline. Modern cities and locations are shown for orientation.

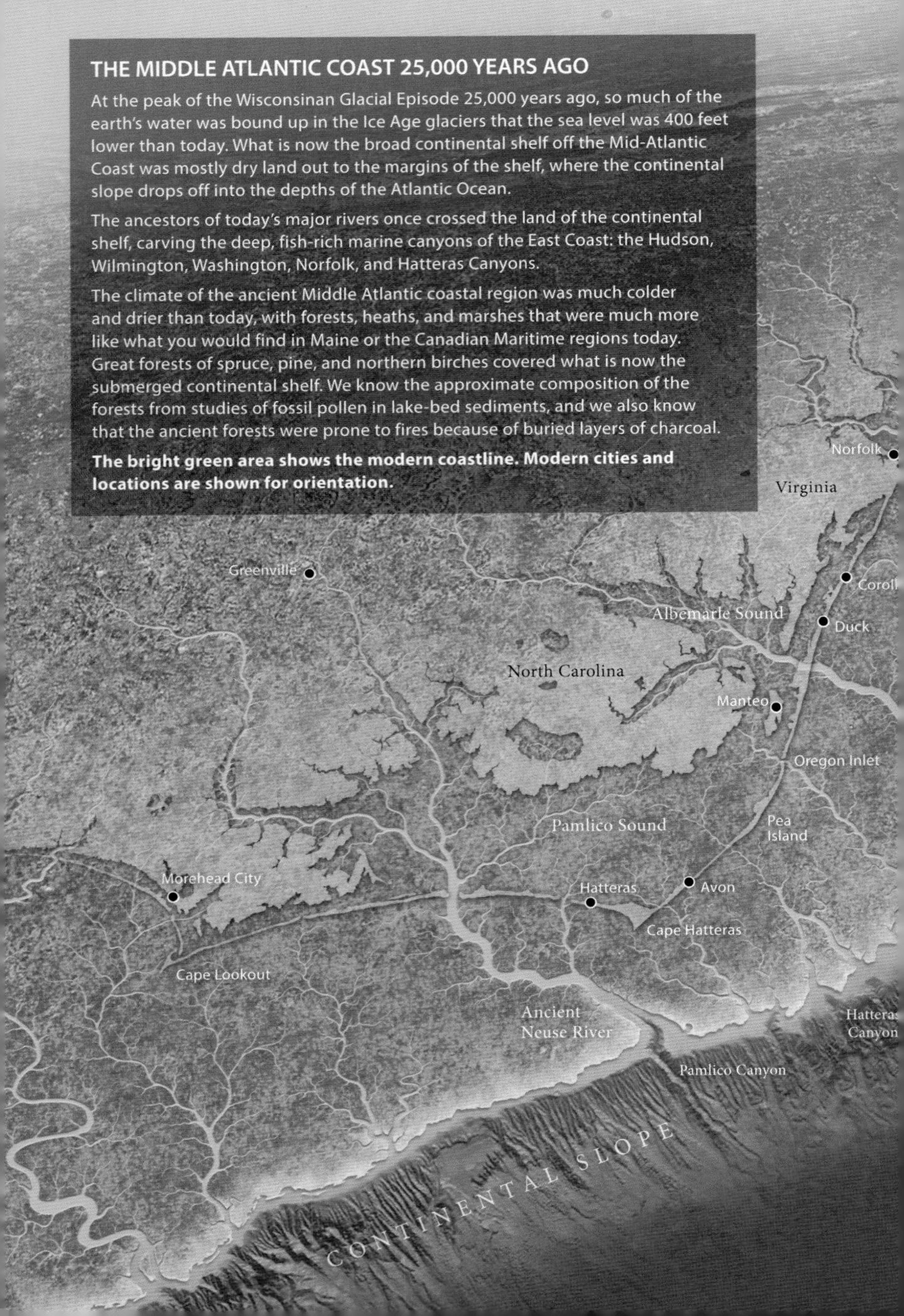
Norfolk
Virginia
Greenville
Coroll
Albemarle Sound
Duck
North Carolina
Manteo
Oregon Inlet
Pamlico Sound
Pea
Island
Morehead City
Hatteras
Avon
Cape Hatteras
Cape Lookout
Ancient
Neuse River
Hatteras
Canyon
Pamlico Canyon
CONTINENTAL SLOPE

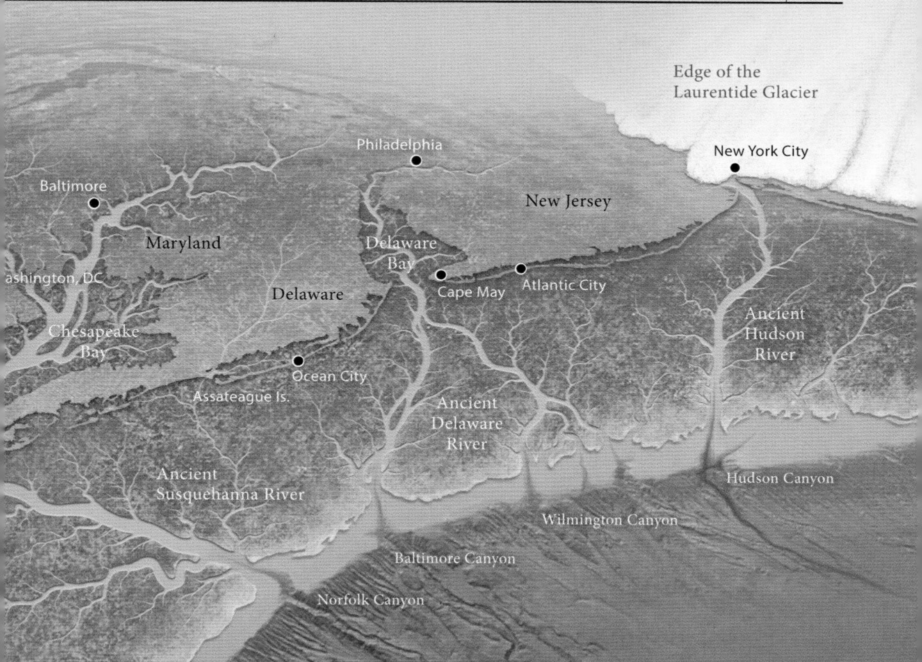
Edge of the
Laurentide Glacier
New York City
Philadelphia
Baltimore
New Jersey
Maryland
Delaware
Bay
ashington, DC
Delaware
Cape May
Atlantic City
Ancient
Hudson
River
Chesapeake
Bay
Ocean City
Assateague Is.
Ancient
Delaware
River
Ancient
Susquehanna River
Hudson Canyon
Wilmington Canyon
Baltimore Canyon
Norfolk Canyon
eller Canyon
GULF STREAM

Petrov Vadim

The ancient forests of the continental shelf resembled this area of modern Nova Scotia.

The cool, dry climate probably supported fire-prone coastal heathlands like these in today's Cape Cod.

the ultimate source for most of today's beach-building processes and the place sand goes to when storms erode beaches and barrier islands. Think of the whole complex of offshore sandbars, beaches, barrier islands, bayside inlet deltas, dunes, and ocean waves and currents as an interrelated system for circulating sand. Sand eroded from beaches by storm waves enters the offshore sand deposits, only to be moved back onto beaches and into inlets by later storms. Wind plays a part here as well. The steady but relatively gentle southeast winds of the warmer months move some sand off north-south–oriented beaches and into the ocean shallows, but then the strong northern winds of winter bring sand inland from beaches to build up dune areas. The most significant builders of barrier islands and sandspits are the inlets in barrier islands, which carry vast amounts of sand landward to the bay sides of islands, forming large inlet flood tidal deltas that are eventually incorporated into the bayside shores of barrier islands. As the oceanside shores of the barrier are eroded, the bayside shore grows landward as inlet delta sands accrete on the bayside shore, often as salt marshes or shallow sand flats. Barriers also gain

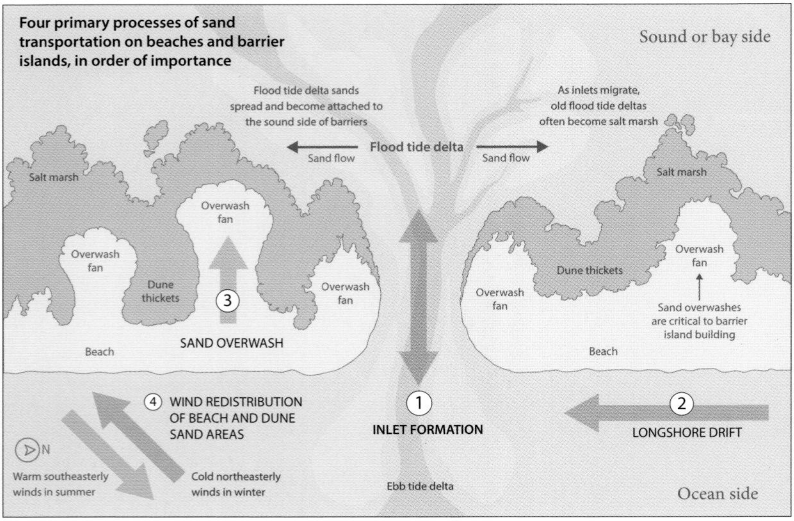
Four primary processes of sand transportation on beaches and barrier islands, in order of importance
Sound or bay side
Flood tide delta sands spread and become attached to the sound side of barriers
As inlets migrate, old flood tide deltas often become salt marsh
Flood tide delta
Sand flow
Sand flow
Salt marsh
Salt marsh
Overwash fan
Overwash fan
Overwash fan
Overwash fan
Overwash fan
Dune thickets
Dune thickets
3
SAND OVERWASH
Sand overwashes are critical to barrier island building
Beach
Beach
4 WIND REDISTRIBUTION OF BEACH AND DUNE SAND AREAS
1
INLET FORMATION
2
LONGSHORE DRIFT
N
Warm southeasterly winds in summer
Cold northeasterly winds in winter
Ebb tide delta
Ocean side

height through storm surges that bring deep, broad overwashes of sand onto the surface of barrier islands, maintaining their height above sea level.

NOAA

Storm overwashes are critical to build and maintain barrier islands. Here multiple sand overwashes invade the vegetation on the Core Banks in North Carolina after Hurricane Isabel in 2003.

Overwash areas also help islands migrate landward, as significant overwashes reach far into the dunes and salt marshes of the landward side of islands, building both the height and width of the island. The landward retreat of natural barrier island beaches in the face of sea level rise does not mean that the above-water area of the island must shrink—in fact, undeveloped islands may grow in size as they migrate toward land. It is only since we have built so much human infrastructure on these sandy barriers that we have come to regard natural coastal evolutions as erosion and destruction, because we insist that our shorelines must not change once we have built on them.

Off the shores of the Mid-Atlantic Coast, there is a broad band of sand deposits averaging 10 feet in thickness on the continental shelf and extending 20–30 miles out to sea. Much of this sand originated in the Appalachian Mountains and Piedmont region of the coastal plain and was carried down to the sea by the regional rivers millions of years ago. The US Army Corps of Engineers estimates that there are some 450 billion tons of sand on the continental shelf off the East Coast. On the bottom of the New York Bight, between Long Island and New Jersey, the corps estimates that there are 270 billion tons of sand.

Near the Outer Banks, there are three vast, famous, and deadly sand deposits: Diamond Shoals off Cape Hatteras, Lookout Shoals off Cape Lookout, and the Frying Pan Shoals off Cape Fear, as well as smaller sandbars such as Wimble Shoals off Pea Island. Although these notorious offshore sandbanks nourish the sand cycle of the Outer Banks, each has been responsible for dozens of shipwrecks. Diamond Shoals, the "graveyard of the Atlantic," has claimed hundreds of ships over the centuries, mostly in the days of sail, when nor'easters and hurricanes forced ships onto the shoals as they tried to pass Cape Hatteras.

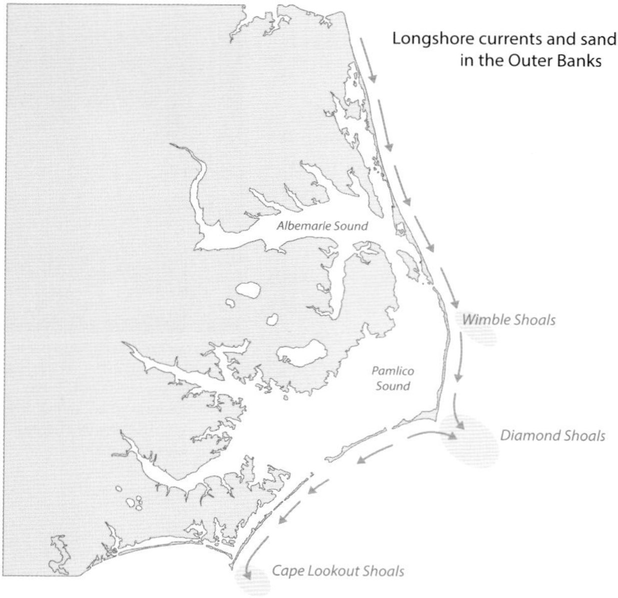
Longshore currents and sand shoals in the Outer Banks
Albemarle Sound
Pamlico Sound
Wimble Shoals
Diamond Shoals
Cape Lookout Shoals

Longshore currents and beach drifting

Sand particles don't just move straight up the beach as waves swash in and straight down the beach as the backwash slides away again. Because of the effects of wind and ocean currents, waves rarely meet the beach in perfectly parallel lines, and they almost always come in at some angle to the line of the beach. The constant angle of waves to the beach has two major effects. First, the angled waves create a current just offshore of the beach, called a longshore current. Second, the angled waves in the foreshore zone of the beach move sand particles along the beach in the direction of the longshore current.

Typical longshore currents flow at two to three miles per hour along the shore. If you've ever been swimming in the ocean surf for a while and ended up coming ashore well down the beach from your towel and umbrella, blame the longshore current. Although the amount of sand moved by one fair-weather wave is modest, the accumulated action of thousands of waves a day is enough to drive many millions of tons of sand down the beach over the course of a year. Coastal geologists estimate that the south-running longshore current off the ocean side of the Outer Banks moves as much as 1.3 million cubic yards of sand per year. To visualize this amount, consider that a dump truck can hold about 15 cubic yards of sand. The amount of sand carried along the ocean shores of the Outer Banks every year is about 87,000 dump truck loads.

Where the coastline bends sharply and the water deepens, such as at the mouth of a bay or the end of a peninsula, the longshore current slows and the sand particles it carries settle out, gradually forming a sandbar. Over time this sandbar accumulates more sand and becomes a sandspit or peninsula above the high-tide level. Each year more sand accumulates at the free end of the sandspit, further lengthening the spit. Once the sand is permanently above the high-tide level, vegetation moves in and helps accumulate yet more wind-driven sand grains that are trapped and held by the roots, leaves, and stems, forming dunes on the spit. Sandy Hook, Atlantic City, and Cape May in New Jersey, Cape Henlopen in Delaware, and the Maryland

Beach sand movement and the longshore current.

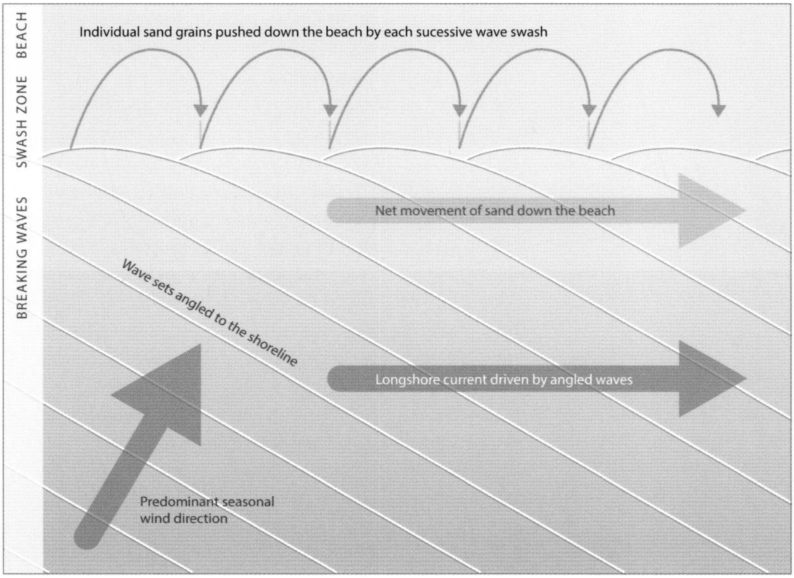
BEACH
SWASH ZONE
BREAKING WAVES
Individual sand grains pushed down the beach by each sucessive wave swash
Net movement of sand down the beach
Wave sets angled to the shoreline
Longshore current driven by angled waves
Predominant seasonal wind direction

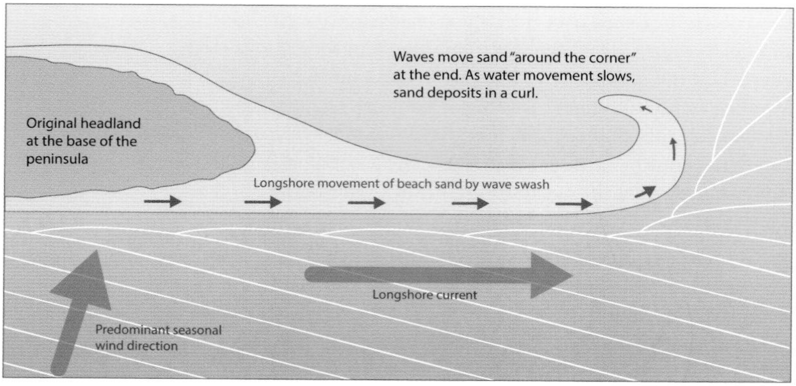
Waves move sand "around the corner" at the end. As water movement slows, sand deposits in a curl.
Original headland at the base of the peninsula
Longshore movement of beach sand by wave swash
Longshore current
Predominant seasonal wind direction

Formation and extension of sandspits on coastal peninsulas and barrier islands.

shore's long Fenwick peninsula are all examples of sand peninsulas formed by longshore drift.

When long sand peninsulas extend from eroding headlands and begin to enclose bays or lagoons between the peninsula and the mainland, they are known as barriers. Overwash from storms often cut off sand peninsulas from their original headland sources, and the sandspits become barrier islands, and the process of erosion and sand deposition continues.

Similar longshore processes created Maryland's long Ocean City peninsula and the barrier islands of Assateague in Maryland and Chincoteague in Virginia. The fate of Assateague Island makes an excellent example of what happens when humans interfere with the longshore movement of sand. Extended rock structures called groins, built perpendicular to the beach, are designed to trap sand from the longshore current and build the beach near the groin. (See illustration, pp. 170–71, for a definition of beach structures.) To try to stabilize the Ocean City beaches and the Ocean City Inlet, a set of groins was built to capture sand from the south-flowing longshore current. But these structures have robbed the north end of Assateague Island of its former sand supply, and as a result Assateague is migrating more quickly toward the Maryland shore. Jetties built to keep the Ocean City Inlet open and stabilize the north end of Assateague Island have only exacerbated the island's sand supply problems. We'll delve into the effects of human development on barrier

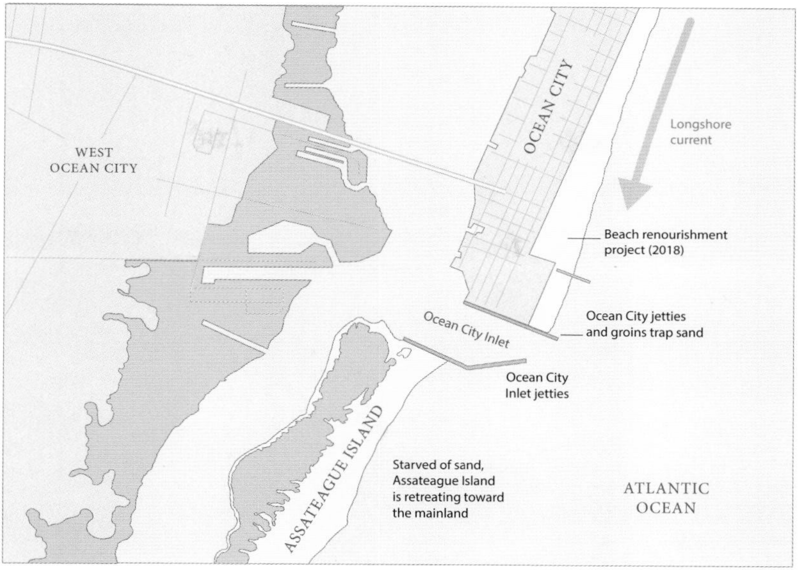
WEST OCEAN CITY
OCEAN CITY
Longshore current
Beach renourishment project (2018)
Ocean City jetties and groins trap sand
Ocean City Inlet
Ocean City Inlet jetties
ASSATEAGUE ISLAND
Starved of sand, Assateague Island is retreating toward the mainland
ATLANTIC OCEAN

islands in the chapter on the Environmental History of the Mid-Atlantic Coast.

The ordinary wind-driven ocean waves that break roughly 6,000 times per day on Atlantic beaches are the primary drivers of the longshore current, and storm waves can either build up a beach by depositing sand or tear away a whole beach in a single bad night. Storm waves are powerful. One large storm wave about 250 yards long and about five to six feet high can move as much as 1.5 million pounds (~24,000 cubic feet) of sand. The wave itself would contain approximately 140,000 cubic feet of water and might weigh about 4,000 tons.

Types of waves and sand movement

Three common types of waves drive the sand transportation system offshore of beaches, and each type influences sand movement. Plunging breakers are the classic surfer's wave, large, powerful rollers that curl into a tubular form just before breaking. Plunging breakers usually form in offshore storms or with strong onshore breezes. Most fair-weather waves don't create a large, dramatic curl as they break; instead, they seem to fall

Hard structures built along sandy coasts to trap sand usually bring unintended consequences. Here the large jetties and groins that protect Ocean City, Maryland, and the Ocean City Inlet are starving Assateague Island of its sand supply. As a consequence, wild Assateague Island is migrating toward the coast much more quickly than the Ocean City area.

For more information on beach erosion and public policy, I recommend these books:

Against the Tide: The Battle for America's Beaches, by Cornelia Dean. New York: Columbia University Press, 2011.

The Last Beach, by Orrin H. Pilkey and J. Andrew G. Cooper. Durham, NC: Duke University Press, 2014.

The Battle for North Carolina's Coast: Evolutionary History, Present Crisis, and Vision for the Future, by Stanley R. Riggs et al. Chapel Hill: University of North Carolina Press, 2011.

The fate of a barrier island is determined by every wave swash. Is the wave bringing new sand to build the beach or pulling sand away? Pea Island National Wildlife Refuge, North Carolina.

Noradoa

The slope angle of a beach has a major effect on the size and nature of breaking waves. In summer the broader, less steep beaches mostly have spilling breakers. The steeper, narrower beaches of winter cause more waves to break in the classic curl.

apart as they pass over the offshore sandbar, curling slightly with white water spilling down the face of the wave as it swashes onto the beach—a spilling breaker. The third type of ordinary wave surges onto beaches with a steep slope. These surging types of waves may also be called collapsing waves.

Plunging and spilling waves tend to remove sand from beaches because they both have a split personality. The top level of the plunging or spilling wave passes over lower "undertow" currents that slide down the face of the beach in the swash zone. The undertow is the flat sheet of fast-moving water that rushes seaward past your feet as you stand in the wave swash. Most sand carried onto the beach by plunging or spilling waves is immediately pulled into the undertow current and off the beach face. Much of the eroded sand in the undertow immediately drops onto the first offshore sandbar (that's what builds the sandbar), but the net movement of sand is still away from the beach.

Surging waves form on more steeply sloping shores, where incoming waves don't have a chance to break because they hit the shallow water so quickly and merely surge up the beach. In surging waves, all the water within the wave moves up the beach at the same time and then slides down off the beach. Because water surging onto a shore has more energy than water sliding off the beach, the net effect of surging waves is to carry sand onto the beach.

April 20, 2018
July 24, 2018
Photo courtesy of Ryan Torrance
October 3, 2018

A single storm can dramatically change an ocean beach. In April 2018 (top image) the beach just north of Jennette's Pier in Nags Head, North Carolina, had its normal width and profile. On a single night in a nor'easter storm on July 24, 2018, the waves cut a 10-foot escarpment into the beach (middle image), removing thousands of tons of sand in just a few hours.

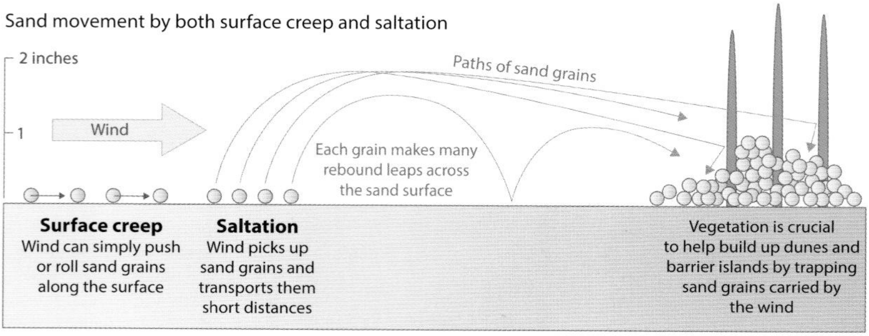
Sand movement by both surface creep and saltation
2 inches
1
Wind
Paths of sand grains
Each grain makes many rebound leaps across the sand surface
Surface creep
Wind can simply push or roll sand grains along the surface
Saltation
Wind picks up sand grains and transports them short distances
Vegetation is crucial to help build up dunes and barrier islands by trapping sand grains carried by the wind

Sand and wind

Fine sand grains are transported up the beach by winds blowing from the ocean onto the shore (onshore winds), which are generally stronger than winds that blow from the land to the sea (offshore winds). Wind-borne sand grains deposited in dunes are much finer than beach sand because the sand in dune areas was moved there entirely by the wind. Normal sea breezes move sand particles short distances over the surface of a beach or dune. When wind speeds exceed 25 miles per hour, large amounts of fine sand particles are lifted from the beach surface into the wind, where they can travel much longer distances. Such wind-blown sand is eventually trapped and brought to the ground when the sand grains hit existing dunes or beach or dune plants. Even a small beach bush or shrub can collect hundreds of pounds of sand around itself in a year (see the illustration of a sand shadow on p. 49).

All dune sand originated on beaches and was carried inland by the wind. Dune sand is much finer than beach sand because only small sand grains can be carried for a distance by the wind.

Wind directions

All along the US Atlantic Coast, the dominant seasonal winds follow a pattern: in warm weather winds originate mostly from the southwest (winds are named for the direction they come from), whereas winter is dominated by north winds (see illustration, facing page) and significant storm winds from the northeast. Although winter winds are typically stronger than summer winds, the seasonal shifts in predominant winds are roughly in balance. This relative stability in annual wind directions allows large dune systems to persist on barrier islands, as sand blown to the northeast by summer winds is blown back south and southeast across beaches and dunes by winter winds

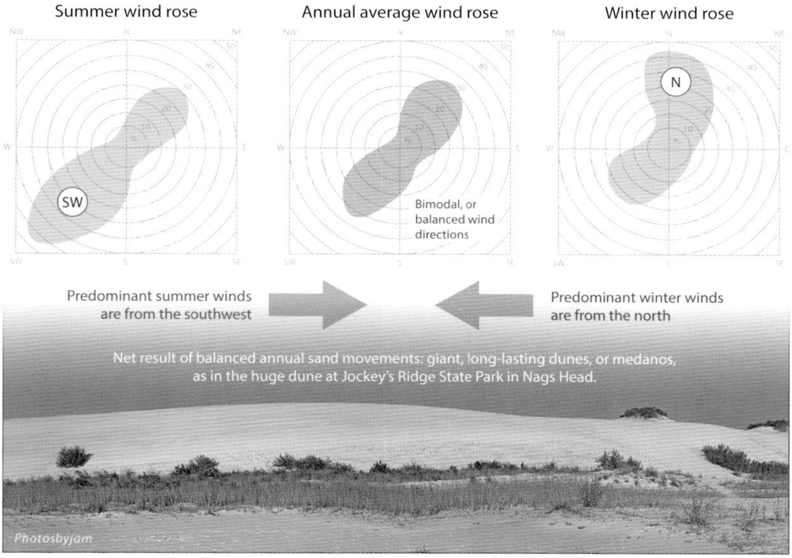
Summer wind rose
Annual average wind rose
Winter wind rose
SW
N
Bimodal, or balanced wind directions
Predominant summer winds are from the southwest
Predominant winter winds are from the north
Net result of balanced annual sand movements: giant, long-lasting dunes, or medanos, as in the huge dune at Jockey's Ridge State Park in Nags Head.
Photosbyjam

The seasonal winds that build and maintain large dune fields are roughly in balance through the year—winds are mostly from the north and northeast in the cold months, then shift to a southwest origin in the warm months.

and storms. If average annual winds were dominated by winds from a single direction, dune sand blown onto a barrier island or sandspit would quickly be scoured off the land, and barrier islands would be far lower and smaller. See the chapter on dunes for more information on the origin and structure of sand dune communities.

Artificial dune lines

One warning about reading the shape of dunes along the Mid-Atlantic Coast: most primary dune lines (the first dunes at the tops of beaches) that you see along Atlantic beaches today are artificial structures, built, reinforced, and heightened by human construction, not by natural forces. This includes dune lines in such natural-seeming areas as the Pea Island National Wildlife Refuge and Cape Hatteras National Seashore in North Carolina. The dune lines along most of the Outer Banks and many other areas along the East Coast were created by Works Progress Administration and Civilian Conservation Corps work crews in the 1930s to stabilize the shoreline and prevent large overwashes in storms. For example, the 50-mile dune line on the ocean side of NC Highway 12 from Whalebone

The dune lines along NC 12 on Pea Island are artificial, maintained by bulldozers to protect the only road south to Cape Hatteras. However, the dune plants are the same species that you would see on wild natural dunes.

Junction south to Cape Hatteras was created to protect the then-new highway from storm overwashes. Many subsequent dune reinforcement projects line the coast, mainly where houses and other structures are situated near beaches.

Although most primary dune lines at the tops of Atlantic beaches are artificially high and steep, they are usually covered and stabilized by the same wild beach and dune plants that live on wholly natural dunes. Environmentalists and geologists have long questioned the value of artificial dune lines. The dune barriers do prevent overwash damage to homes and buildings, but the wall of sand also prevents the island-building process. Without receiving new layers of sand from storm overwashes, our barrier islands are shrinking and eroding away, and they now rely almost entirely on beach nourishment and artificial dune walls to preserve beaches and prevent storm damage.

Barrier islands and peninsulas

Barrier islands and peninsulas are long bodies of unconsolidated sand—that is, loose sand and shell materials that have not compressed over time into rock. Along the shores of the Middle Atlantic Bight (see map, pp. x–xi), over 85 percent of the ocean beaches are on barrier islands and thin sand peninsulas. Barrier islands and peninsulas are typically separated from the mainland by long, narrow lagoons or sounds. In the Outer Banks, the islands sit seaward of large, shallow bodies of water: the Currituck, Albemarle, and Pamlico Sounds.

The Mid-Atlantic Bight barrier islands sit on a gently sloping continental shelf, with coastal tides generally ranging from one to five feet. This modest tide range is crucial to the formation of extended, narrow barrier sand structures such as those found on the Outer Banks and along the Delmarva Peninsula. A larger volume of tidal flow would create many more inlets in the barriers, resulting in the formation of much shorter islands closer to the mainland, such as those found along the South Carolina and Georgia coasts.

NASA

The borough of Mantoloking, New Jersey, sits near the base of a 21-mile-long barrier peninsula that runs from Bay Head in the north to Barnegat Inlet at the south. This very long, narrow barrier peninsula exists only because of the moderate five-to-six-foot tide ranges in the area. Higher tide ranges would result in much shorter islands, closer to the mainland coast.

Formation of barrier islands

Barrier islands form along coastlines where three elements are present: a slowly rising sea level, a sand supply sufficient to build sandy peninsulas and islands, and strong ocean waves and winds that can move large amounts of sand around. When sea levels rose after the Wisconsinan Glaciation began to fade 25,000 years ago (see map, pp. 20–21), the ocean began to flood the ancient river valleys of the East Coast (see illustration, p. 36). On the Middle Atlantic Coast, the valleys of the Chesapeake and Delaware Bays flooded, along with many smaller rivers. In the Outer Banks region, the ancient Chowan, Pamlico, and Neuse River valleys flooded, marking the beginnings of today's Albemarle and Pamlico Sounds. Sandy beaches formed around the headland areas of the ancient coast (see p. 36, stages 1 and 2), and coastal currents modified these sandy beaches into extended sandspits (stage 3). As the sea level continued to rise, the spits evolved into barrier islands separated from the mainland shore (stage 4).

Evolution of barrier islands

Natural barrier islands exist in a dynamic balance of waves, currents, winds, and local sand supply. Although our barrier islands may seem fragile, it's worthwhile to remember that many of today's islands have existed for thousands of years in roughly their present form, although not in the same positions. Barrier islands evolve in the face of sea level rise in many ways. Their primary response to rising sea levels is to migrate toward the land. This landward movement brings islands closer to the land, of course, but the rising seas also affect the mainland shore, so the net effect

Barrier island formation

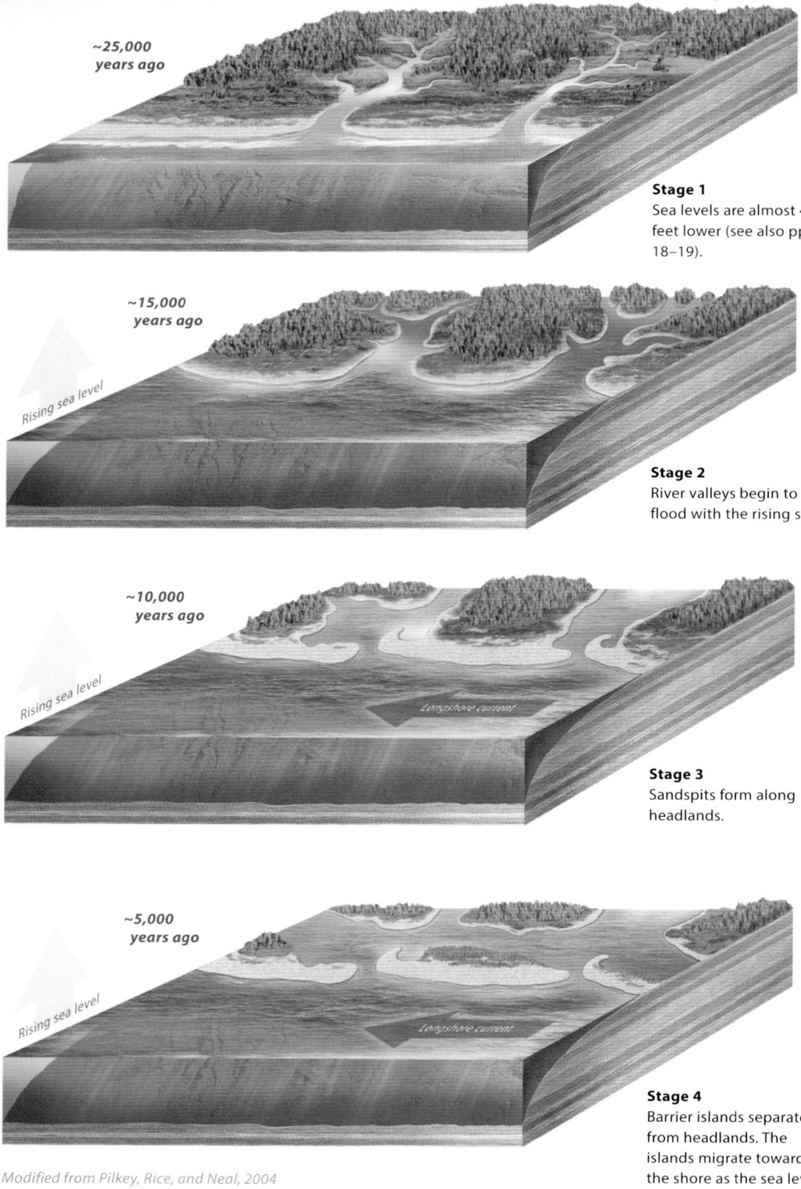
~25,000
years ago
~15,000
years ago
Rising sea level
~10,000
years ago
Rising sea level
Longshore current
~5,000
years ago
Rising sea level
Longshore current

Stage 1
Sea levels are almost 400 feet lower (see also pp. 18–19).

Stage 2
River valleys begin to flood with the rising sea.

Stage 3
Sandspits form along headlands.

Stage 4
Barrier islands separate from headlands. The islands migrate toward the shore as the sea level continues to rise.

Modified from Pilkey, Rice, and Neal, 2004

of barrier island migration is not always noticeable, especially on wild, undeveloped islands without fixed structures.

Four-foot-thick overwash fans of sand from Superstorm Sandy bury a salt marsh on the inland side of a sandspit. Overwashes smother salt marshes and other island vegetation but also help build the height of coastal barriers.

Overwash fans and inlet deltas build islands

Overwashes—where broad fans of new sand are washed onto the surface of the island, sometimes in depths of three to five feet over many acres—are the primary means by which islands build height above sea level. Overwashes used to be seen as just another bad effect of storms, but overwashes and the sand they bring onto land are now recognized as a crucial mechanism in island building and island migration in the face of rising seas.

If you prevent overwashes by building artificially high primary dunes—as is the practice in most developed areas of barrier islands—you effectively starve the island of new sand, causing the island's overall width and height above sea level to shrink. Instead of the bulk of island sand gradually moving landward via periodic overwashes, developed barrier islands erode on both the ocean and sound sides, requiring massive sand-replenishment projects on the ocean side to restore the width of beaches and prevent houses from washing away.

Three large overwash fans from Hurricane Irene on Pea Island. The light horizontal band is the NC 12 highway, with salt marshes on the sound side of the island. In major storms the overwash fans often cover the highway and smother the salt marshes.

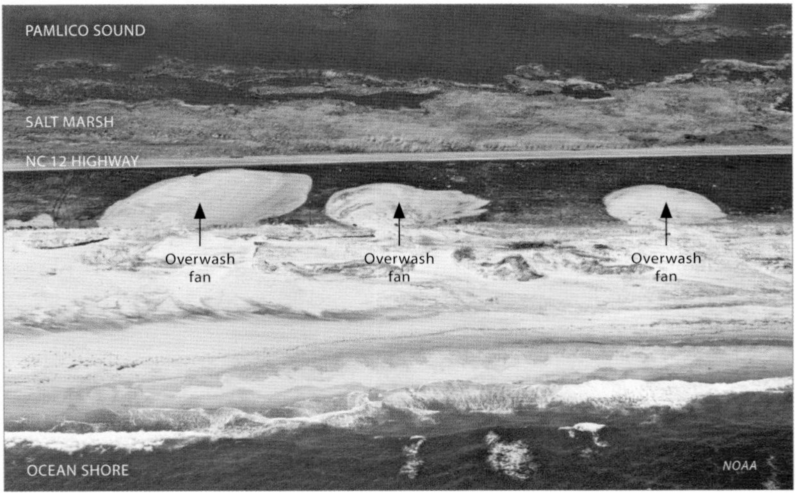
PAMLICO SOUND
SALT MARSH
NC 12 HIGHWAY
Overwash fan
Overwash fan
Overwash fan
OCEAN SHORE
NOAA

Islands change shape, sometimes in response to storms and rising seas, but mostly through the routine daily movements of sand along the shorelines and around inlets. The most obvious kind of change in island shape is the formation of new inlets, which divide an island into two smaller islands. The development of inlets is not a random process. Inlets that divide barrier islands exist in a sensitive balance between the currents and sand supply that build islands and the height, flow volume, and flow speed of both normal and storm tides in the area.

On the northern Outer Banks, lunar tide ranges are a modest two to four feet, and there are long barrier islands with only three inlets in the 126 miles between the Virginia border and the south end of Ocracoke Island. In contrast, on the southern North Carolina coast near Cape Fear, the tidal range is higher at five to seven feet. As a result, the barrier islands in this area are much shorter and the inlets are much more nu-

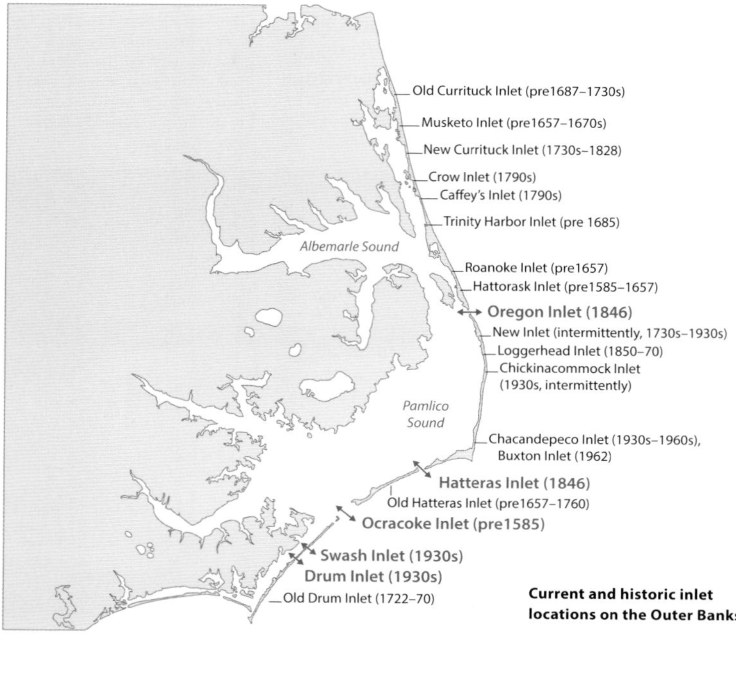
Old Currituck Inlet (pre1687–1730s)
Musketo Inlet (pre1657–1670s)
New Currituck Inlet (1730s–1828)
Crow Inlet (1790s)
Caffey's Inlet (1790s)
Trinity Harbor Inlet (pre 1685)
Albemarle Sound
Roanoke Inlet (pre1657)
Hattorask Inlet (pre1585–1657)
Oregon Inlet (1846)
New Inlet (intermittently, 1730s–1930s)
Loggerhead Inlet (1850–70)
Chickinacommock Inlet
(1930s, intermittently)
Pamlico
Sound
Chacandepeco Inlet (1930s–1960s),
Buxton Inlet (1962)
Hatteras Inlet (1846)
Old Hatteras Inlet (pre1657–1760)
Ocracoke Inlet (pre1585)
Swash Inlet (1930s)
Drum Inlet (1930s)
Old Drum Inlet (1722–70)

Current and historic inlet locations on the Outer Banks

merous to handle the larger tidal flow volumes. Most new inlets are cut by storm surges from the ocean side, but sometimes the seaward-flowing pressure of wind-driven tides and massive flows of rainwater in the sounds can cut or enlarge new inlets (see illustrations, p. 45).

Barnegat Inlet, at about the midpoint of the Jersey Shore's chain of barrier peninsulas and islands. Barnegat is notorious among boaters for its strong currents, frequent windy conditions, and the many sand shoals just outside of the main channel markers.

Storms may temporarily open small inlets in barrier islands, but significant inlets are very durable coastal structures, persisting for decades or sometimes centuries, although over long periods even major inlets migrate in the direction of the longshore drift. For example, since a hurricane opened it in 1846, Oregon Inlet on the Outer Banks has been both a vital regional navigation channel and a notorious hazard to boat traffic because its sands are always changing shape and position.

Later in this chapter, we'll look at the sand deltas that form around barrier island inlets, but inlets aren't just relief valves to allow tidal flows between the ocean and sounds or bays. Inlets and the large sand deltas that form around them are crucial to building islands and helping them to migrate. In particular, the large, shallow flood-tide deltas that form on the landward side of inlets help barrier islands build sand on the sound side of the islands.

Whether inlets are formed from storm surge pressure from the ocean side or from storm runoff on the sound side, they last only if they help balance the daily inflow and outflow of lunar tides and wind-driven tides. Most storm-cut inlets have relatively short lives because they aren't needed to maintain the balance of normal tidal flows around the barrier islands, and therefore they don't carry much water flow in daily tides. Eventually, the sand carried by longshore currents builds a sandbar across the new inlet, closing the inlet mouth. Overwash events bring new sand onto the island to further fill in the former inlet area, restoring the continuity of the island. This inlet closing process has happened many times in the recorded history of the Outer Banks and probably hundreds of times in the older geologic history of the Mid-Atlantic Coast (see map, opposite page).

Barrier island inlets

Inlets are narrow channels between barrier islands that allow the exchange of water between the open ocean and the lagoons or sounds on the landward side of islands. Inlets create coastal estuaries, places where freshwater and salt water mix to create extremely productive habitats for coastal fish and wildlife. Ocean tide water passes through inlets to bring salty water, nutrients, and marine organisms into coastal estuaries, enriching the productivity of coastal waters. Water from rivers mixes with lunar and wind-driven tidal water and flows out from the lagoons and sounds to the ocean, again enriching local marine waters with the nutrients and organisms of the estuary.

Tidal deltas around inlets

The swift flows of tidal water and shallow sand deltas near inlets make coastal inlets dangerous to navigate. Of the 445 vessels reported wrecked off the Outer Banks between 1841 and 1930, 41 percent foundered on offshore sandbanks, but another 25 percent sank while navigating the inlets. Even today the US Coast Guard regularly rescues boats damaged or capsized from collisions with bridge pilings, groundings, or trouble with the rough currents in Oregon and Hatteras Inlets.

Swift currents and ever-changing navigation channels through the tidal sand deltas make Oregon Inlet a challenge to boaters. To remain navigable, the inlet requires constant dredging.

Mark Van Dyke Photography

Aside from the swift current in the central throat of an inlet, the primary dangers to navigation are the shallow tidal deltas on both the ocean and landward sides of inlets. Longshore currents bring large volumes of sand into the inlet area, where tidal currents redistribute the sand into deltas. As tide water flows into the inlet's throat, it picks up sand from the oceanside longshore drift. The speed of the flood tidal current flow usually carries much of the sand through the inlet into the sound, where the water flow slows, causing the waterborne sand to drop out of the current, forming a flood tidal delta shoal just landward of the inlet (see illustration on facing page). As the tide changes and water flows seaward out of the sound, sand from the landward side passes through the inlet and is then dropped on the seaward side of the inlet, creating an ebb tidal delta. The notorious shallow bar that causes rough seas just seaward of Oregon Inlet is part of an

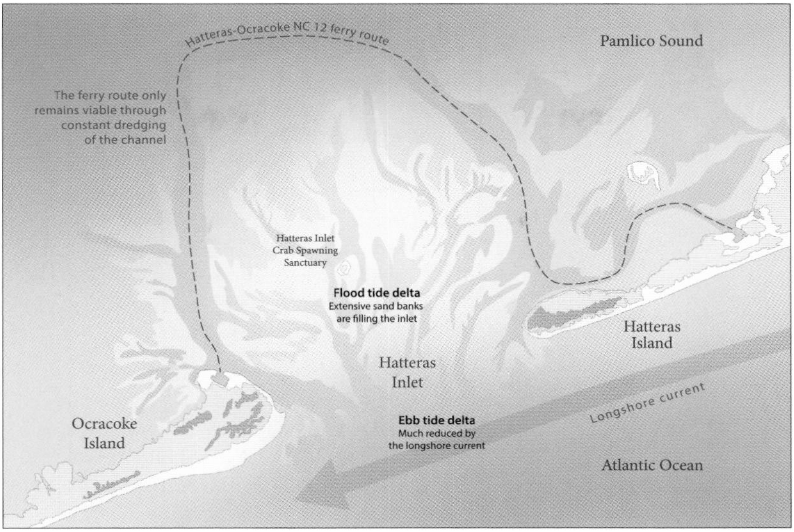
Hatteras-Ocracoke NC 12 ferry route
Pamlico Sound
The ferry route only remains viable through constant dredging of the channel
Hatteras Inlet Crab Spawning Sanctuary
Flood tide delta
Extensive sand banks are filling the inlet
Hatteras Island
Hatteras Inlet
Ocracoke Island
Ebb tide delta
Much reduced by the longshore current
Longshore current
Atlantic Ocean

The large flood tidal delta on the sound side of Hatteras Inlet is now so shallow it is almost becoming a new set of islands, with marsh vegetation moving into the shallower areas. Flood tidal deltas are larger and more persistent than ebb tidal deltas because the longshore current on the ocean side sweeps away much of the sand on that side.

ebb tidal delta. Because the currents in flood tides are usually stronger, the flood tidal delta on the sound side of an inlet is often much larger and shallower than the ebb tidal delta. Ebb tidal deltas are also exposed to strong ocean waves and to the oceanside longshore current, which tends to pick up sand from the ebb tidal delta as it passes the mouth of the inlet. When vessels navigate passages such as Oregon Inlet, it is usually the flood tidal delta that causes groundings, because the navigable channels through the flood tidal delta change almost daily. Only continuous dredging and channel re-marking keep Oregon and Hatteras Inlets navigable today.

The flood and ebb tidal deltas that form around inlets are a significant force in island building and island migration. As large flood tidal deltas form on the sound side of major inlets like Oregon and Hatteras Inlets, the areas become so shallow that marsh grasses can root and trap yet more sediment, and eventually the flood tidal delta becomes a series of marshy islands. These marsh islands grow until they eventually bond with the sound side of the barrier islands on either side of the inlet. The inlet begins to migrate away from the restricted water flow through the flood tide island complex, leaving behind new marshy land on the sound side of the barrier islands.

Migrating inlets

The longshore current continually moves sand around an inlet, pulling sand away from the upstream ocean coast and depositing new sand on the downstream side of the inlet. Aside from its considerable navigational challenges, Oregon Inlet is notorious for its southward movement. The current Bodie Island Lighthouse marked the inlet's northern shore when it was built in 1872. Today the lighthouse stands more than 3.4 miles north of the inlet it was built to signal.

Oregon Inlet is moving because of southward longshore drift. Steadily accumulating sand on the northern (Bodie Island) side of the inlet has created a sandspit that has grown southward into the inlet. Meanwhile, longshore drift and inlet currents have steadily eroded the southern edge of the inlet. For its part, the northern tip of Pea Island was quickly migrating south before a massive rock terminal groin was built in 1989. The groin keeps the southern side of Oregon Inlet stationary, but the northern inlet edge continues to grow southward, narrowing the inlet and requiring continuous dredging of the sand that accumulates in the navigation channel. Despite the construction of the groin, the powerful currents

A view south from the top of Bodie Island Lighthouse shows how far Oregon Inlet has migrated since it formed in 1846. The Basnight Bridge over today's Oregon Inlet is on the center horizon (arrow), more than three miles south of the lighthouse. The salt marshes on the right formed from flood tidal deltas that grew shallow enough to support marsh grasses. Gradually those delta marsh islands bonded to the soundside shores of Bodie Island, enlarging the island on its Pamlico Sound coast.

Oregon Inlet and bridge
Ocean side
Oregon Inlet has migrated 3.4 miles south in the 174 years since it formed in 1846

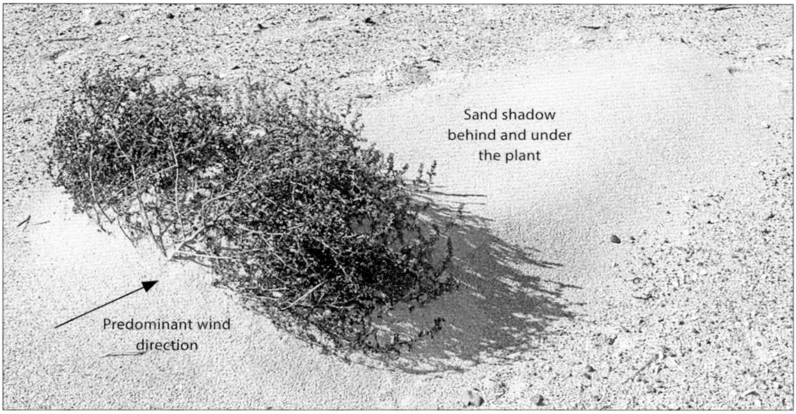
Sand shadow
behind and under
the plant
Predominant wind
direction

Even a single plant (here Common Saltwort, *Salsola kali*) can be effective in catching and holding windblown sand on the beach. Just two feet wide, this plant has captured almost a cubic yard of sand in its lee as a sand shadow, almost an embryonic dune. Note the fine texture of the sand in the shadow. The windblown sand is much finer than the coarse beach sand around it.

against wind erosion. Both grasses also propagate through rhizomes—underground stems that grow horizontally to develop new clumps of grass next to the original plant. Beachgrass is the more effective plant at building dunes for protecting barrier islands, because its rhizome spreading patterns tend to produce solid lines of frontal dunes at the top of the beach. Seaoats is equally tenacious at holding sand but tends to grow in discrete clumps, producing dune lines with many gaps. On undeveloped islands, these gaps in the Seaoats

American Beachgrass
Ammophila breviligulata

Seaoats
Uniola paniculata

dune lines are an advantage, as they allow storm surges to easily overwash new sand onto the top of the island. In developed areas of the coast, the solid lines of dunes produced by Beachgrass are favored to prevent overwash, which can flood neighborhoods and streets with layers of sand as well as water.

Barrier island movement and evolution

In response to rising sea levels, barrier islands migrate toward the mainland coast. Over time storms gradually drive overwash sand from offshore sandbars and oceanside beaches across the surface of the barrier islands, building up the elevation of the islands and moving the oceanside tide lines toward the mainland. Inlets also help islands migrate landward, as old flood tidal deltas become covered with marsh grasses and bond to the landward side of the islands. As the sea level rises, each new overwash event moves some of the older beach sand landward while depositing new sand. Storm overwash often smothers some existing dune plants and forests on barrier islands, but unless the overwash event is catastrophically large, the plant communities respond over time by gradually shifting landward as the island sands shift.

The landward-moving island sand buries older forests and salt marshes, entombing the remains of tree stumps and marsh peat as the new sand layers roll over the islands as they migrate. These older plant remains often reappear on the ocean beaches of the islands. From time to time near Corolla and Nags Head, North Carolina, old tree stumps of a long-vanished forest

Searocket (*Cakile edentula*) is one of the few plants that can thrive in the harsh conditions of the upper beach. Searocket plays a critical role in stabilizing and holding beach sand.

Photo courtesy of Dianna K

The remains of an ancient forest, buried hundreds of years ago as the sand peninsula migrated landward. Tree stumps of the old forest are now visible on the beach near Corolla, North Carolina, on the Outer Banks.

are revealed on the ocean beaches, only to be reburied later by shifting beach sands.

It is common to find oyster shells on the ocean beaches of the Mid-Atlantic Coast. How can this happen when we know that oysters grow only in the protected waters of bays and sounds? The mystery is solved when we realize that these oyster shells are ancient. They were buried hundreds or even thousands of years ago when the island migrated over oyster beds on the sound side of the island, and they have reappeared today because the migrating island has shifted further to reveal the ancient oyster beds.

An oyster shell on the ocean beach at Bodie Island, blackened by burial for thousands of years as the barrier island migrated landward over ancient oyster beds that were originally on the sound side of the island.

Although most attention to sea level rise is focused on ocean-facing shores, the sea rises everywhere along the coast, including on the shores of Roanoke Sound, North Carolina. Here the edges of the maritime forest at Nags Head Woods are eroding at three to four horizontal feet per year.

Weather, Water, and Climate

As the sea level rises, salty water rises in the ground under plants close to the shoreline. Here mature hardwood trees that once thrived on the earthen dikes of Prime Hook National Wildlife Refuge on Delaware Bay are succumbing to saltwater damage to their roots.

The Mid-Atlantic Coast is under the influence of both continental and oceanic weather patterns. In this region, the continental weather patterns generally come from the west and southwest during the warmer months, and from the west and northwest during the cold months. The ocean and large bodies of water like the Delaware and Chesapeake Bays and Pamlico and Albemarle Sounds generally moderate coastal temperatures. In autumn and early winter, the relatively warm waters buffer the effects of increasingly cold continental air masses. In the spring the cool coastal waters keep the arrival of spring along the coast at least two to three weeks later than inland areas, which warm much faster as spring progresses.

Sea breezes play a significant role in moderating temperatures along the coast in the warm months. In summer the air over the relatively warm land rises, drawing cool breezes (also called onshore winds) from the sea toward the coast. Onshore winds are most common in the late spring, summer, and early fall months.

Wind and water patterns

As landforms surrounded by large bodies of water, the barrier islands and beaches of the Mid-Atlantic Coast are always windier than inland areas. The predominant wind patterns in the Mid-Atlantic region are strong cold northwesterly winds* in the winter and early

*We name winds by the direction they come from. Northwesterly winds come from the northwest.

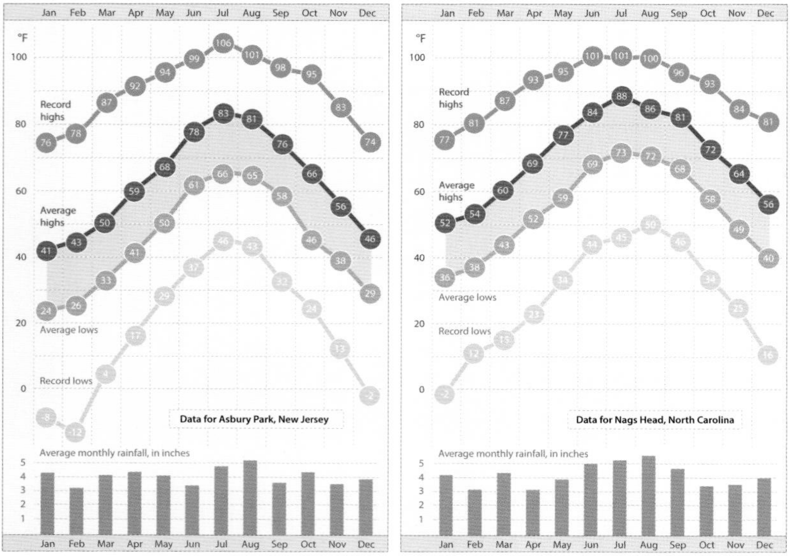
Jan Feb Mar Apr May Jun Jul Aug Sep Oct Nov Dec
°F
100
80
60
40
20
0
Record highs
76 78 87 92 94 99 106 101 98 95 83 74
Average highs
41 43 50 59 68 78 83 81 76 66 56 46
Average lows
24 26 33 41 50 61 66 65 58 46 38 29
Record lows
-8 -12 4 17 29 37 46 43 32 24 13 -2
Data for Asbury Park, New Jersey
Average monthly rainfall, in inches
5 4 3 2 1
Record highs
77 81 87 93 95 101 101 100 96 93 84 81
Average highs
52 54 60 69 77 84 88 86 81 72 64 56
Average lows
36 38 43 52 59 69 73 72 68 58 49 40
Record lows
-2 12 13 23 34 44 45 50 46 34 25 16
Data for Nags Head, North Carolina
Average monthly rainfall, in inches

The average temperature and rainfall profiles for Asbury Park, New Jersey, and Nags Head, North Carolina.

spring, and gentler, warm southwesterly winds in the late spring through early fall. The shape and character of the sand hills in major coastal dune areas like the Outer Banks or the long, sandy peninsulas of the Delaware and Maryland coasts are created and shaped primarily by northwesterly winter winds, which are seldom seen by tourists and beachgoers. In late spring, summer, and early fall the predominant southwesterly winds bring the warmth and moisture of the southeastern United States and the Gulf of Mexico northward into the region, acting to balance the northwestern winds of winter (see illustration, p. 33).

Although the ocean generally moderates weather along the Mid-Atlantic Coast, two major oceanic weather patterns are the great exception to the rule: nor'easter storms and tropical hurricanes.

Nor'easters

Nor'easters are strong storms that typically originate in the Gulf of Mexico as warm, moist, low-pressure systems that are then steered northeast across the south-central United States by the prevailing jet stream winds, eventually tracking north-northeast to parallel the Atlantic Coast. Nor'easters are particularly likely when a large high-pressure system sits over the Bahamas area, as this forces the storms off their usual eastward track and toward the northeast. Although a nor'easter can appear at any time of year, these storms are more common in the cold months between October and March, when they can bring destructive winds, large coastal storm surges, and blizzard conditions to coastal regions of the United States and the Canadian Maritime provinces. A large nor'easter can be as destructive as any hurricane and can cause significant erosion in the soft sandy and earthen coastlines of the Mid-Atlantic Coast.

As a low-pressure system, a nor'easter circulates in a counterclockwise motion and can be pictured as a circular clock face for points of reference (see illustration, below). As the storm tracks along the coast, the counterclockwise winds circulating from about 5 o'clock to 10 o'clock blow freely across the ocean and pick up speed and moisture. Observers along the coast will experience high winds coming onto shore from the northeast direction—hence the name "nor'easter." In a powerful nor'easter the winds off the ocean can

A nor'easter moving up the Atlantic Coast, showing a typical storm track and counterclockwise wind circulation.

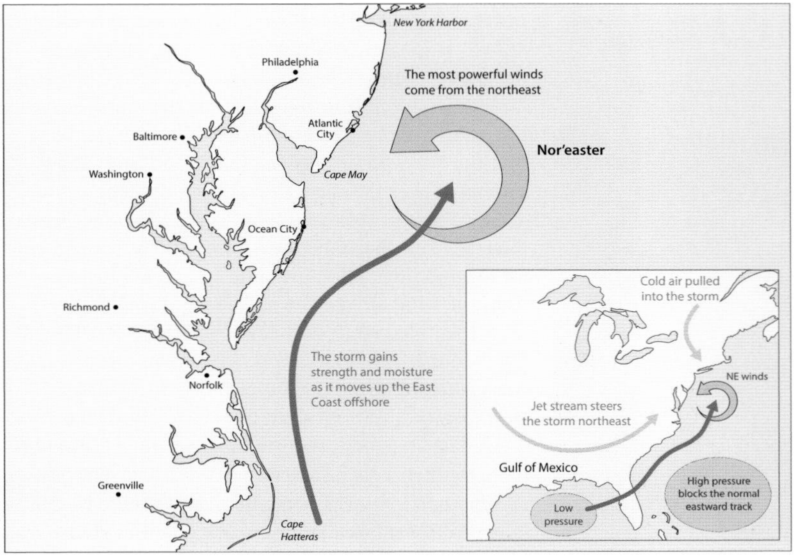
New York Harbor
Philadelphia
The most powerful winds come from the northeast
Atlantic City
Baltimore
Nor'easter
Washington
Cape May
Ocean City
Richmond
The storm gains strength and moisture as it moves up the East Coast offshore
Norfolk
Greenville
Cape Hatteras
Cold air pulled into the storm
NE winds
Jet stream steers the storm northeast
Gulf of Mexico
Low pressure
High pressure blocks the normal eastward track

pile up large waves and hurricane-like storm surges of up to 20 feet on ocean shores, flooding coastal communities and causing shoreline erosion. Winter nor'easters also bring snow. The largest recorded blizzards along the East Coast were nor'easters, such as the famous blizzards of 1978 and 1996, which both dumped two to three feet of snow along large sections of the East Coast in just a few hours. Winter storm Nemo in February 2013 was a classic blizzard-generating nor'easter, where a huge, moist, low-pressure system traveled north along the Eastern Seaboard and met another low-pressure system coming east out of the central United States, triggering a large blizzard that dumped record amounts of snowfall over New England, New York, and the New Jersey coast. Severe nor'easters don't just bring snow. The winds and waves from nor'easters accelerate erosion along the coast and can make long-lasting changes, particularly in barrier islands, sandspits, and coastal cliffs.

The broken ruins of what was once Baltimore Boulevard, on Assateague Island. The road was destroyed by the Ash Wednesday Storm in March 1962. Developers had planned to create a neighborhood of houses along the road, but the storm devastated all of the structures on Assateague Island, Maryland, and the development project was abandoned.

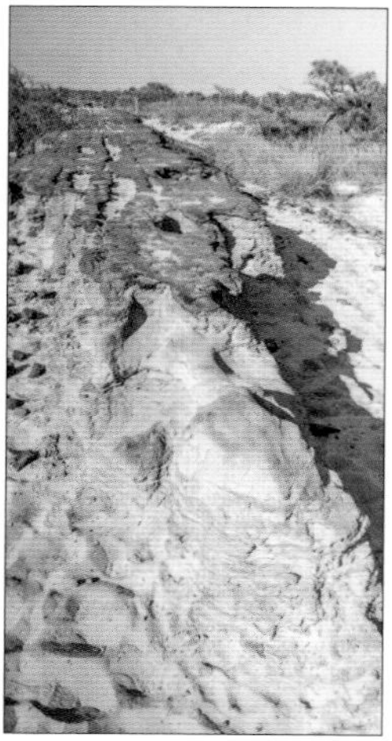

The Ash Wednesday Storm

One of the most devastating oceanic storms ever to hit the Mid-Atlantic region was a nor'easter that made landfall on North Carolina's Outer Banks on March 5–9, 1962. The National Weather Service does not formally name nor'easter storms, but the storm is widely known as the Ash Wednesday Storm, or sometimes the Great Atlantic Coastal Storm. Aside from bringing hurricane-strength sustained winds and storm surges, nor'easters can be particularly destructive because they are often slower moving than hurricanes and can hover over the coast through multiple high-tide cycles. Many people called the Ash Wednesday Storm the High Five Storm because it lingered over the coast for five full tide cycles, bringing coastal floods both from the wind-driven storm surge and from heavy rains that filled rivers and bays from the Outer Banks north to the New Jersey coast. The storm caused major coastal erosion from the Outer Banks to southern New England. Atlantic City, New Jersey, and Ocean City, Maryland, both reported that waves of 25 feet or more hit their beaches. Before it moved off the coast on March 9, 1962, the nor'easter had destroyed 1,793 houses and damaged another 16,782 homes across six

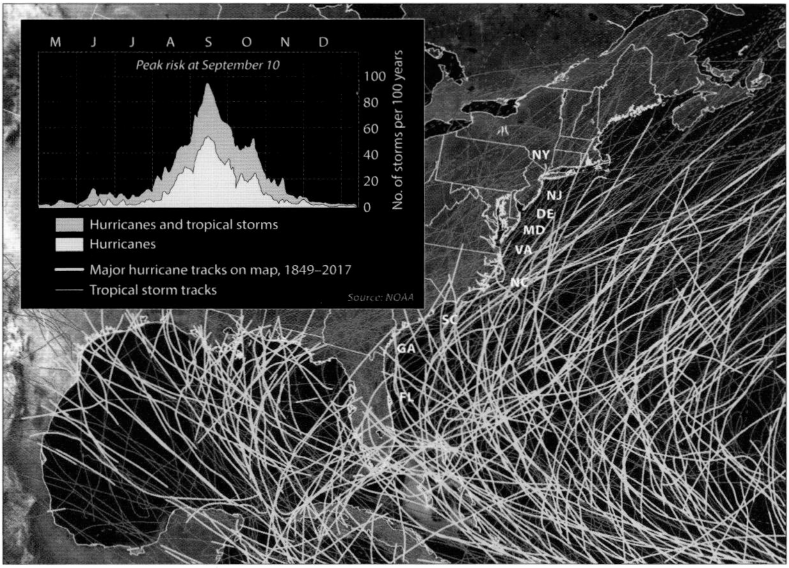
M J J A S O N D
Peak risk at September 10
100
80
60
40
20
0
No. of storms per 100 years
Hurricanes and tropical storms
Hurricanes
Major hurricane tracks on map, 1849–2017
Tropical storm tracks
Source: NOAA
NY
NJ
DE
MD
VA
NC
SC
GA
FL

Major hurricane and tropical tracks from 1849 to 2017. Note the general pattern of a large arc, approaching the United States from the southeast and then typically making a sweeping turn toward the northeast before making landfall on the Mid-Atlantic Coast.

states, at the cost of more than $1.7 billion in 2019 dollars. On Maryland's Assateague Island, a new coastal housing development with hundreds of planned homes was destroyed. Perhaps the only bright spot in the aftermath of the storm was that this Assateague development project was abandoned, and the whole barrier island is now the Assateague Island National Seashore, famous for its natural coastal habitats and wild ponies.

Hurricanes and tropical storms

Hurricanes are tropical cyclones that are typically born in late summer as low-pressure systems off the west coast of Africa that then track westward across the Atlantic, gaining heat energy and moisture from the tropical midocean and arriving on our side of the Atlantic with storm-force winds and heavy seas. Tropical storms generally originate the same way that hurricanes do but do not reach the strength and wind speeds of hurricanes. The storms are differentiated by wind speed—tropical storms are named and tracked by the National Weather Service Hurricane Center once they reach sustained winds of 34 miles per hour; the storm becomes a hurricane once sustained winds

A combined coastal nor'easter and winter blizzard rips up the Mid-Atlantic Coast on January 4, 2018. Informally named Winter Storm Grayson, the storm was so powerful that the National Weather Service called it a bomb cyclone, meaning that it developed extremely rapidly into a major storm.

reach 74 miles per hour or above. As they approach the Atlantic Coast, the north-tracking hurricanes gain additional energy from the hot Florida Current at the base of the Gulf Stream, and almost every year these storms hit parts of the East and Gulf Coasts.

In the Mid-Atlantic region, these summer and fall storms are the warm-weather counterparts to winter nor'easters and are a major factor in changing and eroding local coastlines. A single major hurricane can cut more sand from the coast than a decade's worth of slow and steady erosion from the usual weather and waves. In hurricanes and tropical storms, the wind pattern is very similar to a nor'easter: heavy winds arrive on the coast from the northeast due to the counterclockwise circulation in these low-pressure storms.

The barrier islands of the Outer Banks of North Carolina and points south are particularly vulnerable to hurricanes because they extend far into the Atlantic, just north of where most storms begin their turns toward the northeast. The Mid-Atlantic Coast north of Hampton Roads, Virginia, typically receives fewer direct strikes from major hurricanes because it is north of where most hurricanes turn toward the northeast, and probably also because the colder waters of the Virginia Current don't energize storms the way the Gulf Stream does further south. However, major storms like Superstorm Sandy (2012) do sometimes make landfall in the northern Mid-Atlantic region, and the Delmarva and New Jersey coasts are also vulnerable to nor'easters.

MAJOR REGIONAL CURRENTS

In the Mid-Atlantic Coast region, both the major offshore currents and the longshore currents near the coast generally flow from north to south. The combination of south-flowing longshore currents and moderate tide heights (see illustration, p. 68) create conditions that are ideal for the formation of long, sandy barrier peninsulas and islands.

The Middle Atlantic Bight coastal regions are affected by two major ocean currents: the cold Labrador Current that flows south from the Arctic Ocean along the Atlantic Coast, and the warm Gulf Stream that flows

Tides

Apart from the moment-by-moment action of waves on the shoreline, the tides most strongly define the movements of water along our coasts. The tidal movements of ocean water convey life and nutrients to such shoreline environments as salt marshes, estuaries, beaches, and tidal flats. Tidal water movements are also important farther offshore, where tidal currents sweep nutrient-rich water into and out of the major estuaries of the Mid-Atlantic Coast: the Delaware Bay, Chesapeake Bay, and Albemarle and Pamlico Sounds of the Outer Banks.

Alfredo

Tides are powered primarily by the rotation of the moon around the earth and to a lesser extent by the relationship of the moon, earth, and sun.

Ocean tides are caused primarily by the gravitational pull of the moon and to a lesser extent by that of the sun (see illustration, p. 66). The gravitational effects of the moon and sun on earth's waters are complex, and the shape and depth of local landforms and the sea bottom further influence the depth and timing of tides. The moon's gravity and position relative to the earth are the strongest influences on the height and timing of ocean tides. As the moon rotates around the earth once every 27.3 days, its gravitational pull creates a slight bulge in the ocean surface closest to the moon. The lunar day—the time it takes the moon to rotate once around the earth—is 50 minutes longer than the solar day, and so the tide cycle advances 50 minutes every day according to our clocks and calendars. These lunar or astronomical tides are also semidiurnal, rising and falling twice during each 24-hour-and-50-minute lunar day.

The relative positions of the earth, moon, and sun also modify tidal height throughout the month. Twice a month, at the new and full moon cycles, when

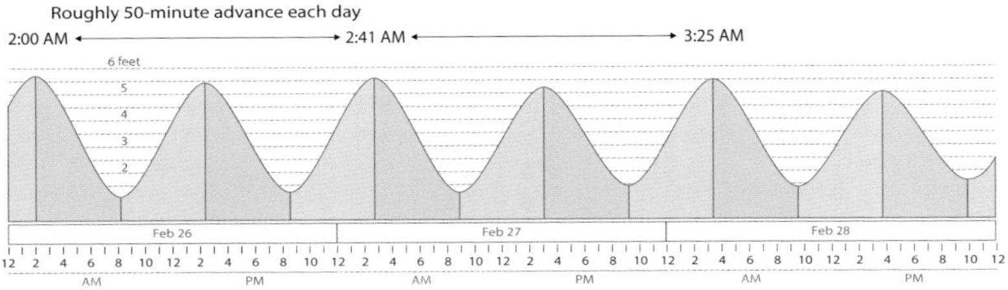
Roughly 50-minute advance each day
2:00 AM
2:41 AM
3:25 AM
6 feet
5
4
3
2
Feb 26
Feb 27
Feb 28
12 2 4 6 8 10 12 2 4 6 8 10 12 2 4 6 8 10 12 2 4 6 8 10 12 2 4 6 8 10 12 2 4 6 8 10 12
AM
PM
AM
PM
AM
PM

Albemarle Sound near Manns Harbor, North Carolina. Although still a healthy and productive estuary, Albemarle Sound faces increasing threats from polluted runoff from hog, chicken, and other farming, more frequent storms and hurricanes, and continual erosion of its coastline due to sea level rise.

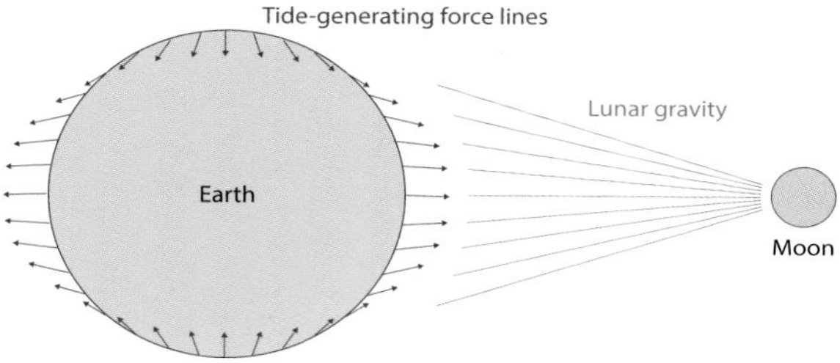
Tide-generating force lines
Lunar gravity
Earth
Moon

Tides spring up when the pull of the moon and sun is aligned

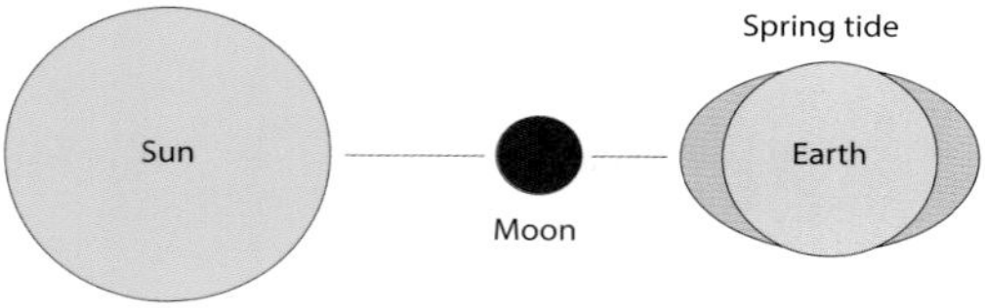
Spring tide
Sun
Moon
Earth

Tides are lower when the moon is not aligned with the sun

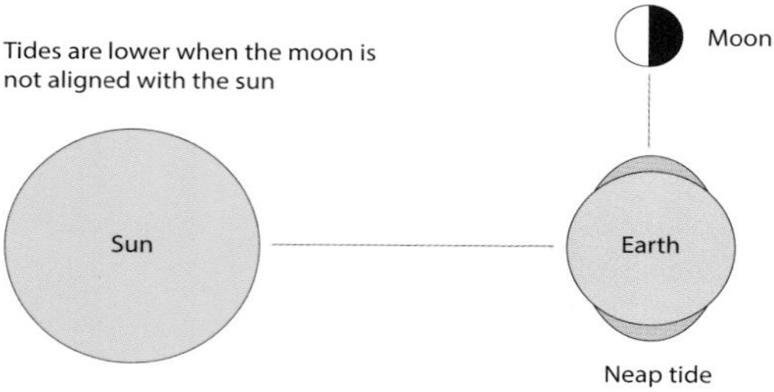
Moon
Sun
Earth
Neap tide

There are two neap tides and two spring tides each lunar month

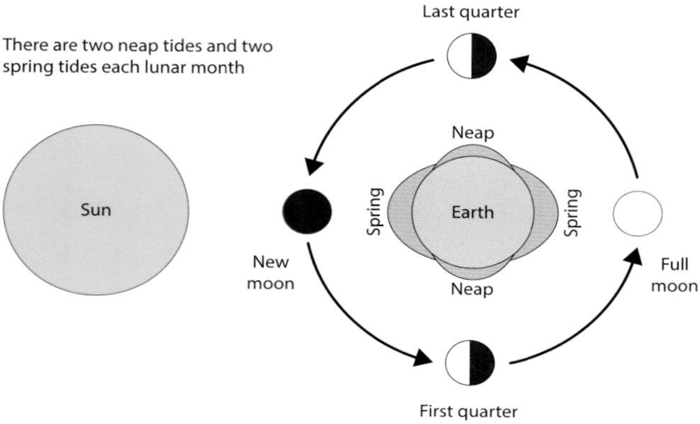
Last quarter
Neap
Sun
Spring
Earth
Spring
New moon
Neap
Full moon
First quarter

the earth, moon, and sun are all in alignment, the combined gravitational pull of the moon and sun cause higher-than-average tides called spring tides. These spring tides have nothing to do with the annual season of spring; rather, they spring up 20–30 percent higher than average high tides. Each spring tide lasts about four days. When the moon and sun are entirely out of phase, during the first and last quarters of the moon, tidal ranges are 20–30 percent lower than average, and the resulting unusually moderate tides are called neap tides.

The marshes of Blackwater National Wildlife Refuge, Maryland, are over 100 miles upstream from the junction of Chesapeake Bay and the Atlantic Ocean but still under the influence of ocean tides.

Tides are also influenced by how close the earth is to the moon. The moon does not rotate around the earth in a perfect circle: it rotates in a slightly oval path that puts the moon closer to the earth twice every 27.3 days. When the moon is closest to the earth in its oval orbit, it is said to be in perigee. Roughly twice a year the occurrence of spring tides in the new or full moon phases will coincide with the moon's closest approach to earth in its orbit, and we get extremely high tides, called perigean spring tides or sometimes king tides.

Winds can also affect tide cycles. In large bodies of shallow water like North Carolina's Pamlico and Albemarle Sounds, a strong opposing wind can temporarily slow or even reverse the lunar tidal flow. A strong wind blowing consistently from one direction for several hours can shift the water within the sounds as much as five feet above normal levels, resulting in temporary but noticeable changes in high and low tides.

The nightmare scenario for wind and weather affecting tides is when a hurricane or nor'easter arrives at the same time as a spring tide or—even worse—a perigean high tide. The combined high tides and storm surge can cause terrible coastal flooding. The Ash Wednesday nor'easter of March 1962 arrived during a perigean high tide and lingered over the Mid-Atlantic Coast through four more perigean high-tide cycles. This created extraordinary flooding damage. The combination of a wind-driven storm surge on the ocean coasts, abnormally high tidal flooding in the bays and sounds behind barrier islands, and record rainfall in the region made a bad storm into a record-breaking storm.

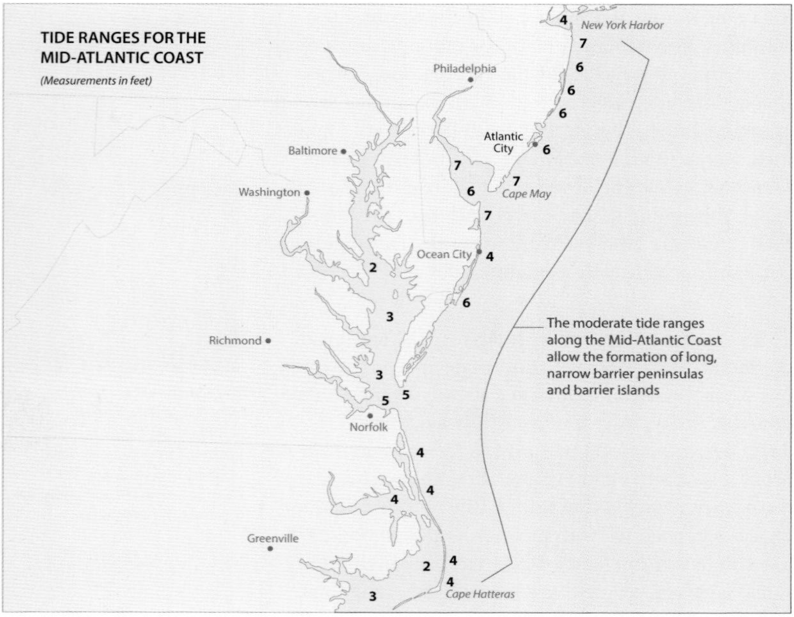
TIDE RANGES FOR THE MID-ATLANTIC COAST
(Measurements in feet)
New York Harbor
Philadelphia
Atlantic City
Cape May
Baltimore
Washington
Ocean City
Richmond
Norfolk
Greenville
Cape Hatteras
4
7
6
6
6
6
7
7
6
7
4
2
6
3
3
5
5
4
4
4
2
4
4
3
The moderate tide ranges along the Mid-Atlantic Coast allow the formation of long, narrow barrier peninsulas and barrier islands

Tidal ranges and barrier islands

The long, narrow barrier islands and peninsulas located some distance from the mainland of the Mid-Atlantic Coast and the Outer Banks are distinctive and very different than the much shorter barrier islands close to the mainland that are typical of the Atlantic Coast south of Cape Hatteras. Long, narrow sand barriers can only exist where the maximum daily tidal ranges are less than 6.5 feet. Oceanographers call these coastlines microtidal coasts, and barrier islands and peninsulas along microtidal coasts can reach 20 miles long and become separated from the mainland by large bays and sounds.

Tidal zonation of marine environments

All coastal marine ecosystems are organized in vertical zones because of lunar tides. Tide levels and the slope of the land as it meets the water determine the zones of marine life in salt marshes, on shoreline rocks, and on beaches, where the difference of a few inches of tide level or degrees of slope can completely alter the vegetation and animal life in a zone.

A tidal marsh on the bay side of Assateague Island National Seashore, Maryland. Saltwater Cordgrass (Spartina alterniflora) lines the immediate shore in the bottom left. Marsh Elder (Iva frutescens), or High Tide Bush, marks the point in the marsh just above the average daily high-tide line. Black Cherry (Prunus serotina), Wax Myrtle (Morella cerifera), and Northern Bayberry (Myrica pensylvanica) fill in the shrub layer just behind. Note that the larger pines and cherries have mostly died, victims of salt infiltration of the soil due to sea level rise.

The thick, leathery leaves of Seaside Goldenrod (*Solidago sempervirens*) are adapted to resist burning from salt aerosols and the constant drying winds near ocean shores.

Coastal environments also have horizontal zones. The most common factors in horizontal zoning are the slope, wave exposure, and distance to freshwater. Groundwater salinity and freshwater flow also influence which plants and animals can survive in a particular habitat.

Salt aerosols (salt spray, see illustrations, p. 134–135), are another horizontal zoning factor. Only a few plant species can thrive in areas that regularly receive salt spray, so distinct zoning patterns form along coastline vegetation (see illustration, pp. 138–39). These zones separate areas that receive a constant spray or dusting of salt from others that are more sheltered from wind-borne salt.

Too much tidal submergence can drown some plants and animals or bring in too much salt. Too little exposure to tides kills many marsh creatures like fiddler crabs and mussels, which need the water for both oxygen and food. Marshes and tidal flow provide important shelter to the young of many species of fish and marine invertebrates. The influence of tidal salt water is especially evident in salt marshes. In the low marsh that is partly submerged twice a day, tall, salt-tolerant grasses like Saltwater Cordgrass predominate. Higher in the marsh, where plants are less exposed to salt water, shorter grasses like Saltmeadow Cordgrass, Spike Grass, and Black Needlerush form vast salt meadows.

Knowledge of average high and low tidemarks is usually sufficient for a quick understanding of most coastal environments, but in salt marshes the monthly variation of spring and neap tides ultimately controls zonation. Luckily, you don't need exotic tide tables to see the zones; you just need to look at the pattern of plants to infer how high the highest high tides get (the Mean Spring High Water, or MSHW, level). In a typical Mid-Atlantic salt marsh, the MSHW level will be marked by Marsh Elder (also called High Tide Bush) and Groundsel Trees, which will grow right to the edge of a salt marsh but cannot tolerate much direct contact with salt water. Spot those two bushes, and you'll know how high the highest normal tides get in that marsh.

CLIMATE CHANGE AND SEA LEVEL RISE

Global sea levels have been rising since the Wisconsinan Glaciation began to end 25,000 years ago, but unfortunately rising sea levels are no longer an ancient geologic curiosity. Global climate change—along with the sharp acceleration of the long-term trend of rising seas—means that sea level rise will have a significant and visible effect on shoreline environments, residents, and visitors in coming decades. The global sea level is now increasing by more than 0.14 inches (3.5 mm) per year, and in the Mid-Atlantic Coast region, the sea level has risen about eight inches (20 cm) since 1960. Experts on climate change predict that the sea level along the Atlantic Coast will increase by approximately four to eight feet by the year 2100, and this rise will have profound impacts on salt marshes, beaches, coastal homes, and other coastal business and transportation infrastructure. Another factor is increasing sea level change along the East Coast: long-term regional geologic trends are causing the land in the Mid-Atlantic region to sink by several millimeters per year, worsening the effects of sea level rise. Based on estimates of a one-foot (30-cm) sea level rise by 2035 in the states of New Jersey, Delaware, Maryland, Virginia, and North Carolina, approximately 66,100 people in 99,400 commercial and residential properties, worth about $14.3 billion and $202 million in annual property taxes, will be severely affected. In this scenario, large sections of such low-lying wild environments as the Chesapeake and Delaware Bay shoreline parks and national wildlife

U.S. Navy

Hurricane flooding at the Naval Station Norfolk, Virginia, during Hurricane Isabel, on September 18, 2003. The US Navy has identified sea level rise as a critical problem for its Norfolk bases, which face a combination of rising seas and subsiding ground levels due to long-term geologic factors and to groundwater extraction in the region.

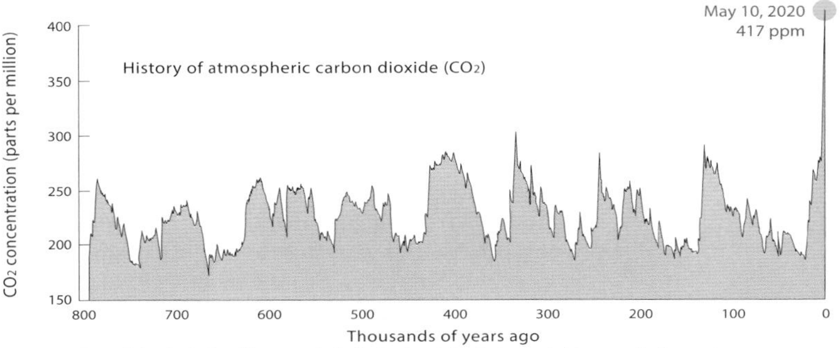
History of atmospheric carbon dioxide (CO_2)
May 10, 2020
417 ppm
CO_2 concentration (parts per million)
400
350
300
250
200
150
800
700
600
500
400
300
200
100
0
Thousands of years ago

Source: Scripps Institution of Oceanography, The Keeling Curve, https://scripps.ucsd.edu/programs/keelingcurve/

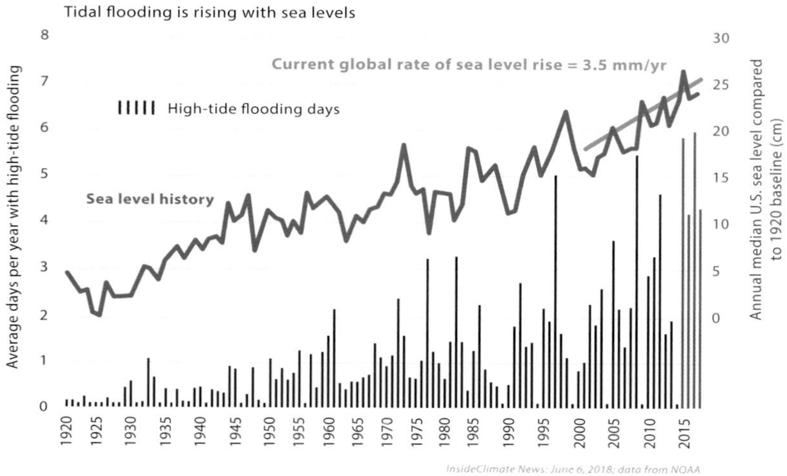
Tidal flooding is rising with sea levels
Current global rate of sea level rise = 3.5 mm/yr
High-tide flooding days
Sea level history
Average days per year with high-tide flooding
Annual median U.S. sea level compared to 1920 baseline (cm)
0
1
2
3
4
5
6
7
8
0
5
10
15
20
25
30
1920
1925
1930
1935
1940
1945
1950
1955
1960
1965
1970
1975
1980
1985
1990
1995
2000
2005
2010
2015
InsideClimate News: June 6, 2018; data from NOAA

refuges, as well as barriers from Sandy Hook, New Jersey, down to Cape Hatteras, North Carolina, will all be profoundly changed. Sections of such major cities as Atlantic City, New Jersey; Philadelphia, Pennsylvania; Ocean City and Baltimore, Maryland; and Norfolk and Newport News, Virginia, will be permanently flooded.

Sea level rise has many harmful effects besides routine daily tidal flooding and shoreline erosion in developed coastal towns and cities. Higher sea levels increase storm damage and the height of storm surges in hurricanes and nor'easters, damage or destroy coastal farmland through saltwater flooding, and damage, disrupt, or drown many natural coastal environments such as salt marshes, estuaries, and the natural communities on barrier islands.

The general warming of the planet over the last century and the increase in atmospheric carbon dioxide (CO_2) are tightly interlinked with sea level rise. Scientists have known since the early 1800s that carbon dioxide in the atmosphere can act as a thermal blanket over the earth, trapping heat energy from the sun in the atmosphere. This greenhouse effect of carbon dioxide is critical to life on earth: it moderates global temperatures that might otherwise be alternately much higher than our normal range during the day and far colder at night. However, the sharp rise of anthropogenic (human-made) carbon dioxide from the burning of fossil fuels like coal and petroleum since the Industrial Revolution, average global temperatures have risen at least 1.2 degrees Celsius (2.16 degrees Fahrenheit) by 2019. Charles Keeling of Scripps Institution of Oceanography was the first scientist to develop a way to measure the level of carbon dioxide in the earth's atmosphere and began keeping records in 1958. Scientists also have obtained good estimates of historical and ancient atmospheric carbon dioxide from air bubbles in ancient ice core samples and other means. The percentage of CO_2 in the atmosphere (see illustration, p. 71) is tightly linked to atmospheric and global warming; in periods of high carbon dioxide, the atmosphere retains more solar heat.

Warmer global temperatures increase the sea level in two ways: through the thermal expansion of ocean water because warm water occupies more volume than cold water, and the melting of mountain glaciers and

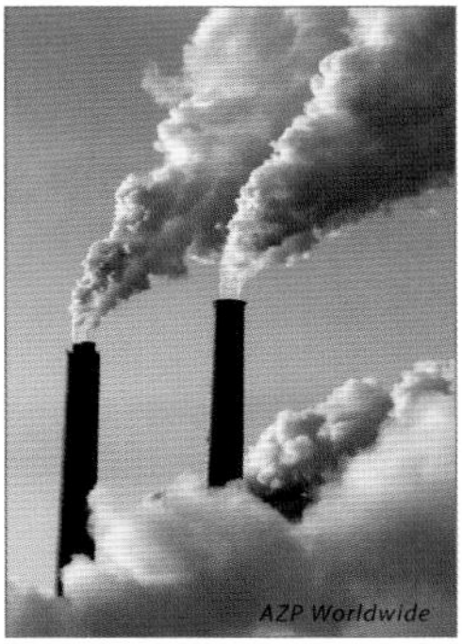
AZP Worldwide

Human-made carbon dioxide emissions have grown to critical levels in recent decades. Although carbon dioxide levels have been rising since the widespread use of coal in the nineteenth century, fully half of the carbon in today's atmosphere was emitted in the past 30 years.

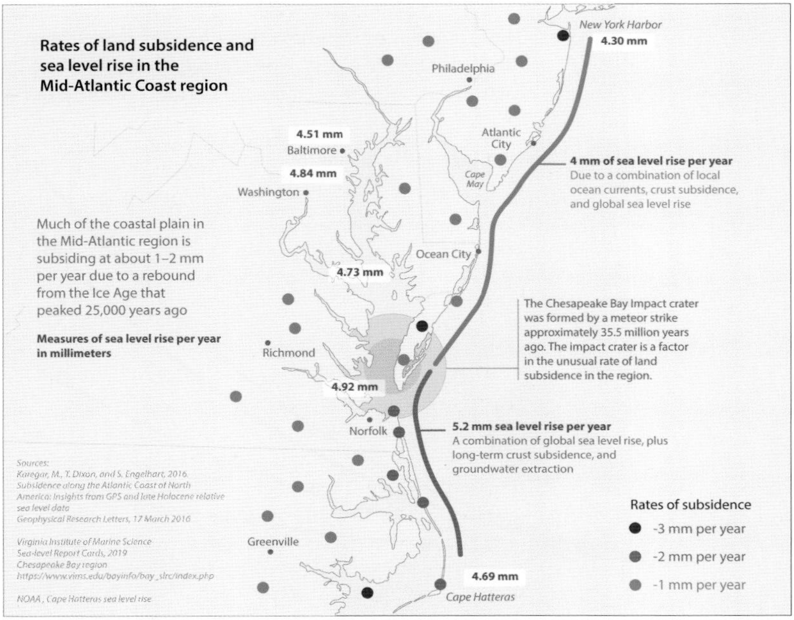
Rates of land subsidence and sea level rise in the Mid-Atlantic Coast region
New York Harbor
4.30 mm
Philadelphia
4.51 mm
Baltimore
4.84 mm
Washington
Atlantic City
Cape May
4 mm of sea level rise per year
Due to a combination of local ocean currents, crust subsidence, and global sea level rise
Much of the coastal plain in the Mid-Atlantic region is subsiding at about 1–2 mm per year due to a rebound from the Ice Age that peaked 25,000 years ago
Ocean City
4.73 mm
Measures of sea level rise per year in millimeters
Richmond
The Chesapeake Bay Impact crater was formed by a meteor strike approximately 35.5 million years ago. The impact crater is a factor in the unusual rate of land subsidence in the region.
4.92 mm
Norfolk
5.2 mm sea level rise per year
A combination of global sea level rise, plus long-term crust subsidence, and groundwater extraction
Sources:
Karegar, M., T. Dixon, and S. Engelhart, 2016.
Subsidence along the Atlantic Coast of North America: Insights from GPS and late Holocene relative sea level data
Geophysical Research Letters, 17 March 2016
Virginia Institute of Marine Science
Sea-level Report Cards, 2019
Chesapeake Bay region
https://www.vims.edu/bayinfo/bay_slrc/index.php
NOAA, Cape Hatteras sea level rise
Greenville
4.69 mm
Cape Hatteras
Rates of subsidence
-3 mm per year
-2 mm per year
-1 mm per year

the land-based ice sheets in Greenland and the Antarctic. The oceans absorb 90 percent of the additional heat the earth now absorbs due to the greenhouse effect. Like most substances, water expands when it is heated, and that extra volume of the warmer water in today's oceans is the primary driver of sea level rise.

The rising sea level

We think of the shorelines we have known all our lives as permanent, but that is only because of our limited time perspective. Many cities along the Mid-Atlantic Coast were founded in the early to mid-1600s when the earth's crust in the region was geologically 1.5 feet higher than it is today and global sea levels were almost two feet lower (0.6 m). This historical perspective on sea level rise and land subsidence is vital to understanding the difficult circumstances facing many older Mid-Atlantic port cities. For example, when they were first built in the early 1700s, Annapolis, Maryland, and Norfolk, Virginia, were situated well above even the highest tide ranges. Today both cities face constant high-tide flooding because the seas have risen and the land beneath them has subsided.

Three factors contribute to the subsiding land along the Mid-Atlantic Coast: isostatic rebound of the earth's crust after the last glacial period, groundwater

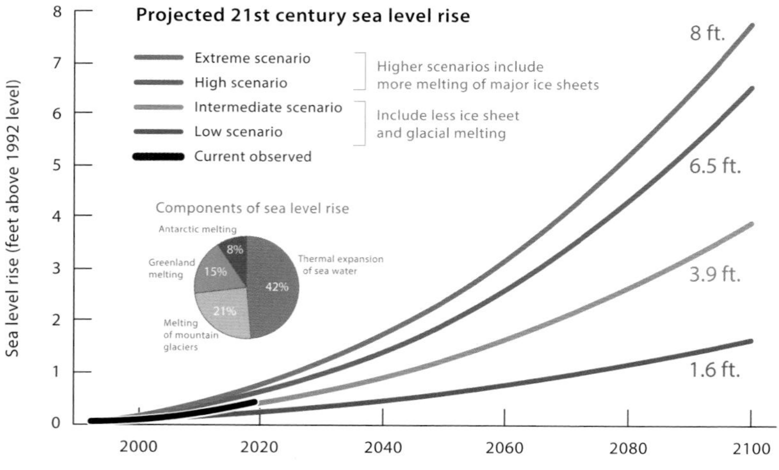
Projected 21st century sea level rise
Extreme scenario
High scenario
Intermediate scenario
Low scenario
Current observed
Higher scenarios include more melting of major ice sheets
Include less ice sheet and glacial melting
Components of sea level rise
Antarctic melting
8%
Greenland melting
15%
Thermal expansion of sea water
42%
21%
Melting of mountain glaciers
8 ft.
6.5 ft.
3.9 ft.
1.6 ft.
Sea level rise (feet above 1992 level)
0
1
2
3
4
5
6
7
8
2000
2020
2040
2060
2080
2100
Adapted from Union of Concerned Scientists (2018), Underwater: Rising Seas, Chronic Floods...

pumping in some areas, and the impact of the meteor crater that underlies the Hampton Roads region (see illustration, p. 73). During the Wisconsinan Glaciation the massive weight of the continent-sized Laurentide Ice Sheet caused the earth's crust to sag downward under the ice sheet. The downward pressure on the crust under the ice sheet caused the unglaciated parts of the East Coast south of New York to bulge upward, roughly like a playground seesaw. Since the ice sheet melted away the upward bulge along the Mid-Atlantic Coast has been gradually subsiding (geologists call this isostatic rebound), and the sinking land has now combined with global sea level rise to accelerate the overall rate of sea level rise along the Mid-Atlantic Coast. In the Norfolk–Hampton Roads region, the pumping of groundwater to supply cities with drinking water has contributed further to land subsidence.

Alexey Seafarer

The melting of the Greenland and Antarctic ice caps currently contribute about 23 percent to rising sea levels, but climate scientists expect this contribution to rise quickly during the twenty-first century.

The Chesapeake Bay Impact crater was formed by a meteor strike approximately 35.5 million years ago. The crater is a recent discovery (1983) and was first described in detail in 1997. The meteor punched a deep hole into the bedrock of the Hampton Roads area and left a massive pit of crushed rock that is now under modern river sediment layers from the Chesapeake Bay. The impact crater is important today because it contributes to the unusual rate of land subsidence in the region, as the surface land sags into the ancient crater.

Currently, the thermal expansion of ocean water accounts for most sea level rise (42 percent). Other contributors to the rising seas are the melting of mountain glaciers (21 percent) and the melting of the major ice sheets of Greenland (15 percent) and Antarctica (8 percent). Later in the twenty-first century, climate scientists expect the melting in Greenland and Antarctica to contribute a much larger percentage to sea level rise, and the more pessimistic sea level forecasts are based primarily on significantly increased melting from those major land-based ice sheets. The melting of sea ice in the Arctic Ocean doesn't play a direct role in sea level rise because Arctic ice is floating and therefore already displaces its volume of seawater. However, the major loss of the ice cover of the Arctic

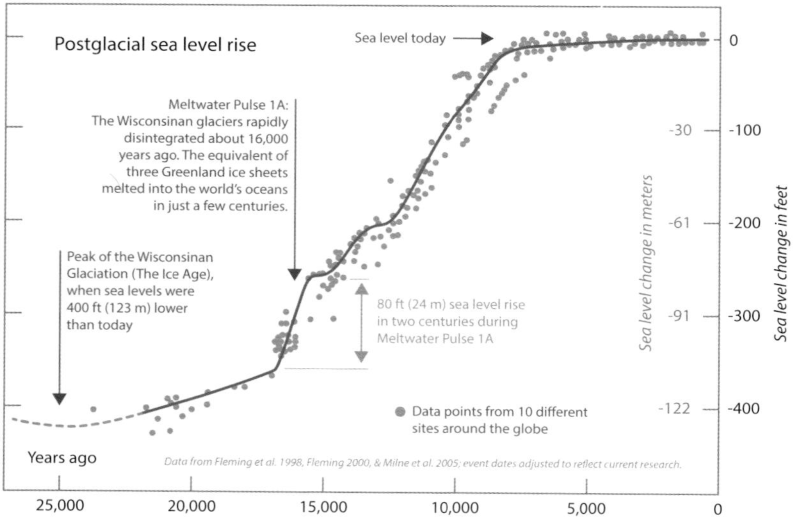

Postglacial sea level rise
Sea level today
Meltwater Pulse 1A: The Wisconsinan glaciers rapidly disintegrated about 16,000 years ago. The equivalent of three Greenland ice sheets melted into the world's oceans in just a few centuries.
Peak of the Wisconsinan Glaciation (The Ice Age), when sea levels were 400 ft (123 m) lower than today
80 ft (24 m) sea level rise in two centuries during Meltwater Pulse 1A
Data points from 10 different sites around the globe
Years ago
Data from Fleming et al. 1998, Fleming 2000, & Milne et al. 2005; event dates adjusted to reflect current research.
25,000
20,000
15,000
10,000
5,000
0
Sea level change in meters
-30
-61
-91
-122
Sea level change in feet
0
-100
-200
-300
-400

In a warming climate glacial ice doesn't melt away at a steady rate. The geologic record shows that there were times after the most recent glacial period when the sea level rose at a dramatically higher rate, called a meltwater pulse.

Ocean does contribute to global warming, because the bright white of Arctic ice used to reflect more sunlight and heat back into space. The Arctic Ocean is now the most rapidly warming region of the planet because of the loss of sea ice.

Evidence from the past

We don't have to imagine what effects our current level of atmospheric carbon dioxide and global warming might bring. We have a detailed geological record of what happened 15 million years ago, the last time atmospheric CO_2 levels were this high (over 400 ppm) for a sustained period. Average global temperatures then were about 5–10 degrees Fahrenheit warmer than today, and the sea level was 75–120 feet higher. The Arctic Ocean had no permanent ice, and most of the ice in Antarctica had melted into the sea.

So why aren't sea levels higher now? Time. Our current rate of increase in atmospheric carbon is rising so fast that the global climate will likely take several centuries or more to catch up with the new conditions. The ice in the Antarctic, Greenland, and the world's mountain chains hasn't had time enough to melt away, but all indications are that today global melting rates are now

Salt marshes along Sinepuxent Bay at Assateague Island National Seashore, Maryland. The species composition and ecological structure of salt marshes are sensitive to mere millimeters of sea level rise.

POWHATAN
this state & fashion when Capt. Smith
was deliuered to him prisoner
1607
MANNAHOACKS
Cape Henrie
Cape Charles
THE
VIRGINIAN
SEA

Environmental History

Brooklyn and Manhattan as seen from Sandy Hook, New Jersey, looking across the entrance to New York Harbor. Sandy Hook is a part of the Gateway National Recreation Area.

The early European settlement of the Mid-Atlantic region was a clash of empires that spanned the Atlantic Ocean: the English, the Dutch, the Spanish, and even the Swedes laid claim to parts of the coastline that then belonged to an entirely different empire, that of the Algonquian-speaking peoples of the Atlantic Coastal Plain. Europeans didn't settle the New World as much as unsettle it, through cultural and military clashes with native peoples, the introduction of Eurasian diseases that decimated the indigenous population, the rapid growth of slash-and-burn land clearance, and the exploitation of local resources for lumber, fur pelts, waterfowl, and seafood.

Early European explorers of the Mid-Atlantic Coast found the region to be a paradox—a land of wild, sandy coasts offering few natural harbors but punctuated by huge, almost unbelievably rich bays and estuaries teeming with seafood and wild game. Inland from the coast, dense virgin forests of hardwood and pines grew on the deep, fertile soils of the Atlantic Coastal Plain. As explorers traveled up the Chesapeake and Delaware Bays, they found the coastal plain laced with fine rivers that were navigable for long distances inland, even by large ships, a major advantage to early settlers at a time when networks of roads were rudimentary at best.

Opposite: A replica of the English ship *Susan Constant*, the largest of the three ships of the 1606–7 voyage that founded the colony of Jamestown, Virginia. The Chesapeake Bay and its major rivers were critical to the development of Virginia, Maryland, and other Mid-Atlantic colonies, allowing large ships and cargoes to move as far as 200 miles inland at a time when roads were few and primitive.

The split personality of the Mid-Atlantic Coast is reflected in the environmental history of the region. Most of the coast is composed of sandy barrier islands and peninsulas that offer few natural harbors, treacherous shoals, and small inlets unsuitable for large ships. Thus much of the immediate shoreline remained unknown and undeveloped for hundreds of years after European contact, until the rise of recreational use of the shore in the mid-1800s. While the coasts remained undeveloped, the major bays, estuaries, and rivers of the Mid-Atlantic Coast enabled the rapid development of the European colonies. New York Harbor, Delaware Bay, and the Chesapeake Bay all offered excellent shelter for large oceangoing ships as well as access to major rivers.

The Mid-Atlantic Coast before European settlements

When the glaciers retreated from New York and New England about 15,000 years ago and the climate warmed, Paleo-Indian hunter-gatherers likely moved into what was then a fairly harsh, cold landscape in the Mid-Atlantic region, similar to that of the Canadian Maritime provinces today. Radiocarbon-dated evidence of human activity in the area dates back to 10,000 years ago, and other evidence indicates that people were in the region well before then. At that time the sea level was 150–200 feet lower than it is today

The huge Chesapeake and Delaware Bays, New York Harbor, and the Pamlico and Albemarle Sounds behind the Outer Banks—as well as the deep rivers that drained into them—offered early mariners and settlers easy, safe access into the riches of the Mid-Atlantic Coastal Plain. In many cases, the rivers and sounds were navigable for a hundred miles or more inland.

(see map, pp. 20–21), and early people probably moved into coastal areas on what is now the continental shelf east of the current Atlantic Coast, but evidence of their settlements has long since been submerged by the Atlantic Ocean.*

Native Americans in the period just before European contact

In the 1500s most of the indigenous peoples in the Mid-Atlantic region spoke closely related variants of the Algonquian language and inhabited distinct territorial areas along the Mid-Atlantic Coast and the Chesapeake and Delaware Bays and rivers. Coastal tribes mostly lived in permanent villages, although some migrated between shoreline settlements in warmer weather and more sheltered inland locations during winter. The Lenape (also called the Delaware) complex of clans dominated the southern New York, New Jersey, eastern Pennsylvania, and northern Delaware region. The Lenape culture had ancient roots in the area, and the broader Algonquian culture considered the Lenapes the "grandfathers" from whom other Algonquian peoples originated. The Powhatan Confederacy (or Virginia Algonquians) dominated the shores of the Chesapeake Bay in Maryland and Virginia. Many Powhatan place-names live on in the region, including the Rappahannock, Pamunkey, Chickahominy, and Nanticoke Rivers. Chesapeake is a word derived from the Algonquian "Chesepiooc" for "great waters," or "at a big river."

Native American land use

After the Wisconsinan Glaciation (what we generally call the Ice Age) began to melt 25,000 years ago, Paleo-Indians who moved into the Mid-Atlantic Coast region wiped out many large mammal species, such as woolly mammoths, giant sloths, and giant beavers, that previously populated eastern North America. The disappearance of these large Pleistocene animals surely changed the ancient environment, but most of those extinctions took place by 10,000 years ago.

Native Americans in the Mid-Atlantic region are known to have used fire extensively to remove undergrowth in favorite game hunting areas and to clear

*The long, complex history of the Native American peoples of the Mid-Atlantic Coast is beyond the scope of this guide. For more information, I recommend these books:

The Powhatan Landscape: An Archaeological History of the Algonquian Chesapeake, by Martin D. Gallivan. Gainesville: University Press of Florida, 2016.

The Saltwater Frontier: Indians and the Contest for the American Coast, by Andrew Lipman. New Haven: Yale University Press, 2015.

First People: The Early Indians of Virginia, by Keith Egloff and Deborah Woodward. Charlottesville: University of Virginia Press, 2006.

Changes in the Land: Indians, Colonists, and the Ecology of New England, by William Cronon. Rev. ed. New York: Hill and Wang, 2003. *The best book on Indians, colonists, and their relationship to the natural world of the Atlantic Coast.*

land for planting crops. The fire-cleared woodland edges, with patches of open grassland, were especially appealing to White-Tailed Deer, a major game animal for Native Americans. However, because indigenous populations were relatively small and scattered, the overall ecological impact of their settlements, agriculture, hunting, shellfish gathering, and fire use was environmentally benign compared to what came after Europeans arrived. Except near large villages and permanent settlements along the coast, and aside from commonly using fire to clear forest undergrowth, Native American land use in the millennium before European contact made relatively few widespread or long-term changes in the natural environments of the Mid-Atlantic coastal region.

Epidemics and disease

As Europeans began contact with the peoples of the Americas in the 1500s, they introduced diseases that immediately began to devastate native populations along the Atlantic Coast. Because of long isolation from Eurasian diseases, Native Americans had little genetic immunity to smallpox, measles, influenza, and other diseases common among the crews of early exploration and fishing vessels. Epidemics ran rampant through indigenous populations, sometimes wiping out settlements within days, leaving empty villages full of corpses. Aside from the terrible psychological trauma of seeing family and neighbors die within days, imagine trying to carry out daily life when 90 percent of the population has died within a few weeks. In such circumstances, the social infrastructure—food, medicine, clothing, commerce, religion, cultural activities, power and water systems, public safety—would quickly collapse. And so it was for many of the indigenous societies of the Mid-Atlantic: whole cultures, languages, and belief systems vanished within a few decades of first contact with Europeans.

For an excellent environmental history of the Virginia Tidewater region, see:

Nature and History in the Potomac Country: From Hunter-Gatherers to the Age of Jefferson, by James D. Rice. Baltimore: Johns Hopkins University Press, 2009.

Population estimates for Native Americans in the Mid-Atlantic at the time of contact are rough at best and are typically derived from early explorer accounts. There may have been 12,000–15,000 Algonquian-speaking people in the Chesapeake Bay region in the late 1500s. Perhaps 15,000–23,000 Lenapes lived in the

New Jersey–New York Harbor area, living in about 80 settlements. Epidemiologists estimate that Eurasian diseases killed 70–80 percent of the indigenous people along the Mid-Atlantic Coast; in many areas, mortality rates exceeded 90 percent.

Weakened by disease and depopulation, and quickly overwhelmed by thousands of settlers from Europe, the indigenous peoples of the Mid-Atlantic Coast were marginalized and forced into reservations that were later dismantled by legal maneuvers. Many Native Americans were eventually pushed into western reservations by the Indian Removal Act of 1830, essentially a form of ethnic cleansing that left little cultural legacy in the Mid-Atlantic region besides place-names. For example, the centers of Lenape culture are now in Moraviantown and Muncey, Ontario, and in the Anadarko and Bartlesville areas of Oklahoma, both many hundreds of miles from the original lands of the Lenape. Today in the Chesapeake Bay region there are surviving centers of Native American cultures of the Chickahominy, Mattaponi, Monacan, Nansemond, Pamunkey, and Rappahannock groups. The surviving Maryland and Virginia tribes are increasingly recognized for their ancient cultures, and many important

***The Treaty of Penn** with the Indians*, by Benjamin West, 1772. The painting depicts William Penn's treaty of peace with Tamanend, chief of the Lenape, in 1683. West reconstructed the scene almost a century later from descriptions and an old portrait of William Penn, but the Native Americans' appearance was mostly conjecture. Although the treaty lasted for 70 years, the Lenape became embroiled in the French and Indian Wars, and through later land seizures and forced migrations they were driven from their traditional lands along the Delaware Bay and River by 1800.

Benjamin West

Worthington Whittredge, Metropolitan Museum

Today all we have left is the artistic imagining of how the vanished old-growth forests of the Atlantic Coastal Plain might have looked. *The Brook in the Woods*, by Worthington Whittredge, 1885.

native archaeological sites, such as Werowocomoco in Gloucester County, Virginia, are now protected and preserved.

The land at the time of first contact

Explorers encountered thick old-growth forests that were far older and more biologically diverse than any current woodlands in the region. The forests of the precontact Mid-Atlantic Coast contained the same basic mix of tree and shrub species as today, so we can make educated guesses about how they looked based on prehistoric pollen evidence as well as modern woodlands. On the immediate coastline and barrier islands were maritime forests of Pitch Pine, Loblolly Pine, American Holly, Canadian Serviceberry (Shadbush), Sassafras, and Black Tupelo (Black Gum). Along the southern Virginia and North Carolina coasts, there were dense coastal forests of Live Oak, Laurel Oak, Loblolly Pine, Pitch Pine, American Holly, Sassafras, Black Tupelo (Black Gum), Redbay, Atlantic White Cedar, and Flowering Dogwood. On higher mainland ground along the banks of the Chesapeake and Delaware Bays were 7,000-year-old cathedral-like coastal plain forests of American Chestnut; Black, Northern Red, and Southern Red Oaks; hickories, American Beech; and pines. Almost every forest on the Atlantic Coastal Plain has been clear-cut at least once (some as many as three times) since European settlers arrived. These ancient woodlands, though they had a familiar range of trees, were unimaginably larger, older, and more complex than anything present today.

The one major exception to the mostly vanished Mid-Atlantic Coast's ancient forests is the immense New Jersey Pine Barrens, where the Pitch Pines were too small and thinly scattered to attract many woodcutters, and the poor sandy soil and shrub-heath ground cover were not suitable for grazing livestock or conversion to farmland. The Pine Barrens cover 1.1 million acres of south-central New Jersey, occupying 22 percent of the state and making the forest the most extensive intact wilderness area in the Mid-Atlantic coastal region. See the chapter on maritime forests for more on this unique habitat.

Bays and wetlands

Behind the barrier islands and long coastal peninsulas there were huge salt marshes. Salt marshes are one

A mature maritime Pine Barrens forest at Island Beach State Park, New Jersey. Coastal Pine Barrens is a unique ecological community with sandy, acidic, nutrient-poor soils that support a unique coastal forest community dominated by Pitch Pines (*Pinus rigida*). Similar coastal forests exist south of Delaware Bay, but there the dominant tree is the Loblolly Pine (*Pinus taeda*).

of the most ecologically productive environments on earth, exceeded in sheer biomass production only by tropical mangrove forests and rain forests (see the chapter on salt marshes). Ecologists estimate that the Chesapeake Bay and its major tributaries have lost 58 percent of its wetlands over the past 400 years, so the original salt, brackish, and freshwater marshes were far more extensive than we see today.

The huge Chesapeake and Delaware Bays are estuaries (see the chapter on estuaries), semi-enclosed bodies of water where the salt water of the ocean meets freshwater draining from coastal rivers and streams. North Carolina's Albemarle and Pamlico Sounds behind the Outer Banks barrier islands are also major estuaries, as are the many smaller bays and sounds behind the Mid-Atlantic Coast's barrier islands and peninsulas. Estuaries offer critical food and shelter to all kinds of fish, invertebrates such as crabs and oysters, and millions of migratory waterfowl. Although the Chesapeake Bay today has many problems due to pollution and siltation from the loss of forests and wetlands, the bay remains the third largest producer of seafood products in the United States, behind the Atlantic and Pacific Oceans.

The Chesapeake Bay

With its 48 principal rivers and 1,750 miles of navigable waterways, the Chesapeake Bay had a profound effect on the history and development of significant portions of colonial Virginia and Maryland as well as parts of Delaware and Pennsylvania, opening over 10,000 square miles of territory to commerce and freight movement at a time when roadways were scarce. This vast network of streams and rivers made possible the development of the Chesapeake region's first major commercial crop—tobacco. Without the ability to transport this bulky but delicate commodity by water, colonial Virginia and Maryland would have developed very differently, and much more slowly. Ironically, the easy transport of tobacco inhibited the development of towns and cities around the Chesapeake, because the usual local infrastructure of transportation, port, and trading facilities supported by towns wasn't necessary. With easy access to waterways, tobacco farmers could bring transport barges right up to the riverfront, load

Opposite:
The Blackwater National Wildlife Refuge, Bucktown, contains one-third of Maryland's tidal wetlands. The refuge is one of the most vibrant examples of what the Chesapeake coasts might have looked like before development, but there is no refuge from the realities of modern development and climate change. Blackwater and its river watershed lose over 300 acres of marsh grasses every year due to sea level rise. The refuge itself has lost 5,000 acres of wetland since 1938.

the tobacco, and send it directly to such large ports as Norfolk, Virginia, and later Baltimore for transport to England.

The major cities of the Mid-Atlantic Coast region mostly developed along the fall line where the earthen coastal plain met the rocky Piedmont. On coastal plain rivers, the fall line is typically marked by rocky rapids or even waterfalls, and farther upstream the rivers are not navigable. Thus major towns often developed at the fall line, to support the transfer of cargo from river ships and barges into warehouses, or onto wagons for movement inland.

The Fall Line

Most of the major towns and cities that developed along the Mid-Atlantic Coastal Plain were located along the regional fall line of the Piedmont region. The fall line was the last point upstream where rivers on the coastal plain were easily navigable. Upriver from the fall line was the rocky Piedmont region of Appalachian foothills, where rivers flowed on a much steeper gradient. Where the steeper, rocky Piedmont met the coastal plain rivers, there were often waterfalls

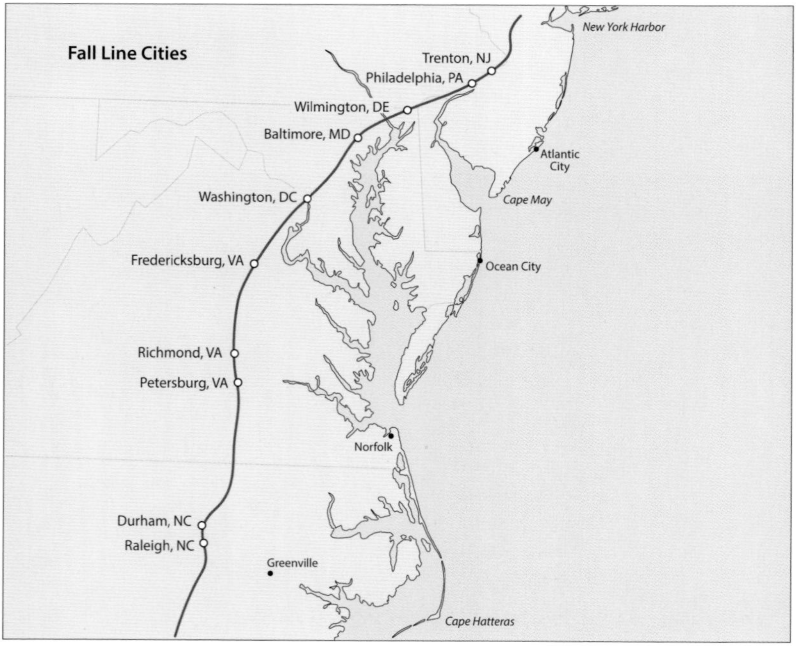
Fall Line Cities
New York Harbor
Trenton, NJ
Philadelphia, PA
Wilmington, DE
Baltimore, MD
Atlantic City
Cape May
Washington, DC
Fredericksburg, VA
Ocean City
Richmond, VA
Petersburg, VA
Norfolk
Durham, NC
Raleigh, NC
Greenville
Cape Hatteras

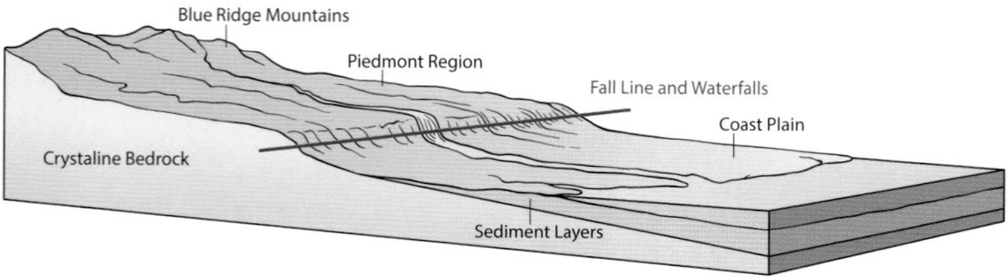
Blue Ridge Mountains
Piedmont Region
Fall Line and Waterfalls
Coast Plain
Crystaline Bedrock
Sediment Layers

or rapids on the river, hence the name "fall line." At the fall line river cargo would need to be unloaded onto wagons for further transportation or temporarily stored in warehouses. Thus major cities and towns naturally developed along the fall line (see map, facing page). The Little Falls of the Potomac at Washington, DC, the falls of the James River at Richmond, Virginia, and the rapids on the Delaware River at Trenton, New Jersey, are all instances where rivers ceased to be easily navigable, and major cities grew up to support the shift to land transportation.

jonbilious

The Potomac River Rapids perfectly illustrate the fall line. For most of its length the Potomac is a wide, slow-flowing river that empties into the Chesapeake Bay. The southern section of the Potomac was ideal for early river navigation and commerce. Just northwest of Washington, DC, however, the Potomac meets the rugged bedrock of the Piedmont, and the river becomes a series of swift-flowing channels and rapids. The capital area developed near the fall line because that's where river traffic halted.

THE LOST COAST

European settlers quickly recognized the unparalleled riches of the region, with its large bays and estuaries, the flat, fertile soils of the coastal plain, and the abundance of coastal and river fish and game. But the Mid-Atlantic Coast presented many challenges to settlement. From a deepwater sailor's perspective, the ocean coasts were a nightmare, with sandy offshore shoals, long stretches of islands and peninsulas with few natural ports to accommodate even a small ship, and small and treacherous inlets. In the 375 miles of coast from Sandy Hook, New Jersey, south to Cape Hatteras the Mid-Atlantic Coast is composed of 305 miles of sandy barrier islands and peninsulas, 20 miles of bay mouth, and 50 miles of mainland beaches providing no harbor or shelter for ships. The Delaware and Chesapeake Bays offer a refuge from ocean storms and access to inland regions, but even the bay shores presented early settlers with only a few locations where large, deepwater ports were easy to build, in Philadelphia on the Delaware River and in Norfolk, Baltimore, and Annapolis on the Chesapeake Bay.

The dangerous sand shoals, treacherous inlets, and vast salt marshes of the barrier islands and bays along the Mid-Atlantic Coast were a lost coast, largely ignored and only lightly populated through the first few centuries of European colonization. If the islands and long peninsulas were used at all, it was for the grazing of cattle and horses. Barrier islands made ideal natural corrals, and the islands offered plenty of marsh grass

Overleaf:
Today we see the sand coast as an inviting playground, but the early explorers and sailors saw most of the Mid-Atlantic Coast as a hostile wasteland, full of dangerous shoals and lacking safe harbors for oceangoing vessels.

A late summer dawn and a Sanderling (Calidris alba) at Assateague Island National Seashore, Maryland.

Although their origin stories are more romantic legend than provable fact, the wild pony herds of the Mid-Atlantic barrier islands are a favorite with visitors. The most famous herds are at Assateague Island National Seashore in Maryland (above), Chincoteague National Wildlife Refuge in Virginia, and in the Currituck National Wildlife Refuge of North Carolina's Outer Banks. The large, rich salt marshes of Assateague offer the local wild ponies plenty of forage all year.

Opposite:
The legends that swirl around Edward Teach ("Blackbeard") are wildly exaggerated, but his crimes were real and numerous enough to warrant a place in history. After pursuing a pirate career mostly in the West Indies, Teach retreated to the Atlantic Coast to evade the Royal Navy—and the hurricanes of the Caribbean. Depicted here is *The Capture of the Pirate Blackbeard* (1920), by famed American illustrator and history painter Jean Leon Gerome Ferris.

for forage. Legend has it that the wild ponies of Assateague Island and the Outer Banks originated from ancient Spanish shipwrecks now lost to history, but it's far more likely that the ponies—though charming—are the feral descendants of colonial-era farm animals that were pastured on the islands to avoid fencing regulations and the taxation of livestock.

Pirates, privateers, and rumrunners

The isolated Mid-Atlantic Coast, without deep ports or roads and with confusing and dangerous inlets and shoals, was perfect for one form of eighteenth-century commerce: piracy. From the late 1600s through the mid-1700s the Mid-Atlantic colonies depended on trade with England for almost all manufactured goods, as well as for shipping their tobacco, tar, pitch, and other bulk commodities to traders in England. The heavy ocean traffic of lightly armed cargo ships proved irresistible to nautical criminals throughout the Caribbean and Mid-Atlantic. The Royal Navy lacked sufficient ships to patrol the entire region, and piracy thrived. In the fall months the pirates of the Caribbean favored the Mid-Atlantic Coast because it offered them places to hide and hunt away from the frequent hurricanes in the tropics.

The most notorious pirate along the Mid-Atlantic Coast was Edward Teach (ca. 1680–1718), known sometimes as Edward Thatch but best by his nickname Blackbeard. Teach's most famous vessel was a captured

Queen Anne's Revenge, 1717

Jean Leon Gerome Ferris painting; pistol JRB

Jennifer

In Blackbeard's time Ocracoke Island on the Outer Banks was mostly a tangle of Live Oak and Loblolly Pine maritime forest. The isolated island was an ideal hiding spot for pirates.

French frigate he renamed the *Queen Anne's Revenge.* After a decade of raiding West Indies shipping, Teach retreated to the remote coasts of the Outer Banks in what is now North Carolina. It was easy to hide among the barrier islands, and the many sand shoals and shallow inlets made it impossible for large warships to follow him there.

Edward Teach's reality was more complicated than the legends suggest. Teach could be charming as well as ruthless. In early 1718, he accepted a royal pardon for his crimes and settled in Bath, North Carolina. He soon became embroiled in the political rivalry between the commercial proprietary colony of North Carolina and the crown colony of Virginia. The independent, hardscrabble North Carolinians resented the perceived arrogance of the Virginia colony, and many viewed the pirates of the Outer Banks area as local folk heroes. To North Carolinians, Blackbeard and his trained sailors were also potentially useful allies against both local Native Americans and the efforts of the Virginia colony to dominate the region. To Virginians, Blackbeard—who quickly returned to piracy after his pardon—was a mortal threat to royal shipping on the Mid-Atlantic Coast.

In November 1718, the British authorities in Virginia sent a pair of small warships to the Outer Banks to find and kill the pirate Blackbeard. They found Teach hiding near the southern end of Ocracoke Island, attacked his ship, killed him after a day's battle, and captured much of his crew for later execution. Virginia's governor illegally sanctioned the expedition that killed Blackbeard without the knowledge of North Carolina's governor, who had tolerated (or at least ignored) Blackbeard's return to raiding Virginia's shipping.

Edward Teach's experience as both the notorious pirate Blackbeard and (effectively) a privateer whose actions against shipping were sometimes overlooked by local government was to become a model for later raiding along the Mid-Atlantic Coast. In colonial times privateers with warrants from the British government were encouraged to attack any ships from enemy countries like France and Spain. Some former pirates became privateers in service to the Crown, and thus the tradition of raiding commerce along the Mid-Atlantic Coast continued well after the age of piracy ended in the early 1700s. The isolated coasts and inlets sheltered American privateers and smugglers evading British taxes up to and during the Revolutionary War. After the War of 1812, as they lost government sanction and the coast became less isolated, privateers faded away on the Mid-Atlantic Coast. A later echo of the days of piracy emerged during the Prohibition era of the 1920s, when rumrunners in small boats again used the complex and isolated parts of the shoreline to land cases of alcohol from offshore cargo ships to supply illegal speakeasy bars in towns and cities up and down the East Coast.

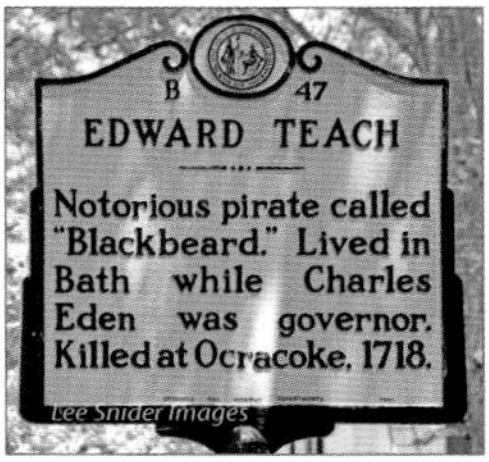
B 47
EDWARD TEACH
Notorious pirate called "Blackbeard." Lived in Bath while Charles Eden was governor. Killed at Ocracoke, 1718.
Lee Snider Images

Bath, North Carolina, was an early coastal settlement on the Pamlico River. Edward Teach ("Blackbeard") briefly used Bath as a base of operations for privateering along the North Carolina coast. Bath still celebrates its association with the pirate, illustrating the complex relationship Teach had with the government of colonial-era North Carolina.

Whales and whaling on the Mid-Atlantic Coast

The waters off the Mid-Atlantic Coast are spring and fall migration pathways for North Atlantic Right Whales and Humpback Whales. Before New England's whaling fleet heavily hunted them, substantial groups of Humpback Whales and Right Whales likely lived most of the year off the Mid-Atlantic Coast and in the deeper southern reaches of the Delaware and Chesapeake Bays. Today the summer populations of Right Whales and Humpback Whales are centered primarily off New England, in the Gulf of Maine, and off the Canadian Maritimes. However, in recent years, as the stocks of Atlantic Menhaden have improved, some Humpbacks have returned to their historical feeding grounds in the New York Bight, off Long Island, and off New Jersey. When the northern waters cool in late fall, the whales migrate south along the coast toward warmer southern waters to mate and give birth. The calving grounds for North Atlantic Right Whales are centered off Georgia and northern Florida; East Coast Humpback Whales travel farther south to Silver Bank, just north of the Dominican Republic, to mate and calve their young.

Dollar Photo Club

A breeching North Atlantic Right Whale (*Eubalaena glacialis*). Right Whales were once common in the waters of the Mid-Atlantic Coast, but were hunted almost to extinction in the nineteenth century. Today there are only about 400 North Atlantic Right Whales, and over the past few years their population has shrunk due to fishing gear entanglements and ship strikes.

These whale migration pathways have come to wider public attention as companies interested in offshore drilling on the continental shelf have sought permits to do seismic testing for oil deposits. The air guns used for seismic testing produce sounds louder than a jet

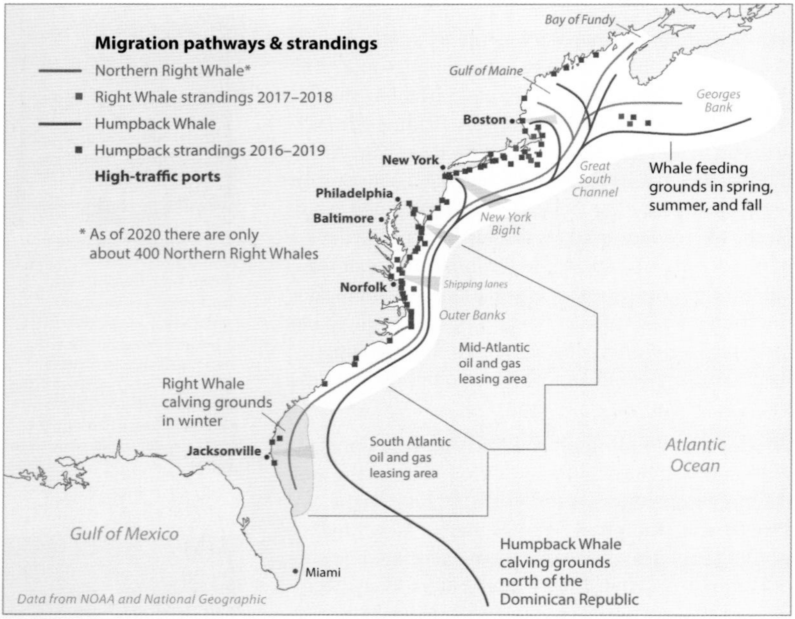

Migration pathways & strandings
Northern Right Whale*
Right Whale strandings 2017–2018
Humpback Whale
Humpback strandings 2016–2019
High-traffic ports
* As of 2020 there are only about 400 Northern Right Whales
Bay of Fundy
Gulf of Maine
Georges Bank
Boston
New York
Philadelphia
Baltimore
Norfolk
Great South Channel
Whale feeding grounds in spring, summer, and fall
New York Bight
Shipping lanes
Outer Banks
Mid-Atlantic oil and gas leasing area
Right Whale calving grounds in winter
Jacksonville
South Atlantic oil and gas leasing area
Atlantic Ocean
Gulf of Mexico
Miami
Humpback Whale calving grounds north of the Dominican Republic
Data from NOAA and National Geographic

engine at maximum power, drowning out all natural sounds in the marine environment, with strong potential to injure, deafen, or even kill marine mammals. From January 2016 through February 2019 the National Oceanic and Atmospheric Administration recorded 88 Humpback Whale strandings along the US Atlantic Coast, which the agency declared to be "an unusual mortality event" because this figure was dou-

Humpback Whale
Megaptera novaeangliae

ble the number of whales stranded between 2013 and 2016. Although many whale deaths are known to be caused by fishing gear entanglement and ship strikes, the addition of seismic testing to coastal waters only increases environmental stress on marine mammals.

New England may be renowned for its nineteenth-century whaling industry, but as early as the late 1600s some small, shore-based whalers operated along the Mid-Atlantic Coast, principally in New Jersey on Barnegat Bay and at Cape May. In shore-based whaling, the whalers hunted whales from small coastal vessels and then towed their captures to shore to process the blubber and baleen. The Cape May whaling community was founded by whaling families that migrated from Massachusetts ports around 1685. The much larger New England ship-based whaling operations quickly eclipsed these shore-based whalers, however, and most Mid-Atlantic whaling faded by the mid-1700s.

New England whalers were well aware of the presence of whales off the Mid-Atlantic Coast. As whales became scarce in New England waters, whalers were attracted to the Mid-Atlantic Coast and what they called the Hatteras Grounds, though these whaling grounds extended from New Jersey south to Cape Hatteras. The larger whale species became hard to find off the East Coast by the early 1800s, yet New England whaleships often stopped on the Hatteras Grounds to train new crew members by running practice hunts for Long-Finned Pilot Whales.

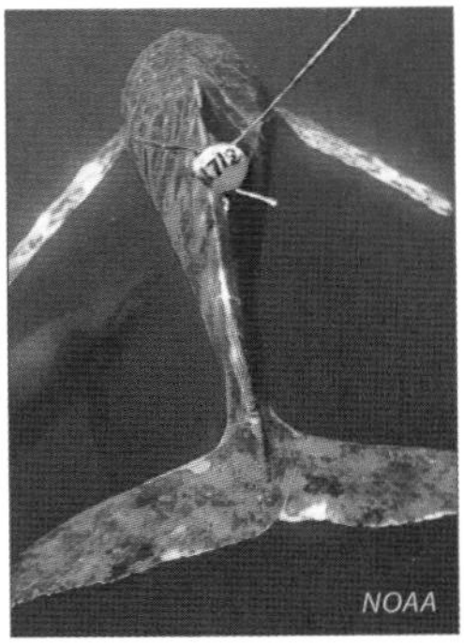
1719
NOAA

Entanglement in fishing gear is a serious problem for both Humpback Whales and North Atlantic Right Whales. Here a Humpback Whale is dragging a heavy line and floats from an offshore fishing net. Whales can sometimes be cut out of their entanglements, but many whales die each year from exhaustion before they can be rescued and cut free.

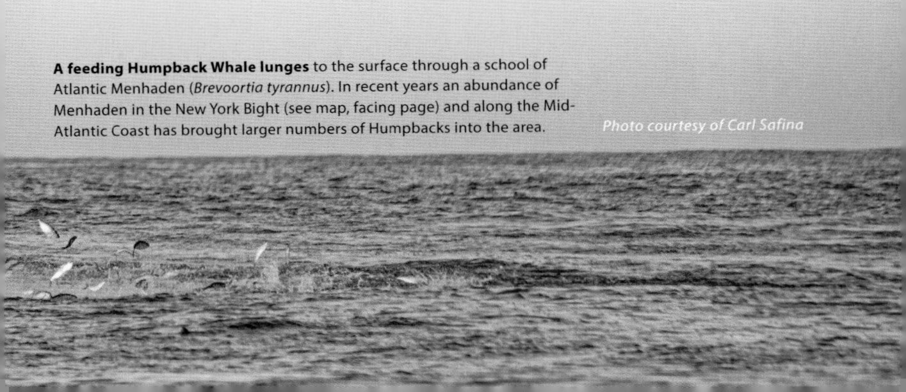
Photo courtesy of Carl Safina

A feeding Humpback Whale lunges to the surface through a school of Atlantic Menhaden (*Brevoortia tyrannus*). In recent years an abundance of Menhaden in the New York Bight (see map, facing page) and along the Mid-Atlantic Coast has brought larger numbers of Humpbacks into the area.

Cape Hatteras and the Graveyard of the Atlantic

Cape Hatteras juts 30 miles from the mainland into the Atlantic Ocean and presents a significant physical barrier to Atlantic Coast shipping traffic. East of the cape are the shallow, sandy Diamond Shoals, which reach a further nine miles into the Atlantic. The cape is also the point where two of the Mid-Atlantic Coast's most powerful currents collide over Diamond Shoals: the cold, south-flowing extension of the Labrador Current, locally known as the Virginia Current, and the warm, northbound South Atlantic Shelf Water current that parallels the Gulf Stream. This clash of currents means that the waters just off Cape Hatteras can boil with chaotic and disturbed wave patterns on even the calmest summer day. The western edge of the Gulf Stream flows about 20 miles east of Cape Hatteras, further complicating navigation in the area.

The dangers of Cape Hatteras waters result from the clash of ocean currents, the extensive shallow sandbanks of Diamond Shoals, and the frequent storms that produce northeast winds that push vessels toward the shoals and coast.

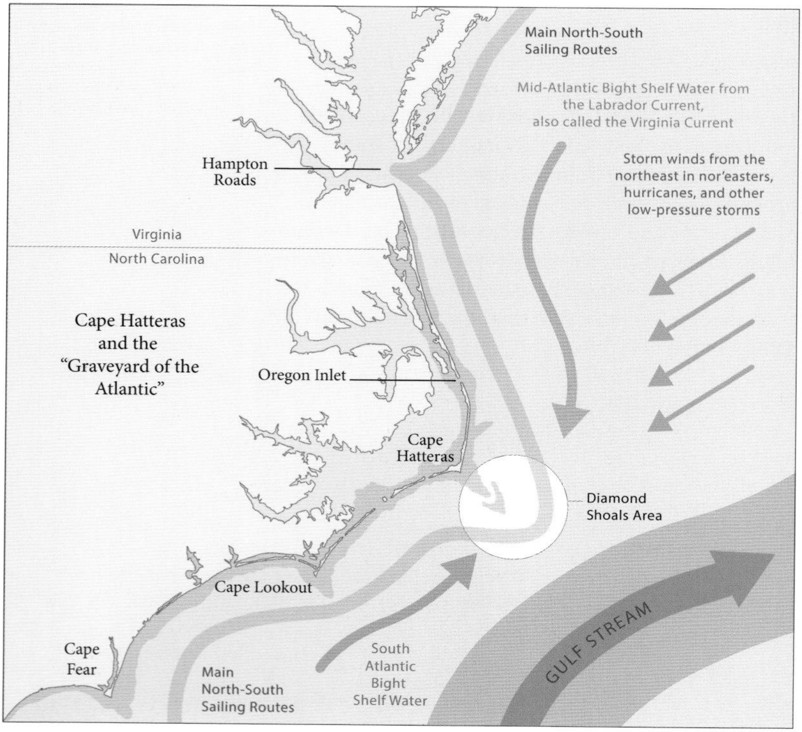
Main North-South
Sailing Routes
Mid-Atlantic Bight Shelf Water from the Labrador Current, also called the Virginia Current
Storm winds from the northeast in nor'easters, hurricanes, and other low-pressure storms
Hampton Roads
Virginia
North Carolina
Cape Hatteras and the "Graveyard of the Atlantic"
Oregon Inlet
Cape Hatteras
Diamond Shoals Area
Cape Lookout
Cape Fear
Main North-South Sailing Routes
South Atlantic Bight Shelf Water
GULF STREAM

William Bradford, Metropolitan Museum

When grounded on a sand shoal in stormy weather, even the largest ship can be quickly destroyed by waves. In *Shipwreck on the Nantucket Shoals* (1861), William Bradford depicts a scene very similar to wrecks off Cape Hatteras: a ship grounded on offshore sand shoals in a violent storm.

Before the mid-twentieth century, coastal ships preferred to sail within sight of the coast. Navigation charts were inexact and often out-of-date, particularly on the position and depth of sand shoals. Although the compass and sextant were available for navigation, neither tool is of much use in establishing an exact location in fog, under overcast conditions, or at night. Most captains preferred to use lighthouses and other visual landmarks to judge their position and progress, but staying within sight of shore presented a dilemma: the closer a ship cleaved toward shore, the more likely it was to run aground on a sandbank. Vessels sailing south also faced another obstacle—the Gulf Stream—which flows northeast off Cape Hatteras at about five to six miles per hour. Most sailing cargo vessels were lucky to make five to six miles per hour at full sail. If the vessel ran too far offshore while sailing south, it would run head-on into the northbound Gulf Stream 20 miles east of Hatteras, and forward progress against the current could drop to zero. So even in good weather, rounding Cape Hatteras meant that southbound captains had to thread a chokepoint about 10 miles wide between Diamond Shoals and the Gulf Stream.

All vessels, heading north or south, also faced the perils of stormy weather. The Cape Hatteras region is notorious for hurricanes in summer and fall and for nor'easters in winter and spring. In this region, both kinds of storm produce violent northeast winds blowing onshore (see illustration, p. 104) that are strong enough to push even the largest sailing ship onto the offshore shoals or the beach. Sailors call this dreaded condition of being helplessly pushed onto the coast a lee shore, and storm conditions like these caused most shipwrecks. Once a ship was pushed onto Diamond Shoals or the shallows near a beach, the storm waves typically pounded the vessel to pieces within hours. Over a thousand wrecks have been documented from the Cape Hatteras area alone, more than justifying its title as the Graveyard of the Atlantic.

A second graveyard

In the twentieth century, steam-driven cargo ships became the norm, with good navigation charts and radio communication. However, north-south shipping traffic along the Atlantic Coast still faced the physical obstacle of Cape Hatteras and the need to avoid running aground on shoals or getting tangled in the Gulf

Stream. In World Wars I and II German submarines (U-boats) took advantage of this coastal shipping traffic bottleneck to concentrate their attacks on American and Allied shipping. During World War I, U-boats attacked Mid-Atlantic coastal ships sporadically, but after Germany declared war on the United States in December 1941, the Germans mounted a concentrated submarine campaign. In 1942 U-boats sank over 200 cargo ships and tankers, many within sight of land. The initial US Navy response to the U-boats was ineffective, and the U-boats operated with little risk. However, the navy gradually mounted more determined air- and ship-based antisubmarine warfare techniques, and by mid-1943 US ship losses off the coast were sharply reduced.

In the 1930s and 1940s, the US military built roads, observation towers, radar facilities, coastal bunkers, and army bases, particularly at potential strategic points like Cape May and Cape Henlopen on the Delaware Bay and on the Outer Banks. The new roads,

Occasionally during World War I and again in 1942 at the beginning of World War II, German submarines targeted shipping in the Cape Hatteras region. Although the ships of the day were equipped with accurate charts and radio navigation, they still had to pass the traffic bottleneck at Cape Hatteras, where the submarines waited for them.
Sea paintings by German illustrator Willy Stöwer (1864–1931).

A coastal watchtower and artillery spotting tower built just before World War II at Cape May, New Jersey. During the war the federal government created bases, roads, and bridges along what had been a fairly isolated coast. The new infrastructure and influx of people helped spur the postwar boom in coastal development.

bridges, and other connections to the mainland made coastal regions much more accessible to development after the war ended, and by the 1950s much of the previously remote Mid-Atlantic Coast was growing quickly with new housing, recreation, and commercial development.

THE ESTUARY EMPIRES

From 1609 through 1900 the development of the Mid-Atlantic Coast is chiefly the story of four estuaries and how the biological riches of those harbors, bays, and sounds and the lands surrounding them influenced the development of the United States as a whole. For the first 300 years of European presence in the Americas, New York Harbor, Delaware Bay, Chesapeake Bay, and the Albemarle and Pamlico Sounds were the foundation for commercial empires built on tobacco, lumber, seafood, shipping, agriculture, and manufacturing, all directly or indirectly the gifts of the Mid-Atlantic estuaries.

The rich history of New York Harbor and its surroundings are beyond the scope of this guide, but even though they are seldom mentioned as such, New York Harbor and the lower Hudson River Valley comprise one of the largest estuaries and tidal river systems in North America and were vital to the early settlement of New York and New Jersey. New York Harbor and the surrounding New Jersey marshlands were once important food sources for the growing populations of the region, because the harbor and lower Hudson River were formerly rich in fish, oysters, and migratory waterfowl.

The Delaware Bay, though much smaller than the Chesapeake Bay, offered many of the same river transportation advantages to early settlers of Delaware, New Jersey, and Pennsylvania. In particular, the fall line ports of Wilmington, Delaware, and Philadelphia, Pennsylvania, quickly became major Mid-Atlantic Coast transportation hubs in the colonial era. Today the Delaware Bay is the nation's second busiest transportation waterway, after the Mississippi River. Forty percent of the shipping traffic to and from the

The Dismal Swamp Canal between Norfolk, Virginia, and the Albemarle Sound of North Carolina was critical to opening up the Albemarle and Pamlico Sounds and their associated rivers to transportation of passengers and cargo. Today the canal is part of the Atlantic Intracoastal Waterway.

Port of Baltimore passes through the Chesapeake and Delaware Canal, which joins the two huge bays across northern Delaware and Maryland.

North Carolina's Pamlico and Albemarle Sounds were less immediately useful to early settlers because the sounds were isolated by the Outer Banks, the long string of sandy barrier islands that separate the sounds from the Atlantic Ocean (see map, p. xiii). Although there are several inlets south of Cape Hatteras, the shallow, constantly changing inlets were hazardous to larger ships. The sounds remained isolated from early colonial development until the completion of the Dismal Swamp Canal in 1805. The Dismal Swamp Canal was the first significant canal completed in early America and connected the Chesapeake Bay near Norfolk, Virginia, with the Albemarle Sound in North Carolina. The canal quickly opened up the large Pamlico and Albemarle Sounds and the major rivers of North Carolina to trade and transportation, and it allowed smaller ships to avoid the dangerous ocean passage around Cape Hatteras.

Overleaf:
The vast Pamlico and Albemarle Sounds behind the Outer Banks were difficult to access before the building of the Mid-Atlantic's first canal, the Dismal Swamp Canal, finished in 1805. The canal connects Norfolk and the Chesapeake Bay with the Albemarle Sound in North Carolina.

The Albemarle Sound near Manns Harbor, North Carolina.

The 38-foot replica ship *Discovery* at Jamestown Settlement museum in Virginia. The *Discovery* was the smallest of the three ships that sailed in the expedition that founded Jamestown in 1607.

The early colonial period, 1600s–1750

The English settlement on the James River at Jamestown in 1607 quickly evolved into the royal colony of Virginia along the banks of the Chesapeake Bay. Initially, the English settlers faced considerable challenges to feed themselves, because the land was thickly forested right to the edge of marshes and rivers. Settlers quickly adopted the Native American custom of swidden agriculture, in which an area of forest is cut to fell the major trees and then burned to remove the remaining tree debris and use the ashes as fertilizer. Early settlers farmed mixed crops until the soil was exhausted in five to 10 years, then moved on to a new plot to start again. The farms were planted in the indigenous fashion, with mixed crops of corn (maize), beans, tobacco, squash, and other vegetables, in relatively small farms run by family groups. Although they eventually became numerous, these small swidden burn-and-clear farms had a limited impact on the huge forests around estuaries and did not cause significant pollution or soil erosion.

However, as soon as the early colonists could feed themselves, they joined the international drug trade—in tobacco, one of the most addictive substances ever discovered and one that was wildly popular in Europe at the time. The early Mid-Atlantic colonies of Virginia, North Carolina, and Maryland were founded as commercial ventures, with investors and royal sponsors who were eager for a return on their considerable investments. Early colonial farms were quickly embedded in a complex web of international trade with Europe and the English colonies of the West Indies, joined later by trade in enslaved Africans.

The Little Ice Age and early European settlements

Modern readers may wonder at the extreme weather hardships described by early settlers at Jamestown and later settlements throughout the Mid-Atlantic coastal region. Settlers in the 1600s and 1700s often struggled with severe winter cold and extended summer droughts, conditions that are not common in the relatively moderate climate of today's Mid-Atlantic Coast. Unfortunately for early colonists their trans-

Atlantic voyages and North American settlements occurred during the Little Ice Age, an extended period of unusually cold and often dry weather that lasted from 1300 to 1850. Climate researchers have found that there were large and unpredictable temperature swings in the Chesapeake Bay region during this time, as well as complex temperature-related changes to the offshore currents in the Mid-Atlantic region, a further hazard to early sailors there.

For more on the influence of the Little Ice Age on the settlement of North America, see:

A Cold Welcome: The Little Ice Age and Europe's Encounter with North America, by Sam White. Cambridge, MA: Harvard University Press, 2017.

Early impacts on the environment

As early settlements and farms matured and more land was cleared, grazing animals imported by the colonists, such as cattle, pigs, sheep, and horses, became a more important factor in the landscape. The introduction of feral hogs was destructive to native Longleaf Pines, which had vulnerable seedlings and young trees. Feral hogs also routinely destroyed indigenous people's farm plots, which typically were not fenced. This crop destruction—and the subsequent killing of marauding hogs—became a continuing source of tension between Native Americans and the European settlers. Fossil pollen studies from this period show an explosion of Ragweed and other alien weed species, indicative of large areas of disturbed ground that were quickly over-

Colonial Williamsburg in Virginia has been criticized by some as portraying an unrealistic, sanitized version of colonial life in the Chesapeake region, but, along with the reconstructions of the Jamestown settlement, the site does give visitors a flavor of what life was like for the white European settlers and residents of early America.

dedtonphotos

run by introduced plants. In addition to raising domestic animals, the settlers preyed on local wildlife. All types of birds from hawks to shorebirds and songbirds were heavily hunted because they damaged crops, as well as for food, including early market gunning of the huge flocks of waterfowl in estuaries.

In this period the endemic wolf populations of the Mid-Atlantic Coast were extirpated by hunting and trapping, principally because wolves were a danger to livestock. Gray Wolves became extinct in Tidewater Virginia by 1800, through hunting, but also because White-Tailed Deer were heavily hunted, too, and the wolves had much less prey available to them. The closely related Red Wolf persisted in small numbers in the southern reaches of the Atlantic Coastal Plain. Research has shown that the Red Wolf is a distinct canid species and not a hybrid of Gray Wolves and Coyotes. Small numbers of Red Wolves were reintroduced in 1986 in the Alligator River National Wildlife Refuge in North Carolina, but the experiment has been controversial and poorly supported by the US Fish and Wildlife Service.

Feral hogs remain a problem today in some wild coastal areas, such as the Currituck Banks Reserve on the Outer Banks of North Carolina. Feral hogs degrade local water quality, reduce forest regeneration by eating young trees and shrubs, and displace or kill many kinds of native wildlife.

Tobacco farms on the Atlantic Coastal Plain quickly developed into vast plantations that were viable only because of the labor provided by imported enslaved Africans.

Expanded farming and an agricultural revolution, 1750–1820

This was a time of rapidly increasing exploitation of the natural resources of the Mid-Atlantic region. Better ports and early road networks made it easier to transport the lumber, agricultural, and the seafood riches of the Chesapeake and Delaware Bays to the growing cities of the East Coast. However, two new factors marked a sharp turning point in the development of the Mid-Atlantic coastal region: the importation of Africans as slaves to create larger plantation-style agriculture, and more sophisticated agricultural practices imported from England.

Methods of fertilization and crop rotation developed during the British Agricultural Revolution of the late 1700s were quickly imported to the Mid-Atlantic Coast, resulting in vastly expanded crop yields. Early farmers typically farmed a cleared area for five to 10 years, until the soil nutrients were exhausted and crop yields became poor. They would then burn a new section of forest and let the old farmland revert to natural vegetation. Growing crops this way depended on a constant supply of new forest land, which eventually

Abeselom Zerit

The Red Wolf (*Canis rufus*) was a unique native species in the Virginia and North Carolina region before being extirpated through hunting. In 1980 the US Fish and Wildlife Service declared the Red Wolf extinct in the region. In the late 1980s the service began a reintroduction of Red Wolves into the Alligator River National Wildlife Refuge, and conservation efforts continue.

The vast oyster reefs of the Chesapeake Bay are only a memory now, due to severe overharvesting with mechanical dredges over the past 150 years. The oyster diseases MSX and Dermo devastated what was left of the oyster beds. Today there are efforts to restore oysters to the Upper Chesapeake Bay. See the chapter on estuaries for more on the Eastern Oyster (*Crassostrea virginica*).

became scarce. The new British farming methods emphasized the use of such fertilizers as animal dung, marl (calcium mineral rock), and rock phosphate, along with more sophisticated crop rotation methods that used nitrogen-fixing fodder crops such as turnips and clover to both feed farm animals and restore the nitrogen and other nutrients of the soil.

These new practices led to a massive increase in farm productivity. Atlantic Coastal Plain farms became a food-rich breadbasket to support the growing cities of the Mid-Atlantic Coast. Much more land was cleared for more substantial row-crop farming, well beyond the size and scale of the earlier family farms that dominated the colonial era. With the vastly expanded land clearance came the problems of deforestation, soil erosion, farm runoff polluted by artificial fertilizers, and the siltation of rivers and estuaries—the beginnings of the problems that now plague the major bays and estuaries of the Atlantic Coast.

In an age well before farm machinery, these new plantation-scale farms demanded far more human labor than an English-style family farm could supply. The first laborers were often English indentured servants working alongside farmers, but African slaves soon began to replace these European farmworkers. By 1700 large numbers of Africans were being imported

Kelli

Although its riches have been abused and overharvested for centuries, the Chesapeake Bay still supports a major Blue Crab (*Callinectes sapidus*) fishery. Long favored by locals, the crabs did not become a significant commercial fishery until the rise of canning and rapid rail transport in the late 1800s.

by Dutch and English slavers, working as part of the international "triangle trade" that brought tobacco, sugar, rum, and cotton from the Americas to Britain, and textiles, guns, and manufactured goods from Britain to West Africa, where the goods were traded for Africans bound for slavery in the New World.

The land clearing, sowing, tending, harvesting, and drying of huge amounts of tobacco required large teams of laborers and was efficient only on sizable estates, worked with large teams of enslaved Africans. After the Revolutionary War, the region underwent its first environmental crisis: decades of tobacco crops had exhausted the soil on major estates. Poor agricultural practices that left bare fields exposed to the elements had caused many of the small river tributaries to silt up and become unnavigable for tobacco transport. Coastal plain farmers abandoned tobacco for crops more locally useful and easier to transport on land, such as corn, wheat, and vegetables. As better roads developed, tobacco farms moved inland into the Piedmont region, and eventually railroads were used to transport bulk tobacco. The small, regional river-based transportation centers of the Chesapeake region faded as Baltimore and Norfolk absorbed both the river trade and international shipping and became the two major trading centers of the Chesapeake Bay area.

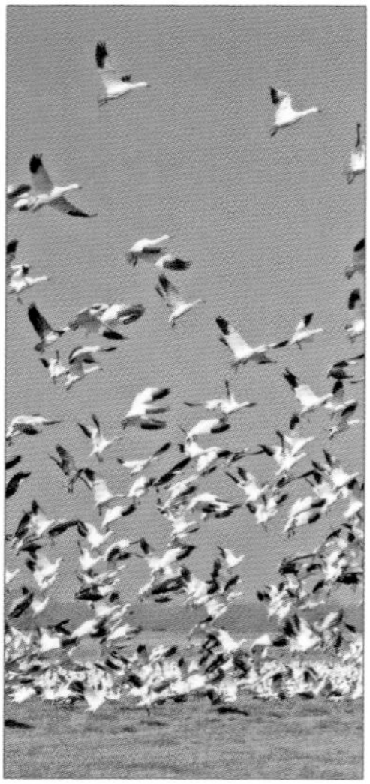

Snow Geese in a farm field on the Eastern Shore of Maryland.

Exploitation of resources, 1820–1920

The nineteenth-century history of the Mid-Atlantic Coast is mostly a story of vastly expanded resource exploitation, made possible by new regional transportation technologies such as canals, road networks, and railroads. The region saw unprecedented growth in deforestation and lumbering, oyster harvesting, market gunning for waterfowl, and heavy shipments of grain and produce to city markets. Land clearance for agriculture reached its peak just before the Civil War (1861–65). Grain production and farming in general began to fade as canals and then railroads made Phragmites cheaper, more abundant midwestern grain supplies available to growing eastern cities. Farmers on the Atlantic Coastal Plain began a gradual shift away from grains to vegetables, orchards, and dairy farming. By 1840 the Chesapeake region was shipping 20 million bushels of live oysters annually to urban markets via fast coastal sloops and schooners. In the fall migration, season market gunners killed thousands of ducks each day. Before, during, and particularly after the Civil War, railroad networks grew across the Mid-Atlantic region, enabling fast and efficient transportation of perishable seafood and ducks to major city markets.

Even in an age before refrigerated railroad cars, fresh produce and seafood could move remarkably fast. In the late 1880s the New York, Philadelphia, and Norfolk Railroad, which ran the length of the Delmarva Peninsula, connected towns of the Chesapeake's Eastern Shore to the urban markets of Philadelphia and New York. The fresh fruits, vegetables, and seafood of the Eastern Shore could be delivered to New York City in 12 hours, Boston in 20 hours, and Montreal in 30 hours. In spring the Peninsula Strawberry Express sent as many as 150 railroad cars per day to East Coast urban markets. In 1886 the NYP&N Railroad alone sent north 125,000 barrels of potatoes, 275,000 barrels of sweet potatoes, 50,000 boxes of green peas, 100,000 barrels of kale and cabbage, 100,000 barrels of oysters, 6,000,000 quarts of strawberries, 50,000 sacks of peanuts, 10,000 boxes of fish, and 12,000 baskets of peaches.

For a wonderful history of the oyster and its importance to the development of East Coast cities like New York, I highly recommend:

The Big Oyster: History on the Half Shell, by Mark Kurlansky. New York: Random House, 2006.

The rise of the tourism economy

In 1854 several local businesspeople on the obscure southern New Jersey barrier island of Absecon created a concept for a beach resort town with a railway that would bring vacationers straight from Philadelphia and Camden, New Jersey, to the island in about three hours. In 1854 they christened their newly built group of small hotels "Atlantic City" and began passenger rail traffic with the Philadelphia area. By 1870 over 300,000 visitors annually were making summer trips to Atlantic City, and the first version of the Atlantic City Boardwalk was opened. By 1880 the city had 50 hotels, and a second rail line was built to Philadelphia to accommodate the heavy summer passenger traffic.

The northern New Jersey seaside town of Long Branch developed along similar lines to Atlantic City. Although Long Branch had been a modest New York region seaside resort since the late 1700s, two factors caused Long Branch to become the premier New Jersey coast resort of the late 1800s. The construction of new railroad networks linking the New York City area and the New Jersey shore made reaching the resort much easier and safer than using the coastal steamers that were formerly the only way to reach Long Branch conveniently. Long Branch also attracted the attention of

Overleaf:
Although the ocean is nominally the star at "beach" resorts, it plays an increasingly minor part in the overall experience of boardwalk cities such as Atlantic City, New Jersey (shown here); Ocean City, Maryland; and Virginia Beach, Virginia.

The opening of the Garden State Parkway enabled the large populations of the New York Harbor region to reach New Jersey's beaches quickly and easily, creating the famous Jersey Shore we know today.

EQRoy

BUD LIGHT

The Boardwalk, Atlantic City, New Jersey.

This a sandy barrier island, barely seven feet above sea level. Wildwood, New Jersey, is a residential and vacation community with urban levels of density and development. Shoreline communities like Wildwood can be maintained only with massive public subsidies for beach replenishment and are highly vulnerable to the combination of sea level rise, constant erosion of the ocean shoreline, and the storm surge flooding that results from even minor hurricanes and nor'easters.

political celebrities of the time. Mary Lincoln stayed at Long Branch in 1861, and later Ulysses S. Grant made Long Branch the first "summer White House," moving the core personnel of his government to the resort for the summer months. Later presidents through Woodrow Wilson favored Long Branch for its resort life and its proximity to New York City and easy train access to Washington, DC. Like other New Jersey coastal communities developed as resorts, Long Branch faded in prominence in the early 1900s, and Asbury Park and Atlantic City became the primary New Jersey seaside resorts.

New Jersey's Garden State Parkway (built 1946–57) was the primary factor that converted New Jersey's string of minor seaside resort communities into the famous Jersey Shore we know today. The parkway is constructed just inland but parallel to the coastline, to draw long-distance north-south traffic away from the congested town centers along the immediate coast and to speed access to the many resort towns then developing along the Jersey Shore. The new road also allowed people who worked in the New York City area to conveniently reach the Jersey Shore for daily commutes. The Garden State Parkway facilitated the residential shoreline building boom of the 1950s to 1970s, when New Jersey barrier island towns such as Seaside Heights and Surf City went from small summer resort communities to dense, semiurban neighborhoods of closely packed family houses that mimicked inland urban communities but were within a few blocks of the ocean or bay shores.

Superstorm Sandy

In 2012 Superstorm Sandy brought all the warnings about coastal development into sharp focus, as the hurricane-turned-extratropical-megastorm slammed into the New Jersey, New York City, and Long Island coastlines. Sandy made landfall at Brigantine, New Jersey, on Sunday, October 28, 2012, just as the full moon brought spring high tides to the coast. Sandy's storm surge was measured at 8.5 feet at Sandy Neck, New Jersey, and the ocean-facing coast of Staten Island, near the entrance to New York Harbor. Within New York Harbor the funnel-shaped coastline brought the surge to 14 feet near the tip of Manhattan Island. In Wildwood, New Jersey, the surge was just under five feet, with sustained winds near hurricane strength, at 74 miles per hour, gusting to 91 miles an hour.

Unfortunately, New Jersey chose to deal with the aftermath of Superstorm Sandy by waiving or fast-tracking rebuilding permits, which largely wasted an opportunity to rebuild with revised coastal zoning and resiliency strategies designed to live with the reality of increasing storms and sea level rise. New Jersey governor Chris Christie's vow that "we will rebuild" was comforting

The derelict Star Jet steel roller coaster may be the best-known image of the devastation that Superstorm Sandy left behind on the Jersey Shore. The Star Jet operated for ten years (2002–12) at the Casino Pier in Seaside Heights, New Jersey, before Sandy swept it into the surf.

to a traumatized community but locked in a commitment to make the same coastal development mistakes over again, guaranteeing future heartaches for the New Jersey shoreline.

Although it is hard to predict the exact courses, severity, and frequency of future coastal storms, we know these things for sure:

– The current data show that storms are increasing in severity and frequency (see illustration, p. 79).

– Sea level rise will overwhelm many low-lying Mid-Atlantic Coast communities in the next few decades.

– Society must learn to live with a rapidly evolving shoreline environment, either by retreating from vulnerable areas or by adopting resiliency strategies that use natural environments and such structures as artificial reefs, artificial dune lines, and other "soft" coastal structures that mimic the natural world to mitigate storm damage.

Beach replenishment on the New Jersey Atlantic Coast has cost taxpayers $475 million since 1990 and billions more up and down the Atlantic Coast from New Jersey to Florida. Every developed shoreline beach must be replenished periodically to compensate for the natural erosion of sand due to storms and longshore drift, or the first lines of houses would have long since been washed away by storms. As the sea rises, we as a society cannot possibly sustain those expenses.

Opposite:
New Jersey isn't the only area of the Mid-Atlantic where intensive development of the shoreline has caused problems. This is a view of the Outer Banks vacation town of Corolla, North Carolina. In season the town hosts over 50,000 vacationers and summer residents in houses built on a sand bar barely 10 feet above the high-tide line on a barrier peninsula only 0.4 miles wide. Access to Corolla is via a single two-lane road, 25 miles by car from the nearest mainland town at Harbor Point, North Carolina.

A Brown Pelican in the spindrift at dawn, Coquina Beach, Nags Head, North Carolina.

Barrier Island Environments

The primary dune line at Coquina Beach in the Cape Hatteras National Seashore, Outer Banks, North Carolina. Here the chief grasses holding the dune line together are Seaoats (*Uniola paniculata*) and Coastal Panic Grass (*Panicum amarum*).

All natural ecological communities are structured in zones that reflect the various physical and biological forces that act upon plants and animals to limit or encourage their growth. The physical forces that shape coastal barrier communities include elevation above sea level, temperature, availability of freshwater, light and heat intensity, the physical stresses of wave and wind action, sand abrasion, and, most of all for plants, exposure to salt aerosols (salt spray).

But physical forces alone do not fully determine the nature of plant and animal communities. The mix of species in a given community is also determined by competition for living space and resources among various organisms. The dominant or best-adapted species in the community tend to overwhelm weaker competitors or force them into more marginal living conditions. Each ecological zone on a barrier results from a mix of physical forces and biological competition among the inhabitants.

Ecology of a typical barrier island or peninsula

Barrier islands and peninsulas along the Mid-Atlantic Coast have a predictable general physical and ecological structure (see illustration, pp. 46–47). This is determined primarily by the exposure to salt aerosols in the wind blowing in from the ocean. Salt marshes depend

General Habitats of a Mid-Atlantic Barrier, Bay, and Adjacent Mainland

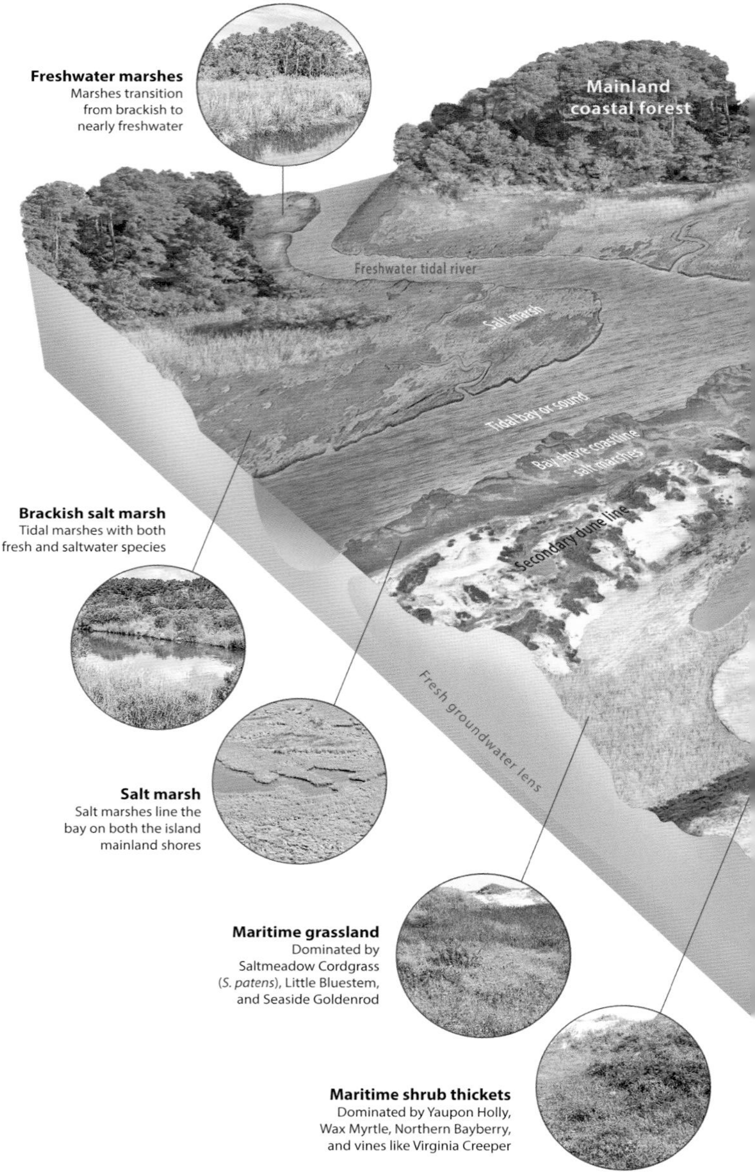
Freshwater marshes
Marshes transition from brackish to nearly freshwater
Mainland coastal forest
Freshwater tidal river
Salt marsh
Tidal bay or sound
Bayshore coastline salt marshes
Secondary dune line
Brackish salt marsh
Tidal marshes with both fresh and saltwater species
Fresh groundwater lens
Salt marsh
Salt marshes line the bay on both the island mainland shores
Maritime grassland
Dominated by Saltmeadow Cordgrass (*S. patens*), Little Bluestem, and Seaside Goldenrod
Maritime shrub thickets
Dominated by Yaupon Holly, Wax Myrtle, Northern Bayberry, and vines like Virginia Creeper

shielding the plant from drying out. Searocket is a common upper beach plant that uses a combination of strategies to ward off salt and conserve water. The leaves and stems of Searocket are thick and succulent, to absorb water during rains, and then to store the water in dry spells of summer heat. Searocket also uses a thick, waxlike coating or cuticle on its leaves and stems to shield it from salt aerosols and prevent water evaporation. Many beach and dune plants, such as Dusty Miller, use a coating of fine (dusty) hairs on their leaves and stems to hold off salt aerosols, which deposit salt on the tips of the hairs, away from the plant surface. The fine, almost white fuzzy hairs also help Dusty Miller by reflecting sunlight and resist drying winds by holding an insulating blanket of still air around the surface of the leaves.

The fine white "dusty" hairs on the leaves of Dusty Miller (*Artemisia stelleriana*) are an adaptation to the harsh beach and dune environment. The hairs protect the leaves from excess sunlight and hold a layer of air near the leaf surface that helps trap moisture and collects salt aerosol droplets before they hit the leaves.

In addition to salt spray, beach and primary dune plants must occasionally contend with storm overwashes of salty water. Many dune plants, such as Eastern Prickly Pear, are limited in their distribution by intolerance for salt water on their roots, so they are confined to sheltered areas behind the first line of dunes. However, the soils on barrier islands aren't necessarily salty: the sandy soil drains so quickly that rain tends to wash the salt from the surface.

Barrier plant communities

The geological origin of barrier islands is explored in an earlier chapter. Here we'll look briefly at the general structure of barrier islands and the plant communities they support. Plants don't just live on barrier structures: by trapping and holding sand, plant communities are a fundamental part of the structure and

Salt aerosols from the ocean
Classic wedge-shaped thicket
of Yaupon Holly and Wax Myrtle
Stunted growth from salt exposure
More normal growth where sheltered from salt

Cross section of a typical Atlantic Coast barrier island or peninsula

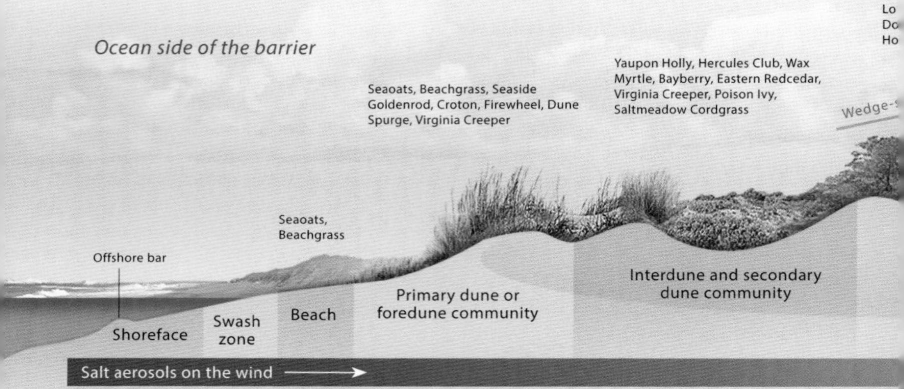
Ocean side of the barrier
Seaoats, Beachgrass, Seaside Goldenrod, Croton, Firewheel, Dune Spurge, Virginia Creeper
Yaupon Holly, Hercules Club, Wax Myrtle, Bayberry, Eastern Redcedar, Virginia Creeper, Poison Ivy, Saltmeadow Cordgrass
Seaoats, Beachgrass
Offshore bar
Shoreface
Swash zone
Beach
Primary dune or foredune community
Interdune and secondary dune community
Salt aerosols on the wind

Upper Beach

Foredune Community

Interdune Shrubs and Grasslan

Upper Beach

Northern areas
American Beachgrass
Rough Cocklebur
Searocket
Red Goosefoot
Seaside Spurge
Common Saltwort
Sandbur
Dusty Miller

Southern areas
Seaoats
American Beachgrass
Rough Cocklebur
Searocket
Sandbur
Dusty Miller
Seaside Spurge
Dune Pennywort

Foredune Community

Northern areas
American Beachgrass
Beach Plum
Northern Bayberry
Eastern Redcedar
Rugosa Rose
Marsh Elder
Seaside Goldenrod
Switchgrass
Beach Heather
Beach Pea
Virginia Creeper
Poison Ivy

Southern areas
Most of the above, plus:
Seaoats
Coastal Panic Grass
Sea Elder
Yaupon Holly
Dune Pennywort

Interdune Shrubs and Grasslan

Northern areas
Saltmeadow Cordgrass
Virginia Creeper
Catbrier
Poison Ivy
Eastern Prickly Pear
Switchgrass
Little Bluestem
Northern Bayberry (more common)
Wax Myrtle (less common)
Marsh Elder
Winged Sumac
Black Cherry
Bear Oak

Southern areas
All of the above, plus:
Wax Myrtle (more common)
Northern Bayberry (less common)
Yaupon Holly
Dune Pennywort
Bristly Foxtail

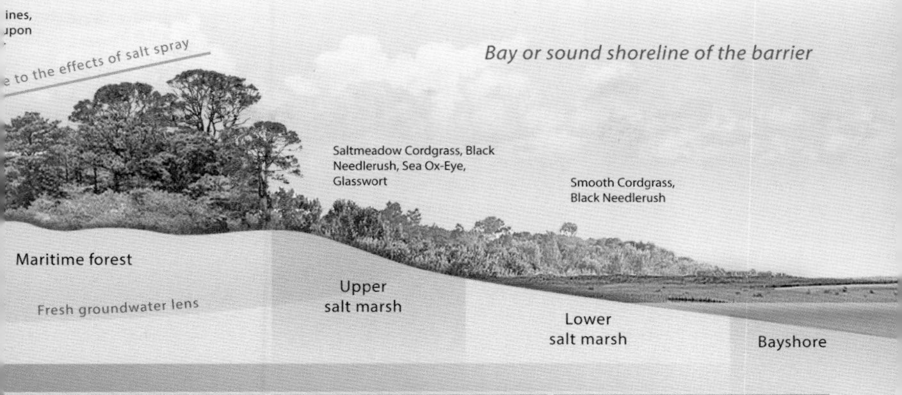
e to the effects of salt spray
Bay or sound shoreline of the barrier
Saltmeadow Cordgrass, Black Needlerush, Sea Ox-Eye, Glasswort
Smooth Cordgrass, Black Needlerush
Maritime forest
Fresh groundwater lens
Upper salt marsh
Lower salt marsh
Bayshore

Maritime Woodlands

Upper Salt Marsh Border

Salt and Brackish Marshes

Northern areas
Pitch Pine
blolly Pine (less common)
Atlantic White Cedar
Eastern Redcedar
American Holly
Canadian Serviceberry (Shadbush)
Sassafras
Red Maple
Black Tupelo (Black Gum)

Southern areas
All of the above, plus:
Live Oak
Sweetgum
Redbay
Southern Magnolia

Northern areas
Saltmeadow Cordgrass
Switchgrass
Spike Grass
Blackgrass
Common Reed (*Phragmites*)
Narrow-Leaved Cattail
Marsh Elder
Groundsel Tree
Northern Bayberry
Black Cherry
Loblolly Pine
Eastern Redcedar
Red Maple
Seaside Goldenrod
Perennial Saltmarsh Aster

Southern areas
All of the above, plus:
Black Needlerush
Live Oak

Northern areas
Saltwater Cordgrass
Saltmeadow Cordgrass
Spike Grass
Blackgrass
Sea Lavender
Glasswort
Erect Sea Blight
Marsh Orach
Perennial Saltmarsh Aster

Southern areas
All of the above, plus:
Black Needlerush

American Beachgrass (*Ammophila breviligulata*) is the most important stabilizer of dunes north of Chesapeake Bay. Beachgrass is so good at holding sand that it is planted well south of its native range and is now found as far south as Florida.

origin of barriers, allowing what would otherwise be ephemeral shoals of loose sand to support biological communities over thousands of years.

The barrier islands and peninsulas of the Mid-Atlantic Coast typically have moderate temperature and rainfall amounts, governed by the ocean and the bays and sounds on the landward side of coastal barriers. However, barriers islands usually have a much lower diversity of plant and animal species because the marine climate is harsh, ocean winds are constant, water is often scarce due to the fast-draining sand, and salt aerosols are always raining from above.

Plants must also be able to cope with burial in sand. Beachgrass and Seaoats have deep vertical roots and rhizomes (underground stems) that help them cope with sudden burial in sand or sand blow-outs, where storm winds erode large parts of a dune, leaving the grass roots partially exposed.

Only a few well-adapted species can survive so near to the ocean. The mainland species that do well on barrier islands tend to be what ecologists call early succession plants—forbs (smaller herbaceous plants), bushes, and trees that specialize in quickly colonizing disturbed

The picturesque wild ponies of the northern Outer Banks near Corolla, North Carolina. Like their northern cousins on Assateague Island, these ponies are most likely descendants of farm horses that were pastured on barrier islands.

ground. In many beach, dune, and grassland areas only a few species are dominant, and the total plant species count may be a few dozen. On smaller coastal barriers this early succession stage is permanent and may never produce a climax successional community because of the harsh and unsettled conditions.

Beaches, dunes, and maritime grasslands tend to be dominated by three kinds of plants: grasses such as American Beachgrass, Seaoats, and Saltmeadow Cordgrass, annual herbaceous plants that reproduce each year via seeds, and very tough, salt-adapted shrubs such as Northern Bayberry, Wax Myrtle, and Yaupon Holly (south of Chesapeake Bay).

In addition to their tough underground rhizomes, the grass species produce extremely deep root systems, capable of extending 30–60 feet below the surface to the fresh groundwater level. Beach and dune annuals do not invest in perennial stems and roots but trust in a wide dispersal of seeds each year. Being an annual may seem like a risky strategy, but some of the toughest, most salt-resistant—and most successful—beach plants, such as Searocket and Rough Cocklebur, are annuals that leave behind only seeds to overwinter.

Seaoats (*Uniola paniculata*) is the most important beach grass south of Chesapeake Bay. Seaoats naturally grows in discontinuous clumps. American Beachgrass is often planted with Seaoats, because Beachgrass forms a continuous dune line. The solid dune line helps prevent storm overwash on developed beaches.

Photo courtesy of Dianna K

The primary dune line at Coquina Beach, Cape Hatteras National Seashore, North Carolina.

Sandy barrier islands and peninsulas are created by four forces that move sand: flood tidal deltas near inlets, sand that is both deposited and eroded by longshore currents just off the beach, sand overwashes created by storm surges, and the movement of finer sand grains by the wind.

The shoreface is a combination of the lower wet beach and the first 30–60 feet of sand that extends out from the beach under the water. Think of the shoreface as a system for continually circulating sand: fair weather waves usually bring sand from offshore shoals onto the beach. The larger waves of stormy weather often strip sand from the beach, taking the eroded sand back out to sand shoals on the submerged shoreface.

The beach extends from the low tide line up to the base of the first or primary dune line at the top of the beach. We'll look in detail at beach structure and ecology in the next chapter.

The primary dune line on a natural beach is created by two factors: winds from the ocean that constantly move fine sand particles up the beach surface and away from the water, and the tough, salt-adapted grasses and other plants that grow at the top of the beach, well above the normal highest tides. Remember: the plants of the primary dune line don't just live on the dune;

If a beach is lined with houses, the primary dune is artificial. Bulldozers are used to create an unusually steep dune profile to help prevent storm overwash. The wooden stairs prevent foot traffic from harming the dune vegetation, which is the usual mix of wild grasses such as American Beachgrass and Seaoats. There is irony here: storm overwashes of sand are how barrier islands are built and renewed. By preventing overwashes of new sand, developed barrier islands are always shrinking, as well as losing their beaches.

Pine, Live Oak dominates other oaks, and Redbay and Black Tupelo (Black Gum) enter the mix. Groves of maritime forest are sometimes called coastal hammocks, maritime hammocks, or hardwood islands, mainly where they occur on higher dune ridges surrounded by lower wetlands in dune swales.

Atlantic White Cedar (*Chamaecyparis thyoides*) is a maritime forest tree that favors wet, acidic ground and often creates small cedar swamps in valleys and hollows near the coast. Unfortunately, the dense, rot-resistant wood of White Cedar was highly valued to make house shingles. Many coastal White Cedar swamps were destroyed in the nineteenth century.

Fire is an unusual but important factor in shaping mature maritime forest areas, and most mature forests have had some fire damage in the past. Today modern communications allow authorities to discover and quickly control most wildfires on barrier islands. Barrier plant communities are always vulnerable to fire because on sandy soils rainwater drains away fast and the constant ocean winds both evaporate moisture and fan the flames of wildfires. Most wildfires are caused naturally by lightning strikes, but human carelessness is always a factor near park campgrounds and developed areas.

Salt marshes develop in sheltered waters along the bay shore or sound shoreline. Marshes often form on deposits of sand from old inlet flood deltas, where the

A maritime forest at Chincoteague National Wildlife Refuge, Virginia, dominated by Loblolly Pines (*Pinus taeda*).

A salt marsh at Assateague Island National Seashore, Maryland. Although the marsh is very healthy, signs of sea level rise are evident. The line of Loblolly Pines (Pinus taeda) along the park road in the background is quickly becoming a ghost forest of trees being killed by saltwater infiltration of what used to be high ground. A dead Loblolly Pine trunk rises in the foreground.

sand deltas eventually become so shallow that marsh grasses colonize the delta sand, and eventually the whole complex of sand flat and marsh becomes attached to the bay shore side of the barrier. This absorption of inlet deltas along the bay shore coasts of barrier islands is important to island building and migration. As inlets migrate over time, they leave behind their old, shallow inlet deltas. The extensive salt marshes of the bay shore area south of Bodie Island Light in the Cape Hatteras National Seashore were formed in this way (see illustration, p. 43). As Oregon Inlet has migrated south since it was formed in 1846, the old inlet flood deltas became covered with marsh grasses, and the areas eventually bonded with the bay shore coast of Bodie Island.

Groundwater along the coast

Most mainland beaches and coastal barrier islands along the New Jersey, Delaware, and Maryland shores benefit from deep underground layers of water-bearing sediment that slope from the Piedmont region down toward the coast and extend well beyond the current shoreline out under the continental shelf. In New Jersey, wells that tap the immense Kirkwood-Cohansey aquifer that underlies most of the state's coastal plain supply drinking water to Jersey Shore barrier islands

Atlantic Ocean
Pamlico Sound
Old flood tidal deltas from earlier positions of Oregon Inlet
Basnight Bridge
Salt marshes created from old inlet deltas

Bodie Island, north of Oregon Inlet, looking south. As Oregon Inlet has migrated south it has left behind old inlet deltas of sand that have gradually accreted to the main island on the Pamlico Sound side and now support salt marshes that help the island migrate landward as the sea level rises.

and peninsulas. Similar large aquifers supply most of the Delaware and Maryland coast.

The Norfolk–Virginia Beach–Newport News area has historically drawn heavily on groundwater supplies, and this has exacerbated the region's problems with ground subsidence and sea level rise (see illustration, p. 73). In southeastern Virginia the combination of excess reliance on local groundwater wells, the complications of an ancient meteor crater under Hampton Roads, and ground subsidence due to aftereffects of the most recent glacial period have all combined to create significant challenges to supplying drinking water to the state's most populous region.

Groundwater on barrier islands

Given the porous, sandy soils, limited land area for drainage into groundwater aquifers, lack of rivers, and surrounding ocean waters, it seems remarkable that

The American Avocet is one of our most beautiful shorebirds. The long, upturned bill is used to sweep through shallow waters in search of small insects and crustaceans. Fairly common in marshes and estuaries south of Chesapeake Bay, Avocets are present most of the year in good numbers at Pea Island National Wildlife Refuge, North Carolina. Adult birds have a striking cinnamon wash across the head and neck in breeding season that fades to a cool gray in winter.

American Avocet
Recurvirostra americana

A small but mature freshwater pond at Buxton Woods, at Cape Hatteras, about 30 miles out to sea from the nearest mainland shore. Cape Hatteras—and many other barrier islands made entirely of sand—support substantial ponds, thanks to the fresh groundwater within the sand. Ponds form in low areas where the ground meets the local freshwater table, and support a wide variety of freshwater plants and animals.

barrier islands have much fresh groundwater at all. Without a significant reservoir of groundwater, the smaller and more isolated Mid-Atlantic Coast barrier islands and peninsulas would be almost uninhabitable. Rainfall and, to a much more limited extent, snowmelt are the only natural sources of freshwater on sandy barriers. Luckily, two factors combine to provide freshwater in these salty surroundings.

Freshwater is lighter (has a lower specific gravity) than saltwater, and in the ground a body of freshwater will float above a surrounding body of saltwater, preventing a mixing that would make the resulting brackish water undrinkable. Also, the sandy soils quickly absorb rainwater from the ground surface, but the deep, porous layers of sand also hold significant quantities of water for long periods, acting both as a giant underground sponge and as a huge natural filter to clean impurities from the groundwater. Thus the ground under a barrier island or peninsula acts like an enormous invisible freshwater reservoir—a much larger store of water than any of the visible lakes and ponds on the surface. Geologists call these groundwater pools lenses owing to their shape: thick in the middle of land areas and tapering to thin edges near the shorelines.

However, the freshwater lens under barrier islands is surrounded by salty groundwater on both the ocean and bay shore coasts, and if too much groundwater is pumped out of the freshwater lens, its edges become contaminated with salt, and the water must be desalinated before it can be distributed through municipal water systems. There are other complications for depending on barrier island groundwater to supply communities. The fresh groundwater is tidal

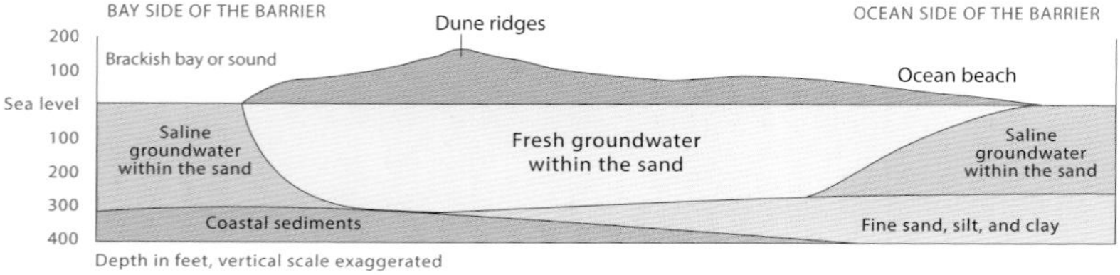
BAY SIDE OF THE BARRIER
Dune ridges
OCEAN SIDE OF THE BARRIER
200
100
Sea level
100
200
300
400
Brackish bay or sound
Ocean beach
Saline groundwater within the sand
Fresh groundwater within the sand
Saline groundwater within the sand
Coastal sediments
Fine sand, silt, and clay
Depth in feet, vertical scale exaggerated

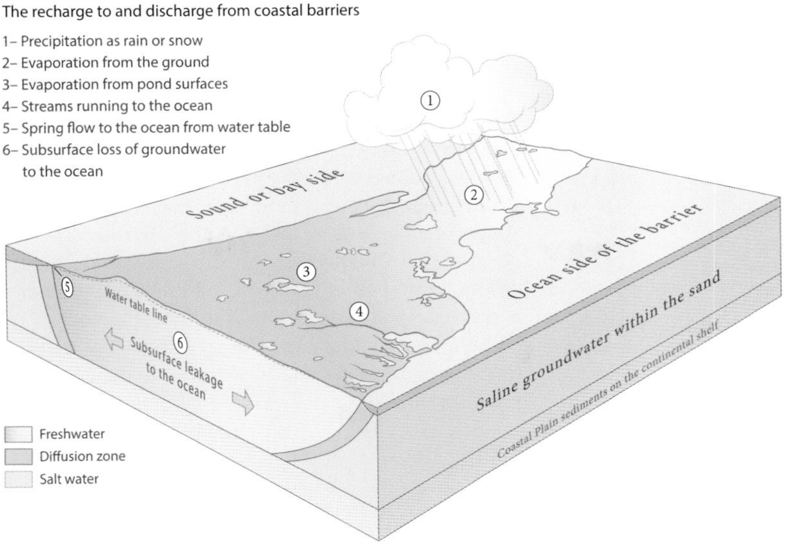
The recharge to and discharge from coastal barriers
1– Precipitation as rain or snow
2– Evaporation from the ground
3– Evaporation from pond surfaces
4– Streams running to the ocean
5– Spring flow to the ocean from water table
6– Subsurface loss of groundwater to the ocean
Sound or bay side
Ocean side of the barrier
Water table line
Subsurface leakage to the ocean
Saline groundwater within the sand
Coastal Plain sediments on the continental shelf
Freshwater
Diffusion zone
Salt water

on smaller barrier islands, and this daily up-and-down movement increases the contamination with salt water. In storm surges and island overwashes a substantial amount of seawater infiltrates the groundwater and can at least temporarily render the groundwater too salty to drink.

On wild barrier islands, the thickness of the groundwater lens can be as much as 40 times the height of the island above sea level. However, on developed barrier islands with many wells, the fresh groundwater supply will shrink if it is withdrawn faster than rain or snow can replenish it. As the groundwater lens thins, it can also become contaminated by the surrounding pool of salt water, making the groundwater too saline for household use. In some coastal communities with relatively large populations and small land areas, such as Cape May, New Jersey, and Nags Head, North Carolina, so much groundwater has been withdrawn by wells that the local underground aquifers have become too salty for household use, and the groundwater must be desalinized before entering the municipal water system.

Just as they do in mainland forests, small vernal pools develop in maritime forests on sand barriers. Vernal pools form during spring rains and are critical to forest amphibians like the Common Toad and the coastal Fowler's Toad. Toads spend most of their lives on the dry forest floor, but as amphibians they are still tied to the water for mating, egg laying, and the development of their tadpoles. Most vernal pools only last for a few months and are dry ground by midsummer.

Opposite: Nags Head Woods Preserve on North Carolina's Outer Banks.

The pool of fresh groundwater under sandy barriers is a finite resource that is only slowly replenished by precipitation. Unfortunately, on developed islands, many of these groundwater sources are under stress due to the enormous demands of commercial development and new housing. Every year more of the shoreline's natural ground cover disappears under buildings, parking lots, driveways, and home lawns and septic systems that leak nitrogen (from lawn fertilizers), phosphorous (mainly from home soaps and cleaning products), and other pollutants into the groundwater and surface ponds. Impervious surfaces like roads, building roofs, and parking lots also impede the absorption of rainwater and snowmelt into the groundwater supply.

Fowler's Toad
Anaxyrus fowleri

Jeff Holcombe

Dawn at Assateague Island National Seashore, Maryland. Note the size gradient from coarse shell hash and pebbles in the swash zone to fine-grained sand just a few feet up the beach.

Beaches

Sanderlings (*Calidris alba*) on the beach at Southern Shores on the Outer Banks of North Carolina.

Beaches are rough and turbulent places, built and eroded by winds, waves, and coastal currents. It's easy to see that the breaking waves and swash on the beach are fluid, but the beach sand itself is also in constant motion, flowing with the forces of both water and wind. Every beach is a sand circulation system, bringing in sand from offshore sandbars in fair weather and stripping away sand in storms. Sand supply, the shape of local landforms, the size and frequency of waves, and the rising sea level are all elements in the flowing geometry of the beach. Wind also plays a significant role in shaping the form of beaches, continually moving and sorting sand grains by size and weight. At the top of the beach, plants become a crucial element in building beaches, catching and holding sand to form lines of vegetated dunes that create and sustain barrier islands. For plants, fast-draining beaches are dry as deserts, and leaves are sprayed continuously with blasts of sand and salt.

Beaches respond with great sensitivity to all these forces, and each ripple line or small ridge of sand reflects those shaping energies like a sculptor's handprint. Everything on a beach is in constant motion, whether under the blazing sun of summer or in the tearing waves of winter. The ultimate fate of the beach lies in the thin swirl of sand within each wave swash.

Searocket
Cakile edentula
One of the most important sand-holding plants on Mid-Atlantic beaches.

The structure of beaches

The actions of waves on sandy beaches over the seasons produce a consistent and predictable beach structure. The foredune is a raised portion at the back of a beach that is a transition point from the beach into a vegetated dune. The foredune is higher because the beach plants there are dense enough to trap and hold sand, and over time the foredune rises over the height of the upper beach. The upper beach is mainly created by wind action and is a repository for sand grains blown up from lower areas, although unusually high tides may bring wave swash onto the upper beach. The upper beach is usually bare of plants, though it may harbor a few very hardy species, such as American Beachgrass, Dusty Miller, Seaside Goldenrod, Searocket, Rough Cocklebur, and Common Saltwort (see illustrations, pp. 198–201).

Wrack lines

The wrack line (also called the wet-dry line) marks the average high-tide line. Incoming waves are more forceful than the backwash off the beach, and as they

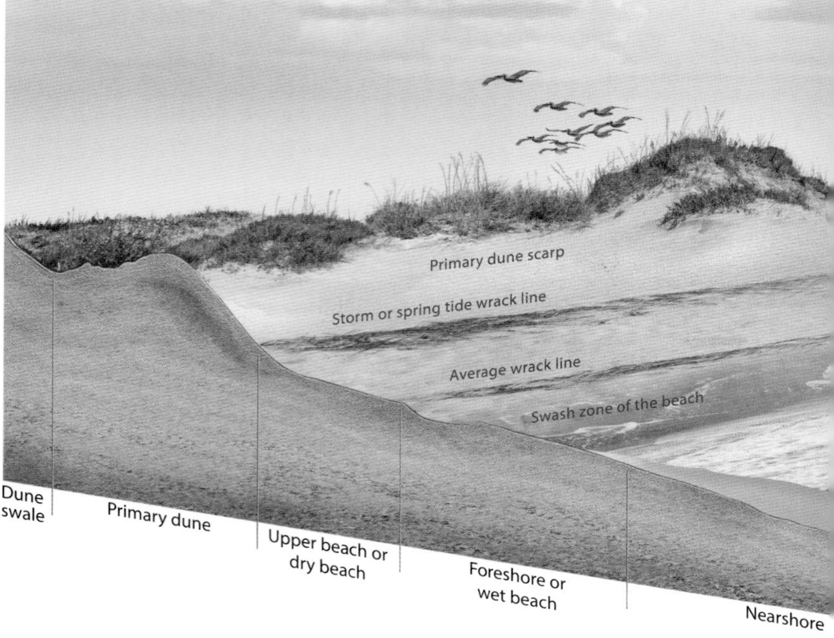
Primary dune scarp
Storm or spring tide wrack line
Average wrack line
Swash zone of the beach
Dune swale
Primary dune
Upper beach or dry beach
Foreshore or wet beach
Nearshore

Brown Pelican
Pelecanus occidentalis

Structure of an ocean beach

Ocean beaches on the Mid-Atlantic Coast have a remarkably consistent general structure that varies only where beaches have been recently nourished (filled in with new sand from offshore). Although most recreational beaches along the Mid-Atlantic have been nourished at some point in recent decades to combat sand erosion, the waves quickly reshape the beach into this general pattern.

Longshore current
arshore bar
Offshore

Seaweed fly
Fucellia sp.

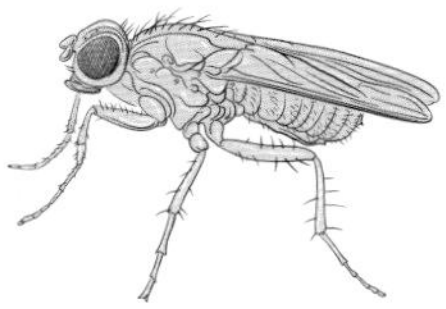

Small wrack line invertebrates such as seaweed and beach flies (*Fucellia* sp.) play a crucial role in the beach food chain, converting detritus, bacteria, small microorganisms, and plant debris into animal matter. The flies are important food sources for migrating shorebirds, as well as resident songbirds and other dune birds nesting near the beach. *Seaweed flies do not bite or sting people.*

come in, the surges sweep material from the tidal zone and onto the beach up to the high-tide line. This wave action leaves a collection of plant and animal debris called the wrack line. Wrack lines are usually composed of broken stalks of Common Reed (*Phragmites*) and Saltwater Cordgrass, strands of Eelgrass, molted crab shells, Sea Lettuce and other algae, and bits of other floatable debris. In the mix may be clam and scallop shells, egg cases from whelks and skates, and the carcasses of small fish and invertebrates. Any intact crab shells you see in the wrack line are not from dead crabs but are the molted shells that crabs shed as they grow. Crabs killed by birds or other predators have smashed shells and scattered legs and pieces.

Wrack lines are inhabited by beach flies, wolf and other spiders, beach fleas (amphipods), and beetles, all essential sources of food for shorebirds that feed on the beach. Most wrack line animals are nocturnal, feeding at night when the beach is cooler and damper. Wrack line shells and plants are a good indication of what plants and animals are abundant just offshore in the subtidal environment. Dead and partially dismem-

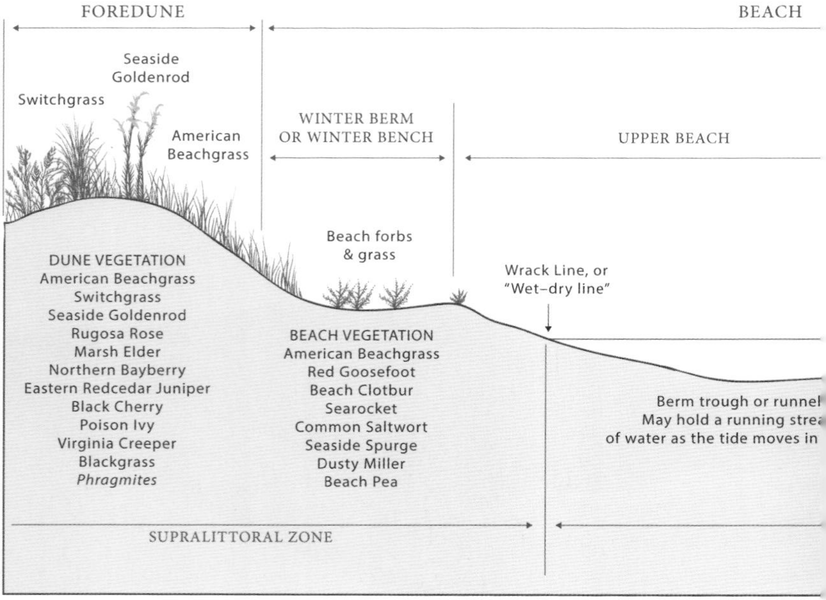
FOREDUNE
BEACH
Seaside Goldenrod
Switchgrass
American Beachgrass
WINTER BERM OR WINTER BENCH
UPPER BEACH
Beach forbs & grass
Wrack Line, or "Wet–dry line"
DUNE VEGETATION
American Beachgrass
Switchgrass
Seaside Goldenrod
Rugosa Rose
Marsh Elder
Northern Bayberry
Eastern Redcedar Juniper
Black Cherry
Poison Ivy
Virginia Creeper
Blackgrass
Phragmites
BEACH VEGETATION
American Beachgrass
Red Goosefoot
Beach Clotbur
Searocket
Common Saltwort
Seaside Spurge
Dusty Miller
Beach Pea
Berm trough or runnel
May hold a running strea
of water as the tide moves in
SUPRALITTORAL ZONE

bered Northern Searobins are common in the wrack line because they are easily caught by fishers and make excellent bait for Bluefish and Striped Bass.

The seeds of many annual beach plants are also mixed into the wrack line, and their dispersal by tides, wind, and wave action are an important way that these plants spread, particularly on more sheltered beaches away from heavy ocean waves. Seaside Spurge, Common Saltwort, Red Goosefoot, and Searocket are annual plants that spread their seeds this way. Wrack debris aids a beach by trapping and holding windblown sand, contributing to dune formation. Many foredunes begin as sand and seeds trapped in a high storm wrack line that gradually accumulates enough sand to support plant life.

Many bathing beaches sweep away the wrack line to leave "clean" sand. Unfortunately, beach grooming to suit sunbathers tends to sterilize the beach, removing food sources, shelter, and seeds for plants and animals. Ironically, it also makes the sand more mobile and thus more prone to being blown or swept away

Wrack lines provide food and shelter for many small beach organisms. Beach fleas (amphipods), small crabs, wolf spiders, many other kinds of spiders, beetles, and even foxes and raccoons scavenge in wrack lines. Wrack lines also trap and hold windblown sand on beaches.

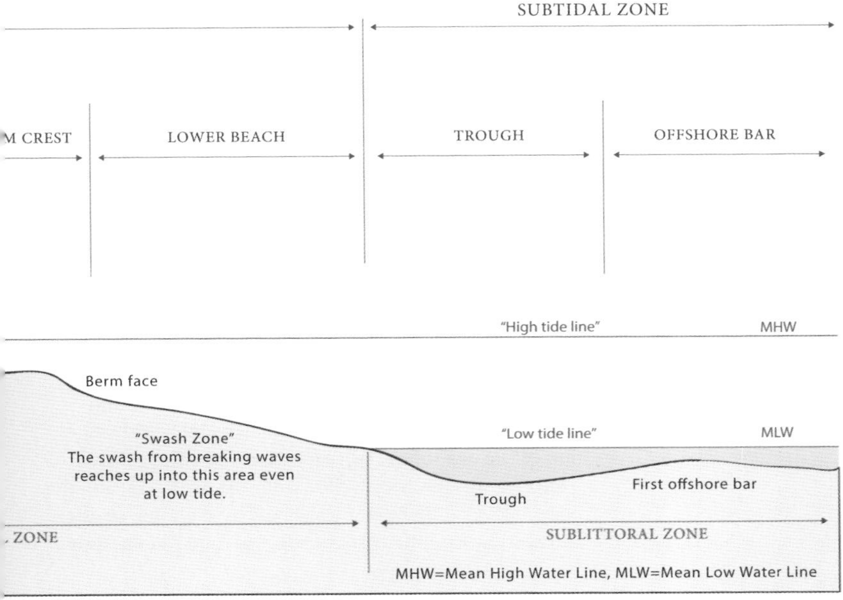
SUBTIDAL ZONE
M CREST
LOWER BEACH
TROUGH
OFFSHORE BAR
"High tide line"
MHW
Berm face
"Swash Zone"
The swash from breaking waves reaches up into this area even at low tide.
"Low tide line"
MLW
First offshore bar
Trough
. ZONE
SUBLITTORAL ZONE
MHW=Mean High Water Line, MLW=Mean Low Water Line

Piping Plover
Charadrius melodus

by tides. Grooming is particularly bad for two of the Mid-Atlantic Coast's most endangered birds, the Piping Plover and the Least Tern, both of which nest on beaches. The Piping Plover also feeds frequently in the wrack line near where it nests, and beach grooming often destroys Piping Plover nests.

The lower beach or foreshore

The lower beach, the swash zone, and the submerged area below the low tide line is the transition area where waves meet the beach, swashing up the sand and sliding back with each new wave set. Farther up the beach, a summer berm typically forms where the relatively gentle summer waves pile up an accumulation of sand, building the width and height of the beach. Often the beach becomes steeper on the seaward side of the summer berm.

Just below the foreshore area of beaches, below the low tide line, there is typically a trough in the beach profile where heavier gravel and shells accumulate, and just beyond that dip area is a shallow bar area composed of a mix of the coarse materials and sand brought in from deeper waters. It seems that every child at the beach makes the surprise discovery that if you head out into the water and brave the first line of breakers and the deep trough under them, you'll suddenly be in much shallower water when you reach the sandbar beyond the breaking waves. Offshore sandbars form when sand pulled off the lower beach by wave swash is drawn into the water just offshore, where wave action below the surface is less intense. The sand milling in the backwash drops out of the water column, forming a sandbar just seaward of the beach trough.

Rough shell hash, pebbles, and intact shells in a beach trough exposed at low tide. Finer sand sediments are washed either up the beach or toward the offshore bar.

Seasonal beach profiles

If you visit your favorite summer beach during the winter months, you might be shocked at how unfamiliar it looks: the wide, dry beach of summer may have vanished, replaced by a much narrower, lower, and wetter beach where the high-tide wrack backs right up to the base of the primary dune line. The gentler waves of summer push sand onto the beach, raising the beach level and widening the beach. In winter, or after a severe storm in any season, waves tend to tear away the beach sand, pulling it off the wet and dry beach areas onto sandbars just offshore of the low tide line. The regular waves in good weather then begin to push the submerged sand back onto the beach, gradually restoring the wide summer beach profile.

Beach sand

Most Atlantic Coast beaches from New York Harbor south to Georgia's Sea Islands are created by sand that eroded from upland areas of the Piedmont and Appalachians and was ferried to the coast by major rivers millions of years ago. In more recent times, the sand that is carried by the major Mid-Atlantic Coast rivers is mostly deposited in the many bays and sounds behind coastal barrier islands and does not contribute directly to beach building or offshore sand deposits.

In general, beach sediments range in particle size from coarse gravel and shell fragments near the low tide line to very fine particles of sand in the dunes at the top of the beach. The constant action of waves and currents sorts rocks and sand by size, forming large areas of consistent sediments. Water sorts sediments into coarse pebble areas, finer sand zones, and, finest of all, silty clay sediments. The fine particles of silt move the farthest and can drift in the water column for years before settling either deep offshore in the ocean bottom or as muddy sediments in bays and other protected areas with slower, gentler wave action. Sand accumulates along shores because it is composed of such

A "shining beach" at low tide. The sand of the lower beach still contains so much water from the previous high tide that the surface of the sand has a coating of draining water. You usually see shining only on beaches with a very shallow slope, because they drain so slowly.

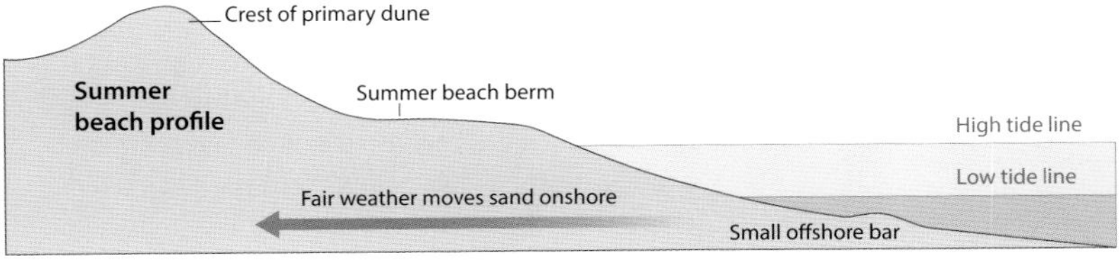
Crest of primary dune
Summer beach profile
Summer beach berm
High tide line
Low tide line
Fair weather moves sand onshore
Small offshore bar

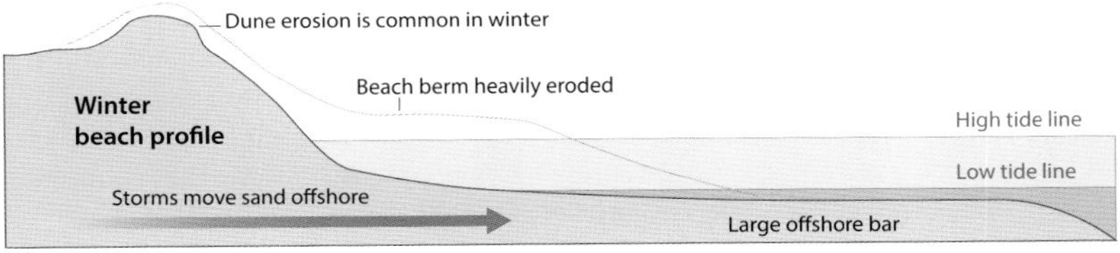
Dune erosion is common in winter
Winter beach profile
Beach berm heavily eroded
High tide line
Low tide line
Storms move sand offshore
Large offshore bar

Lower beach gravel
Middle beach sand
Dune area sand

Beach sand varies in both size and color, depending on where you are on the beach. On the lower beach sand grain size is large, and the sand is typically mixed with broken shells and small pebbles. The middle beach has finer sand because the wind blows finer particles inland from the swash zone. Middle beach sand is also lighter in color than lower beach sand because it is drier, and it consists mostly of quartz and feldspar. Dune sand is the finest of all in grain size, because all dune sand is driven inland by the wind, leaving large sand grains on the beach. The tiny sand grains on dunes are mostly made of quartz, which is bright white.

hard minerals as quartz and feldspar, in particles small enough to be easily moved by ocean waves but also durable enough to persist along the coastline rather than be washed immediately into deep water.

Beach sand also contains shell fragments of various sizes. About 1 percent of the sand from upper areas of Mid-Atlantic beaches is composed of tiny shell fragments. This does not include the many larger gravel-sized shells on the lower beach (often called shell hash) or where wind and wave action has concentrated shells. Many of the intact shells and shell fragments that you find on the beach are fossil shells that may be hundreds or even thousands of years old. Shells from ancient animals are often pulled offshore and buried and preserved in sand shoals for long periods before they are washed ashore onto the beach. These ancient shell fragments are often stained by burial, in colors ranging from light yellow to almost black. Shells from the Assateague Island National Seashore average about 1,700 years old, and shells from the Outer Banks of North Carolina average about 7,800 years old.

Wave size determines the size of sand grains on a beach. Beaches with larger waves will have larger grains of sand, because the wave energy tends to sweep smaller sand grains into the longshore current or seaward into offshore sand shoals. Highly exposed beaches such as those around Capes May, Henlopen, and Hatteras also tend to have larger, heavier sand grains because of all the wave action.

Wind also plays a role in structuring beach sand. Onshore winds carry smaller, lighter grains of sand up the beach, where they settle, often because dune plants at the top of the beach capture the flying sand grains (see illustration, p. 234). These small sand grains are usually made of white quartz, which is lightweight but very hard as well as lighter in color than most other sand minerals. If you stand in the middle of a beach and gaze from the water line up the beach toward the dune line, you'll usually see a distinct change in sand color.

Dry sand near the wrack line is a mix of medium-sized and larger sand grains, composed of many kinds of sand minerals. Up near the dunes at the top of the beach, the sand grains are much smaller, and lighter in color because the sand is mostly quartz. Once the wind has swept most smaller sand grains off the dry beach, a crusty lag deposit of larger sand grains, shell fragments, and small stones often forms above the high-tide line. See the "common beach features" section later in the chapter for more on the details of sandy beaches.

Most sand on Mid-Atlantic beaches is light brown or tan, but streaks of darker or colored sand often appear, particularly in the wet sand near the swash zone. Pollution is often blamed for dark patches of sand, but the cause is almost always clean and natural. The dark or black streaks are heavier minerals such as magnetite, ilmenite, and pyrite. The swash water from waves sorts the lighter-weight quartz and feldspar sand grains from the heavier magnetite, leaving dark streaks. Red

Colored mineral sands

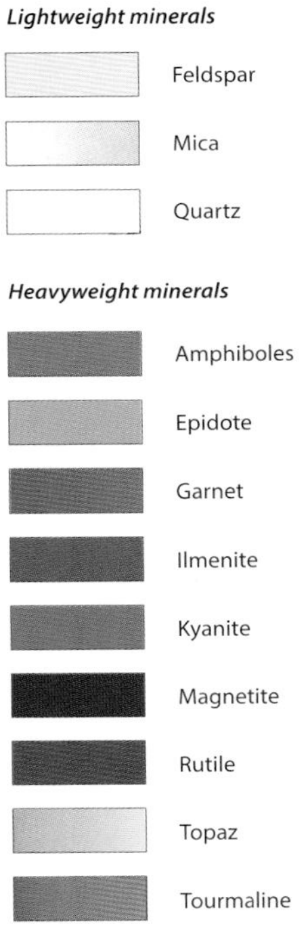
Lightweight minerals
Feldspar
Mica
Quartz
Heavyweight minerals
Amphiboles
Epidote
Garnet
Ilmenite
Kyanite
Magnetite
Rutile
Topaz
Tourmaline

Beach sand close-up showing many-colored mineral grains.

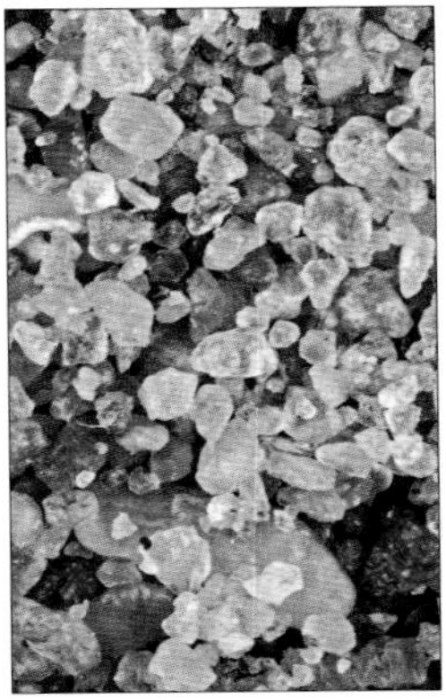

or purple streaks may be caused by garnet grains, and green streaks can be caused by grains of the mineral hornblende.

Nourished beaches

Beach nourishment—also called beach replenishment—is the process of replacing eroded sand with new sand to widen and elevate beaches where storms and routine coastal erosion have worn away the old beach sand. Almost all recreational beaches along the Mid-Atlantic Coast have been nourished and artificially reshaped, both to restore the width of the beach and to create an artificially high primary dune line to protect houses and other built structures. If your favorite Jersey Shore, Delmarva, or Outer Banks beach is fronted by houses, a boardwalk, or other structures, then it has almost certainly been artificially nourished at least once over the past few decades.

Sand to nourish eroded beaches almost always comes from offshore sand shoals, which are abundant on the continental shelf of the East Coast. Giant hydraulic pumps vacuum sand from the seafloor onto barges, which then transport the sand closer to shore, where large hydraulic pipes are used to spray the new sand from the barges onto the beach. Bulldozers then grade and smooth the new sand and often shape the sand at the top of the beach to create or reinforce a high dune

Most recreational beaches along the Mid-Atlantic Coast have been nourished with sand at least once in the past few decades, creating artificially high primary dune lines to protect beachfront houses. Wooden walkways protect the dune vegetation from foot traffic. Duck, North Carolina.

travelview

CAT

Army Corps of Engineers

In a beach nourishment project on the Jersey Shore, a huge hydraulic pipe brings sand and water ashore from a dredging ship in the background. Bulldozers move and shape the new sand to form the desired beach profile. Gulls flock to catch dead and dying invertebrates from the pumped sand.

line. These artificial dunes help prevent storm waves and sand overwash from invading seaside houses and streets.

Nourished beaches can look quite natural if the replacement sand is clean and of high quality (good grain size, with little silt or mud) and the nourishment was done years before, allowing time for natural shoreline processes to create a typical beach profile (see illustration, pp. 160–61). However, all beach nourishment projects destroy the ecology of sand beaches, and it may be years before the inshore fish, crabs, shellfish, plants, and wrack line animals repopulate a nourished beach. This lack of a natural beach ecosystem in nourished shorelines has important implications for beach-nesting birds and for migratory shorebirds that feed on beaches.

Beach nourishment is controversial because it is expensive and because most sand-replacement projects last as little as five years (often less), requiring a constant cycle of nourishment to preserve the beach. The US Army Corps of Engineers does most beach nourishment, and these projects often amount to a lavish federal subsidy in support of a relatively small number of owners of seasonal beach houses. Most of these seaside homes were built in areas well known to be flood-prone and vulnerable to storms.

Poorly executed beach nourishment projects can result in beaches with muddy, mucky sand, and the artificial beaches sometimes contain hazards you don't see on natural beaches. A newly deposited nourished beach often has a normal profile on the dry beach, but then drops off very steeply below the wave line, without the typical near-shore sandbars of a mature beach. The shifted or absent sandbars may create rip currents or cause shore breaks, in which large waves break directly onto the beach because no natural sandbars have yet developed on the nourished beach. It may take as long as a year for the nourished sand to redistribute into a typical beach profile. Sand pumped in from offshore often contains fossil shells that have been sheltered from normal erosion and weathering, and these shells are often very sharp and a hazard to bare feet.

Breakwaters, jetties, and groins

In the past, various kinds of hard structures have been built to try to stabilize sand beaches and protect them from storm damage. Breakwaters are long rock structures built offshore and roughly parallel to the shoreline to reflect storm waves and protect harbors. Jetties

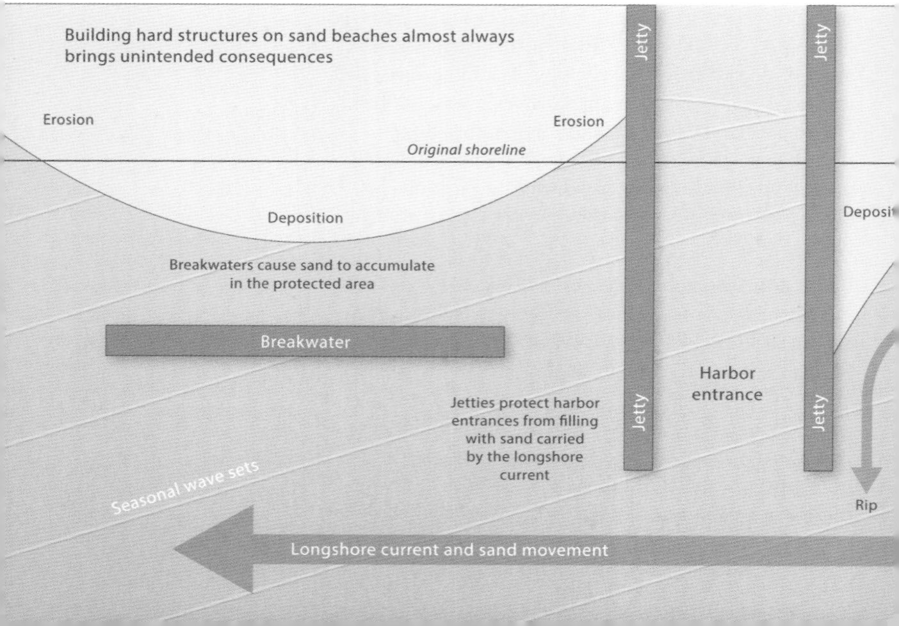
Building hard structures on sand beaches almost always brings unintended consequences
Jetty
Jetty
Erosion
Erosion
Original shoreline
Deposition
Deposi
Breakwaters cause sand to accumulate in the protected area
Breakwater
Harbor entrance
Jetties protect harbor entrances from filling with sand carried by the longshore current
Jetty
Jetty
Seasonal wave sets
Rip
Longshore current and sand movement

are walls built on either side of a harbor entrance to prevent the navigation channel from filling with sediment carried by longshore currents. Groins are stone, wood, or metal walls built perpendicular to sandy shores to stabilize and widen beaches that are losing sand to erosion from longshore currents. Groins are no longer considered effective for shoreline engineering because although they trap some sand locally along the upstream face of the wall, they rob downstream areas of their sand supply. Over time, groins worsen the overall problem of beach erosion.

Local longshore current

A rock groin at Herring Point Beach, Cape Henlopen State Park, Delaware. Note the extensive sand collected against the groin on the right upstream side and the lack of sand on the downstream side. The local longshore current here moves north (right to left in the photo).

Avoid swimming close to beach groins, especially on the upstream side of the groin—the side where the sand accumulates. Groins stick out into the longshore current, and this often generates small rip currents near the seaward end of the groin.

How to read a beach

Although all ocean beaches share superficial similarities, each has differences in wave energy, sand origin and supply, and weather regime that together determine its unique shape and character. Before swimming at a new beach, it is always wise to get advice on local conditions from the lifeguards, particularly on where

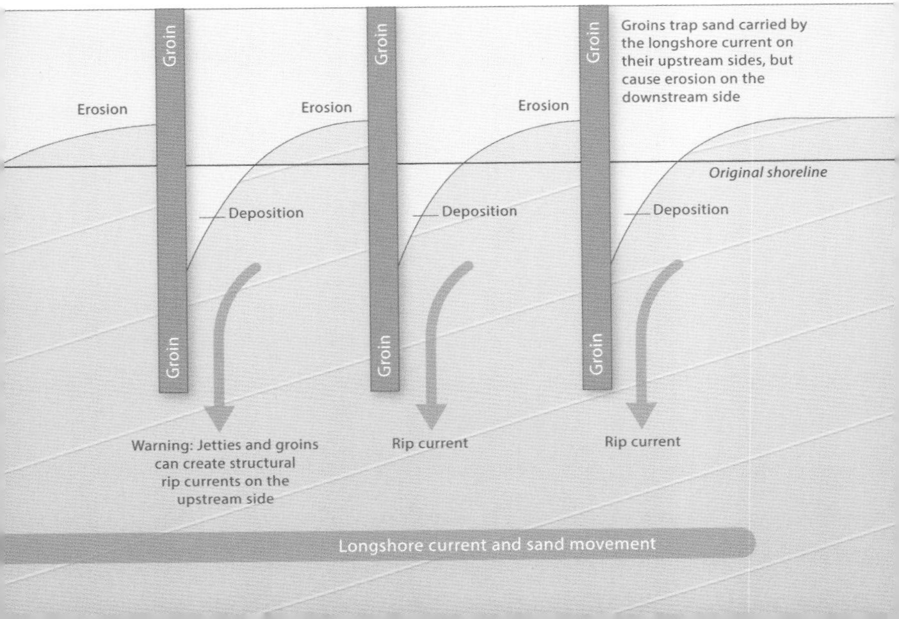
Groin
Groin
Groin
Groins trap sand carried by the longshore current on their upstream sides, but cause erosion on the downstream side
Erosion
Erosion
Erosion
Original shoreline
Deposition
Deposition
Deposition
Groin
Groin
Groin
Warning: Jetties and groins can create structural rip currents on the upstream side
Rip current
Rip current
Longshore current and sand movement

Willets at dawn at Pea Island National Wildlife Refuge on the Outer Banks of North Carolina. The Willets are hunting for Atlantic Sand Crabs in the wave swash.

Reading a wave set
Deep offshore
Shallow nearshore
Spilling breakers at the offshore bar
Trough
Spilling breakers at the nearshore bar
Wave swash
Final surge waves at the waterline

dangerous rip currents might develop.

Sandbars and the waves they generate

If you look carefully at the waves approaching an ocean beach on a day with moderate weather, you'll see a number of general patterns in the position and timing of breaking waves, as well as in the shape of the breakers themselves. The location of sandbars determines the first pattern to notice. Two sandbars form at most ocean beaches. The nearshore bar forms close to the beach, just seaward of the wave breaks nearest the shoreline. A second line of breakers marks the offshore bar. Offshore bars are widespread on beaches exposed to strong ocean waves, such as the beaches along the Jersey Shore, the Delmarva area, or on the Outer Banks of North Carolina. On exposed ocean beaches with large waves, the offshore bar may be 100–200 yards from shore, particularly in winter, but on most beaches and in summer, the offshore bar is much closer to shore. As ocean waves approach a beach, they begin to slow, and the spacing between waves decreases, causing the wave shapes to steepen, and finally, the steep structures topple forward and break. As with sandbars, the position of wave breaks can tell you a lot about the beach profile under the water, and the pattern of breaking waves can also reveal the overall wave energy as they interact with the bottom profile. Most smaller

Surfers work the offshore bar near Jennette's Pier on the Outer Banks at Nags Head, North Carolina. The wave breaks over the offshore bar are much larger than the waves closer to shore over the inshore bar.

Spilling breakers
Surging breakers
Plunging breakers

The slope angle of a beach also has a major effect on the size and nature of breaking waves. In summer the broader, less steep beaches mostly have spilling breakers. The steeper, narrower beaches of winter cause more waves to break in the classic curl.

ocean waves approaching a beach have a period (time in seconds between wave crests) of about 8–15 seconds, with larger storm waves showing a longer interval of 15–20 seconds.

Types of wave breaks

Wave breaks fall into three general patterns. Most fair-weather ocean waves are medium-energy waves known as spilling breakers. As each breaker approaches the shallows, its steepening crest curls just a bit as it spills down the front, taking a relatively long time to break entirely. Spilling breakers seem to fall apart as they hit the shallows. Surging breakers are another form of a fair-weather wave, often seen passing over the offshore sandbar without breaking. These long-period, low-profile waves push quickly over the shallows without much white water, then hit the wave swash from the previous waves and disintegrate into a low surge of white water, again without much force. Plunging breakers are the classic high-energy storm or wind-driven waves that heave into a near-vertical wall as they approach the shallows and then form the classic tubular curve that surfers love and most people fear. Plunging breakers are usually the result of offshore storms, which can send long-period waves across vast distances of ocean. Plunging breakers hit the shallows with tremendous force, sometimes pounding the beach so hard that you can feel the break through your feet, even many yards away up the beach. A major storm or powerful onshore winds can cause a storm surge, creating a dangerous wave pattern called a shore break, in which large waves pass over the sandbars without breaking (because of the deeper surge waters) and break directly onto the beach. Swimming in a stormy shore break is dangerous: the large waves breaking onto the beach can sweep you up and pound you directly into the sand with enough force to cause injury.

Rip currents

If you swim on ocean beaches, it is critical to understand rip currents: what they are, how they form, and, most important, what to do if you are caught in one. Rip currents (sometimes incorrectly called rip tides) form when strong sets of waves drive more water up a beach than can easily drain away through the normal

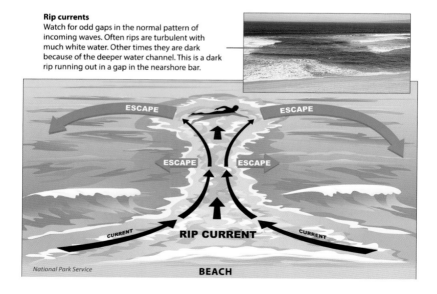

Rip currents
Watch for odd gaps in the normal pattern of incoming waves. Often rips are turbulent with much white water. Other times they are dark because of the deeper water channel. This is a dark rip running out in a gap in the nearshore bar.

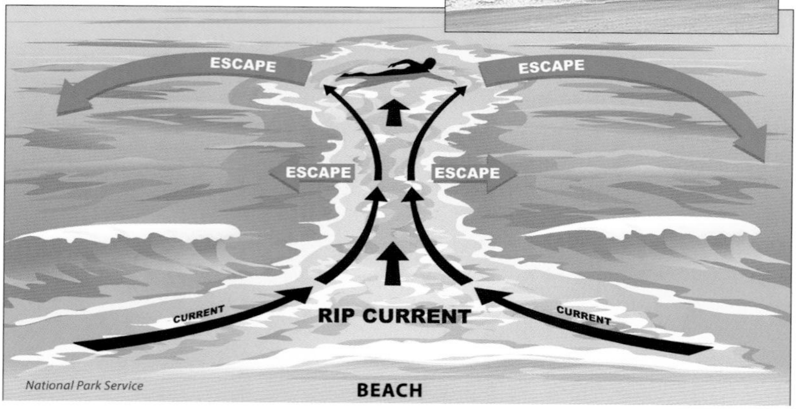
ESCAPE
ESCAPE
ESCAPE
ESCAPE
CURRENT
RIP CURRENT
CURRENT
National Park Service
BEACH

A dark rip current running in a deep channel

A lighter rip carrying sand offshore

swash of waves. As each succeeding wave breaks and slides down the beach, the next wave blocks the back-flow of water and raises the overall level of water on the beach. Eventually, too much water is well above the current tide level. To release the pent-up water, a swift current forms in a low spot or channel on the beach and drains the excess water out to sea. This channel of fast-flowing water, usually running perpendicular to the shoreline, is a rip current (see diagram, opposite). Rip currents are powerful and can flow at three to five miles per hour. Even an Olympic-caliber swimmer could not swim against a current that strong. If you are caught in a rip current, don't panic and try to swim directly back to the beach. Instead, tread water and let the current carry you out a short distance: the force of most rips dissipates quickly away from the beach. Then swim parallel to the shore to exit the main rip flow; most rip currents are narrow channels. In the United States rip currents kill about 50 people a year as the victim tries to fight the current, and this leads to exhaustion and drowning. Swim only on beaches with lifeguards, and ask the lifeguards if any rips or other

Some rip currents are visible if you know what to look for. Beware of deceptively calm areas where waves are not breaking. Watch for a dark or light gap in the normal wave sets coming onto a beach. Sometimes a strong rip current kicks up a lot of white water.

Rip currents are sometimes a darker color than the water around them because they run in a deeper channel or because they are drawing silt and sand off the beach. *In rough surface conditions, a strong rip current may be invisible from the shore, so be especially wary around large waves.*

Surf fishing is often better on days when offshore winds have brought colder water toward the shore. Larger gamefish often follow the cool water close to the beach.

hazards have been reported in the area.

Winds

Beaches are windy for the same reason that open waters are windy: there are no landforms or tall vegetation to break the force of the wind. Beaches are also windy because of the very different ways that land and sea heat and cool over the seasons. This differential heating and cooling along the coast generates onshore winds as well as their opposite, offshore winds, particularly in summer when the contrast between land and sea temperatures is the greatest.

Onshore winds form when the land heats up during the day, creating columns of rising warm air. As the warm air mass rises, it draws in air from the lower, cooler air over the sea, creating winds that blow in from the sea, usually in the afternoon and early evening. While these cool sea breezes may feel great on land, the onshore winds can be strong enough to kick up three-to-four-foot waves even in sheltered waters, sometimes creating a rough ride for small boats. Onshore winds happen almost daily along ocean coastlines in summer and early fall.

Offshore winds result when the ocean is warmer than the land and rising air over the sea pulls air from the land. Offshore breezes occur most often in late fall, when the water is still relatively warm but the land is cooling quickly with the approach of winter.

Wind and water temperatures at the beach

Most beachgoers have noticed that the water temperature at a beach can vary widely from one day to the next. Onshore and offshore winds play a significant role in determining water temperature. When the wind blows from the ocean toward the land, it blows surface water that has been warmed by the sun toward the beach. When the wind blows from the land toward the ocean, warm surface water is pushed out to sea, and cold water from depths rises to take its place at the shore. Warm water from onshore winds tends to be clear but may contain more drifting marine life, such as sea jellies. While the water may be mild, onshore winds can also produce rough surf and larger beach waves. Cold water upwelling near the beach caused by

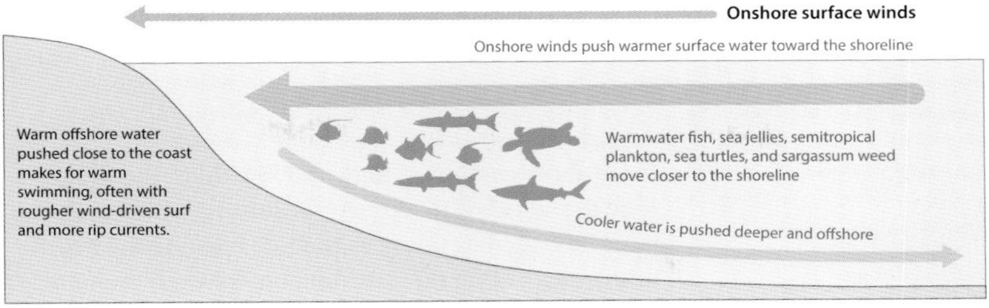
Onshore surface winds
Onshore winds push warmer surface water toward the shoreline
Warm offshore water pushed close to the coast makes for warm swimming, often with rougher wind-driven surf and more rip currents.
Warmwater fish, sea jellies, semitropical plankton, sea turtles, and sargassum weed move closer to the shoreline
Cooler water is pushed deeper and offshore

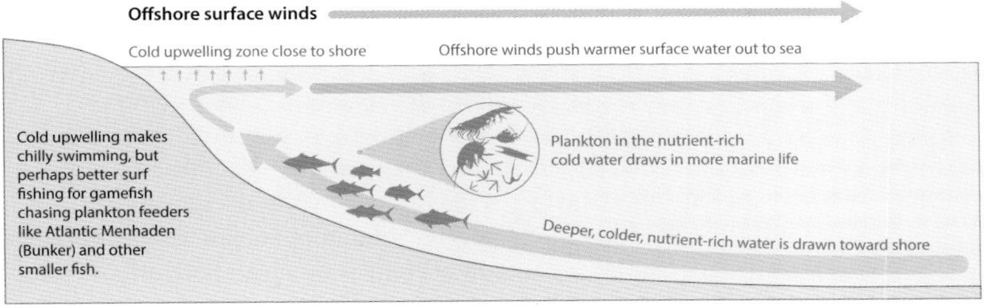
Offshore surface winds
Cold upwelling zone close to shore
Offshore winds push warmer surface water out to sea
Cold upwelling makes chilly swimming, but perhaps better surf fishing for gamefish chasing plankton feeders like Atlantic Menhaden (Bunker) and other smaller fish.
Plankton in the nutrient-rich cold water draws in more marine life
Deeper, colder, nutrient-rich water is drawn toward shore

offshore winds tends to carry more bottom sediment and plankton and can be murky, but cold upwellings often bring gamefish closer to the beach, making for better surf fishing conditions.

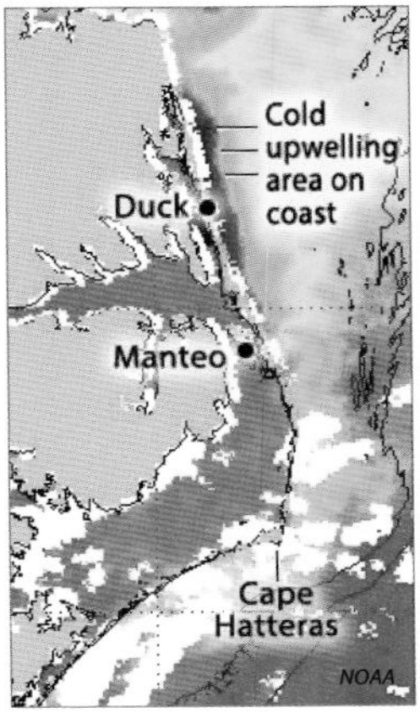
Cold upwelling area on coast
Duck
Manteo
Cape Hatteras
NOAA

A satellite sea surface temperature image of the Outer Banks, July 23, 2016, after strong offshore winds in the area. Note the blue upwelling of cold water near the beaches of Duck, North Carolina. The water in previous days had been very warm, but the offshore winds caused an upwelling of cooler waters.

Common beach features

Knowing more about the physical, geological, and biological processes in beach ecology can make a visit to the shore much more enjoyable. Both wind and water can create interesting patterns, as well as mysteries: How were given set of marks formed? Items in boldface are illustrated on the next series of pages.

Physical details of beaches

Many of the things you see on beaches are created by purely physical forces of air and water. **Swash lines** on the wet beach are tiny ridges of sand grains, small rocks, and shell fragments. Swash marks are like miniature wrack lines, formed at the landward edge of each wave swash. Sea foam is common on beaches during storms or strong onshore winds. The foam is formed from dissolved organic matter in the seawater, churned up from the shallows and turned into bubbly foam by the surface tension created by the organic matter, much the way dish soap creates bubble masses if you

Beach escarpments (or scarps) are generally small, vertical erosion cuts in the beach, such as this one-foot escarpment. Storm waves that come onto the beach at a sharp angle can remove large amounts of sand. A single offshore storm on July 24, 2018, cut a 10-foot scarp into the beach at Nags Head, North Carolina, removing tens of thousands of square yards of sand overnight.

spray water into it. The sticky sea foam attracts fine silt particles that give the foam its characteristic light brown color.

Air and water within the beach

In the daily rhythm of high and low tides, the beach sand acts like a giant sponge, absorbing water as the tide rises, then draining as the tide falls. As the beach drains in a falling tide, air replaces water in the sand. Once the tide starts to rise again, the water forces the air out of the beach, and the displaced air rises to the surface in various ways. On a rising tide, look for **nail holes** in the beach near the wave swash. These small holes are about the size of a hole from a common building nail. Although you might think that animals make them, in fact they are air vents formed as air in the sand is pushed upward by the rising seawater. A common variation is miniature **volcanoes or bubble holes,** essentially nail holes in which both air and sand are expelled from the beach, forming tiny volcano-like cones of sand around the hole.

Sometimes air forced out of the beach by the rising water of high tide doesn't reach the beach surface but forms soft or bubbly sand full of air cavities, almost like a light sand sponge. **Soft sand** forms most readily in relatively coarse sand up near the wrack line of the beach. Soft sand can be an annoyance when you are walking on the beach, as suddenly your footsteps sink 3–6 inches or more into the sand. Soft sand can be particularly hazardous to beach vehicles, which can quickly sink axle-deep when they hit a patch of soft sand.

Water within beaches drains away at low tide, and you can often see the drainage directly in **rill marks**, drainage marks that show the water flowing out of the beach. The top of the rill can also give you a sense of how high the water table line is relative to the slope of the beach. On relatively flat beaches that absorb a lot of water at high tide, the rills drain into **beach runnels**, larger streams of draining water that often flow at an angle across the top of the lower beach before draining into the sea. In very flat, fine-sand beaches, the drainage from the beach may form a thin sheet of water

ash marks on the lower beach

Sea foam at the edge of the swash zone

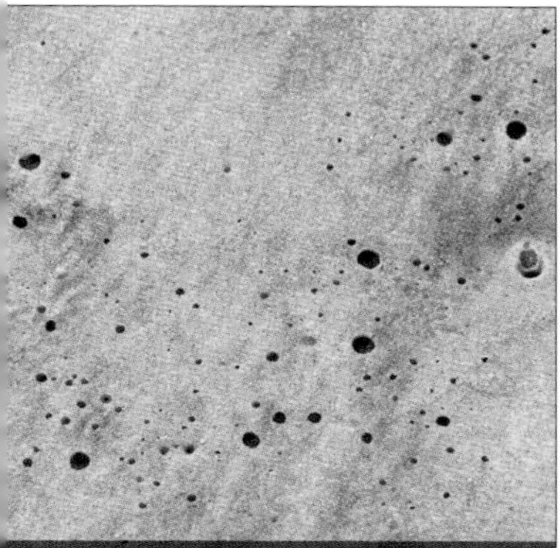
il holes are channels that let air out of the beach

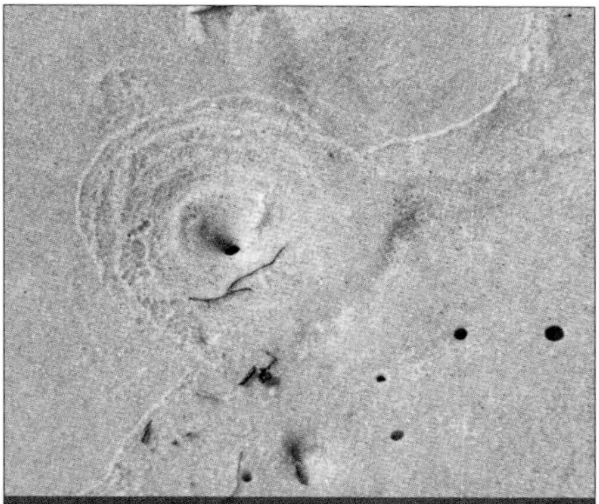
Bubble holes or volcanoes are also air channels

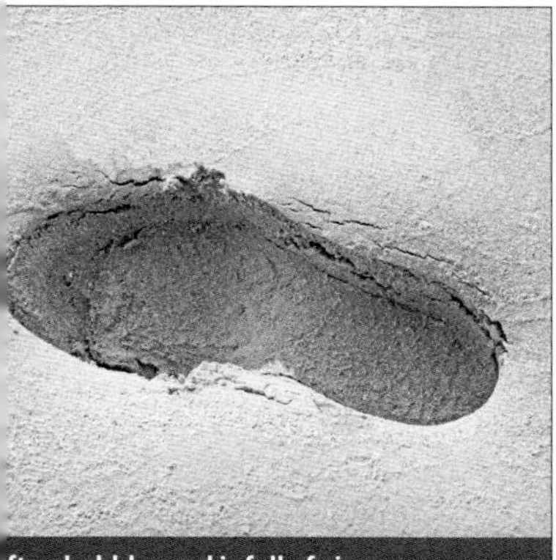
ft or bubbly sand is full of air

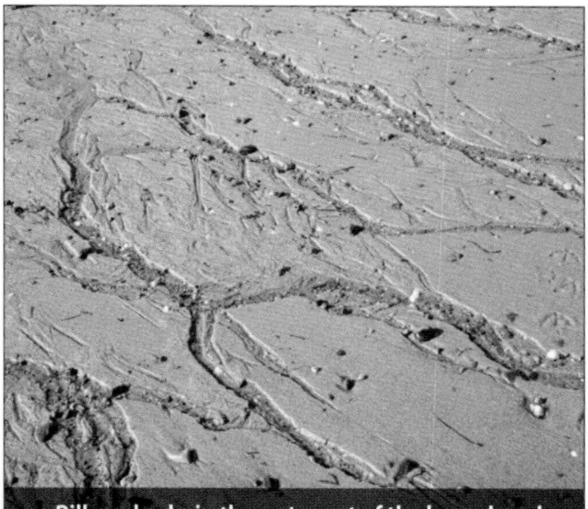
Rill marks drain the water out of the lower beach

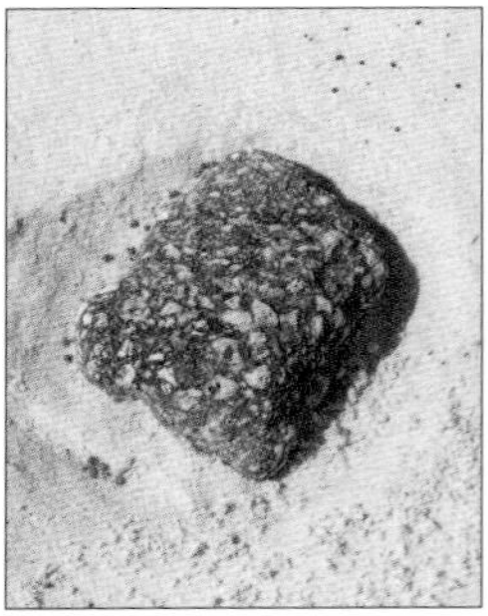

Not all black lumps on the beach are coal. On the Outer Banks south of Whalebone Junction, NC 12, the only highway leading to Cape Hatteras, has been torn up and repaved many times to repair storm damage. Asphalt lumps on the beach are not just evidence of old storms. At Pea Island National Wildlife Refuge, North Carolina, they indicate the former position of the highway. Beach erosion and island migration constantly push the island—and thus the highway—westward, leaving pieces of old road scattered about what is now the beach.

across the top of the sand, a shiny, wet beach.

One commonly found black beach stone tells a sadder story. On the beaches of the Mid-Atlantic Coast and Outer Banks, you may find rounded, **sand-smoothed lumps of coal**. When coal was used for home heating in the nineteenth century, great four- and five-masted wooden sailing ships transported coal up and down the East Coast. The massive ships were often wrecked in nor'easters and hurricanes, driven onto offshore sandbars by easterly winds and then pounded to pieces by storm waves. Offshore currents and waves have long since destroyed the ships, but their loads of coal remain offshore, and occasionally pieces come ashore, like small memorials to their vanished crews.

On days with large breaking waves, the lower beach may be wet with **spindrift**, water that is blown off the tops of breaking waves by a strong onshore wind. Although sprays of spindrift can certainly wet both you and the lower beach if you stand in the swash zone, spindrift is not the origin of the salt aerosols (salt spray) that can leave a fine coat of salt on your glasses, phone, or car and can kill or damage plants for miles inland (see illustration, p. 134, on salt aerosols).

SAND FEATURES

Beach sand is composed of **minerals**, each with a characteristic color. Dry sand on Mid-Atlantic beaches tends to be light brown or tan because the most commonly occurring minerals are quartz and feldspar, which range in color from white to light brown. Other minerals contribute to the overall color of beach sand, and sometimes they give parts of the sand distinct colors (see color chart, p. 167). The most common heavyweight minerals in beach sand are **magnetite and ilmenite, both almost black**. These minerals cause the black streaks and patches in beaches that people often mistake for evidence of oil pollution or other human-made contaminants. The dark minerals are much heavier than the relatively lightweight quartz and feldspar, and both wind and water act to separate the minerals on the beach. This sorting of sand grains by weight is the cause of the intricate swirling patterns

ɔeach runnel draining the beach

A weathered lump of coal from an offshore wreck

indrift blown from the top of a wave

Sand is composed of many different minerals

per beach sand with black magnetite grains

Wind sorts heavy magnetite from lighter quartz

Dark streaks in beach sand are rarely the result of pollution. The streaks are caused when swash water sorts the heavy, dark mineral grains from the lighter grains. See the chart on p. 167 for the colors of common beach sand minerals. The dark streaks in this photo are caused by black sand grains of magnetite, which are much heavier than the lightweight quartz grains surrounding the streak.

you often see on beaches and dunes.

Water or wind moving over sand can create intricate **ripple patterns.** If you look closely at the ripple shapes, you can infer water or wind direction, as well as whether the pattern was created by flow in one direction or in two directions, as when a tide changes or wind changes directions. Both water and wind flowing in one direction create asymmetric ripples, with a gentler slope on the up-current side and a steeper slope on the down-current side. Tidewater that flows in two directly opposite directions creates flat-topped ripples. When water changes direction at an angle, a new **cross-ripple or rhomboid ripple** pattern can form. As the water or wind flows over the sand, it sorts the lighter-weight, light-colored minerals from heavier black minerals like magnetite, which can create **bold patterns** in beach runnels or in the dunes at the top of the beach.

Both wind and water can also create laminations or layers in beach and dune sand, where layers of darker and lighter sand alternate. When later winds or tides cut through the layered sand, they can create **bold lamination or contour patterns** on the beach or dunes.

One widespread beach and dune feature is usually created by the wind: **sand shadows** on the downwind side of any clump of plant or animal matter on the beach. These sand shadows are typically seen near the dry tops of beaches above the high-tide line. Sand shadows and the blowing sand they collect are significant for conserving and holding sand on a beach that might otherwise blow away into the dunes or the sea.

Beach shells

The shells and shell fragments you find on the beach and in the intertidal accumulations of **shell hash** (jumbled broken shells) often vary in color from the nearly pure white of modern shells to black in shells that were buried for centuries. Modern light-colored shells on a beach that hasn't been nourished recently are often a pretty good reflection of the clam, snail, and crab populations just offshore. But what about all the yellow, brown, and black shells you encounter? **Yellow**

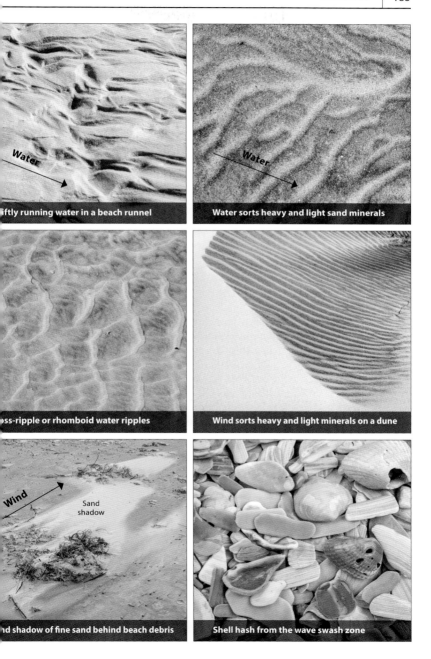

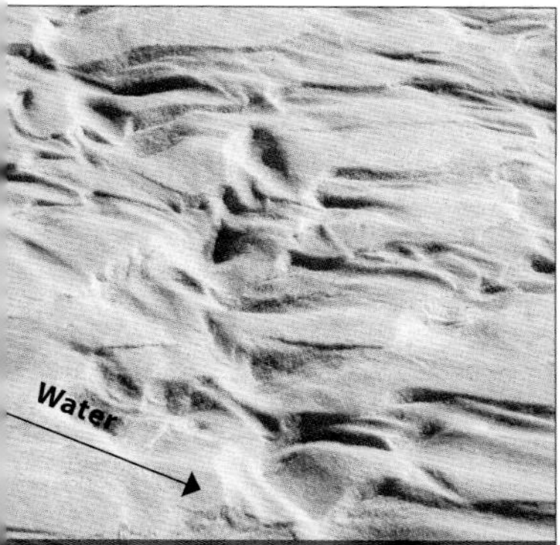
Water
iftly running water in a beach runnel

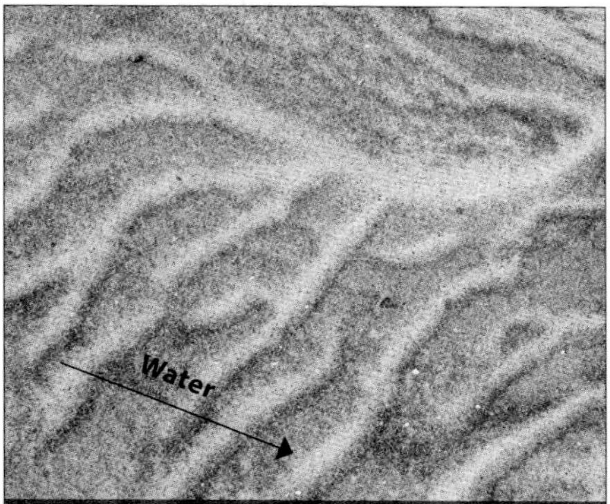
Water
Water sorts heavy and light sand minerals

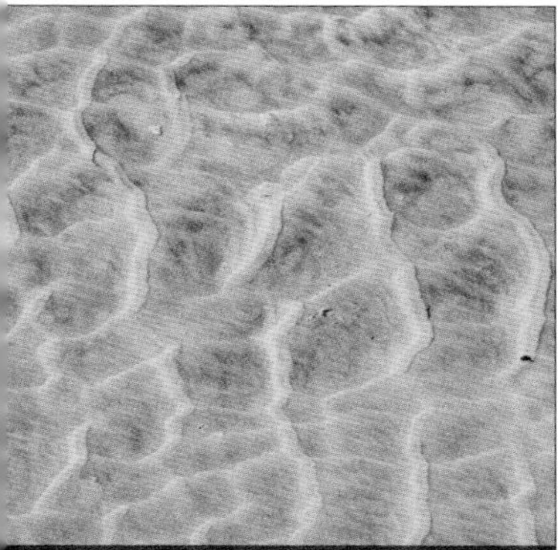
ss-ripple or rhomboid water ripples

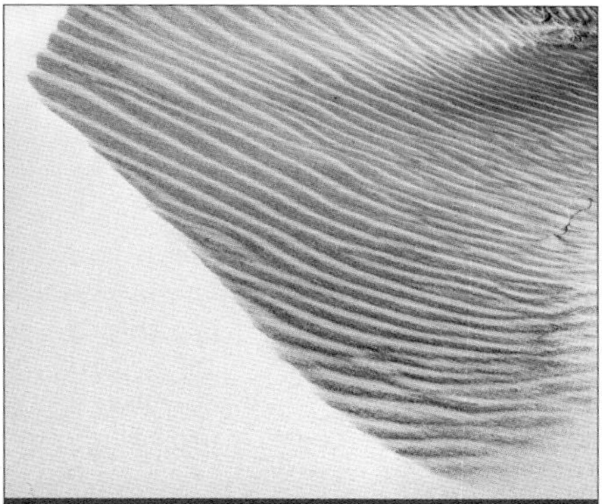
Wind sorts heavy and light minerals on a dune

Wind
Sand shadow
nd shadow of fine sand behind beach debris

Shell hash from the wave swash zone

and brown shells and shell fragments were likely buried in shallow beach sand or in shallow offshore sand shoals, where they were stained by organic matter in the presence of oxygen. The darkness of the staining is roughly in proportion to the age of the shell over time spans of decades to many centuries. **Black shells** were deeply buried in mud, sand, or sand mixed with mud and ancient plant material, in the absence of oxygen.

Blackened oyster shells are particularly common on barrier island ocean beaches. In addition to being ancient, the oyster shells on ocean beaches also tell an interesting story of sea level rise and barrier island migration. Oysters do not live near ocean beaches—they live in the protected waters of bays and estuaries. So, where did the oyster shells on the ocean beaches come from?

Our modern Mid-Atlantic Coast barrier islands have been migrating toward land for thousands of years. As the sandy islands shift landward through storm overwashes, the overwashed sand buries the island vegetation and forests, as well as any oyster reefs, on the bay side of the islands. Over hundreds of years, the islands migrate past the buried ancient forests and oyster reefs, and the **old tree stumps, marsh peat**, and oyster shells get exposed on the ocean-facing side of the islands (see pp. 50–51 for more on this process). The many oyster shells you find on island beaches—especially on the Outer Banks—thus show us how much natural barrier islands have moved over time.

Ancient shark teeth are a common biologic component of beach sand, particularly as you travel south along the US Atlantic Coast. Like clam shells, shark teeth range in color from relatively recent, almost white teeth to teeth that were deeply buried and have turned dark brown or black over time. Virtually all the shark teeth we see on beaches are ancient—some are over 1,000 years old. Shark teeth are common not because sharks themselves were so abundant but because the teeth are very hard and can survive the constant erosion of sandy environments. Most shark teeth in beach sand are only about a quarter inch in size, and

ost colored shells on a beach are ancient

A fossil scallop shell deeply buried without oxygen

'ossil oyster shell, evidence of island migration

Photo courtesy of Dianna K

An ancient forest reemerges from the sand

ncient salt marsh peat uncovered in a storm

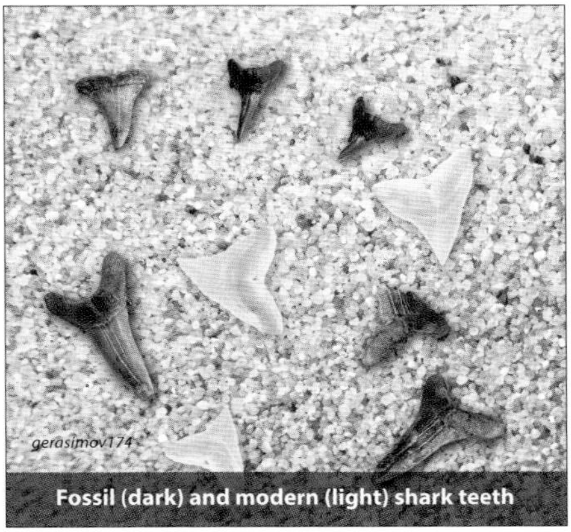

gerasimov174

Fossil (dark) and modern (light) shark teeth

Shells on an Outer Banks beach. Research shows that many of the shells on Mid-Atlantic Coast beaches are hundreds of years old. Some are over 1,000 years old. The ancient shells get preserved when they are buried in sand. Years later the sand shifts in storms, and the old shells are exposed again.

many teeth are broken and heavily worn with time.

The Mid-Atlantic Coast is rich in interesting shells (see illustrations, pp. 192–95). This region mixes the northern mollusk species of New England and the New Jersey region with warmer-water species found on the Outer Banks and Cape Hatteras.

Offshore animals and plants on the beach

In addition to interesting shells, ocean beaches are great places to look for signs of marine life washed up on or living on the beach. These are animals that live offshore, not on the beach itself, but are commonly seen by beachcombers.

Sargassum Weed is the most common marine algae seen on beaches around and south of the Chesapeake Bay. Sargassum Weed is the most common marine algae on earth, and giant mats of the weed circulate so densely in the Middle Atlantic Ocean that the area is called the Sargasso Sea. The smaller bits and pieces of Sargassum that we see on Mid-Atlantic beaches mostly comes up with the Gulf Stream and are then transported inshore by local currents and offshoots of the Stream.

Animal sailors on the Gulf Stream and local currents include wonderfully unique marine animals that float with the breezes and tides, eventually washing up on our coasts. Our most common sea jellies seen stranded on ocean beaches include the **Moon Jelly** (the white ones), the **Lion's Mane Jellyfish** (the red ones), the **Portuguese Man o' War,** and the **Cannonball Jelly**. Beware of all sea jellies on the beach, even the obviously dead ones. Some, like the Portuguese Man o' War, are notorious for retaining their ability to sting long after they are dead. But all sea jellies sting, and even animals with weaker stings, such as the Moon Jelly, may cause an allergic reaction in some people.

Other drift animals seen on beaches are colonial animals only distantly related to sea jellies. **By-the-Wind Sailors** and **Blue Buttons** wash up on Mid-Atlantic beaches, although they may be very worn from tumbling in the surf and sand. Blue Buttons have often completely lost their blue fringe by the time they get to

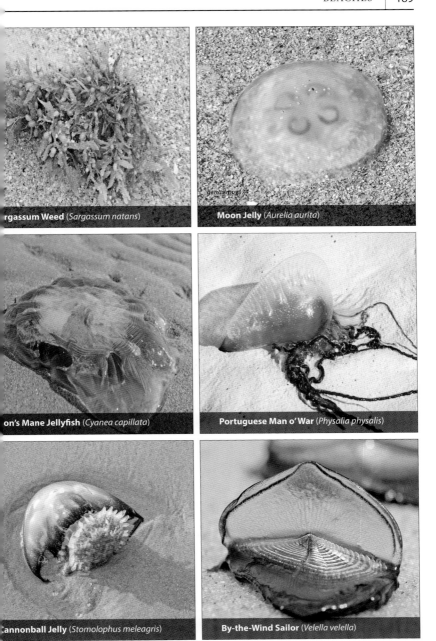

rgassum Weed (*Sargassum natans*)

Moon Jelly (*Aurelia aurita*)

on's Mane Jellyfish (*Cyanea capillata*)

Portuguese Man o' War (*Physalia physalis*)

annonball Jelly (*Stomolophus meleagris*)

By-the-Wind Sailor (*Velella velella*)

CANNONBALL JELLY
Stomolophus meleagris

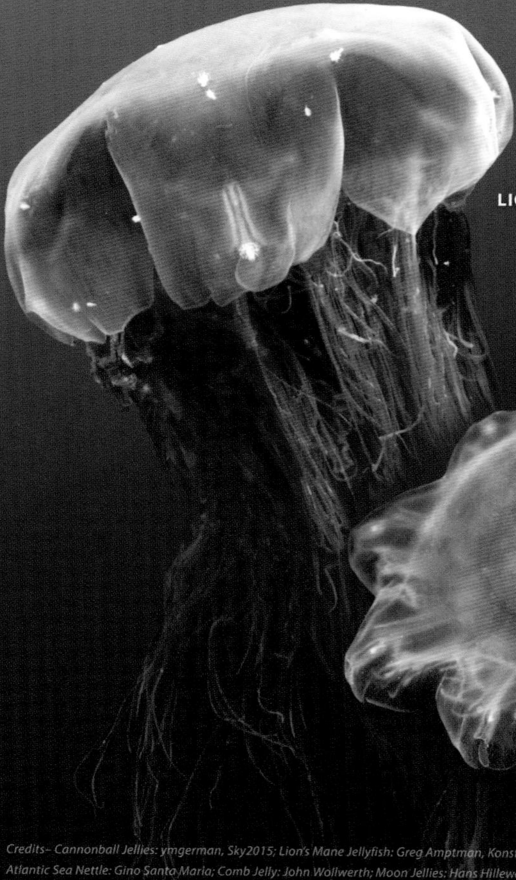

LION'S MANE JELLYFISH
Cyanea capillata

Seen from above, as in shallows or on a beach

Credits– Cannonball Jellies: ymgerman, Sky2015; Lion's Mane Jellyfish: Greg Amptman, Konstantin Novikov; PMOW: MSNN, sciencepics; Atlantic Sea Nettle: Gino Santa Maria; Comb Jelly: John Wollwerth; Moon Jellies: Hans Hillewaert.

Portuguese Man o' Wars are sea jelly–like animals that appear sporadically in regional waters, usually in late summer. These jellies have a powerful sting and very long tentacles, so stay well away from them. The tentacles can sting long after the animal has died or has washed up on the beach.

PORTUGUESE MAN O' WAR
Physalia physalis

ATLANTIC SEA NETTLE
Chrysaora quinquecirrha

MOON JELLY
Aurelia aurita

COMMON NORTHERN COMB JELLY
Bolinopsis infundibulum
(A ctenophore, not a true jelly)

Not to scale

KNOBBED WHELK
Busycon carica

NORTHERN MOON SNAIL
Euspira heros

RIBBED MUSSEL
Geukensia demissa

BAY SCALLOP
Argopecten irridians

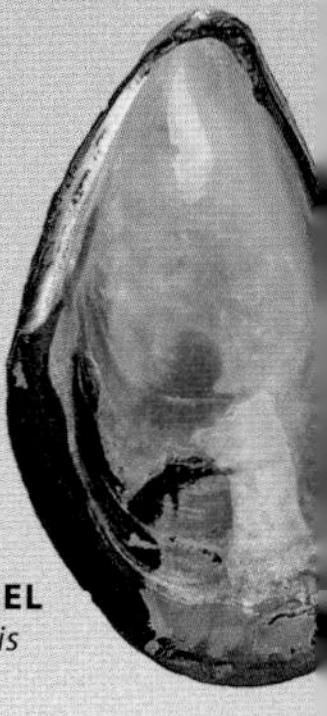

BLUE MUSSEL
Mytilis edulis

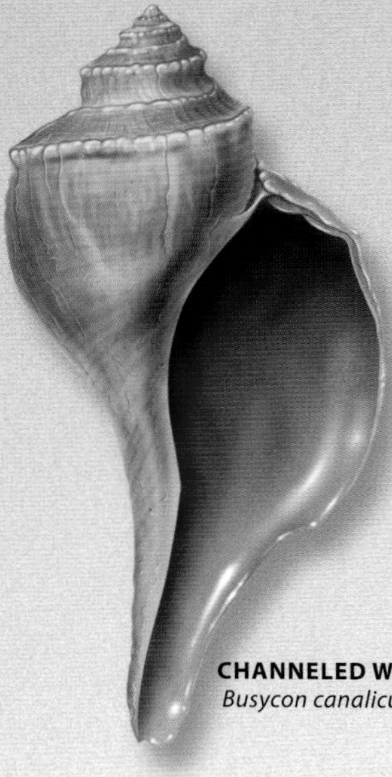

CHANNELED WHELK
Busycon canaliculatus

ATLANTIC SURF CLAM
Spisula solidissima

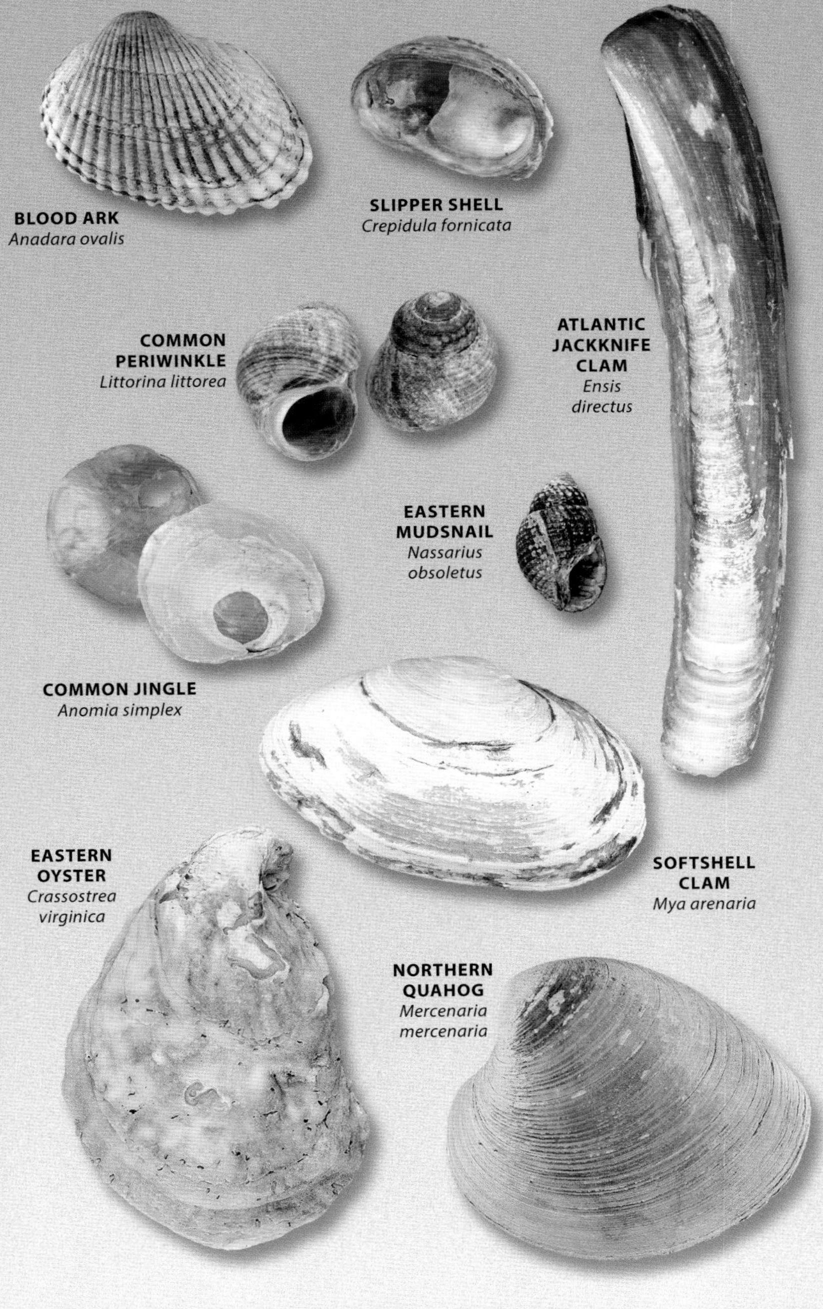

BLOOD ARK
Anadara ovalis

SLIPPER SHELL
Crepidula fornicata

ATLANTIC JACKKNIFE CLAM
Ensis directus

COMMON PERIWINKLE
Littorina littorea

EASTERN MUDSNAIL
Nassarius obsoletus

COMMON JINGLE
Anomia simplex

SOFTSHELL CLAM
Mya arenaria

EASTERN OYSTER
Crassostrea virginica

NORTHERN QUAHOG
Mercenaria mercenaria

COQUINA CLAM
Donax variabilis
GIANT EASTERN MUREX
Hexaplex fulvescens
FLORIDA FIGHTING CONCH
Strombus alatus
COMMON NUTMEG
Cancellaria reticulata
ANGEL WING
Cyrtopleura costata
LIGHTNING WHELK
Sinistrofulgur perversum

SCOTCH BONNET
Semicassis granulata

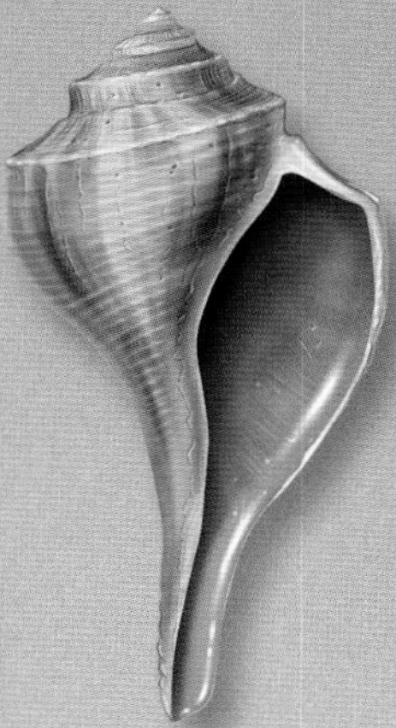

PEAR WHELK
Sinistrofulgur perversum

ATLANTIC AUGUR
Terebra dislocata

LETTERED OLIVE
Oliva sayana

GIANT ATLANTIC COCKLE
Dinocardium robustum

DISC DOSINIA
Dosinia discus

SOUTHERN QUAHOG
Mercenaria campechiensis

CALICO SCALLOP
Argopecten gibbus

For photo credits, see p. 417

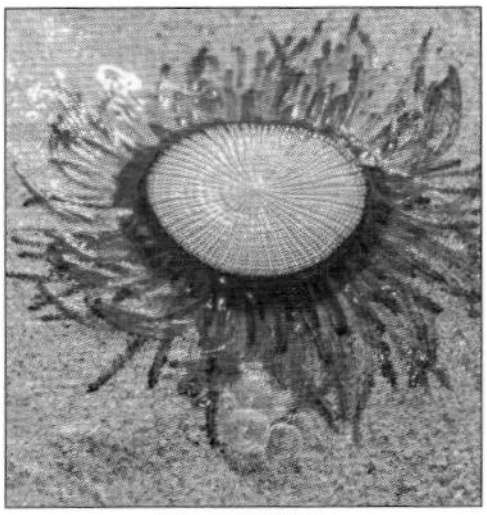

Blue Button
Porpita porpita

Clearnose Skate egg cases
Raja eglanteria

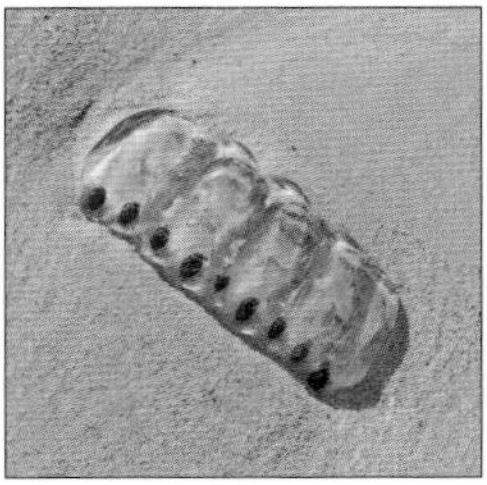

Salps
Family Salpidae

Lightning Whelk egg cases
Sinistrofulgur perversum

the beach and look more like interesting white bottle caps than animals. **Salps** are colonial marine animals that look like bits of clear jelly when they wash up and are easy to overlook.

A few marine animals have interesting, durable egg cases that frequently wash up on beaches. **Skate egg cases** (also called Mermaid's Purses) are dark, leathery pouches with curly extensions that are meant to entangle the cases in marine algae to keep the eggs submerged. **Whelk egg cases** are coiled masses of angular egg pouches attached to a central spine.

BEACH PLANTS

Few plants and animals are well adapted to the dry conditions, sandy substrate, and salt aerosols of beach environments. No plants can survive below the wrack line except Saltwater Cordgrass on very sheltered beaches, and few plants can survive the first stretch of upper beach behind the wrack line, primarily because only a few plants can tolerate having their roots periodically immersed in salt water. Most true beach plants live in the dry upper beach area just before the rise of the foredunes behind the beach, where American Beachgrass begins to dominate.

American Beachgrass

American Beachgrass is the most common plant on the upper beach, and it becomes even more dominant in the foredune and back dune areas beyond the upper beach. To conserve moisture in dry winds, its leaves curl into vertical tubes. Beachgrass can spread by seed, but it generally spreads over a beach through underground stems or rhizomes, with roots that extend deep into the sand—six feet or more is not unusual. With its rhizomes and deep roots safe under the sand, American Beachgrass can survive storm damage, sand blowouts, and winter exposure.

American Beachgrass is often the first plant to colonize an empty stretch of beach or dune. Once its seeds take root, the grass spreads rapidly through its rhizomes, and as the grass spreads, it begins to build dunes or sandspits by accumulating windblown sand particles.

As the leaves trap the sand grains, a small mound forms around each grass cluster. One of this grass's most essential adaptations is the ability to grow upward quickly, which keeps it from being overwhelmed by the growing pile of sand around it. Many other beach plants have similar vertical growth adaptations for the same reasons. As American Beachgrass moves into a beach or sandbar, the grass builds its environment by accumulating and stabilizing the sand with its roots and rhizomes. The grass does not just grow on sandspits and dunes—American Beachgrass creates the dunes of the upper beach.

American Beachgrass (*Ammophila breviligulata*) is the most important shoreline plant north of Chesapeake Bay in stabilizing coastal dunes, sandspits, and barrier islands.

Other common beach plants

Saltwater Cordgrass is one of the few land kinds of grass that can tolerate having its roots soaked in salt water, and on protected beaches, without much wave action, you'll often see small stands of Saltwater Cordgrass running right down the beach to at least the low tide line and sometimes a little beyond.

In late summer and fall, Seabeach Orach lines upper beaches, gradually turning red as the weather cools. Seabeach Orach seeds are highly salt-tolerant, and they overwinter in the wrack line to start a new generation the following spring.

Rough Cocklebur (*Xanthium strumarium*) seeds are a common sight on Mid-Atlantic beaches in summer and fall.

Dusty Miller, Rough Cocklebur, Searocket, Common Saltwort, and Seaside Spurge are all species adapted to living on beaches and dune faces. They have tough, leathery leaves that are sometimes also waxy or hairy, all strategies to prevent moisture loss. Seaside Spurge grows in a flat disc just above the level of the sand to conserve water by staying out of the wind. If you look closely at Seaside Spurge plants in late summer or fall, they seem to grow on top of little mounds. As with American Beachgrass, the spurge creates the hill by trapping sand between its leaves and stems and thus must continuously grow upward or be buried under the sand captured by its leaves.

Seaside Goldenrod is one of the most common beach specialists and seems to dominate the upper beaches in the late summer and fall with its showy yellow sprays of flowers. This hardy perennial goldenrod has tough, waxy evergreen leaves over a deep set of roots that

AMERICAN BEACHGRASS *Ammophila breviligulata*

South of Chesapeake Bay

SEAOATS *Uniola paniculata*

ROUGH COCKLEBUR *Xanthium strumarium*

SEASIDE GOLDENROD *Solidago sempervire*

COMMON SALTWORT *Salsola kali*

COMMON SALTWORT, detail

ASIDE SPURGE *Chamaesyce polygonifolia*

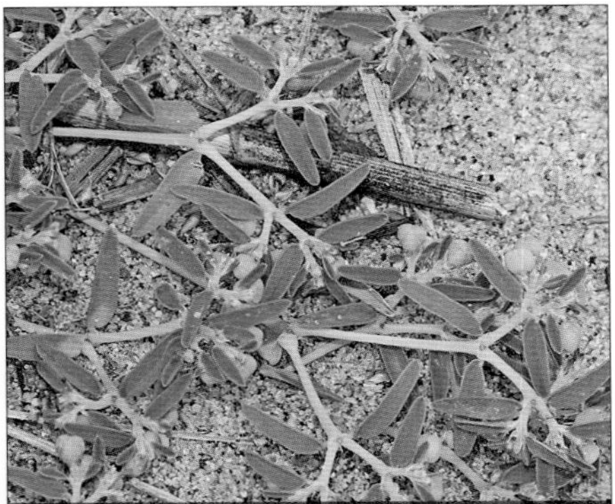

SEASIDE SPURGE, detail

D GOOSEFOOT *Chenopodium rubrum*

South of Chesapeake Bay

DUNE PENNYWORT *Hydrocotyle bonariensis*

AROCKET *Cakile edentula*

SEAROCKET, detail

SANDBUR *Cenchrus longispinus*

SWITCHGRASS *Panicum virgatum*

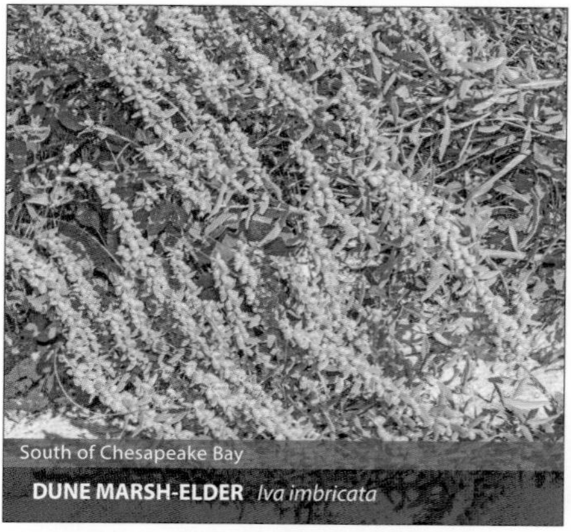

South of Chesapeake Bay

DUNE MARSH-ELDER *Iva imbricata*

DUSTY MILLER *Artemisia stelleriana*

FIREWHEEL (Indian Blanket) *Gaillardia pulchella*

SEABEACH ORACH *Atriplex pentandra*

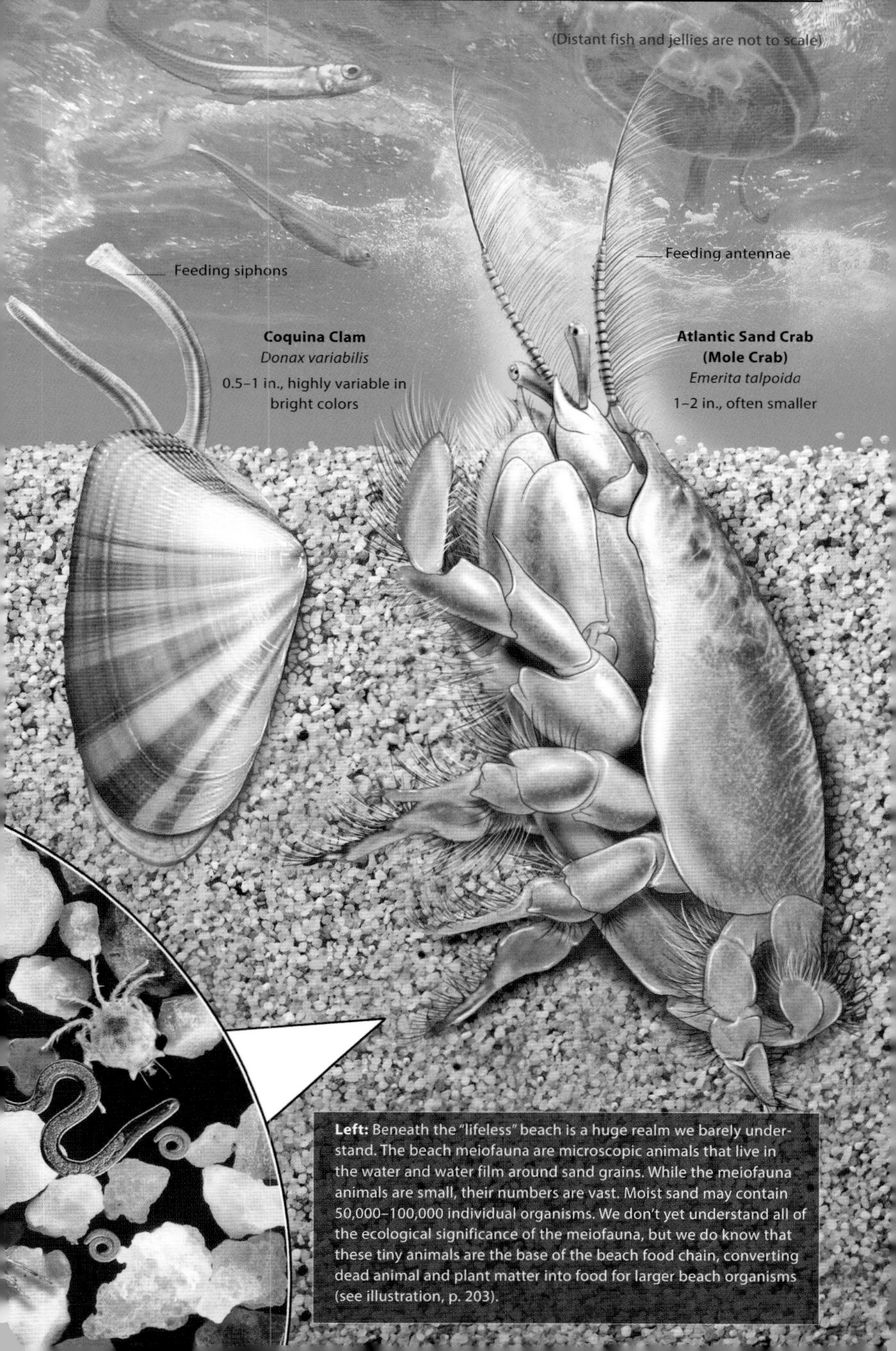
(Distant fish and jellies are not to scale)
Feeding siphons
Feeding antennae
Coquina Clam
Donax variabilis
0.5–1 in., highly variable in bright colors
Atlantic Sand Crab (Mole Crab)
Emerita talpoida
1–2 in., often smaller

Left: Beneath the "lifeless" beach is a huge realm we barely understand. The beach meiofauna are microscopic animals that live in the water and water film around sand grains. While the meiofauna animals are small, their numbers are vast. Moist sand may contain 50,000–100,000 individual organisms. We don't yet understand all of the ecological significance of the meiofauna, but we do know that these tiny animals are the base of the beach food chain, converting dead animal and plant matter into food for larger beach organisms (see illustration, p. 203).

On an early spring morning, tens of thousands of Double-Crested Cormorants (Phalacrocorax auritus) crowd the beach at Cape Hatteras National Seashore. Although beaches and the shallow waters around them may sometimes appear barren, they support an incredible abundance of wildlif

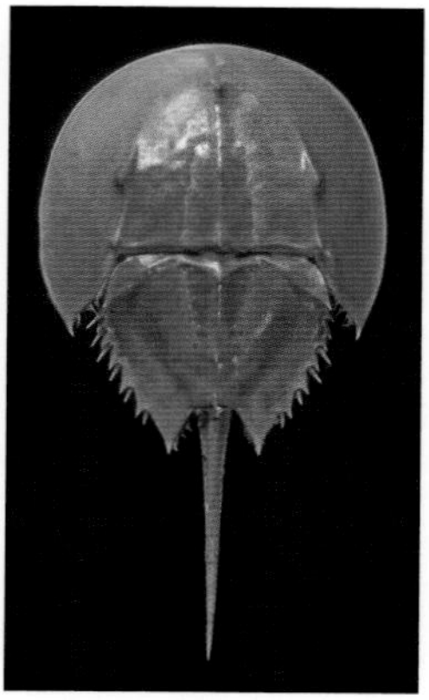

Atlantic Horseshoe Crab
Limulus polyphemus

they often appear in great numbers, but many beaches in their range don't have either species, especially if the beach has been nourished with new sand in the past few years.

Horseshoe Crabs

The Atlantic Horseshoe Crab is a large but utterly harmless creature often spotted on beaches, unfortunately not always alive, because these crabs have been overharvested as fishing bait. Their long, tapered tails are not weapons and are used only to help the crabs turn over when they are knocked upside down by waves. Only recently, as their numbers have dwindled, have Horseshoe Crabs attracted conservation support and research interest. In May and June, often during a spring (unusually high) tide, Horseshoe Crabs travel up into the low tidal zone to lay their eggs. These eggs are very attractive to shorebirds, and often the best indication that the crabs are breeding is the sight of flocks of shorebirds and gulls avidly picking at the eggs in the surf line.

Horseshoe Crab eggs (*Limulus polyphemus,* top) in spring, and juvenile Horseshoe Crabs in late summer.

USFWS

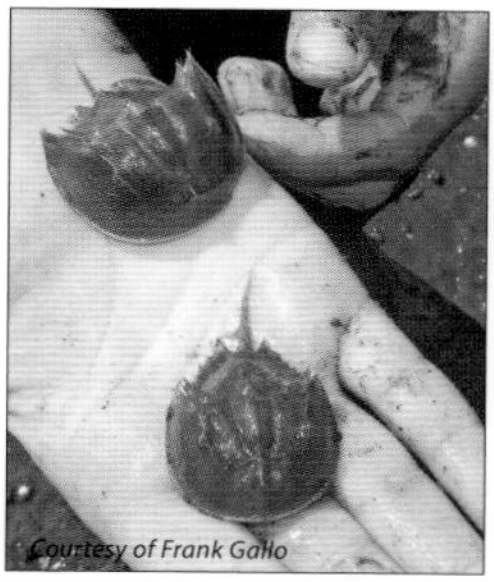

Courtesy of Frank Gallo

Northern Moon Snails and Atlantic Oyster Drills are predators on bivalves in the intertidal region of beaches. Both species drill neat, round holes in shells, usually near the umbo, or hinge point, of a clam or oyster. Once the snail finds a suitable live clam, it uses its sharp, toothy radula to scrape a hole in the clam's shell as it secretes a strong acid to help dissolve the shell. When the radula breaks through to the interior of the clamshell, the snail injects powerful enzymes that digest the clam's interior organs and muscle. The snail then sucks up the dissolved clam through the hole in the shell.

Clam or oyster shells that you find on beaches are often riddled with holes from snails but may also be eaten away into a honeycomb of tunnels through the action of Boring Sponges. The Boring Sponge doesn't prey on clams and oysters directly, but the slow dissolving of its shell is usually fatal to an oyster if the sponge attacks an occupied shell.

Atlantic Ghost Crabs

Ghost Crabs are some of the most common and entertaining beach inhabitants, and once you know what to look for, you'll see their burrow holes and tracks everywhere on the dry beach. Ghost Crabs are often active during the day when beachgoers can easily see them, but the crabs are most energetic at night. Ghost Crabs are entirely harmless, and they have excellent eyesight. Once you get closer than about 15 feet from their burrows, the crabs will dive into their holes and won't return to the surface for many minutes. If you want to see Ghost Crabs in their element, visit the beach at night with a flashlight. Walk down to the waterline, and you'll typically see dozens of crabs hunting for prey and carefully walking up to the swash lines to wet their gills.

Atlantic Ghost Crab (*Ocypode quadrata*) tracks, top, and a Ghost Crab burrow hole and surrounding diggings on the dry beach, well above the high-tide line.

Sea turtle nesting

Four sea turtle species are found in the near-shore waters of the Mid-Atlantic Coast (see illustration, p. 213), but only the Loggerhead Sea Turtle nests in the region, and most of its nests are on the Outer Banks south of Oregon Inlet. Smaller numbers of Loggerheads nest north of the Outer Banks. In 2017 park rangers at Assateague Island National Seashore in Maryland observed over 100 Loggerhead nestlings hatch and move into the sea. As both the climate and the ocean warm, we might expect the Loggerhead's nesting range to extend north, but unfortunately, in the Mid-Atlantic Coast region, few stretches of beach are undisturbed enough to attract nesting Loggerhead Turtles.

An adult Ghost Crab.

arinahabich

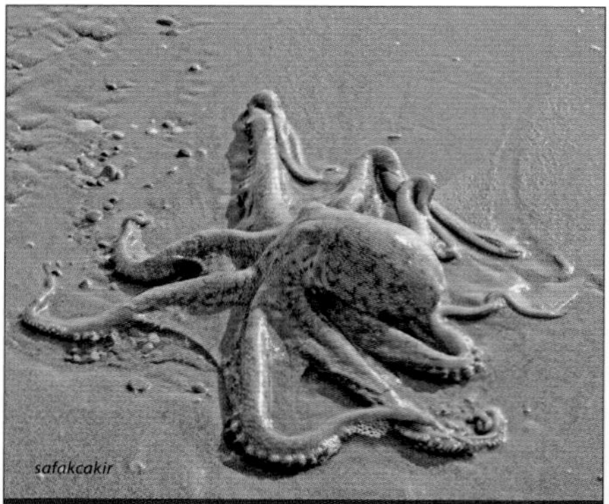
safakcakir
COMMON OCTOPUS *Octopus vulgaris*

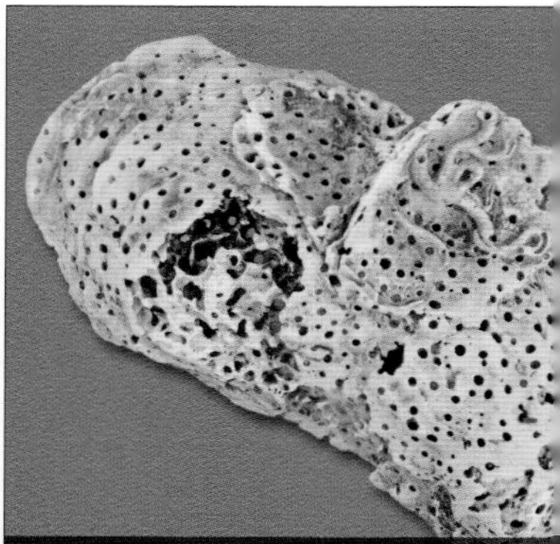
BORING SPONGE damage *Cliona* sp.

Egg mass
Matthew R McClure
NORTHERN MOON SNAIL *Euspira heros*

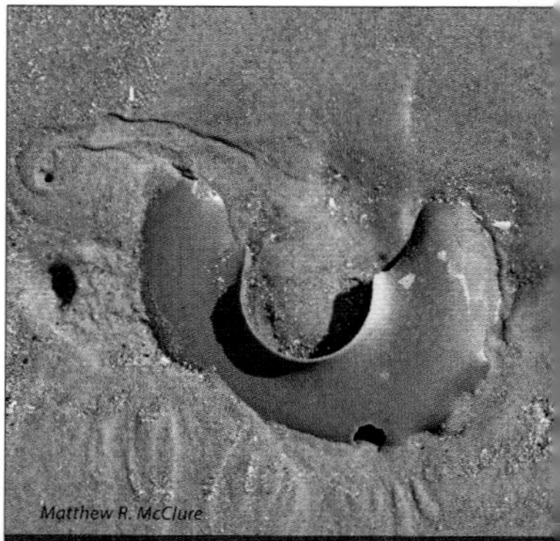
Matthew R. McClure
MOON SNAIL egg mass or "sand collar"

Vagabondivan
HERMIT CRAB *Pangurus* sp.

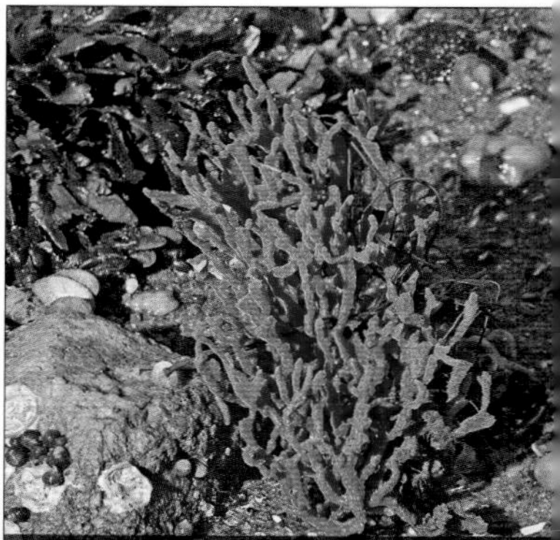
RED BEARD SPONGE *Microciona prolifera*

hereswendy

...ANTIC SLIPPER SHELLS *Crepidula fornicata*

SAND DOLLAR *Echinarachnius parma*

...EEN FLEECE *Codium fragile*

SEA LETTUCE *Ulva lactuca*

...CKWEED *Fucus distichus*

KNOTTED WRACK *Ascophyllum nodosum*

HARBOR SEAL
Phoca vitulina
Harbor Seal pup
GRAY SEAL
Halichoerus grypus
The pelage colors and patterns of young Gray Seals vary from almost pure white to yellow or gray.

GRAY SEAL
Mark Bridger

HARBOR SEAL
Wim Claes

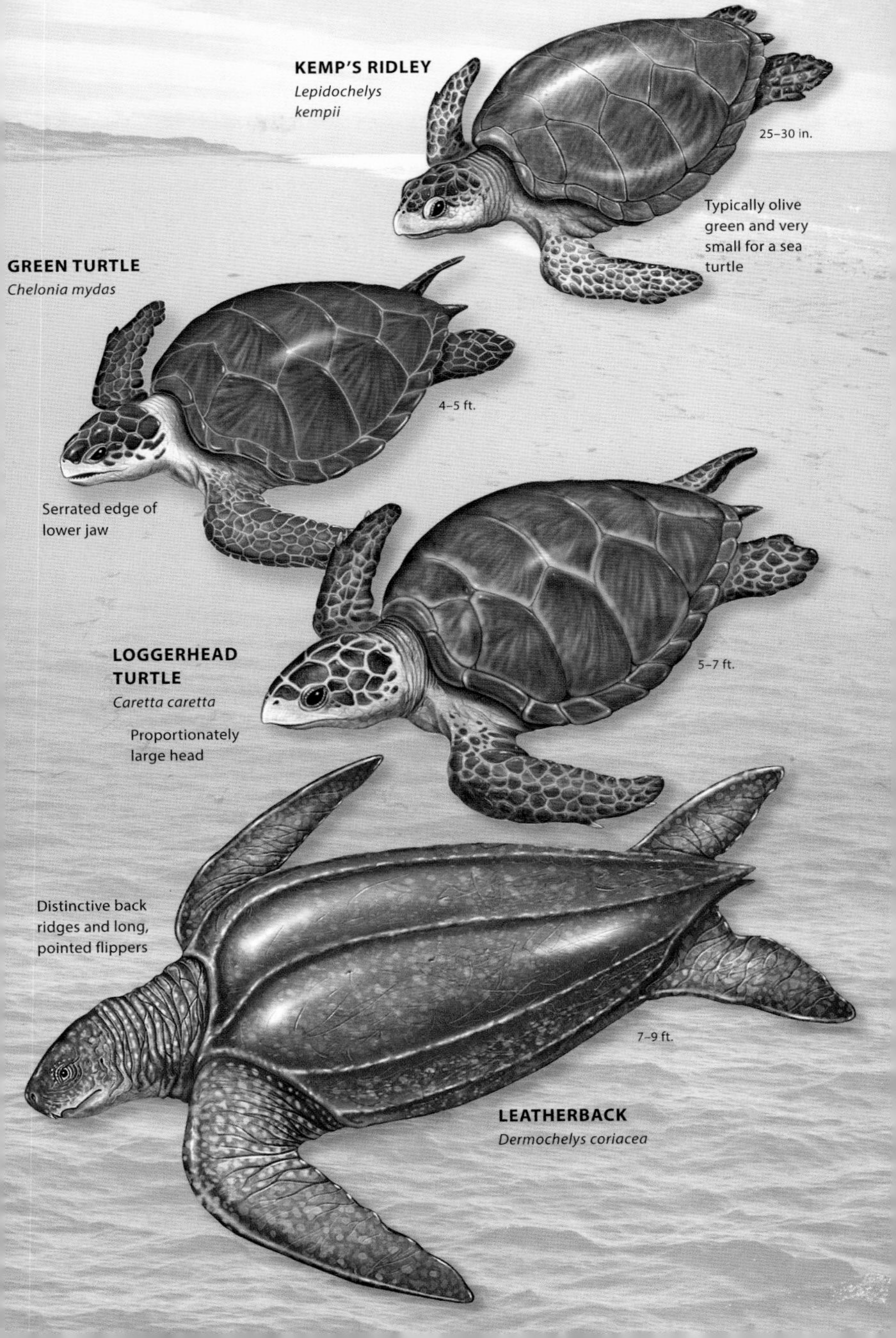
KEMP'S RIDLEY
Lepidochelys kempii
25–30 in.
Typically olive green and very small for a sea turtle
GREEN TURTLE
Chelonia mydas
4–5 ft.
Serrated edge of lower jaw
LOGGERHEAD TURTLE
Caretta caretta
5–7 ft.
Proportionately large head
Distinctive back ridges and long, pointed flippers
7–9 ft.
LEATHERBACK
Dermochelys coriacea

Thomas Barrat

Loggerhead Turtle hatchling (*Caretta caretta*) on the beach at Pea Island National Wildlife Refuge on the Outer Banks of North Carolina.
Top: The tracks and nest site digging of a Loggerhead Turtle on the Outer Banks.

Loggerhead Turtles mate in offshore Atlantic waters, and females begin to come ashore on nights in early May; nesting may last into early September. Loggerheads typically dig their nests above the average high-tide line, just inland from the main wrack line of the beach. Just after nesting, you'll see the distinctive tread marks of the adult turtle on the beach, leading from the swash zone up the beach to a roughly circular nest area where the eggs are covered with sand (see illustration, above). Hatchlings emerge from the nest at about 45 days, but late nests in cooler weather may incubate longer. Healthy adult females may lay as many as five nests over the summer. At hatching time, the sand around the nest erupts with miniature Loggerheads, which immediately race for the ocean to avoid being eaten by predators like gulls, herons, raccoons, and foxes. You may encounter hatchlings on the beach any time from late June into early November.

Bottlenose Dolphins

One of the best and most common pleasures of Mid-Atlantic beaches is watching small schools of Bottlenose Dolphins parade past the beach. Dolphins travel inshore following schools of small prey fish like Atlantic Herring and Sand Lance, which move into shallows near the beach at night. Although dolphins may appear off the beach at any time of day, the best time to see groups of Bottlenose Dolphins near shore is in the early morning.

Common Bottlenose Dolphins (*Tursiops truncatus*) cruise at dawn off Pea Island National Wildlife Refuge, on the Outer Banks of North Carolina.

Seals

You should never expect to see a Harbor Seal or Gray Seal along the Mid-Atlantic Coast, but both species are becoming more frequent as seal populations in New England expand. Every winter more and more seal sightings occur, possibly because forage fish populations have been expanding along the Atlantic Coast.

Biting animals at the beach

The insects that bother you at the beach are the same biting flies and mosquitos that bite you in other environments. The tiny sand "fleas" (*Orchestia agilis* and others) you see in the beach wrack do indeed jump like fleas when disturbed, but they cannot bite humans. Other common wrack line beetles and spiders are also harmless, and the tiny seaweed flies around wrack lines (*Fusellia* sp.) do not bite and are a valuable food source for migrating birds. Unscrupulous exterminators and beach cleaners often try to persuade homeowners to use pesticides to combat so-called beach fleas, but the insecticides they spray are lethal to ***all*** small animals in the wrack line.

The worst offenders among biting beach flies are also the smallest. No-See-Ums and Stable Flies may be tiny and easy to overlook, but both can leave you with painful, itchy welts that can last a week. Greenhead Flies, Deer Flies, and Horse Flies are common in all coastal

For Ruddy Turnstones (*Arenaria interpres*) and other shorebirds that feed on the beach, the small invertebrates in the wrack line—often called beach fleas— are an extremely important part of their diets. Beach fleas are completely harmless to people.

FLIES AND MOSQUITOS THAT BITE AT THE BEACH *Flies shown 3x life size for clarity*

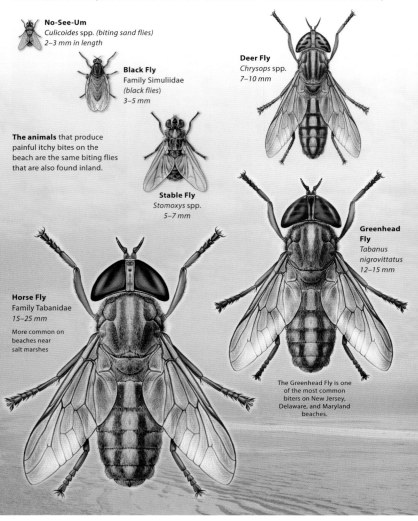

No-See-Um
Culicoides spp. *(biting sand flies)*
2–3 mm in length

Black Fly
Family Simuliidae
(black flies)
3–5 mm

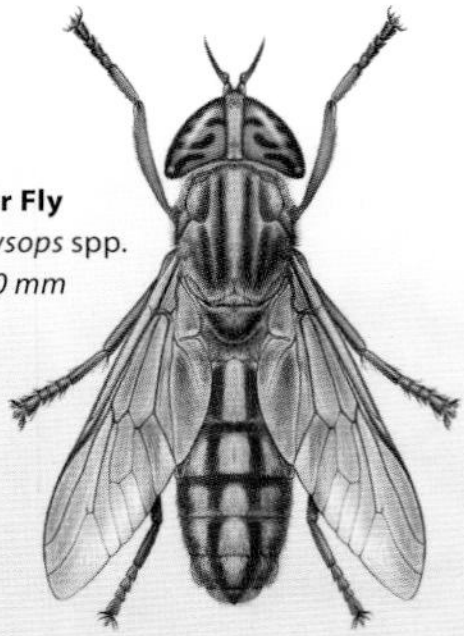

Deer Fly
Chrysops spp.
7–10 mm

The animals that produce painful itchy bites on the beach are the same biting flies that are also found inland.

Stable Fly
Stomoxys spp.
5–7 mm

Greenhead Fly
Tabanus nigrovittatus
12–15 mm

The Greenhead Fly is one of the most common biters on New Jersey, Delaware, and Maryland beaches.

Horse Fly
Family Tabanidae
15–25 mm

More common on beaches near salt marshes

COMMON MOSQUITOS *Shown 4x life size for clarity*

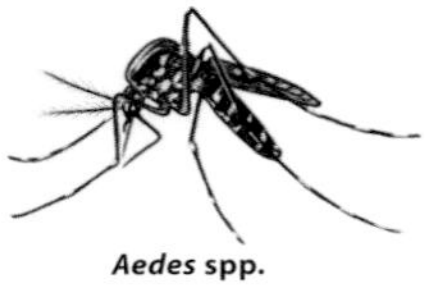

***Aedes* spp.**

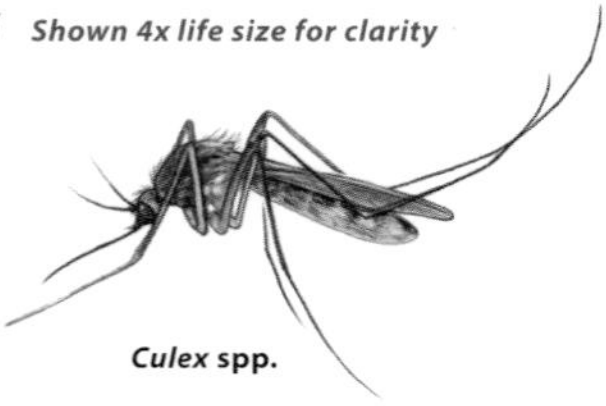

***Culex* spp.**

***Anopheles* spp.**

environments but are especially prevalent in and near salt marshes in summer.

Try to avoid the beach in the twilight hours of dawn and dusk, and always keep insect repellent handy for days when mosquitos are abundant. Covering up with clothing or a towel is more effective for biting flies, which tend to ignore most repellents. If your beach is near a salt marsh, try to avoid days when an offshore wind blows flies and mosquitos from the marsh toward the beach. Wearing light-colored clothing also seems to help with Greenhead, Deer, and Horse Flies: these species are instinctively drawn to dark moving objects.

Beach or sand flea, 5x life size

Some beach fleas can jump, but none of the tiny invertebrates found in the wrack line or wet lower beach can bite or sting.

These little animals are totally harmless to humans but extremely important to shorebirds, Ghost Crabs, and other wildlife that feed on the beach.

Beach flea: Paul A. Carpenter

THE INVERTEBRATES OF THE WET WRACK LINE DO NOT BITE OR STING

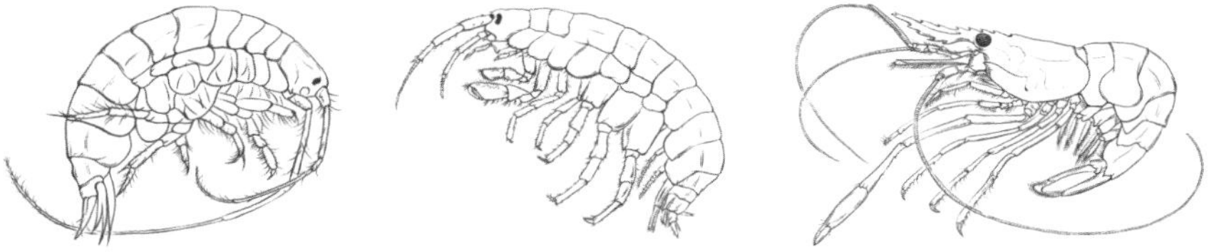

Laughing Gull
Summer (breeding) plumage
Leucophaeus atricilla

Laughing Gull
Winter (nonbreeding) plumage
Leucophaeus atricilla

BEACH BIRDS

The dominant birds of Mid-Atlantic beaches are gulls, particularly the Herring Gull, Ring-Billed Gull, Laughing Gull, and Great Black-Backed Gull, joined in the winter months by the more unusual white-winged Iceland and Glaucous Gulls. Gulls are intelligent and watchful predators of all small beach animals (including nestling birds of many species), taking their prey from the immediate shoreline or the shallows near the beach. Their usual prey includes clams, crabs, snails, small fish, and any other animals they can capture or scavenge. Gulls generally do not dive for their prey, which limits their feeding to the shallowest water and the beach and tidal flat areas exposed at low tide and to surface feeding farther offshore.

The gull population of the Mid-Atlantic Coast region expanded rapidly in the mid-twentieth century with the rise of suburban towns using open-air dumps and large-scale commercial fishing offshore. However, in the past two decades, gull populations have shrunk substantially as open-air dumping has become much less common, factory fishing has been pushed offshore beyond the 200-mile limit, and coastal development has reduced suitable nesting areas. Gulls nest on barrier islands along the coast or on the rare isolated sandspits that still exist.

In summer, terns may be seen on most Mid-Atlantic beaches, particularly when the adults and newly fledged young wander the shorelines and coastal waters in late summer in flocks before they migrate south. Terns look like small, delicate gulls with long, swallowlike tails (see illustrations, pp. 226–27). They hunt small fish such as Atlantic Silverside, smaller Blueback and Atlantic Herring, and Sand Lance by diving onto schools of fish near the surface. Historically terns nested both on offshore islands and along mainland beaches and barrier islands. As the beaches and barriers were developed and became summer playgrounds, terns (except for Least Terns) were driven off most mainland nesting sites, and now the only large nesting colonies of terns are on the few Mid-Atlantic barrier islands that have not been developed.

Herring Gull
Summer (breeding) plumage
Larus argentatus

Aside from gulls and terns, Willets, Sanderlings, Ruddy Turnstones, and the Brown Pelican are the most visible birds of the Mid-Atlantic Coast (see illustrations, pp. 228–29). Willets and Sanderlings specialize in picking off small invertebrates in the swash zone of beaches. Willets have a sandy brown plumage that blends into the beach, but when Willets take off, they show bold white wing stripes in flight. Sanderlings are the small toylike shorebirds that run back and forth at the edges of the wave swash. Both Willets and Sanderlings specialize in feeding on the Atlantic Sand Crab (Mole Crab) and other tiny invertebrates the waves toss into the swash. Ruddy Turnstones are plump-looking shorebirds that show bold color patterns, both standing and in flight. Turnstones specialize in feeding farther up the beach in the wrack line, where—as their name suggests—they constantly winnow through wrack line items, overturning vegetation and shells hoping to pick off a hapless baby crab, beetle, or other invertebrate.

Brown Pelicans are the royalty of Mid-Atlantic beaches. No shoreline predator is bolder or more capable. Pelicans can cruise for hours up and down the beach with hardly a wingbeat, looking for schools of fish to plunder just behind the breakers. A feeding flock of pelicans is spectacular, with dozens of birds

Brown Pelicans
Pelecanus occidentalis

Kenneth Keifer

GREAT CORMORANT
Phalacrocorax carbo
First-year
immature
Dark throat,
light belly
First-year
immature
Light throat,
dark belly
DOUBLE-CRESTED
CORMORANT
Phalacrocorax auritus
Adult
Imm.
Double-crested
in flight
Imm.
Adult
Uphill angle
of flight
Great Cormorant
in flight
DOUBLE-CRESTED
CORMORANT
GREAT
CORMORANT
Double-Crested
and Great adults in
breeding plumage

NORTHERN GANNET
Morus bassanus

Outer wings are black to the wrist, unlike the more limited black wingtips of gulls
Second- or third-year immature
First-year juvenile
Adult plumage (at least five years old)
The heavy bill, shielded nostrils, and thick head plumage are adaptations to diving from great heights into the sea
Adult

LARGER BIRDS OF MID-ATLANTIC BEACHES

Gulls dominate most Mid-Atlantic Coast beaches, both in sheer numbers and in their aggressive habits in locating food. Gulls take several years to mature to the classic gray-and-white seagull appearance, and younger gulls will show varying degrees of brown plumage (see the next page spread).

Two other large birds are prominent on beaches. Brown Pelicans and Double-Crested Cormorants are distantly related, and both species are expert swimmers and divers. Cormorants generally dive from the ocean surface to hunt smaller schooling fish such as herring and juvenile Atlantic Menhaden. Pelicans make spectacular dives from the air, folding their wings to plunge deep beneath the surface to snatch up smaller schooling fish. Often you'll see both pelicans and cormorants working the same inshore schools of fish.

DOUBLE-CRESTED CORMORANT
RING-BILLED GULL
LAUGHING GULL

BROWN
PELICAN
GREAT
BLACK-BACKED
GULL
HERRING
GULL
© Pat Lynch 2020

COMMON GULLS

Gulls are one of the most accessible forms of coastal wildlife, with both interesting behaviors to watch and challenges to sort out the various ages and seasonal plumages. For detailed information on gulls, see recommendations for bird field guides in Further Reading.

Relatively small bill at all ages
First winter
Adult winter
Bill ring
RING-BILLED GULL

HERRING GULL

Second winter
Adult breeding
First winter
Pink legs at all ages

GREAT BLACK-BACKED GULL

Third winter
Heavy bill at all ages
First winter
Adult breeding
Pale pink legs at all ages

HERRING GULL
RING-BILLED GULL
WS 65 in.
WS 58 in.
WS 48 in.
GREAT BLACK-BACKED GULL
WS 33 in.
BONAPARTE'S GULL
WS 40 in.
LAUGHING GULL
BONAPARTE'S GULL
First winter
Delicate bill
Adult winter
Cheek spot
First winter
Dark bill
Adult winter
Adult breeding
Dark red bill
Legs dark gray
Deep pink or red legs
LAUGHING GULL
Legs dark red in breeding plumage
Adult breeding

COMMON TERN SPECIES OF MID-ATLANTIC BEACHES

Terns are smaller, more delicate-looking relatives of gulls and are often seen on Mid-Atlantic Coast beaches in multispecies flocks ranging from just a few birds to several hundred birds in migration seasons. And yes, to the casual observer, they do all look alike. But with a little effort it's fairly easy to sort out the more frequently seen tern species.

The quickest method to sort out the various terns is to look first at their overall size and then at their beak colors. The Caspian Tern is the size of a gull, with a bright orange beak. Royal Terns are about half the bulk of Caspians, with an red-orange beak. The Least Tern is easy to identify: it is tiny and the only tern with a bright yellow beak.

Least Terns have received a lot of attention because they are endangered on the Atlantic Coast, due to their habit of nesting on the same sand beaches that people favor. ***PLEASE observe any signs that surround Least Tern nesting colonies. Their nests and sand-colored eggs are almost invisible to all but trained observers.***

FORSTER'S TERN
More orange in bill
Lighter mantle than Common Tern
COMMON TERN
Bill orange-red at base
Darker mantle
Bright yellow bill
LEAST TERN

CASPIAN
TERN
A very large tern,
the size of a gull
SANDWICH
TERN
Yellow tip of bill
GULL-BILLED
TERN
ROYAL
TERN

Brian Kushner

AMERICAN OYSTERCATCHER *Haematopus palliatus*

Nonbreeding plumage (no black belly)

BLACK-BELLIED PLOVER *Pluvialis squatarol*

SEMIPALMATED PLOVER *Charadrius semipalmatus*

KILLDEER *Charadrius vociferus*

Brian Lasenby

Nonbreeding plumage

SANDERLING *Calidris alba*

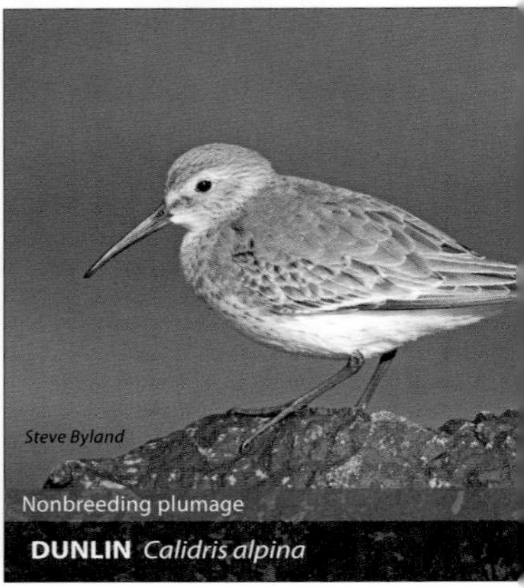

Steve Byland

Nonbreeding plumage

DUNLIN *Calidris alpina*

MIPALMATED SANDPIPER *Calidris pusilla*

GREATER YELLOWLEGS *Tringa melanoleuca*

ESSER YELLOWLEGS *Tringa flavipes*

WILLET *Tringa semipalmata*

OUBLE-CRESTED CORMORANT *Phalacrocorax auritus*

BROWN PELICAN *Pelecanus occidentalis*

wheeling and dive-bombing smaller school fish such as Atlantic Herring. Dawn is the optimal time of day to watch pelicans feed because large schools of fish enter shallow coastal waters at night but then move offshore during the day to avoid both fish and bird predators.

Our endangered beach-nesting birds

Two beach-nesting birds are among North America's most endangered species due to the almost total loss of their former nesting grounds. The Least Tern and the Piping Plover both nest in lightly vegetated upper beach and dune areas—precisely the types of areas that are mostly buried now beneath coastal houses or have been converted to recreational beaches.

In the past decade, both species have received more attention and protection of their nesting grounds in places such as New Jersey's Sandy Hook, Island Beach State Park, and Cape May. In the Delmarva area, there are substantial beach bird nesting colonies at Cape Henlopen and Assateague Island National Seashore. On the Outer Banks, there are Least Tern, Piping Plover, and Black Skimmer colonies, particularly around and south of Oregon Inlet.

If you visit beaches with reserved nesting areas, ***please obey the posted signs and stay away from the fenced-***

Piping Plovers
Charadrius melodus

Ray Hennessy

Ray Hennessy

off areas, and never let a dog on the beach (with or without a leash) during the late spring and summer months when birds are nesting. This small accommodation to these beach-nesting birds has made a real difference in their nesting success rates.

A pair of Least Tern parents feed a Sand Lance (*Ammodytes americanus*) to their chick. Least Tern nests are minimal scrapes in the upper beach and are very easy to miss. *Please stay out of marked nesting areas on the beach.*

Piping Plover nests are really just shallow cups of sand on the dry beach, and their eggs are a speckled sandy color that make the eggs almost invisible against the sand. The nests are very difficult to spot, even for experienced wildlife biologists who work with plovers. ***PLEASE stay out of marked nesting areas***. One careless step could wipe out the yearly nesting cycle for a pair of plovers.

Seaoats on a foredune on the Outer Banks of North Carolina. Without the stabilizing effects of beach grasses and shrubs, dune fields could not persist over time.

Dunes

Dunes in the northern Mid-Atlantic Coast are dominated by American Beachgrass. This foredune on the beach at Assateague Island National Seashore contains Beachgrass, Seaside Goldenrod, and a few very stunted Northern Bayberry bushes. The vegetation is typical of foredunes from New York Harbor south to the Chesapeake Bay, where Seaoats joins the mix.

Dunes occur naturally along sandy beaches. The upper beach above the wrack line receives significant salt aerosols (salt spray), and this constant salt coating kills all but a sparse sprinkling of grasses and other plants high up on the beach. Just up the beach, the salt spray lessens, plants grow more densely, and the stems and leaves of American Beachgrass, Rough Cocklebur, Searocket, and other beach plants begin to trap wind-blown sand. As the sand piles up around the plants, they respond by growing upward, and soon a foredune forms at the top of the beach. Foredunes don't attract plants: the plants themselves create the foredune and give the dune stability through their roots and rhizomes under the surface. On the upper beach, look for sand shadows next to beach plants (see illustration, p. 234). As the windblown sand meets a plant on the upper beach, the wind slows, dropping grains of sand on the leeward side of the plant. Soon a stretched oval shadow of piled sand forms next to the plant. In this way, plants build the dune environment by collecting sand around them and growing upward to stay atop the pile.

Formation of dunes

Beaches and dunes are made of sand, and along the Mid-Atlantic Coast, both environments are tightly linked. Shoreline dunes originate from material eroded from the Appalachian Mountains thousands

Plants accumulate sand to form dunes
Sand shadow
Dominant wind direction blowing inland from the beach

This foredune at Island Beach State Park in New Jersey shows how even sparse plantings of American Beachgrass can help accumulate sand. Notice that each grass clump has a small sand shadow just downwind of the plant. Even larger amounts of sand are trapped and held by the Seaside Goldenrods at the top of the dune.

of years ago. The sand minerals are cut from the land by weather and water and mixed, sorted, and ground down by powerful ocean waves. Then waves throw the most durable small mineral grains back on the shore as beach sand grains. Onshore winds constantly move sand up the beach, where the grains are caught by the stems and leaves of plants. Here they form the primary dunes that give rise to both sandspits and larger dune communities. No matter how large, dune environments were all born on beaches. Water and wind sculpt beaches, but dunes are the province of the wind.

Wind and sand

On the upper beach, just above the splash of waves, sand grains begin to move under the influence of winds. At low tide, the sand dries, and when winds reach a speed of about 12–15 miles per hour, they can move average-sized sand grains long distances across the dry beach.

Several processes transport sand grains inland from the beach. Strong winds pick up surface grains and carry them in short leaps across the sand surface in an action called saltation (from the Latin for "jumping"). Any windy day will move significant quantities of sand, but most beachgoers never see the strong, steady winter winds and blustery storms that move the majority of sand over a year.

American Beachgrass
in flower
Ammophila breviligulata

Even in a relatively moist climate like the Mid-Atlantic Coast, dunes are a dry environment because of how rapidly surface water empties away in the sand. What rain the dunes receive drains quickly in the porous sand toward a groundwater table that might be six to 10 feet or more below the sand surface. Salt spray can damage plants that lack tough leaves, but the constant mist of salt spray also brings minerals to an environment where most nutrients are washed down into the fast-draining sand. Nitrogen especially is in limited supply in dune areas, contributing to poor soil productivity.

Seaside Goldenrod
at peak of bloom in September
Solidago sempervirens

On more mature and stable dune fields farther back from the shoreline, larger plants such as Northern Bayberry bushes, Black Cherries, and Eastern Redcedar junipers provide shade and act as windbreaks. On the Jersey Shore and Delaware and Maryland coasts, you may see small areas of the classic dune ground cover communities of mixed Bearberry, Broom Crowberry, Bear Oak, Gray Reindeer Lichen, and Beach Heather.

The brilliant white appearance of dune sand is no accident: dune sand is lighter, finer-grained, and whiter than typical beach sand on the Mid-Atlantic Coast. As the wind blows sand grains inland, it sorts out mineral particles, and smaller grains of extraordinarily durable but relatively lightweight quartz and feldspar move inland the farthest.

What makes a dune community?

So how do you tell a dune environment from the usual range of plants that inhabit the upper beach? In large dune areas such as on the Outer Banks or at Delaware's Cape Henlopen, the answer is obvious, with sand hills as far as the eye can see. But most dune areas are considerably smaller, and the difference between the upper beach and dune communities can be subtle.

Secondary lines of dunes are farther from direct salt aerosols and can support a wider variety of plant life.

First, there's the physical distance from the ocean waves and the influence of salt spray. Upper beach communities share many of the same hardy plants as true dune environments. Still, beaches are defined by the short distance to water and waves, where plants must be able to survive and thrive with a constant mist of saltwater on their leaves, as well as an occasional salty drenching of their roots by perigean high tides (king tides). A true Mid-Atlantic dune community is defined by the presence of plants that can survive the heat, dryness, and sandblasting of living on sand but have protection from most salt aerosols by distance and a line of primary dunes.

Dunes act as a barrier between the ocean and inland areas, shielding inland areas from the salt aerosols that are so lethal to most plants. With distance from saltwater and the protection of the dune line, a complex and distinctive community of lichens, fungi, grasses, shrubs, wildflowers, and trees can develop and thrive. Watch the ground as you walk (preferably on an established footpath) from the beach and over the first high mounds of sand atop the beach, where bare sand covers the ground between plants.

In the northern areas of the Mid-Atlantic Coast, you know you are in a mature dune community through the presence of two key ground covers: Gray Reindeer Lichen and Beach Heather. The typical upper beach herbs and grasses, Northern Bayberry bushes, Beach Plums, and other upper beach plants also thrive on dunes, but only when you see a mixed carpet of Gray Reindeer Lichen, other lichens, small patches of moss, and Beach Heather in the open areas have you arrived in a mature dune environment.

There are patches of mature northern dune environments on the Jersey Shore at Island Beach State Park and in the southern and western areas of Cape May. Cape Henlopen State Park in Delaware has magnificent mature dune areas. Cape Henlopen's extensive Pitch Pine forests mixed with dune vegetation bring to mind the Provincelands of Cape Cod, as well as the dunes and seaside Pine Barrens of eastern Long Island. All are closely related coastal ecosystems that line the New York Bight region. The dunes at Assateague Island National Seashore in Maryland are constrained by the relatively narrow width of the island, but the southern stretch of the park has one of the few purely natural Atlantic Coast dune communities, unmodified by beach nourishment and bulldozers.

Cape Henlopen State Park in Lewes, Delaware, has many areas where the maritime Pine Barrens forest grades into dune areas.

These are the key plants without which coastal sand dunes such as these at Coquina Beach in Nags Head, North Carolina, could not persist. At the dune tops are Seaoats (*Uniola paniculata*) and Coastal Panic Grass (*Panicum amarum*). The middle band is dominated by Seacoast Marsh Elder (*Iva imbricata*) and more Panic Grass. The foreground is a mixture of Yaupon Holly (*Ilex vomitoria*), Virginia Creeper (*Parthenocissus quinquefolia*), and American Beachgrass (*Ammophila breviligulata*).

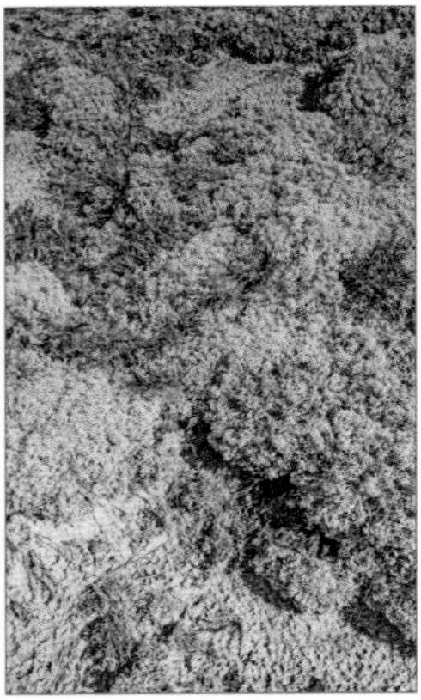

In a combination unique to the Jersey Shore, Long Island, and New England, Gray Reindeer Lichen (*Cladonia rangiferina*) mixes with Broom Crowberry (*Corema conradii*) in Pine Barrens and maritime forests. Island Beach State Park in New Jersey (above and below) is the southern end of the range of Broom Crowberry, but Gray Reindeer Lichen persists in dune pine forests farther south.

In the Outer Banks north of Cape Hatteras, mature dune communities occur in the Cape Hatteras National Seashore, around Coquina Beach, and in the extensive dune areas just north and south of Oregon Inlet.

Southern dune communities are dominated by Seaoats, American Beachgrass, Atlantic Coastal Panic Grass, Seacoast Marsh Elder, and, in sheltered areas, Yaupon Holly and Wax Myrtle. However, on the Outer Banks, you should remember that there are few, if any, natural primary dune lines. All the dune lines from Corolla south to Cape Hatteras have been artificially shaped to be much steeper and higher than natural dunes to protect houses and roadways from storm surges and sand overwashes. Even so, most Outer Banks dunes are covered with the same wild plant species that cover naturally shaped dunes.

Dune plant communities

Dune plants must have robust, flexible leaves, able to withstand the mechanical strain of whipping in the wind, along with impervious waxy or hairy leaves that limit moisture loss. Many dune plants, such as American Beachgrass, also have leaves that curl in high heat, minimizing evaporation.

This primary dune from the Outer Banks of North Carolina shows the classic southern dune pattern in two ways: Seaoats is the dominant grass, and because of Seaoats the dune forms a distinct clump with gaps on either side rather than a solid dune line.

In wild environments the gaps in the Seaoats dune lines allow storms to overwash new sand onto barrier islands, helping to build and preserve the islands. On developed beaches, however, these gaps are considered a vulnerability, and Seaoats is generally mixed with planted American Beachgrass to form a solid dune line.

Many perennial dune flowering plants and grasses spread aggressively through underground stems called rhizomes. Rhizomes both increase the area a plant can cover and allow the plant to respond quickly to burial by drifting sand through rapid upward growth from the rhizomes.

Like most beach plants, many dune plants are annuals. Annual plants invest all of their reproductive energy in seed production, and they are most common in constantly changing or disturbed environments where their seeds can rapidly germinate to take advantage of favorable conditions. With no permanent stems or roots to protect during the harsh winter months, annual plants spread their seeds widely, placing their evolutionary bets on next year's seedlings. Given that such annuals as Seaside Spurge, Common Saltwort, and Searocket are so prevalent on beaches and dunes, the strategy has been successful.

Foredune communities

Foredunes are simply a higher continuation of the upper dry beach and are usually the first place that significant amounts of plants appear. Most foredune plants are the same ones you'll find scattered on the upper beach—American Beachgrass, Seaside Spurge,

Rugosa Rose (*Rosa rugosa*) is often the first shrub to appear in foredune plant communities, where its toughness and resistance to salt spray helps stabilize foredunes throughout the Northeast.

Common Saltwort, Seabeach Orach, Searocket, and Seaside Goldenrod—but here they are more numerous. Other dune community plants begin to appear on the foredune, including Dusty Miller, Beach Pea, and the grasslike Umbrella Sedge. The introduced Rugosa Rose is the hardiest and most salt resistant of the dune shrubs and is common on foredunes and sandy areas throughout the Mid-Atlantic shoreline. Many common inland plants and wildflowers are also rugged enough to live on foredunes, well back from the beach: Yarrow, Evening Primrose, Switchgrass, Virginia Creeper, and Poison Ivy.

Less exposure to salt spray is the main thing that distinguishes true dune environments from the saltier foredune communities. All the foredune plants mentioned above are also present on dunes, but the primary thing you'll notice about true dune environments is the presence of shrubs and stunted trees. Rugosa Rose, Shining (Winged) Sumac, Northern Bayberry, Beach Plum, and Black Cherry are all common dune shrubs. Black Cherry is also a common forest-edge tree that can grow quite tall, but on dunes, the salt aerosols and lack of water keep the Black Cherries small and shrublike. Quaking Aspen appears on dunes that are well away from salt spray, and if present, the aspens are

A classic foredune community, dominated by Seaside Goldenrod (*Solidago sempervirens*) and American Beachgrass (*Ammophila breviligulata*).

often the tallest trees in the dunes. Aspens are more common where dune fields transition to bordering maritime forests, and Black Locust trees will tolerate the arid conditions of beaches. In scattered locations, you'll find shrub-sized American Holly in the dunes.

The Mid-Atlantic's only cactus species also appears in dunes. Eastern Prickly Pear is intolerant of salt spray or saltwater on its roots and is usually found well back from the beach in areas sheltered from salt spray by shrubs or on rocky headlands near the coast. Along with the ubiquitous American Beachgrass, you'll see additional grasses and sedges here, including Switchgrass, Cheatgrass, Nutsedge, and Umbrella Sedge.

In protected dune areas well back from the beach, ground cover plants such as Bearberry, Broom Crowberry, and Beach Heather may form small heathlike carpets, especially when sheltered from wind and salt aerosols by such small trees and shrubs as Northern Bayberry, Black Cherry, Bear Oak, and Beach Plum. These dune heath areas are also home to a few distinctive lichens: Gray Reindeer Lichen and British Soldiers Lichen thrive on sandy soils. Also sometimes seen on bare patches of sand, especially after a rainstorm, is the Hygroscopic Earthstar. Two conifers dominate: Eastern

A grouping of the dominant northern dune shrubs: Eastern Redcedar (*Juniperus virginiana*), Beach Plum (*Prunus maritima*), and the nearly ubiquitous Northern Bayberry (*Myrica pensylvanica*). In wetter areas near beaches and near salt marshes, Marsh Elder (*Iva frutescens*) often joins the mix.

AMERICAN BEACHGRASS *Ammophila breviligulata*

SEASIDE SPURGE *Chamaesyce polygonifolia*

COMMON SALTWORT *Salsola kali*

SEABEACH ORACH *Atriplex pentandra*

SEAROCKET *Cakile edentula*

SEASIDE GOLDENROD *Solidago semperviren*

USTY MILLER *Artemisia stelleriana*

BEACH PEA *Lathyrus japonicus*

NDBUR *Cenchrus longispinus*

RUGOSA ROSE *Rosa rugosa (an invasive species)*

f Chesapeake Bay

ACH HEATHER *Hudsonia tomentosa*

North of Chesapeake Bay

BEACH HEATHER, detail

SWITCHGRASS *Panicum virgatum*

VIRGINIA CREEPER *Parthenocissus quinquefolia*

POISON IVY *Toxicodendron radicans*

CATBRIER *Smilax glauca*

EASTERN PRICKLY PEAR *Opuntia humifusa*

MUSCADINE *Vitis rotundifolia*

ʀAY REINDEER LICHEN *Cladonia rangiferina*

BRITISH SOLDIERS LICHEN *Cladonia cristatella*

ʃSHY BEARD LICHEN *Usnea strigosa*

HYGROSCOPIC EARTHSTAR *Astraeus hygrometricus*

of Chesapeake Bay

ARBERRY *Arctostaphylos uva-ursi*

North of Delaware Bay

BROOM CROWBERRY *Corema conradii*

SWEET FERN *Comptonia peregrina*

MARSH ELDER *Iva frutescens*

UMBRELLA SEDGE *Cyperus strigosus*

RED GOOSEFOOT *Chenopodium rubrum*

BEACH PLUM *Prunus maritima*

BEAR OAK *Quercus ilicifolia*

ACK CHERRY *Prunus serotina*

NORTHERN BAYBERRY *Myrica pensylvanica*

th of Delaware Bay

TCH PINE *Pinus rigida*

South of Delaware Bay

LOBLOLLY PINE *Pinus taeda*

th of Chesapeake Bay

VE OAK *Quercus virginiana*

SASSAFRAS *Sassafras albidum*

SEAOATS *Uniola paniculata*

COASTAL PANIC GRASS *Panicum amarum*

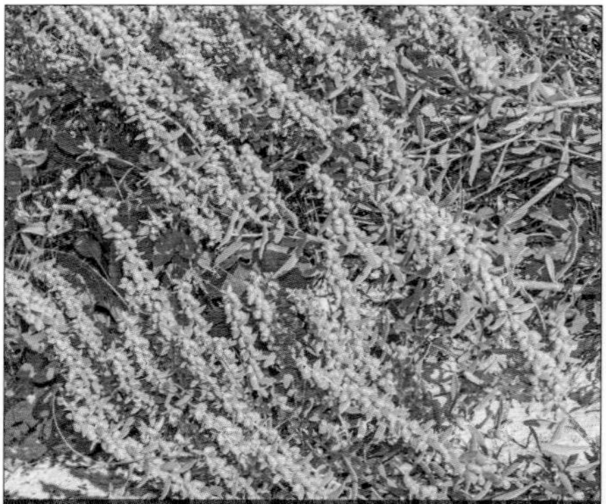

SEACOAST MARSH ELDER *Iva imbricata*

DUNE PENNYWORT *Hydrocotyle bonariensis*

GULF CROTON *Croton punctatus*

SALTMEADOW CORDGRASS *Spartina patens*

X MYRTLE *Morella cerifera*

YAUPON HOLLY *Ilex vomitoria*

NE CAMPHORWEED *Heterotheca subaxillaris*

SAND LIVE OAK *Quercus geminata*

SHY BLUESTEM *Andropogon glomeratus*

ADAM'S NEEDLE *Yucca filamentosa*

Common Dune Shrubs

Marsh Elder
Iva frutescens

Groundsel Tree
Baccharis halimifolia

Northern Bayberry
Myrica pensylvanica

Beach Plum
Prunus maritima

Black Cherry
Prunus serotina

Redcedars are the most common evergreen in many upper beach and salt marsh environments because of their tolerance of salt spray, but farther from the beach Pitch Pines become the predominant conifer. At the inland edges of dune areas, where sandy glacial soil replaces pure sand, Eastern White Pines (*Pinus strobus*) will mix with Pitch Pines. As the Mid-Atlantic's tallest trees, White Pines often shade and outcompete Pitch Pines, but their shallower root systems make White Pines more vulnerable to storm winds, and the hardier Pitch Pine often wins out in the competition with its loftier relative.

Dune swales

Dune swales are low areas in dunes that have more shelter from the wind and moister soils. Most dune swales are seasonal and hold standing water or wet soils only in colder months. In summer, the swales can sometimes be recognized by thin patches of Mud Rush (*Juncus pelocarpus*) and Canada Rush (*J. canadensis*) growing in low areas between dunes. Few other plants can survive a wetland that becomes a blazing-hot desert for three to four months of the year.

More reliably moist swale areas may contain a variety of the usual dune shrubs and small trees, as well as such salt marsh plants as Glasswort, Sea Lavender, Spike Grass, and Saltmeadow Cordgrass (see the chapter on salt marshes). Besides the dune shrubs pictured at left, you may see such common salt marsh border shrubs and grasses as Marsh Elder, Groundsel Tree, and Switchgrass.

In many areas of the Mid-Atlantic Coast, small dune fields are often next to salt marshes on the landward side of sandspits, so salt marsh and dune environments often intermix. You can see this mixing of marsh and dune environments on the landward coasts of Island Beach State Park and southernmost Cape May in New Jersey, at Assateague Island National Seashore in Maryland, and on the sound-side coasts of the Outer Banks of North Carolina.

Animals on the dunes

Most beach animals and birds also frequent dunes, particularly if they nest on beaches. Our two most

Inland
Ocean side
Primary dune line
Secondary dune line
Dune swale

A dune swale area just behind the primary dune. A swale is a small valley between lines of dunes. Here plants are sheltered from the most direct salt aerosols and may grow lushly in swales that collect rainwater or meet the local water line to form small temporary ponds.

endangered beach nesters, the Piping Plover and the Least Tern, both sometimes use adjacent dune areas as nesting sites, particularly if the vegetation remains low and grassy and is not too thick. Other birds that nest in the transition areas from beaches to dunes include the Black Skimmer, American Oystercatcher, and Willet. Many songbirds also nest in dune areas, particularly the Northern Mockingbird, Common Grackle, American Robin, Song Sparrow, and in marshy swales the Red-Winged Blackbird.

In the shadows of dune plants, small animals prowl, including large wolf spiders, Seaside Grasshoppers, field crickets, and (unfortunately) several species of ticks that mostly parasitize wild mammals, including White-Footed Deer Mice, Meadow Voles, Raccoons, and Red Foxes. Always wear long pants if you explore away from trails in sandspits and grassy or brushy dune areas, and apply a DEET-based insect repellent on your clothes, socks, and shoes. Dune and beach vegetation often harbors the primary carrier of Lyme disease, the Black-Legged Tick (often called the deer

Lone Star Tick
Amblyomma americanum

Black-Legged Tick
(Deer Tick)
Ixodes scapularis

tick). The much more common Lone Star Tick can also carry diseases, so always check your clothing and any exposed skin when you exit wild shoreline environments.

The beaches and dunes of the Mid-Atlantic Coast are some of the best places to observe migrating insects in the fall months. On a bright September or October day with a brisk northwest wind sweeping them down to the coastline, hundreds of migrating Green Darner and Black Saddlebags dragonflies move along the shores, often using the dune vegetation for rest and shelter.

Also migrating along the coast at this time are millions of Monarchs. Unfortunately, Monarchs have experienced a significant decline in numbers in recent decades due to several causes, including habitat destruction and pesticide use. All North American Monarch butterfly populations overwinter in just a few valleys in northern Mexico. Those Mexican valleys are now reasonably well protected as conservation areas, and researchers are looking into the increased use of glyphosate herbicides by farmers since 2003 as a possible cause of reduced Monarch numbers. Loss of their chief food source is a third culprit: Monarch caterpillars feed on milkweeds, and the significant reduction in milkweeds (particularly in midwestern farming areas) is suspected to be behind the 59 percent drop in overwintering Monarch populations documented

FALL COASTAL MIGRATORY INSECTS

Black Saddlebags
Tramea lacerata

Green Darner
Anax junius

Monarch
Danaus plexippus

Above: Lone Star Tick: Melinda Fawver; Black-Legged Tick, Sarah2

MMON BUCKEYE *Junonia coenia*

CLOUDED SULPHUR *Colias philodice*

SIDE DRAGONLET *Erythrodiplax berenice*

FOWLER'S TOAD *Anaxyrus fowleri*

ACK SWALLOWTAIL *Papilio polyxenes*

Lisa Hagan
VIRGINIA OPOSSUM *Didelphis virginiana*

Steve Byland

PIPING PLOVER *Charadrius melodus*

LEAST TERN *Sternula antillarum*

BLACK SKIMMER *Rynchops niger*

WILLET *Tringa semipalmata*

SONG SPARROW *Melospiza melodia*

NORTHERN MOCKINGBIRD *Mimus polyglotto*

LOW-RUMPED WARBLER *Setophaga coronata*

Rachelle Vance

AMERICAN ROBIN *Turdus migratorius*

RTHERN CARDINAL *Cardinalis cardinalis*

Steve Byland

AMERICAN GOLDFINCH *Carduelis tristis*

FOX *Vulpes vulpes*

MEADOW VOLE *Microtus pennsylvanicus*

Every fall millions of Monarch butterflies (*Danaus plexippus*) migrate along the US East Coast on their way to their wintering grounds in the mountains of central Mexico. In recent years, a combination of droughts, widespread insecticide use, farm herbicides that suppress Common Milkweed, and habitat loss in Mexico have combined to reduce the North American Monarch population. There is good news, though: in 2019 Monarch migration was up substantially, perhaps due to conservation efforts and the greater awareness of the importance of pollinating insects.

in Mexico in 2012. Public awareness of the Monarchs' plight has led to milkweed planting campaigns and other conservation efforts, and Monarch migration numbers were up significantly in 2019.

As in other environments, most animal activity in the dunes is at night, where the Raccoon, Virginia Opossum, Striped Skunk, Meadow Vole, and Marsh Rabbit are all common. Two less common dune specialists are Fowler's Toad and the Eastern Hognose Snake. Fowler's Toad is the only amphibian typically found on beaches and dunes, where it buries itself in the sand under shrubs to escape the heat of the day. Hognose snakes are nonpoisonous and harmless but will sometimes perform an elaborate rearing and hissing display if surprised. Hognose snakes are very reluctant to bite humans even if handled (but please don't handle them) and are more likely to roll over and play dead if you approach them. The ubiquitous Atlantic Ghost Crab inhabits dune lines and dune swales all along the Mid-Atlantic Coast, although Ghost Crab populations can be spotty. When present, the crabs are numerous, but for unknown reasons—and probably temporarily—some stretches of the coast have few or no Ghost Crabs. Most of the Ghost Crabs that live in dune environments are big adults that make large, noticeable burrows in dune sand. Only the adult crabs are robust enough to make the necessary daily journey from the dunes down to the surf line to wet their gills.

Dunes in winter

In winter, dunes can be productive and interesting areas for birding. Many northern species fly south to winter along the Atlantic Coast, and for species used

The Northern Mockingbird (*Mimus polyglottos*) occurs everywhere along the Mid-Atlantic Coast, but the birds seem especially conspicuous and charming in the open environment of dunes. If you hear a Herring Gull, a Common Crow, a Goldfinch, and a Robin all calling from the same Bayberry bush, it's a Mockingbird.

to the wide expanses of Arctic tundra, beaches must seem like familiar territory. Snow Buntings, Lapland Longspurs, and Horned Larks are all small songbirds that nest in the high Arctic and winter on open fields, beaches, dunes, and marshes near coastlines.

Almost every winter, a few spectacular Snowy Owls visit the marshes and beaches of the northern Mid-Atlantic Coast, but usually not in large numbers. In the winter of 2013–14, and again in the winter of 2014–15, many dozens of Snowy Owls were spotted throughout the Mid-Atlantic Coast area. This was probably due to cyclical increases in the population of their lemming prey in the Arctic. In the breeding season of 2013 and again in 2014, so many young Snowy Owls survived to fledge that many juveniles and young adult birds ventured far south of their usual wintering grounds in search of reduced competition from their peers and adult owls for food. Snowy Owls gravitate to open coastal beach and marsh areas that are similar to their

Snow
Bunting
Lapland
Longspur

The classic winter birds of beaches, dunes, heaths, and open grassy areas throughout the Mid-Atlantic Coast. When winter sets in, look for mixed flocks of Lapland Longspurs (*Calcarius lapponicus*), Snow Buntings (*Plectrophenax nivalis*), and Horned Larks (*Eremophila alpestris*).

typical tundra habitat. Snowys are solitary creatures in winter, and they can be difficult to spot against clumps of snow and ice. On winter beaches, dunes, and salt marshes, these large white owls will often take an exposed perch on a driftwood snag, post, or rock, looking for small mammals to capture and eat. Unlike their nocturnal cousin the Great Horned Owl, Snowy Owls are mostly daytime hunters that locate their prey by sight.

Horned
Lark
Pat Lynch ©2013

Pat Lynch ©2012

Snowy Owl
Bubo scandiacus

Snowy Owls are iconic birds of the Arctic, but in recent years the northeastern United States and even the Mid-Atlantic Coast have seen Snowy Owl irruptions—large movements of primarily young birds into areas well south of their usual range. On the Mid-Atlantic Coast the owls have been seen regularly as far south as the Outer Banks, although never in great numbers. Ornithologists who study the owls have learned that for the past decade lemming populations in the Arctic have been large, and with the abundant prey many more nestling Snowy Owls have survived. These owls are territorial, and the young birds are driven south in winter by competition with their peers, as well as with adult Snowy Owls.

Please never closely approach a Snowy Owl. Wintering birds are typically right on the edge of malnutrition. Forcing a bird off its perch is stressful, wastes the bird's energy, and is viewed as harassment by birders and wildlife authorities. No picture is worth driving a young bird to starvation.

A magnificent Loblolly Pine (Pinus taeda) in the maritime Pine Barrens forest at Cape Henlopen State Park in Lewes, Delaware.

Maritime Forests

Sunset over the Life of the Forest trail and boardwalk at Assateague Island National Seashore, Maryland.

A maritime forest is a plant community dominated by trees that are under the influence of salt aerosols (salt spray, see illustration, p. 134-35). Maritime forests are typically found in the interior or inland side of coastal barriers, in areas that are more protected from strong salt aerosols blowing in from ocean beaches. Salt aerosols can limit an otherwise mature forest to heights of 15–25 feet and cause salt pruning, or distorted growth patterns, in individual trees and other plants. Maritime forests are rare or much reduced on narrow barrier islands and peninsulas that are heavily exposed to salt aerosols. The gnarled, windswept character of coastal trees may be picturesque, but it also demonstrates the struggle all plants have in maintaining growth in a stressful environment.

The presence of mature maritime forest indicates long-term stability in the configuration of barrier islands and peninsulas. Forests occur in areas that are geologically stable and not subject to constant storm damage or sand overwashes.

Fortunately, we do have several well-developed maritime forests along the Mid-Atlantic Coast. This north-south string of outstanding coastal forests shows a gradual transition from the northeastern Pine Barrens forests dominated by Pitch Pines and oaks to a more southern type of forest south of Delaware Bay and dominated by Loblolly Pines.

Loblolly Pines
Pinus taeda

On the Jersey Shore, there are small areas of maritime forests at Island Beach State Park and on the extreme southern tip of Cape May, as well as smaller patches of Pine Barrens forests along the mainland shore. In Delaware, there are extensive coastal forests at Cape Henlopen State Park on Delaware Bay. Here Loblolly Pines replace Pitch Pines as the dominant coastal tree species. There are small to medium-sized Loblolly Pine woodlands at Assateague Island National Seashore in Maryland and at Chincoteague National Wildlife Refuge in Virginia. On the Outer Banks of North Carolina, there are several large tracts of species-rich and globally unique maritime woodlands at Nags Head Woods Preserve and at Buxton Woods near Cape Hatteras.

Northern Mid-Atlantic maritime forests

The maritime forests of the Jersey Shore barrier islands and peninsulas are dominated by a combination of Pitch Pine, Red Maple, and coastal oak species including Bear, Northern Red, White, and Black Oak. Most of these large forest trees are dwarfed or salt-pruned through exposure to salt aerosols, except in areas well away from the beach. Loblolly Pines mix in around the Cape May and Delaware Bay shoreline. Classic coastal forest understory trees include Black Cherry, Sassafras, American Holly, Canadian Serviceberry (Shadbush), Eastern Redcedar, Quaking Aspen, Black Tupelo (also called Black Gum, and found in moist areas), and Flowering Dogwood.

Near the edges of the forest, especially near water or salt marshes, Northern Bayberry, Marsh Elder, Common Juniper, and Groundsel Tree often mix with thickets of Fox Grape, Catbrier, sumacs, and other bramble species. In some areas, the ground cover may include Highbush and Lowbush Blueberries. Muscadine is a southern grapevine species that is gradually moving north as the climate warms and is now found along most of the Jersey Shore. On the Delmarva Peninsula, Northern Bayberry begins to mix with its southern cousin Wax Myrtle (Southern Bayberry). The two bayberry/myrtles look much alike, but one big difference is that Northern Bayberry is deciduous and loses its leaves in winter.

A grove of Loblolly Pines at Assateague Island National Seashore, Maryland. The maritime forests at Assateague are intermediate between the northern-type forest and southern-type forests. Here Loblolly Pines dominate, along with Red Maple (*Acer rubrum*), Sweetgum (*Liquidambar styraciflua*), and Sassafras (*Sassafras albidum*), but there are no Live Oaks (*Quercus virginiana*), which begin to appear in maritime forests south of Chesapeake Bay.

Southern Mid-Atlantic maritime forests

The coastal forests of the Delmarva Peninsula and its barrier islands form an ecological transition area between the northern coastal Pine Barrens forests typical of Cape Cod, Long Island, and the Jersey Shore, and the southern collection of species that dominate coastal forests from Virginia south to Georgia. The most noticeable change from Delaware Bay south is the complete dominance of Loblolly Pines, which replace Pitch Pines from Cape Henlopen down to southern Florida. South of the Chesapeake Bay, Live Oaks join the mix in coastal forests. The combination of Loblolly Pine, Live Oak, Southern Red Oak, and Southern Magnolia form the classic overstory pattern in the maritime forests of southern Virginia, North and South Carolina, and Georgia.

The understory trees of the southern Mid-Atlantic Coast include Redbay, American Holly, Sassafras, and Flowering Dogwood. In the shrub layer, Wax Myrtle becomes much more common than Northern Bayberry, and Wax Myrtle completely replaces Bayberry from the Outer Banks and south. Yaupon

Nags Head Woods Preserve is an extensive maritime forest on the Outer Banks of North Carolina. The forest covers a series of rolling dune ridges interspersed with moist valley areas. Unlike most maritime forests, the trees are full-sized here, and many of the larger oaks, Red Maples, American Hollies, and Sweetgums may be 100–200 years old.

Opposite: Although Assateague Island contains many small but healthy Loblolly Pine–dominated maritime forests, climate change has damaged or destroyed the most vulnerable woods. This former woodland near the beach has been heavily damaged by two recent problems: more severe coastal storms and the northward spread of the Southern Pine Beetle (*Dendroctonus frontalis*), which attacked and killed these trees. The Pine Beetles have moved north along the coast as the climate has warmed.

Holly, American Beautyberry, and Muscadine are all classic southern shrub and bramble species that enter the mix of forest-edge species in southern Maryland and northern Virginia and become increasingly common on the Outer Banks and south. The dangling tree epiphyte Spanish Moss becomes noticeable on trees in southeastern Virginia and the Outer Banks. At the margins of southern maritime forests, especially where the forest meets the salt marsh, thickets of Marsh Elder, Groundsel Tree, and Wax Myrtle grow. Bramble vines of American Beautyberry, Catbrier, Poison Ivy, and Virginia Creeper form an almost impenetrable wall of green at the base of the trees.

Buxton Woods is an extensive maritime forest at Cape Hatteras and contains the northernmost US population of palms. In the relatively mild temperatures of a forest 30 miles at sea from the mainland, Saw Palmettos grow in the understory. On the mainland coast, the closest Saw Palmettos are found in southern South Carolina.

BEACH PLUM *Prunus maritima*

BLACK CHERRY *Prunus serotina*

QUAKING ASPEN *Populus tremuloides*

STAGHORN SUMAC *Rhus typhina*

SHINING (WINGED) SUMAC *Rhus copallina*

BEAR OAK *Quercus ilicifolia*

SSAFRAS *Sassafras albidum*

BLACK OAK *Quercus velutina*

RTHERN RED OAK *Quercus rubra*

WHITE OAK *Quercus alba*

IERICAN HOLLY *Ilex opaca*

RED MAPLE *Acer rubrum*

CANADIAN SERVICEBERRY *Amelanchier canadensis*

COMMON APPLE *Malus pumila*

UMBRELLA SEDGE *Cyperus strigosus*

AMERICAN LINDEN (BASSWOOD) *Tilia amer*

ARROWWOOD VIBURNUM *Viburnum dentatum*

BLACK TUPELO (BLACK GUM) *Nyssa sylvatica*

OWERING DOGWOOD *Cornus florida*

INKBERRY *Ilex glabra*

APLELEAF VIBURNUM *Viburnum acerifolium*

SWAMP AZALEA *Rhododendron viscosum*

MMON MILKWEED *Asclepias syriaca*

WAVY HAIRGRASS *Deschampsia flexuosa*

POISON IVY *Toxicodendron radicans*

VIRGINIA CREEPER *Parthenocissus quinquefolia*

BEAR OAK *Quercus ilicifolia*

CATBRIER *Smilax glauca*

FOX GRAPE *Vitis labrusca*

JEWELWEED *Impatiens capensis*

WBERRY *Rubus* sp.

WINEBERRY *Rubus phoenicolasius*

IATIC BITTERSWEET *Celastrus orbiculatus*

BLACK SWALLOW-WORT *Cynanchum louiseae*

PANESE HONEYSUCKLE *Lonicera japonica*

AILANTHUS (TREE OF HEAVEN) *Ailanthus altissima*

JAPANESE KNOTWEED *Polygonum cuspidatum*

COMMON REED *Phragmites australis*

AUTUMN OLIVE *Elaeagnus umbellata*

MULTIFLORA ROSE *Rosa multiflora*

FIELD BINDWEED *Convolvulus arvensis*

BLACK LOCUST *Robinia pseudoacacia*

ARSH ELDER *Iva frutescens*

GROUNDSEL TREE *Baccharis halimifolia*

VITCHGRASS *Panicum virgatum*

NORTHERN BAYBERRY *Myrica pensylvanica*

GHBUSH BLUEBERRY *Vaccinium corymbosum*

EASTERN REDCEDAR *Juniperus virginiana*

YARROW *Achillea millefolium*

ORCHARDGRASS *Dactylis glomerata*

ORCHARDGRASS, flowers

FOXTAIL GRASS *Alopecurus* sp.

WILD GERANIUM *Geranium maculatum*

PINK AZALEA *Rhododendron periclymenoides*

OLDENROD *Solidago* sp.

RUGOSA ROSE *Rosa rugosa*

ASTURE ROSE *Rosa carolina*

SWAMP ROSE MALLOW *Hibiscus moscheutos*

HITE WOOD ASTER *Eurybia divaricata*

LATE PURPLE ASTER *Symphyotrichum patens*

LIVE OAK *Quercus virginiana*

LOBLOLLY PINE *Pinus taeda*

SWEETGUM *Liquidambar styraciflua*

REDBAY *Persea borbonia*

WAX MYRTLE *Morella cerifera*

In Buxton Woods, Cape Hatteras, and south to Florida
SAW PALMETTO *Serenoa repens*

Maritime forests and climate change

Today coastal forests face several challenges. Like all shoreline environments, maritime forests are under pressure from coastal development of new homes and businesses. Once a section of woodland has been cut down and replaced by buildings and streets, the habitat is lost forever. Even in places where some areas of forest are left undisturbed, the mix of plant and animal species changes in the small remnant patches, and almost invariably, the former diversity of the mature forest is lost.

Climate change and the associated rise in sea levels has quickly become a significant problem in preserving all forms of coastal habitat. As sea levels rise, saltwater infiltration of coastal habitats is killing maritime forest trees that have adapted to salt aerosols in the air but cannot tolerate salty groundwater. Another more insidious problem affects many coastal forests: salt water is denser than freshwater. As the salt water infiltrates the ground under a forest, it raises the fresh groundwater level and drowns tree roots that cannot survive being permanently soaked. As sections of the forest gradually die from salt infiltration, formerly healthy groups of trees become ghost forests of dead trees standing in rapidly eroding salt marshes. Once you know about the problem, you'll notice ghost forests or isolated clumps of dead trees everywhere at the edges of salt marshes all along the Mid-Atlantic Coast.

The warming climate is also changing the distribution ranges of significant insect pests like the Southern Pine Beetle, which is responsible for killing large numbers of Loblolly and other pine species. The Pine Beetle's range is gradually expanding northward, and large tracts of Loblolly Pines as far north as Maryland and Delaware are now at risk. For example, the combination of stress from salt aerosols and physical damage from a series of recent hurricanes has proved fatal for many Loblolly Pines at Assateague Island National Seashore in Maryland (see illustration, p. 269).

Erich G. Vallery

Southern Pine Beetle
Dendroctonus frontalis

meisterphotos

Pine Beetle damage to a Loblolly Pine. The beetles kill trees by digging under the bark and feeding on the vital phloem tissue that carries nutrients throughout the tree. When the phloem has been heavily damaged, the tree dies. Pine Beetles do their damage under the bark where you can't see them, but infested pines usually show a polka-dot pattern of white pitch bleeding out of the tree bark.

Animals of the maritime forests

Although restricted in area, maritime forests can be incredibly rich in wildlife of all kinds. Coastal forests

HALF-BLACK BUMBLEBEE *Bombus vagans*

HONEY BEE *Apis* sp.

PAPER WASP (VESPID) Subfamily Polistinae

HOVER FLY (FLOWER FLY) Family Syrphidae

PEARL CRESCENT *Phyciodes tharos*

GREAT SPANGLED FRITILLARY *Speyeria cybele*

ELAWARE SKIPPER *Anatrytone logan*

SILVER-SPOTTED SKIPPER *Epargyreus clarus*

NOWBERRY CLEARWING MOTH *Hemaris diffinis*

CHINESE MANTIS *Tenodera sinensis*

ARGE MILKWEED BUG *Oncopeltus fasciatus*

RED MILKWEED BEETLE *Tetraopes tetrophthalmus*

Halloween Pennant
Celithemis eponina

Ruby Meadowhawk
Sympetrum rubicundulum

Black-Crowned Night-Heron
Nycticorax nycticorax

offer shelter and a diversity of microhabitats for both year-round residents and migratory birds and insects.

Butterflies, dragonflies, and other insects

Insects are not always the top priority when people visit coastal fields and forests, but if you can look past the biting and stinging bugs—and wear your bug spray and long pants—insects are one of the most visible, accessible, and beautiful forms of wildlife to observe. Large insects are most active during the middle of the day. On a summer afternoon, most forest birds will be roosting out of sight, but open fields, dune grasslands, and the edges of forests, ponds, and marshes will be humming with insect life.

More than 40 species of dragonflies and damselflies are found in and around forests, fields, and ponds of the Mid-Atlantic Coast, as are several dozen common butterfly species, so there is a wide variety of large, colorful, and easy-to-identify insects to seek out. Insect populations have been of particular concern to wildlife biologists in recent years, as many studies have shown a dramatic drop in insect populations worldwide—up to 90 percent in some areas. In particular, important pollinator species such as bees, flower flies that imitate bees, and popular butterfly species such as the Monarch have all seen substantial declines in their populations, due mostly to the widespread use of neonicotinoid pesticides and herbicides such as glycophosphates that kill native plants like milkweed, as well as habitat loss. About 35 percent of our major food crops, including potatoes, onions, apples, cranberries, broccoli, cauliflower, squashes, zucchini, and coffee, are all entirely dependent on bees. If you are not allergic to bee stings, don't be afraid to approach honey bees, bumblebees, and carpenter bees. They rarely sting unless you try to handle them or swat them. Dragonflies are completely harmless—unless you are a mosquito.

Birds

Many of the birds and mammals that feed in coastal dunes and marshes shelter and nest in the adjacent coastal forests. Great Horned Owls, Long-Eared Owls, Screech Owls, and tiny Northern Saw-Whet Owls all hunt in salt marshes, open fields, woodlands, and

FFERENTIAL GRASSHOPPER *Melanoplus differentialis*

COMMON WHITETAIL *Plathemis lydia*

EEN DARNER *Anax junius*

BLUE DASHER (male) *Pachydiplax longipennis*

ATY SKIMMER *Libellula incesta*

EASTERN AMBERWING *Perithemis tenera*

Butterflies are shown at roughly life size

Mourning Cloak
Nymphalis antiopa

Red Admiral
Vanessa atalanta

Question Mark
Polygonia interrogationis

Red-Spotted Admiral
Limenitis arthemis

Eastern Tiger Swallowtail
Papilio glaucus

Spicebush Swallowtail
Papilio troilus

Black Swallowtail
Papilio polyxenes

Butterflies are shown at roughly life size

Variegated Fritillary
Euptoieta claudia

Painted Lady
Vanessa cardui

Common Buckeye
Junonia coenia

Gray Hairstreak
Strymon melinus

Clouded Sulphur
Colias philodice

Wood Nymph
Cercyonis pegala

Northern Pearly-eye
Enodia anthedon

Viceroy
Limenitis archippus

Monarch
Danaus plexippus

Maritime woodlands along the Atlantic Coast are a critical habitat for migrating songbirds such as this Black and White Warbler (*Mniotilta varia*). The birds migrate on evening with winds from the southwest, which sweep the flocks close to the coast. On a big migration day at dawn large flocks descend into coastal woodlands to feed and rest after a long flight. *Photo courtesy of Robin Ladouceur.*

forest margins but roost in nearby coastal forests, as does that versatile predator of all coastal habitats, the Black-Crowned Night-Heron.

Spring migrant birds

In spring, coastal woods attract a variety of migrating woodland birds. Beginning in March, Red-Winged Blackbirds, Common Grackles, Northern Cardinals, and Marsh Wrens announce the coming of warm weather. Noisy gangs of boreal songbirds heading north to the Canadian woods move through the trees, including Golden-Crowned and Ruby-Crowned Kinglets, Brown Creepers, and White-Throated Sparrows.

On a moist, early May morning, with warm-front winds from the southwest, large groups of songbirds will move through the woodlands, including Red-Eyed Vireos, Veerys, Yellow Warblers, Yellow-Rumped Warblers, American Redstarts, and Common Yellowthroats. Carolina Wrens, Marsh Wrens, and Song Sparrows travel through as migrants but also remain to breed in Mid-Atlantic coastal woodlands.

Barrier islands can be an excellent place to view migrating birds in both spring and fall, because the long, narrow islands tend to concentrate groups of birds, particularly in excellent shelter offered by maritime forest areas.

Fall migrants

In autumn, many of the same woodland species move south again, but fall migration also brings large flocks of Blue Jays, Tree Swallows, and all of the common blackbird species. Often the flocks flow over the coasts, heading southwest in a continuous stream across the sky. But if the birds do drop into the trees, the experience can be amazing, as 300–400 noisy Blue Jays suddenly blast a riotous mix of jay calls and blue-and-white blurs across the treetops.

All the songbirds in the trees draw down migrating hawks, particularly forest bird hunters such as the common Sharp-Shinned Hawk. Watch for these sleek, short-winged pursuers as they fast-cruise through the forest canopy, looking for an unwary songbird to pick off.

In autumn, the maritime woodlands can be full of blackbirds, wood warblers, and Cedar Waxwing flocks.

The Baltimore Checkerspot (*Euphydryas phaeton*) is widely known as the official insect of Maryland, but unfortunately it is an unusual treat to spot one in the Chesapeake and Mid-Atlantic Coast region. The Checkerspot ranges widely in the eastern United States but is highly local in distribution and never common.

Boat-Tailed Grackle
Quiscalus major

Carolina Jessamine vine
Gelsemium sempervirens

Chris Hill

Cooper's Hawk
Accipiter cooperii

Hermit Thrush
Catharus guttatus

birdiegal

Yellow-Rumped Warbler
Setophaga coronata

American Redstart
Setophaga ruticilla

Yellow Warbler
Setophaga petechia

Palm and Yellow-Rumped Warblers are common in both spring and fall migration. The thickets along the wood edges draw Gray Catbirds, Northern Mockingbirds, and a range of sparrow species. Later in the fall, Ruby-Crowned and Golden-Crowned Kinglets move through park woods, and some linger well into winter, joining gangs of Black-Capped Chickadees, Tufted Titmice, and Brown Creepers in winter foraging flocks.

In winter, it's worthwhile to scan clusters of Eastern Redcedar junipers and other dense conifers along the edges of the woods near salt marshes or open fields for roosting Northern Saw-Whet Owls.

Spring and fall hawk-watching

New Jersey's Cape May is a world-renowned site for fall hawk-watching, but many places along the Mid-Atlantic Coast offer excellent spots to watch migrating hawks and songbirds in both spring and fall. The best migration birding areas provide a range of habitat types and feature forests that offer food and shelter to tired migrant songbirds and hawks. On the Jersey Shore, the small but interesting American Holly forest at Sandy Hook attracts many migrants, as do the low but dense maritime forest areas of Island Beach State Park. Cape Henlopen's extensive tracts of maritime forest, dune fields, and beaches offer excellent spring and fall migration birding. The small Loblolly Pine forests of Assateague Island National Seashore in Maryland attract many migrants, as do the much larger forests of the Chincoteague National Wildlife Refuge in Virginia.

As the sun heats the landscape, the warm ground heats the air near the ground, and that warm air forms columns of rising air called thermals. Most migrating hawks circle in these thermals to gain altitude and then glide relatively effortlessly on their way, instead of having to use active flapping flight to travel the thousands of miles from northern North America to the southern United States, Central America, and South America. Warm thermals form over solid ground but not over the relatively cold waters of bays or the Atlantic Ocean. Hawks are understandably reluctant to fly out over water, where they get no assist from rising thermals and must actively flap across the water to the next piece of

BROAD-WINGED HAWK
Buteo platypterus

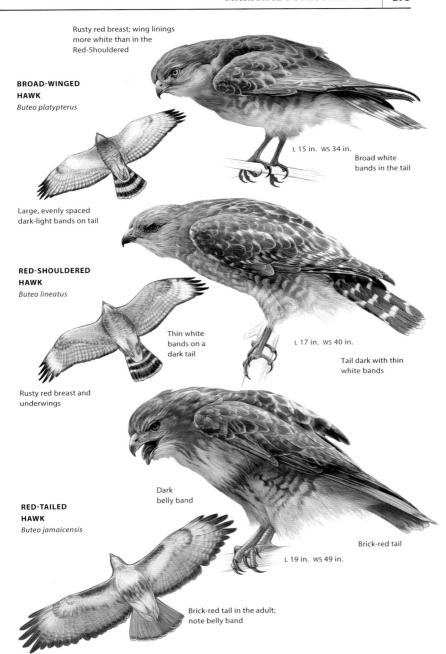

Rusty red breast; wing linings more white than in the Red-Shouldered
L 15 in. WS 34 in.
Broad white bands in the tail

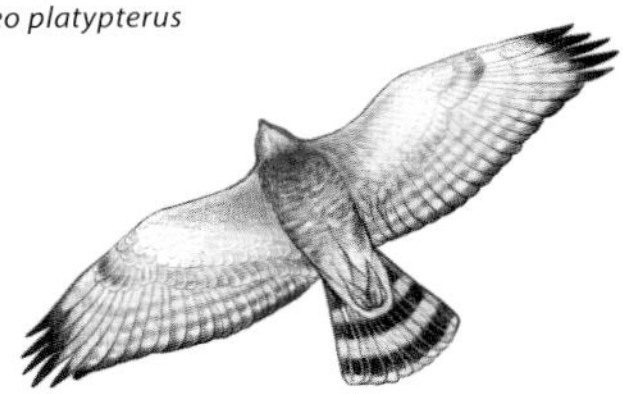
Large, evenly spaced dark-light bands on tail

RED-SHOULDERED HAWK
Buteo lineatus

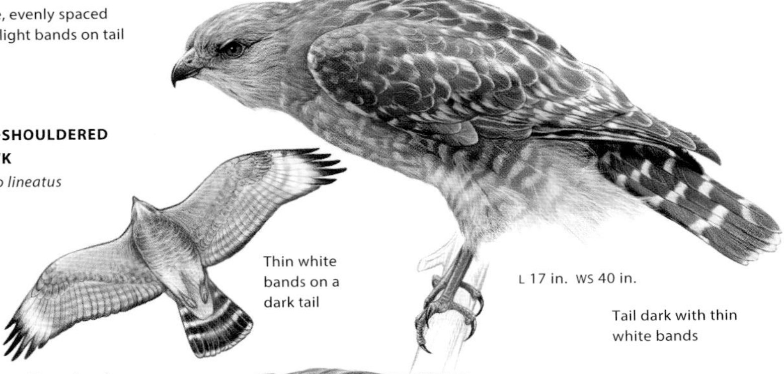
L 17 in. WS 40 in.
Tail dark with thin white bands
Thin white bands on a dark tail
Rusty red breast and underwings

RED-TAILED HAWK
Buteo jamaicensis

Dark belly band
Brick-red tail
L 19 in. WS 49 in.

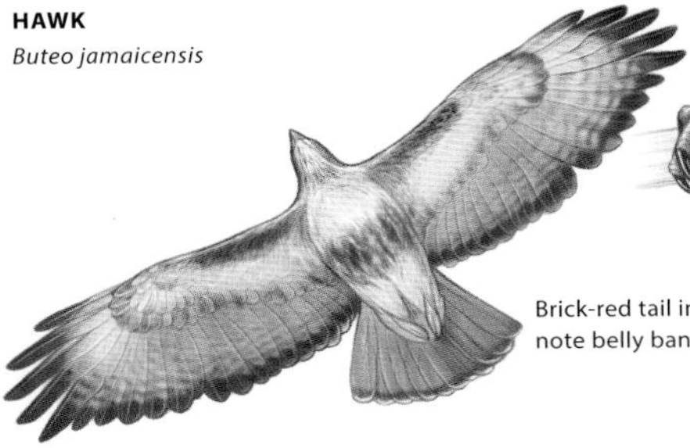
Brick-red tail in the adult; note belly band

GOLDEN-CROWNED KINGLET
Regulus satrapa
L 4 in.
WS 7 in.
RUBY-CROWNED KINGLET
Regulus calendula
L 4.25 in.
WS 7.5 in.
Common in migration, particularly in autumn
RED-BREASTED NUTHATCH
Sitta canadensis
WHITE-BREASTED NUTHATCH
Sitta carolinensis
L 5.75 in.
WS 10.5 in.
L 4.5 in.
WS 8.5 in.
L 5.25 in.
WS 8 in.
CAROLINA CHICKADEE
Poecile carolinensis
L 11 in.
WS 16 in.
BLUE JAY
Cyanocitta cristata

WHITE-THROATED SPARROW
Zonotrichia albicollis

L 6.75 in. WS 9 in.

Common in migration, particularly in autumn

SONG SPARROW
Melospiza melodia

L 6.25 in.
WS 8.25 in.

WHITE-CROWNED SPARROW
Zonotrichia leucophrys

L 7 in. WS 9.5 in.

GRAY CATBIRD
Dumetella carolinensis

L 8.5 in. WS 11 in.

CAROLINA WREN
Thryothorus ludovicianus
L 5.5 in.
WS 7.5 in.
MARSH WREN
Cistothorus palustris
L 5 in.
WS 6 in.
HOUSE WREN
Troglodytes aedon
L 4.75 in.
WS 6 in.
Male
NORTHERN CARDINAL
Cardinalis cardinalis
Female
L 8.75 in. WS 12 in.
NORTHERN MOCKINGBIRD
Mimus polyglottos
L 10 in. WS 14 in.

EASTERN SCREECH OWL
Megascops asio

L 8.5 in. WS 20 in.

SHARP-SHINNED HAWK
Accipiter striatus

Common in migration, particularly in autumn

L 11 in. WS 23 in.

Common Yellowthroats (*Geothlypis trichas*) are one of the liveliest and most noticeable of the resident birds in maritime forests. In coastal woodlands south of the Chesapeake Bay Yellowthroats may be resident all year. *Photo courtesy of Robin Ladouceur.*

land. Cape May is a particularly good spot to view fall migration because the south-going birds funnel into the Cape peninsula, and then mill about the forests and fields because they are reluctant to make the 20-mile journey across Delaware Bay.

Start in the early morning to get the best views of migrating songbirds and hawks moving low over marshes and forests. The early hawks will be looking for a breakfast of songbirds, so a morning walk through coastal woodlands will often be rewarded with views of Sharp-Shinned and Cooper's Hawks rocketing through the woods below treetop level, looking for a meal. Later in the day, the movement of soaring groups of hawks becomes harder to view, because the thermals rising above the coastline bring the hawks up so high that they become difficult to spot even with binoculars.

Resident birds

The breeding coastal woodland birds are the familiar but beautiful residents of most woodlands and forest edges of the Atlantic Coast. Song Sparrows, American Goldfinches, Baltimore Orioles, and Northern Cardinals inhabit forest edges. Birding in bramble areas will often yield White-Throated Sparrows, Eastern Towhees, and the tiny but gorgeous Common Yellowthroat. Overhead in the crown foliage of the trees, look and listen for Red-Eyed Vireos. These vireos are the most common bird species in the deep woodlands during the summer, but they are heard more often than seen because they favor the treetops for feeding and nesting. Scan the trees for flashes of crimson from American Redstart warblers, common but not easy to spot high in the foliage. Forest edges and marshes ring with the calls of Red-Winged Blackbirds from mid-March until these birds depart southward in late fall.

The skies above Mid-Atlantic Coast forests were once filled with millions of Carolina Parakeets, the only parrot native to continental North America. The robin-sized birds inhabited forests all along the Atlantic Coast as well as inland forests. Unfortunately the parakeets had a taste for apples, corn, and other grains, and farmers slaughtered the birds in huge numbers. Habitat loss through the cutting of forests also contributed to their population decline in the late 1800s. Once one of the most numerous birds in the United States, the parakeets were extinct by the 1920s.

CAROLINA PARAKEET
Conuropsis carolinensis (extinct)

CEDAR WAXWING *Bombycilla cedrorum*

brm1949

RED-BELLIED WOODPECKER *Melanerpes carolin*

CAROLINA CHICKADEE *Poecile carolinensis*

Rachelle Vance

AMERICAN ROBIN *Turdus migratorius*

Greg Williams

DOWNY WOODPECKER *Picoides pubescens*

MOURNING DOVE *Zenaida macroura*

Mammals

Most woodland and coastal edge mammal species are nocturnal or active only at dawn and dusk, so you won't often see such familiar residents as White-Tailed Deer, Raccoons, Virginia Opossums, or Northern Flying Squirrels. The structural height complexity of woodland edges (dense foliage from ground level up to the treetops), the diverse range of plant species, and the shelter that thick bramble provides all make coastal woodlands particularly attractive to small mammals—and to the animals that hunt them. White-Footed Deer Mice, Eastern Chipmunks, Raccoons, Gray Squirrels, American Red Squirrels, and Northern Flying Squirrels are all common. Red Foxes were once more common in Mid-Atlantic Coast coastal forests, but with the rise of the Eastern Coyote population in the past 20 years, foxes are now a bit less common. White-Tailed Deer thrive in edge habitats with an abundant supply of shrub-height plants and thus are common in coastal woods, though they are not often seen by casual hikers. Eastern Cottontail rabbits and Groundhogs (Woodchucks) are very common in coastal woodland edges, in open meadows, and along grassy roadsides near bramble thickets, where they can quickly retreat from predators.

Both of the region's vulture species can be seen throughout the Mid-Atlantic Coast. The Turkey Vulture and the smaller Black Vulture are formerly more southern birds that have moved steadily up the Atlantic Seaboard as the climate has warmed over the past 50 years.

Turkey Vulture
Cathartes aura

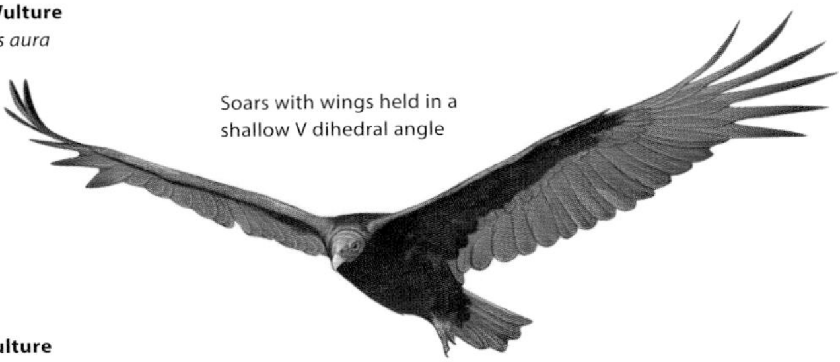
Soars with wings held in a shallow V dihedral angle

Black Vulture
Coragyps atratus

Soars with relatively flat wings; note the light wingtips

Nicolase Lowe

WHITE-TAILED DEER *Odocoileus virginianus*

hkuchera

RACCOON *Procyon lotor*

DMM Photography Art

WHITE-FOOTED MOUSE *Peromyscus leucopus*

elharo

EASTERN CHIPMUNK *Tamias striatus*

Orhan Cam

GRAY SQUIRREL *Sciurus carolinensis*

Anterovium

AMERICAN RED SQUIRREL *Tamiasciurus hudsonic*

ny Campbell

)UTHERN FLYING SQUIRREL *Glaucomys volans*

dannyfox

RED FOX *Vulpes vulpes*

sef Pittner

ASTERN COYOTE *Canis latrans var.*

mandritoiu

EASTERN COTTONTAIL *Sylvilagus floridanus*

rio Beauregard

ROUNDHOG (WOODCHUCK) *Marmota monax*

hakoar

LONG-TAILED WEASEL *Mustela frenata*

A Loblolly Pine (Pinus taeda) at the edge of a salt marsh at Assateague Island National Seashore, Maryland. The tree and its neighbors are slowly succumbing to salt water infiltration due to sea level rise. Note the orange foliage, a symptom of salt burning.

Salt Marshes

Assateague Island National Seashore has some of the most vibrant and accessible salt marshes on the Mid-Atlantic Coast. A large salt marsh creek winds its way to Sinepuxent Bay, which lies between Assateague Island and the mainland.

Salt marshes are North America's most biologically productive ecosystem—only tropical rain forests and coastal mangrove ecosystems are their equals in sheer productivity. Marshes provide significant nutrients to Mid-Atlantic estuaries and are the coastal nursery ground for almost every important commercial and sport fish in nearshore waters. More than 170 fish species and 1,200 invertebrate species live in Mid-Atlantic coastal waters at least part of the year, and most of those species use the salt marshes at some point in their life cycles.

Salt marshes are natural water treatment facilities, cleaning coastal waters through filtering by grasses and by filter feeders that live in and around the marsh, as well as through the activities of the large detritivore community within marshes themselves. The natural salt marsh food chains have a large capacity to absorb and convert dissolved forms of organic matter into grass and animal biomass, cleaning coastal waters and adding vital nutrients to the coastal ecosystem.

Marshes also act as sinks for the excess nitrogen that runs off our highly developed landscapes, and they absorb much of the excess carbon generated from the burning of fossil fuels. Salt marshes work as natural buffers and sponges in stormy conditions, protecting the coastline against storm surges and breaking the full force of storm waves and flooded rivers.

Salt marshes are complex environments, governed both by local tide levels and by the many herbivores that derive some or all of their food from marsh grasses. Many crab species, snail species, and insects feed directly on marsh grass leaves. Predators such as finfish species, Blue Crabs, and birds in turn feed on salt marsh invertebrates. These intricate relationships among grasses, herbivores, and predators can break down when humans remove top predatory species from the environment. For example, overfishing of predatory fish such as Striped Bass and Bluefish has led to population explosions of the salt marsh crabs and snails that the gamefish formerly fed upon. Freed from predation pressures, the crabs and snails can destroy sections of marsh through overgrazing.

Marsh grasses shed their leaves during fall and winter, and this primary source of vegetable matter is broken down by bacteria and fungi into fine detritus that is carried out into the estuary by ebbing tides. Salt marsh grass provides a rich source of energy for tiny planktonic animals, filter feeders such as clams, oysters, and scallops, grass shrimp, amphipods, and other small animals. In turn, these little animals become food for larger predators and scavengers such as crabs, lobsters, fish, birds, and mammals.

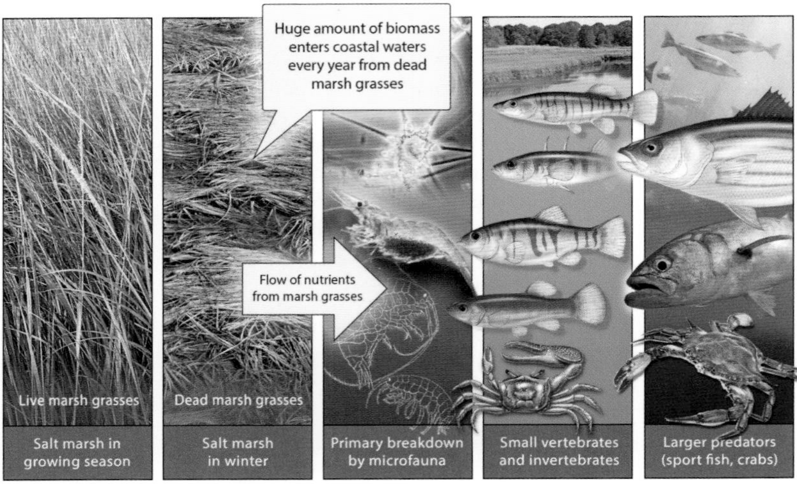
Huge amount of biomass enters coastal waters every year from dead marsh grasses
Flow of nutrients from marsh grasses
Live marsh grasses
Dead marsh grasses
Salt marsh in growing season
Salt marsh in winter
Primary breakdown by microfauna
Small vertebrates and invertebrates
Larger predators (sport fish, crabs)

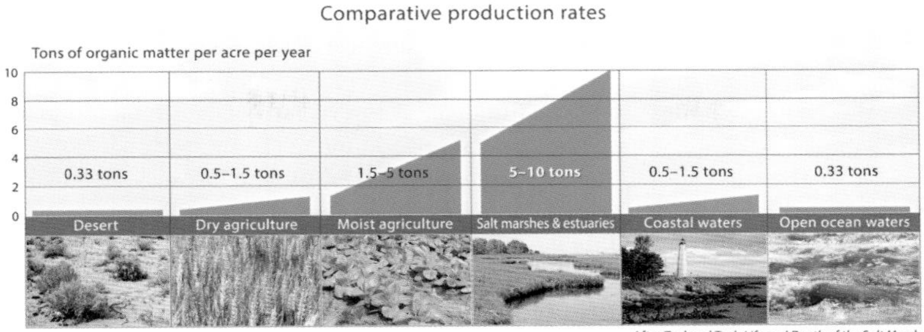
Comparative production rates
Tons of organic matter per acre per year
10
8
6
4
2
0
0.33 tons
0.5–1.5 tons
1.5–5 tons
5–10 tons
0.5–1.5 tons
0.33 tons
Desert
Dry agriculture
Moist agriculture
Salt marshes & estuaries
Coastal waters
Open ocean waters

After Teal and Teal, *Life and Death of the Salt Marsh*

Marshes along the Mid-Atlantic Coast produce five to ten tons of organic matter per acre every year, and that enormous productivity comes from three fundamental marsh components: mud algae, diatoms, and seaweeds at the marsh surface; phytoplankton in the marsh water; and large salt marsh plants, especially grasses.

Salt marshes are a unique form of grassland in that the entire above ground annual growth dies back in winter, leaving only the underground rhizomes to renew the marsh in spring. Ninety percent of a marsh's annual productivity is realized at the end of the growing season in October, when the grass leaves begin to die off, decompose, and then wash into the estuary through tidal flow over winter and early spring. In these tons of dead grass leaves per acre, much of the productivity drains from the marsh as an organic soup of plant detritus to be consumed by bacteria, fungi, and other tiny planktonic animals. Although these microscopic decomposer organisms are not easily visible to us, they are critical to the estuary food chain, because their activity makes the bounty of the salt marsh grasses available to the rest of the food chain.

Animals in the next link of the marsh food chain are detritivores such as fiddler crabs, salt marsh snails, grass shrimp, and marsh amphipods that consume the partially decomposed grass, turning it into animal biomass.

Snails, clams, mussels, and other detritivores and filter feeders form the base of the food chain of predatory animals. Small marsh fish such as killifish and

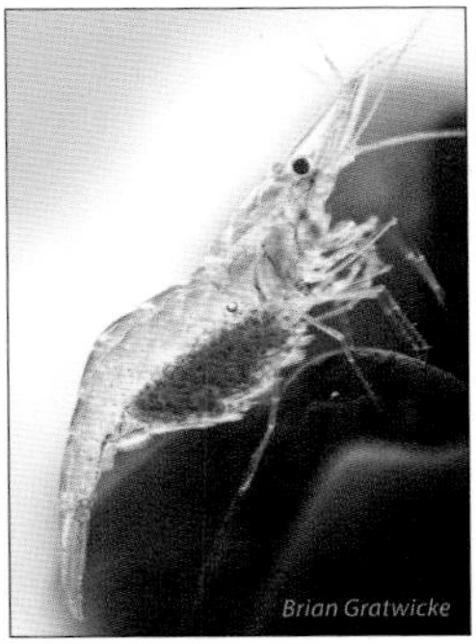
Brian Gratwicke

Daggerblade Grass Shrimp
Palaemonetes pugio

A classic salt meadow composed of Saltmeadow Cordgrass (*Spartina patens*).

sticklebacks feed on detritivores like amphipods and grass shrimp, as do such crustaceans as Green and Blue Crabs. The Diamondback Terrapin, various crabs, and even such birds as the American Black Duck all feed on the abundance of salt marsh snails. Smaller marsh predators become food for larger animals such as Bluefish, Striped Bass, herons, and Ospreys. Although the productivity of the salt marsh may be hard to see directly, wetlands are the most significant contributors to biological wealth in our coastal waters. They are the base of the food chain for most of the birds, fish, and other more visible wildlife along our shorelines.

Energy conversion

Salt marshes capture and convert about 6 percent of the sunlight that falls on them during the year. This figure may sound modest, but the salt marsh compares very well to other plant communities. A farm field of corn captures about 2 percent of the sun's energy; coral reefs capture about 3 percent. Most heavily managed farm crops produce only about half that productivity per year.

Marsh ecosystems depend on tidal flow as well as rivers and streams to deliver raw nutrients along with the mud and sediments washed from inland areas down to the coast. Because marsh vegetation dies back each fall and winter, marshes are quick to convert nutrients into organic matter available to estuary and marine animals. In contrast to forests, where much of the annual productivity is bound up in the wood and roots of trees, shrubs, and other perennials for many years, marshes release almost all of their yearly production when the grasses die back and are washed into the estuary by the tides. The grass leaves and fragments are broken down and gradually converted into microscopic animal biomass at the base of the food chain.

Regional salt marshes

On the ancient, unglaciated Mid-Atlantic Coast, the ancestors of today's salt marshes have probably been in place for millions of years. The coasts have had millennia to accumulate both the sandy barrier islands that protect the shore from wave action and the fertile, deep silt flats that nurture the vast salt marshes of the Mid-Atlantic coastline.

Most large salt marshes on the Atlantic Coast are associated with major rivers or lie behind substantial barrier islands formed at least in part from sediments carried to the coasts by rivers. Silt from coastal erosion settles onto the bottom of tidal areas and eventually builds up to form a stable platform for marsh grasses. As pioneer grasses like Saltwater Cordgrass (*Spartina alterniflora*) take root, they trap yet more silt, building a higher platform of silt and peat from older grass roots. Eventually, the grasses form high salt marsh dominated by Saltmeadow Cordgrass (*S. patens*), along with Spike Grass, Blackgrass, and Black Needlerush.

The low marsh silt is held together by a complex of grass rhizomes, roots, Ribbed Mussels, and both macroalgae such as Sea Lettuce and microalgae on the mud surface.

Origins of salt marshes

Salt marshes typically form when seeds or rhizomes of Saltwater Cordgrass colonize shallow tidal flats. As the cordgrass shoots develop, they slow the movement of water, leading to sediment deposition and limiting erosion during storms and high-tides. As the tidal flats grow into a more mature marsh platform, tidal creeks develop that drain the marsh during low tides. The movement of tidal water acts almost like a breathing mechanism for the marsh, bringing in fresh nutrients and sediment on the flood tide and draining away waste and detritus on the ebb.

Ribbed Mussels (*Geukensia demissa*) play an essential role in the low salt marsh, binding the marsh sediments to resist erosion from tides and storms and contributing nutrients to the *Spartina* through their feces.

High salt marshes are in critical danger from rapid sea level rise because they exist in the very narrow range between the average height of high-tides and the average height of twice-monthly spring tides. The most important high marsh grass, Saltmeadow Cordgrass (*Spartina patens*), cannot tolerate more than the twice-monthly soaking of its roots in salt water. Even a few millimeters of sea level rise can damage and eventually kill high salt marsh meadows.

Marsh grasses propagate primarily by rhizomes—spreading underground stems that both expand the size and area of the original shoot of grass and help bind and stabilize the tidal mud beneath them. Rhizomes also allow marsh grasses to store energy underground for the next growing season.

As the grasses take root, the tangle of rhizomes and stems traps more sediments and sand, gradually building up a robust platform of dense roots, covered by sticky surface mats of blue-green algae that are resistant to normal currents and tides. Once this platform reaches above the mean high-tides, the marsh begins to stratify into a lower marsh area that floods twice a day with the tides and an upper marsh platform that floods only a few times a month during spring high-tides.

Winter ice is a major limiting factor in northern salt

The critical role of tides in salt marsh formation

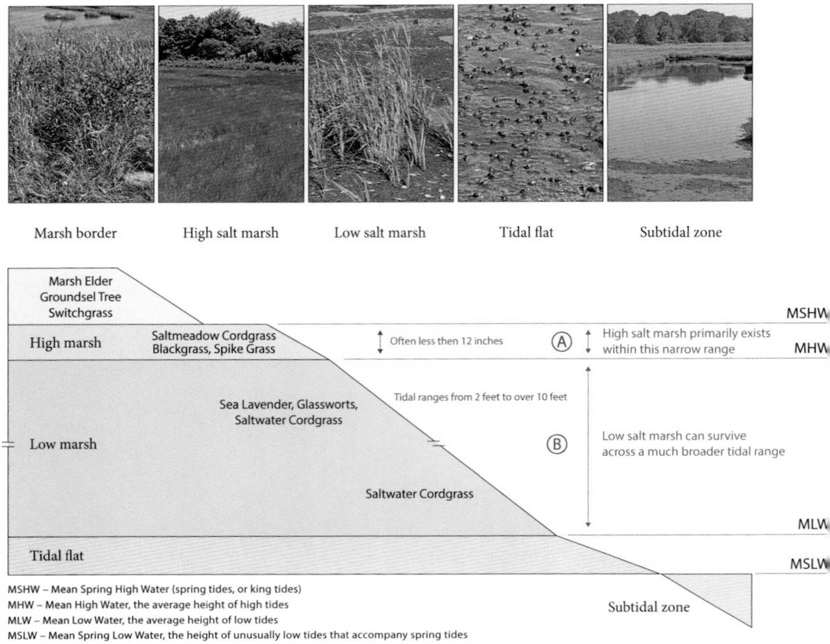
Marsh border
High salt marsh
Low salt marsh
Tidal flat
Subtidal zone
Marsh Elder
Groundsel Tree
Switchgrass
MSHW
High marsh
Saltmeadow Cordgrass
Blackgrass, Spike Grass
Often less then 12 inches
A
High salt marsh primarily exists within this narrow range
MHW
Tidal ranges from 2 feet to over 10 feet
Sea Lavender, Glassworts,
Saltwater Cordgrass
Low marsh
B
Low salt marsh can survive across a much broader tidal range
Saltwater Cordgrass
MLW
Tidal flat
MSLW
Subtidal zone
MSHW – Mean Spring High Water (spring tides, or king tides)
MHW – Mean High Water, the average height of high tides
MLW – Mean Low Water, the average height of low tides
MSLW – Mean Spring Low Water, the height of unusually low tides that accompany spring tides

marshes. Sharp, heavy plates of ice often cover the surface of the upper marsh and line the banks of marsh creeks in winter. These ice plates effectively shear off the stems of taller plants, so trees and bushes that might tolerate the salty water cannot gain a foothold in the upper marsh. The marsh grasses survive the ice shearing because their rhizomes and roots are safe under the mud and peat surface, ready to send up new green shoots in spring. Marsh environments experience a wide range of temperatures as well as rapid temperature changes, as the exposed marsh heats during low tides in warmer months and then cools rapidly when high-tides flood the marsh.

Narrow-Leaved Cattail
Typha angustifolia

Tidal movements, rainwater runoff, and the variable flow rate of rivers all affect the salinity of the water around marshes. Evaporation during low tides increases the salinity of shallow pools and open pannes in the salt marsh, sometimes to levels well above the salinity of ocean water.

Patterns and zonation

The structure of a salt marsh is a direct reflection of area tide levels. Its patterns of vertical zonation are so consistent that you can determine local tide levels merely by looking at the marsh plants. There are four major zones of the salt marsh, and each zone has characteristic vegetation:

Lower marsh

This area lies between the mean low water line (MLW) and the mean high water line (MHW). In northern regions of the Atlantic Seaboard, the lower marsh is dominated by a single grass species, Saltwater Cordgrass, which tolerates flooding at high-tides but cannot thrive where its roots are permanently underwater. South of Delaware Bay, Saltwater Cordgrass mixes with Black Needlerush. Many salt marshes in the Carolinas, Georgia, and Florida are dominated by Black Needlerush.

Upper marsh

This marsh area lies above the MHW and below the mean spring high water line (MSHW), the highest of the monthly high-tides. This area is dominated by a trio of grasses that can tolerate the twice-monthly

Bodie Island salt marshes at Cape Hatteras National Seashore, North Carolina

Salt pannes are low, muddy areas of the marsh with no grass cover. Pannes often flood during spring tides. The water they contain is often far saltier than seawater, owing to evaporation.

flooding of spring high-tides but otherwise must grow above the average high-tide level: Saltmeadow Cordgrass (Salt Hay), Spike Grass (Saltgrass), and, especially south of Delaware Bay, Black Needlerush.

Salt pannes

Salt pannes are shallow, water-retaining, open areas within the marsh, often with a bare, muddy bottom and a sparse collection of plants. At low tide, salt pannes may dry entirely to a hard mud surface dotted with caked salt crystals. Older salt pannes develop a surface crust of algae and bacteria that will crack into plates on hot, dry summer days. Though it isn't pretty, this living crust over the mud is essential to the biological productivity of the salt marsh. Mud Fiddler and Red-Jointed Fiddler Crabs feed directly on the crust, and the tiny crabs often congregate around salt pannes.

Pannes are very high in salinity owing to the evaporation of brackish water. The thin vegetation of salt pannes is usually dominated by especially salt-tolerant plants, including Spike Grass, Glasswort, Sea Lavender, and sometimes a dwarfed, low-growing form of Saltwater Cordgrass.

Marsh borders

Borders are the higher ground surrounding the marsh, above the mean spring high water level, where flooding

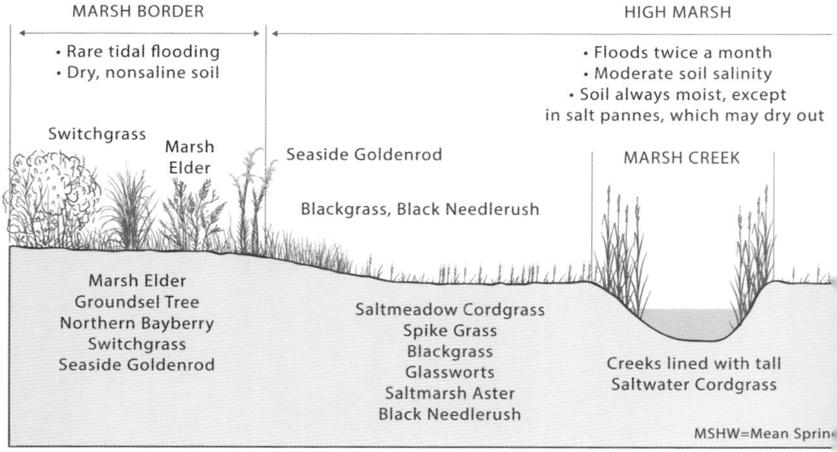
MARSH BORDER
HIGH MARSH
• Rare tidal flooding
• Dry, nonsaline soil
• Floods twice a month
• Moderate soil salinity
• Soil always moist, except in salt pannes, which may dry out
Switchgrass
Marsh Elder
Seaside Goldenrod
MARSH CREEK
Blackgrass, Black Needlerush
Marsh Elder
Groundsel Tree
Northern Bayberry
Switchgrass
Seaside Goldenrod
Saltmeadow Cordgrass
Spike Grass
Blackgrass
Glassworts
Saltmarsh Aster
Black Needlerush
Creeks lined with tall Saltwater Cordgrass
MSHW=Mean Sprin

is rare and less salt-tolerant plants can survive. In most Mid-Atlantic salt marshes, you can spot the marsh border quickly by looking for Marsh Elder (high-tide Bush) and Groundsel Tree, two shrubs that generally line the salt marsh border.

The lower marsh

In New Jersey and much of the Delmarva Peninsula, the lower salt marsh vegetation is composed mostly of Saltwater Cordgrass stands. Besides tolerating saltwater immersion of its roots and rhizomes, Saltwater Cordgrass has a range of adaptations to living between the low and high-tide lines. The waterlogged soils of salt marshes and tidal flats are poorly oxygenated, and all plant roots require oxygen to do the work of transporting nutrients throughout the plant. Saltwater Cordgrass has a specialized honeycomb-like air circulation tissue called aerenchyma within its stems, rhizomes, and roots. This allows the plant to grow on waterlogged soils and still oxygenate its roots. Its leaves also have special salt glands on their surface that excrete excess salt absorbed through the roots. If you look closely at a living cordgrass leaf, you'll see tiny white crystals of salt, excreted by the salt glands, all along the blade (see illustration, p. 318).

Low salt marsh is defined by Saltwater Cordgrass (*Spartina alterniflora*), which grows especially tall where there is a big tidal range.

Although we usually look at the characteristic

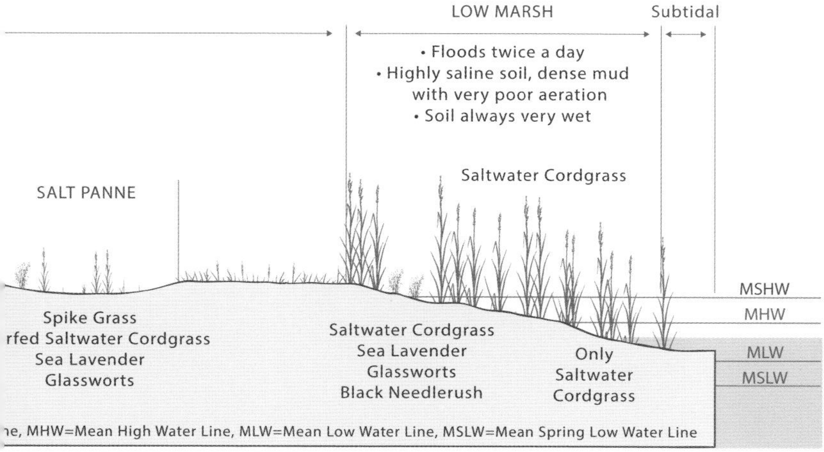
LOW MARSH
Subtidal
• Floods twice a day
• Highly saline soil, dense mud with very poor aeration
• Soil always very wet
Saltwater Cordgrass
SALT PANNE
MSHW
MHW
MLW
MSLW
Spike Grass
rfed Saltwater Cordgrass
Sea Lavender
Glassworts
Saltwater Cordgrass
Sea Lavender
Glassworts
Black Needlerush
Only Saltwater Cordgrass
ne, MHW=Mean High Water Line, MLW=Mean Low Water Line, MSLW=Mean Spring Low Water Line

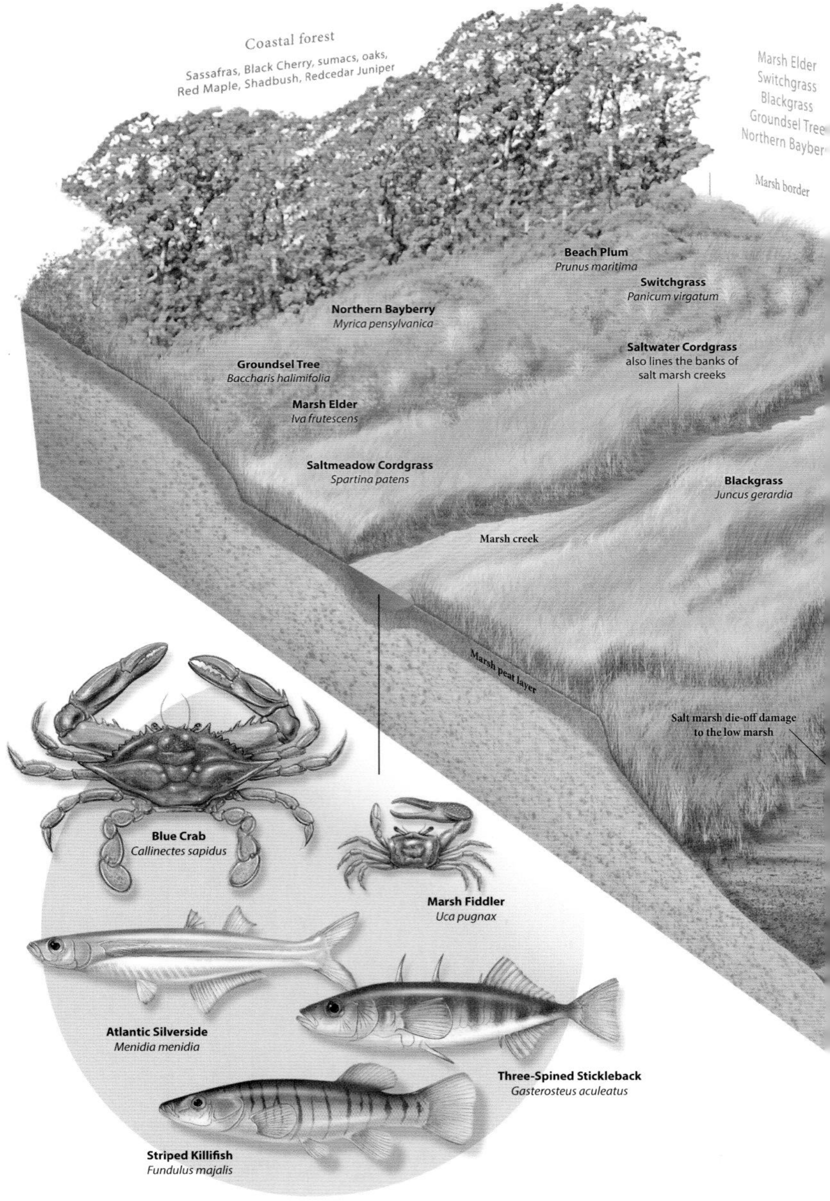
Coastal forest
Sassafras, Black Cherry, sumacs, oaks, Red Maple, Shadbush, Redcedar Juniper
Marsh Elder
Switchgrass
Blackgrass
Groundsel Tree
Northern Bayber
Marsh border
Beach Plum
Prunus maritima
Switchgrass
Panicum virgatum
Northern Bayberry
Myrica pensylvanica
Saltwater Cordgrass
also lines the banks of salt marsh creeks
Groundsel Tree
Baccharis halimifolia
Marsh Elder
Iva frutescens
Saltmeadow Cordgrass
Spartina patens
Blackgrass
Juncus gerardia
Marsh creek
Marsh peat layer
Salt marsh die-off damage to the low marsh
Blue Crab
Callinectes sapidus
Marsh Fiddler
Uca pugnax
Atlantic Silverside
Menidia menidia
Three-Spined Stickleback
Gasterosteus aculeatus
Striped Killifish
Fundulus majalis

ARSH ELDER *Iva frutescens*

South of Delaware Bay

BLACK NEEDLERUSH *Juncus roemerianus*

IKE GRASS (in flower) *Distichlis spicata*

SWITCHGRASS *Panicum virgatum*

ACKGRASS *Juncus gerardii*

BLACKGRASS, flower detail

GLASSWORT *Salicornia* sp.

GROUNDSEL TREE *Baccharis halimifolia*

ERECT SEA BLIGHT *Suaeda linearis*

SEA LETTUCE *Ulva lactuca*

GREEN FLEECE *Codium fragile*

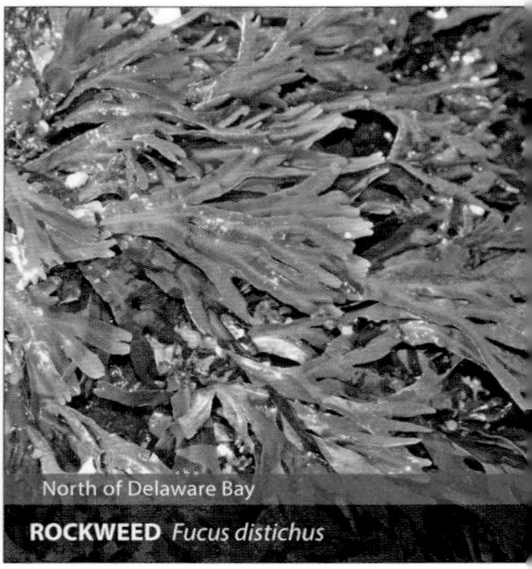

North of Delaware Bay

ROCKWEED *Fucus distichus*

EA LAVENDER *Limonium carolinianum*

SEA LAVENDER, basal rosette

EASIDE GOLDENROD *Solidago sempervirens*

MARSH ORACH *Atriplex patula*

ERENNIAL SALTMARSH ASTER *S. tenuifolium*

COMMON REED *Phragmites australis*

Salt marsh snails (*Melampus* sp.) on a stem of Saltwater Cordgrass (*Spartina alterniflora*).

bring oxygenated water and nutrients into the silty soils. The most common fiddler crab in salt marshes is the Mud Fiddler Crab, but the Red-Jointed Fiddler Crab is also common. Both fiddler crabs feed on the rich layer of algae, bacteria, and plant detritus on the surface of marsh mud.

Purple Marsh Crabs are about the size of a fiddler crab but are dark violet to black and have a more square-shaped body. These little crabs are less visible to the marsh visitor because they are active mainly at night. Although they will prey on fiddler crabs, Purple Marsh Crabs are primarily herbivores that feed on the stalks and leaves of Saltwater Cordgrass. These crabs have been implicated in the die-off of lower marsh grasses in sections of many Atlantic Coast salt marshes. In marsh die-off syndrome, the crabs eat away large patches of Saltwater Cordgrass, leaving bare, muddy creek banks. Research by Brown University professor Mark Bertness and his graduate students has shown that marsh die-off tends to occur in areas where sport fishing has depleted the number of predatory fishes and Blue Crabs that commonly feed on the Purple Marsh Crabs. Released from predation pressure, the enlarged crab population damages the salt marsh by eating far more grass.

Within the marsh creeks, the beautiful Blue Crab is the characteristic salt marsh crustacean. As the climate and water temperatures have warmed over the past few decades, Blue Crabs have extended their range northward and have become more numerous in most areas. Blue Crabs are frequent targets of human crab fishers as well as of the larger herons, and so they are wary of any movements around them. If you stand still by a marsh creek for a few minutes looking carefully under the surface, you will often be rewarded by spotting a Blue Crab or the smaller Green Crab, also common in

Atlantic Silverside
Menidia menidia

An example of salt marsh die-off, at Stony Creek, Branford, Connecticut. Here almost all of the low salt marsh grass, Saltwater Cordgrass (*Spartina alterniflora*), has been chewed away by marsh crabs, leaving large brown banks of exposed marsh peat that erode easily in storms.

salt marsh creeks north of Chesapeake Bay.

Grass shrimp (also called prawns, *Palaemonetes* sp.) are also widespread in salt marsh creeks, and they play an essential role in the salt marsh and estuary food chains. Grass shrimp are detritus feeders that break down larger bits of dead grass leaves. Bits of the reduced leaves that are not eaten by the shrimp are broken down by microbes and become food for filter feeders like clams, mussels, and barnacles. The grass shrimp are eaten by larger fish and birds that move into the marsh creeks at high-tide.

Fish of the lower marsh and marsh creeks

Salt marshes are essential nursery areas for many fish and are also rich in species that spend their lives in and around marshes. Small salt marsh fish eat algae, detritus from the breakdown of marsh grasses, amphipods, copepods, isopods, shrimp, marsh snails, and insects. Mummichogs and killifish are important predators on mosquito larvae, helping to limit populations of marsh mosquitos and other biting insects.

If you quickly approach a salt marsh creek in summer or fall, you'll see an explosion of tiny, panicked fish darting in every direction. The fast-moving fish are mostly a nondescript brownish color, but if you wait until the fish settle down and look closely, you can identify a few species. The Mummichog is the most abundant fish in the lower marsh and marsh creeks.

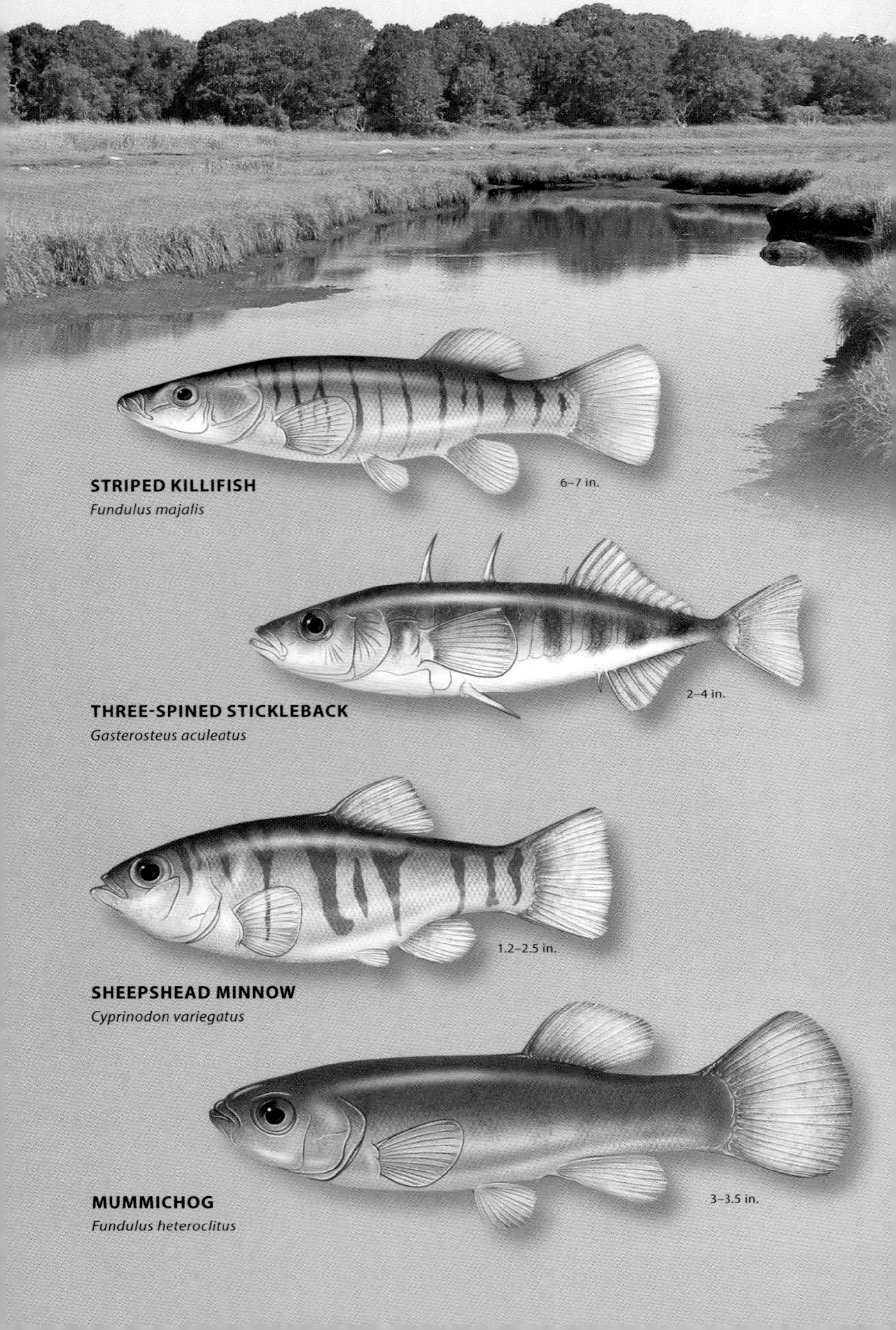
6–7 in.
2–4 in.
1.2–2.5 in.
3–3.5 in.

STRIPED KILLIFISH
Fundulus majalis

THREE-SPINED STICKLEBACK
Gasterosteus aculeatus

SHEEPSHEAD MINNOW
Cyprinodon variegatus

MUMMICHOG
Fundulus heteroclitus

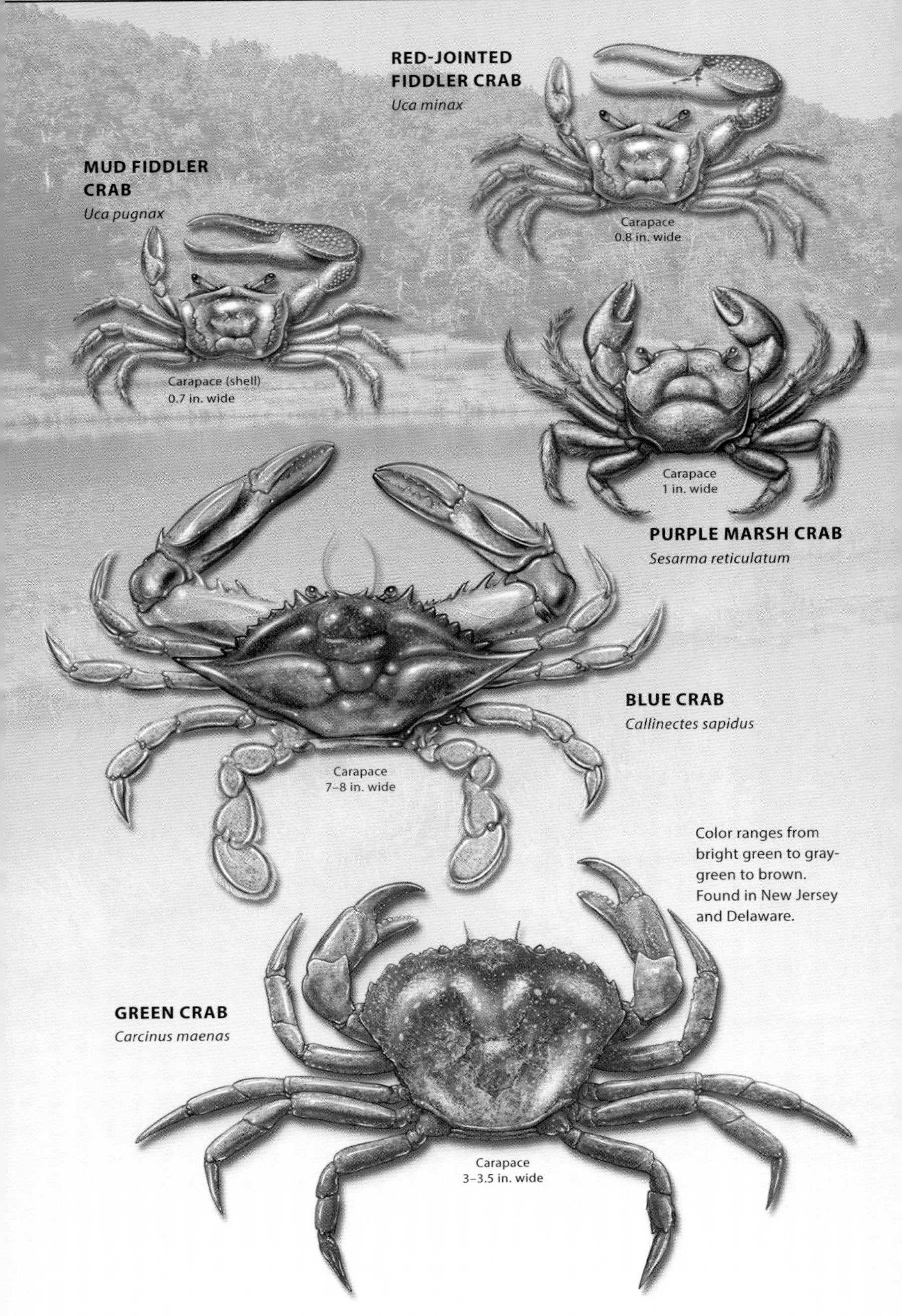
RED-JOINTED FIDDLER CRAB
Uca minax
Carapace 0.8 in. wide
MUD FIDDLER CRAB
Uca pugnax
Carapace (shell) 0.7 in. wide
Carapace 1 in. wide
PURPLE MARSH CRAB
Sesarma reticulatum
BLUE CRAB
Callinectes sapidus
Carapace 7–8 in. wide
Color ranges from bright green to gray-green to brown. Found in New Jersey and Delaware.
GREEN CRAB
Carcinus maenas
Carapace 3–3.5 in. wide

Salt marsh creeks are critical habitat, not only for the thousands of Mummichogs (*Fundulus heteroclitus*) and other small fish, but also for the young of most of our coastal food fish species, including Striped Bass (*Morone saxatilis*).

Mummichogs can grow as long as seven inches, but most individuals in marsh creeks and shallows are one to two inches long. Tiny flashes of silver are usually from the Atlantic Silverside, a fish that also ranges into the coastal and deeper waters. Striped Killifish and Sheepshead Minnows are other familiar residents of salt marsh creeks. Young flounders use the shelter of salt marsh creeks to grow before venturing into deeper waters. The flounders are a favorite target for Ospreys, as are the schools of silvery Atlantic Menhaden and Blueback Herring that also enter tidal creeks in the marsh.

Larger species of coastal fish range into the marsh to feed at high-tide. Smaller Bluefish and Striped Bass enter for the rich pickings of small marsh fish and crabs in tidal creeks. These larger predatory and sport fish species are essential to salt marsh ecology because they limit the populations of plant-eating prey that might otherwise damage the marsh.

Diamondback Terrapins

Northern Diamondback Terrapins are turtles native to brackish and salt marshes ranging from Cape Cod south to the Florida Keys and the Gulf Coast. Their common name derives from the diamond patterns

Diamondback Terrapin
Malaclemys terrapin

Diamondback Terrapin
Malaclemys terrapin

of the shell carapace, the details of which are highly variable but are always in a bold geometric design. The name "terrapin" is derived from the Algonquian word "torope," which the Native Americans used to describe the Diamondback.

Terrapins are shy and are fast, active swimmers with large webbed feet and powerful jaws for crushing their favored prey of small fish, clams, mussels, periwinkles, and mud snails. To see them, approach salt marsh creeks slowly and scan the water for swimming turtles as well as the water's edge along the mudbanks for basking terrapins. In early summer, check roads near marshes for female turtles seeking out nesting sites. Terrapins can survive in the wild from 25 to 40 years, making them one of North America's longest-lived animals. Diamondbacks are also unusual in that they can survive in a variety of water salinities, from freshwater (<5 salt per thousand parts of water, or ppt) to ocean water (32 ppt), but they prefer the brackish water of salt marshes (15–25 ppt). Special lacrimal glands near their eyes allow terrapins to drink salt water and then excrete the salt as tears.

Diamondbacks mate in late spring and lay egg clutches in June and July. The females prefer to lay their eggs in sandbanks but will also dig nests under vegetation in the high marsh. Females often wander long distances from the marsh to find suitable nesting areas, making them vulnerable to cars and domestic animal predation. Young turtles emerge from eggs in August and September and are a favorite food of herons, Bluefish, and Striped Bass. Diamondbacks overwinter by hibernating in deep marsh creeks under mud bottoms or high marsh vegetation, but their winter biology is not well understood.

In the nineteenth and early twentieth centuries, the Northern Diamondback Terrapin was nearly hunted to extinction for its meat, then used in a fashionable soup. As the popularity of turtle soup faded in the early twentieth century, Mid-Atlantic Coast populations of Diamondbacks recovered somewhat. However, all states along the coast ban the hunting or possession of terrapins due to their fragile population status. Today

lightningboldt

Common Snapping Turtle
Chelydra serpentina

the main threat to terrapins is habitat loss. Biologists estimate that almost 75 percent of terrapin marsh habitat has been eliminated since colonial times. Accidental death owing to human activity is another problem: terrapins are often caught and drowned in crab pots and nets or hit by boat propellers or cars.

Another common turtle that often enters salt marshes is the Common Snapping Turtle. Snapping Turtles are readily distinguished from terrapins by a more massive head, lack of strong linear patterns on the shell, and generally darker overall color. Adult Snapping Turtles (up to 18 inches long) are also much larger than adult Diamondback Terrapins (usually five to seven inches long). Snapping Turtles are almost exclusively aquatic. They are more noticeable in late spring and early summer, when female turtles wander into the upper marsh or uplands near marshes to lay their eggs.

Birds of the lower marsh

The lower salt marsh offers a wide variety of animal and vegetal food sources to ducks, wading birds, and aerial divers such as terns and Ospreys. Water is deeper in the lower marsh, so long-legged wading birds such as the Great Blue Heron, Great Egret, and Snowy Egret are common sights there in all seasons except winter—

American Black Duck
Anas rubripes

and there is enough food in salt marshes that some Great Blue Herons hang around even in winter. Wading shorebird species are other frequent marsh visitors, particularly during spring and fall migration. Greater and Lesser Yellowlegs and Glossy Ibis are very common in water less than a foot deep, and Willets both feed and nest in many marsh sites along the coastlines.

Common Snapping Turtle
Chelydra serpentina

American Black Ducks and Gadwalls are year-round residents, and salt marshes are a vital breeding environment for these ducks, which have lost much of their former nesting habitat to coastal development. Other ducks use the marshes primarily in migration and in winter, when marshes offer food as well as shelter from human activity and the weather. Given the relatively shallow water, the lower marsh is used most intensively by dabbling duck species such as Mallards, Gadwalls, Green-Winged and Blue-Winged Teals, American Wigeons, and Wood Ducks. Deeper water near the marsh attracts nonnative Mute Swans, as well as such diving ducks as the Hooded and Red-Breasted Mergansers, Greater and Lesser Scaups, Common Goldeneyes, and Ruddy Ducks. Double-Crested Cormorants also frequently dive for fish in or near salt marshes and can often be seen perched on docks, pilings, and other

Black-Crowned Night-Heron in flight

Yellow-Crowned Night-Heron in flight

Yellow-Crowned Night-Heron
Nyctanassa violacea

Black-Crowned Night-Heron
Nycticorax nycticorax

Herons are the emblematic birds of salt marshes. These water birds are graceful yet fierce predators of virtually all small animals: fish, turtles, voles, crabs, large insects, and the young of other birds are all fair game.

Herons are solitary feeders. You will seldom see large flocks of herons, although Cattle Egrets are more gregarious than most other herons. More typical are small mixed-species clusters of herons feeding along marsh creeks. Great Blue Herons are particularly territorial toward other herons, especially toward fellow Great Blue Herons.

Great Blue Heron
Ardea herodias

Green Heron
Butorides virescens

Little Blue Heron
Egretta caerulea

Great Egret
Ardea alba
Snowy Egret
Egretta thula
Cattle Egret
Bubulcus ibis
Tricolored Heron
Egretta tricolor
© Pat Lynch 2019

FotoRequest
AMERICAN BITTERN *Botaurus lentiginosus*

SPOTTED SANDPIPER *Actitis macularius*

BELTED KINGFISHER *Megaceryle alcyon*

WILLET *Tringa semipalmata*

LESSER YELLOWLEGS *Tringa flavipes*

Glenn Youvng
GREATER YELLOWLEGS *Tringa melanoleuca*

LOSSY IBIS *Plegadis falcinellus*

MALLARD *Anas platyrhynchos*

ve Byland

LUE-WINGED TEAL *Anas discors*

Steve Oehlenschlager

GADWALL *Mareca strepera*

UTE SWAN *Cygnus olor*

pstclair

CLAPPER RAIL *Rallus longirostris*

Wenona Suydam

Short-Eared Owl
Asio flammeus

wildphoto4

Wood Duck
Aix sponsa

Green-Winged Teal
Anas carolinensis

nearby structures.

Coastal diving birds like terns depend on the health of our salt marshes. Terns feed on small fish such as Mummichogs, Atlantic Silversides, Sand Lance, and Sheepshead Minnows, which they take in shallow dives at the water surface. All of these small fish either live entirely in or around salt marshes or depend on the protection of wetlands early in their lives. The endangered Least Tern takes small fish directly from salt marsh creeks and from shallow coastal waters near marshes. Black Skimmers also hunt more open waters near marshes for the same small fish species taken by terns.

Along creek banks in the lower marsh, look for the secretive Clapper Rail in early morning or evening twilight hours. Scanning the same areas of marsh creeks will often turn up a Black-Crowned Night-Heron or the less common but similar Yellow-Crowned Night-Heron. All three birds hunt for fiddler crabs, snails, and other small marsh invertebrates. The night-herons will also take larger crabs and fish from the marsh creeks.

The upper marsh

The upper marsh, or marsh platform, is the area of the salt marsh above the typical high-tide line (MHW) but below the level of the high water in monthly spring tides (MSHW) (see illustration, p. 310). Although the upper marsh is above the average high-tide, it is flooded twice monthly by spring high-tides, and thus the plants in the upper marsh must also be able to tolerate regular immersions in salt water. As with the lower salt marsh, the upper marsh owes its existence to a single dominant grass species, in this case, Saltmeadow Cordgrass (Salt Hay). Saltmeadow Cordgrass is the low-growing grass that forms the open meadow-like expanses most people think of when referring to salt marshes. It is brilliantly green from late spring to early fall and has a peculiar growth habit of not usually growing fully upright. The grass stalks tend to lean over against their neighbors, giving Saltmeadow Cordgrass meadows their typical cowlicked appearance.

In northeastern salt marshes, Saltmeadow Cordgrass

is joined by scatterings of Spike Grass. Spike Grass is not competitive enough with Saltmeadow Cordgrass to dominate most marsh areas, but in areas of the upper marsh where the soil has been disturbed or is particularly salty, Spike Grass may occur in pure stands. Spike Grass is the most salt-tolerant of all high marsh grasses and will also grow in salt pannes in the upper marsh, where because of evaporation, the underlying mud is often much saltier than pure seawater. In typical marshes, Spike Grass is not easy to spot among the more common Saltmeadow Cordgrass. However, from September on, the distinctive white flowers of Spike Grass are visible, making the overall distribution of Spike Grass in the marsh more obvious.

In raised areas of the salt marsh or along the upland rim of the marsh, Blackgrass (Black Rush) mixes in with Saltmeadow Cordgrass and Spike Grass. Areas of the marsh dominated by Blackgrass have a different visual texture and color because Blackgrass leaves are spiky and erect as well as a darker shade of green in summer. In the spring, Blackgrass is the first marsh grass to turn a brilliant spring green, and in the fall, Blackgrass leaves turn the very dark brown or black color that gives the rush its name. The similarly named and related Black Needlerush is a much taller rush, with very dark leaves with sharp tips that make stands of Black Needlerush almost impenetrable to both people and larger animals.

In the less salty conditions of the upper marsh, more plants can tolerate the occasional baths of salt water. Two low, herbaceous plants are widespread in the upper marsh: Glasswort and Sea Lavender. Glassworts have a distinctive twig and leaf structure adapted to conserve water and resist salt spray. Their leaves are much reduced and hug the fleshy stems, but Glassworts are true flowering plants. Unless you are a botanist, the three Glasswort species are difficult to distinguish, and botanists themselves do not always agree on which is which, so we'll just call them Glassworts. Luckily, Glassworts are so distinctive that once you know what they look like, you can easily spot them in the marsh, particularly in the fall, when Glasswort stems turn a brilliant red against the green of the

Common Upper Salt Marsh Border Shrubs

Marsh Elder
Iva frutescens

Groundsel Tree
Baccharis halimifolia

Northern Bayberry
Myrica pensylvanica

Beach Plum
Prunus maritima

Black Cherry
Prunus serotina

Lone Star Tick
Amblyomma americanum

Black-Legged Tick
(Deer Tick)
Ixodes scapularis

Carrier of Lyme disease

American Dog Tick
Dermacentor variabilis

Greenhead Fly
Tabanus sp.

Photos: Melinda Fawver, Sarah2, photobee, Elliotte Rusty Harold, allocricetulus.

marsh grasses around them. When in bloom in the summer and early fall, Sea Lavender adds a beautiful violet haze to the waterside edges of the upper marsh. Sea Lavender is particularly tolerant of salt water on its roots and will even grow slightly below the high-tide line.

Scattered through the upper marsh grasses, you'll see several other flowering plants. In the late summer and fall, the golden flowers of Seaside Goldenrod are unmistakable, and even before they flower, the fleshy, tough leaves of this perennial stand out in the upper sections of salt marshes. The much less conspicuous Common Orach and Perennial Saltmarsh Aster are also common along the upland rim of the high marsh.

Invertebrates of the upper salt marsh

As in the lower marsh, the most visible invertebrates of the upper marsh are the small Purple Marsh Crabs, Mud Fiddler Crabs, and Red-Jointed Fiddler Crabs that scurry into holes or under grasses before you as you walk through the marsh. However, by sheer number, the dominant invertebrate of the upper marsh is the salt marsh snail (*Melampus* sp.), sometimes called the coffee bean snail because of its size and glossy brown color. These tiny snails occur in densities of hundreds per square yard in healthy marshes. Salt marsh snails start their lives as aquatic larvae in nearby estuary waters, but as adults, the snails are air-breathing and avoid immersion in water by climbing grass stems during high-tides. Salt marsh snails are an important link in the salt marsh food chain. They feed on algae and grass debris on the surface of the marsh and in turn are eaten by American Black Ducks, Diamondback Terrapins, and other larger marsh animals.

Inspection of the grass and underlying mud surface will show other upper marsh invertebrates, although not in the same numbers as fiddler crabs and salt marsh snails. Salt marsh isopods and amphipods are small, pillbug-like crustaceans that feed on decomposing salt marsh grasses and algae from the surface of the marsh soils. Wolf spiders are a common upper marsh predator of small insects. You won't have to look for one unfortunately common insect—if they are present in the marsh, the biting Greenhead Flies will find you.

The various species of salt marsh mosquitos are other pests you'll come across in the summer and fall months. It's always wise to bring a DEET-based repellent along for any trip into a salt marsh in summer or early fall, both to avoid the annoyance of insect bites and to prevent more severe problems that can come from insect- or tick-borne diseases. Marsh mosquitos can carry West Nile virus, although the chance of catching the disease from the average mosquito bite is extremely low. A much more serious problem is the presence of ticks. If it's 90 degrees Fahrenheit on a sunny summer day, never "bushwhack" through marsh vegetation with bare legs, even if you are wearing insect repellent. If you plan on straying off established paths, always wear long pants sprayed with a DEET-based repellent. For even more protection, wear long pants and high socks treated with pyrethrin, and bind the bottoms of your pants with bicycle clips. There are too many shrubs, and long grass stems in the marsh to risk wearing shorts, and long pants will also protect you from other common irritants like Poison Ivy in

Seaside Dragonlets (*Erythrodiplax berenice*) are the most common resident dragonfly species in or near salt marshes all along the East Coast. The male is pictured here; the females have more bold orange markings on the abdomen. Seaside Dragonlets are unique among dragonflies because they can breed in salt water.

marsh border areas. Both the Black-Legged Tick and the American Dog Tick are common in salt marshes. The Black-Legged Tick is the vector for the Lyme disease spirochete bacteria *Borrelia burgdorferi*. American Dog Ticks can carry such diseases as Rocky Mountain spotted fever.

Birds of the upper marsh

In spring and fall migration and over the winter, Northern Harriers (formerly called Marsh Hawks) and Short-Eared Owls hunt over the salt marshes. Sadly, in recent decades, the Short-Eared Owl population has been sharply reduced owing to the loss of both freshwater and saltwater marsh habitats. Today the sight of the Short-Eared Owl's low, tilting flight over the marsh is an unusual moment to treasure.

Northern Harriers have a happier story. Predatory birds at the top of the food chain, including harri-

Ospreys (*Pandion haliaetus*) are the most visible and numerous large predatory birds above salt marshes, although Bald Eagles are becoming more common along the Mid-Atlantic Coast. The resurgence of Atlantic Menhaden (*Brevoortia tyrannus*) populations along the coast and in the Chesapeake Bay has been good for a wide range of predators, from Osprey and eagles to Humpback Whales and seals. Here the Osprey has just snagged a Menhaden.

Abeselom Zerit

Steve Byland

Northern Harriers (*Circus cyaneus*, also called Marsh Hawks) are a common sight over Mid-Atlantic salt marshes. The distinctive owl-like round face of the harrier is an adaptation to hunting by ear. Harriers sweep over the marsh barely above the tops of the grasses, hoping to surprise a Meadow Vole feeding out in the open.

ers, were almost wiped out by widespread use of the pesticide DDT in the 1950s and 1960s. DDT is a powerful organic chemical that moves easily through food chains and causes fatal egg shell thinning in top predatory birds such as eagles, Ospreys, falcons, and hawks. The birds would lay eggs as normal, but with thin shells the eggs would usually break and die before hatching. With the banning of DDT in the United States in 1972, birds like the Bald Eagle, Osprey, and Norther Harrier began a long, slow recovery that continues today. Harriers are now a common sight all along the coast in every season except the height of summer.

The nearly ubiquitous Red-Tailed Hawk commonly hunts Meadow Voles in the salt marsh. You'll often see American Kestrels perched on dead snags with a good view of the marsh or hovering over the marsh hunting for their prey of larger insects and small mammals.

Meadow Vole
Microtus pennsylvanicus

The larger heron species are usually the most visible birds within the upper marsh, hunting along natural tidal creeks and the straight, artificial mosquito ditches for crabs and small fish. The Great Blue Heron, Great Egret, and Snowy Egret are the most often spotted, but the smaller Green Heron is also common, if less vis-

Willets (*Tringa semipalmata*) commonly nest within or near salt marshes. If a pair of Willets like this one circles over you, calling noisily, try to back off and choose another path if you can. The birds are protecting a nearby nest.

ible, owing to its size and more secretive habits. The even shyer Clapper Rail both feeds and breeds in the upper marsh but is rarely seen because of its retiring nature and preference for activity at dawn and dusk. Black-Crowned Night-Herons prowl marshes at twilight but also commonly fly and feed during daylight hours. Willets often nest in or near the upper marsh, and if you are near a nest, the Willet pair will circle you, calling loudly and displaying their bright white wing stripes as they fly or land nearby. If this happens, please retreat from the area, because a close approach will stress the nesting adults and any nestlings.

Our common gull species also frequent salt marshes in search of food. Besides the birds themselves, you will often see the footprints of Herring and Ring-Billed Gulls in salt pannes and creek banks of salt marshes, where the gulls particularly relish eating fiddler crabs and the larger crab species.

Small songbirds are a significant part of the bird life of the upper marsh. The Seaside Sparrow and the Saltmarsh Sparrow are salt marsh specialists and are rarely seen in other habitats. These marsh sparrow species cling precariously to the tops of marsh grasses while singing their territorial songs but can also behave more like mice than birds, running head-down and low

SWAMP SPARROW
Melospiza georgiana
SONG SPARROW
Melospiza melodia
SEASIDE SPARROW
Ammodramus maritimus
MARSH WREN
Cistothorus palustris
SALTMARSH SPARROW
Ammodramus caudacutus
NELSON'S SPARROW
Ammodramus nelsoni

The Saltmarsh Sparrow is one of North America's most endangered species, owing to the loss of high marsh areas through sea level rise and habitat destruction.

through grasses to avoid detection. Marsh Wrens are the third of the classic salt marsh songbird species, and they are familiar and noisy residents of both saltwater and freshwater marshes.

Snow Geese and Canada Geese

For thousands of years Snow Geese and Canada Geese have migrated from their breeding grounds in the eastern and central Canadian Arctic to winter in the food-rich bays and sounds of the Mid-Atlantic Coast. However, the gigantic geese flocks we see today are a relatively new phenomenon. They have developed over the past 40 years in a complex interaction with the salt marsh and bay environments, our efforts at wildlife management, and the ways geese have adapted to the modern landscape. In the late nineteenth and early twentieth centuries both goose species were hunted to near extinction in the Chesapeake region by market gunners. Conservation efforts over the past century to

Snow Geese (white morph)
Chen caerulescens

As with a number of bird species, Snow Geese come in two varieties, or color morphs: white and blue. White morph Snow Geese are dominant across North America, but blue morph geese are more common in the western United States. In large Snow Geese flocks it's fun to try to spot the tiny number of "Blue Geese."

Snow Goose (blue morph)
Chen caerulescens

Canada Goose
Branta canadensis

Anne Richard

Snow Goose (white morph)
Chen caerulescens

Agami Photo

Snow Goose (blue morph)
Chen caerulescens

save the geese were successful—some would say too successful.

The Canada Goose is so familiar and iconic a symbol of the waterfowl hunting traditions of the Delaware Bay and Chesapeake regions that it is startling to see that the geese are now regarded by most birders as a nuisance—nonmigratory "golf course birds" that plague corporate campuses, park ponds, or any other place with large, inviting lawns near waterways. Humans have offered up such a smorgasbord of food and living spaces to Canada Geese that most of them have stopped migrating north to breed and are now year-round residents of suburbia. In 2012 there were an estimated 81,000 resident Canada Geese in New Jersey and more than a million residents along the US East Coast. Some small percentage of Canada Geese still migrate to the Mid-Atlantic Coast as their ancestors did, but most Canada Geese you see today are resident in the region.

The large population of Canada Geese causes problems in both the wild and built environments by overgrazing, grubbing, and trampling salt marshes and farm fields and overfertilizing wetland ponds and marshes with their feces. Of course, the geese didn't cause the problems, we did. After hundreds of years of indiscriminate killing and the loss of much of their natural habitat, Canada Geese have simply adapted to their new surroundings, and they are thriving.

The story with Snow Geese is similar, except that Snow Geese have adapted to the modern human addiction to corn products and have found an almost limitless supply of food in the Mid-Atlantic Coast farm fields that surround the Delaware and Chesapeake Bays. The mechanical harvesters that farmers use to manage thousands of acres of cornfields in the region leave behind lots of corn kernels and other edibles. The combination of aquatic habitat conservation, hunting regulations, and a huge new food supply have resulted in a 300 percent increase in Snow Goose populations since the mid-1970s.

So enjoy the vast flocks of waterfowl in our region. We once did almost everything possible to drive them

Salt marsh creek on Sinepuxent Bay, at Assateague Island National Seashore, Maryland.

Eastern Cottontail
Sylvilagus floridanus

moosehenderson

The Marsh Rabbit (*Sylvilagus palustris*) is a dark, stocky relative of Cottontails, but it has a dark tail, not a white one. Marsh Rabbits range from the lower Chesapeake region south to Florida.

Eastern Redcedar (*Juniperus virginiana*) is one of the most common tree species along the borders of salt marshes and at the seaward edges of maritime forests.

to extinction, and yet, against all odds, the birds are florishing. Once in a long while, the wild birds win.

Mammals of the upper marsh

The upper platform of salt marshes creates a dry enough habitat to attract mammals, at least as a hunting ground. A few smaller mammals live in the marsh itself. Although you won't often see them, mouselike Meadow Voles are common in the upper marsh, and these voles attract Northern Harriers, Red-Tailed Hawks, and other predatory birds to the upper salt marsh to hunt for food. Muskrats are common in brackish salt marshes that transition to freshwater wetlands. Raccoons are clever and versatile omnivores that frequently enter the upper salt marsh in search of mussels, crabs, and other small animals. Raccoons are chiefly nocturnal, but you can find their tracks in salt pannes or along creek banks in the marsh.

Although the Eastern Cottontail rarely grazes in the upper marsh, rabbits are very common in coastal parklands with grassy areas next to salt marshes.

The upper borders of the salt marsh

Four dominant border plants allow you to see the marsh border above the maximum high-tide line. Marsh Elder is the classic high-tide bush and the most visible marker for the salt marsh border. Once you can identify Marsh Elder, you will be able to read the marsh quickly, because Marsh Elder typically grows in a narrow band right up against the mean spring high water line, where it must tolerate some salt water in storms. But Marsh Elder is not competitive enough with more terrestrial shrubs and grasses to spread far beyond the MSHW line. Switchgrass joins Marsh Elder along the marsh border but also spreads into more upland areas along the marsh border, and Switchgrass is also common in other coastal environments like upper beaches. Groundsel Tree is another shrub that grows near the MSHW line, but it is usually found on ground a bit higher and farther back from the marsh edge. The fourth highly visible marsh edge plant is Seaside Goldenrod, which is sparse within the high marsh but becomes very common in marsh border areas.

The invasion of Phragmites

BLACK CHERRY *Prunus serotina*

WAX MYRTLE *Morella cerifera*

WINGED SUMAC *Rhus copallina*

STAGHORN SUMAC *Rhus typhina*

NORTHERN BAYBERRY *Myrica pensylvanica*

BEACH PLUM *Prunus maritima*

Common Reed, or Phragmites
Phragmites australis australis

Along virtually all Mid-Atlantic Coast salt marsh borders, there are stands of the invasive Eurasian subspecies of the Common Reed (*Phragmites australis australis*), often called Phragmites. Phragmites is particularly well adapted to disturbed ground that is a little saltier than average, although this reed species is so adaptable that it can live in just about any wetland area except true salt marshes, where it inhabits the marsh border.

Sonja Guijarro

Plants are not the only troublesome invasive species on the Mid-Atlantic Coast. The Nutria (*Myocastor coypus*) is an aquatic rodent similar to, but much larger than, our native Muskrat (*Ondatra zibethicus*). Nutria were introduced into the region by fur farmers. Nutria eat the roots and rhizomes of marsh plants, and their feeding habits cause severe harm to marshes throughout the Chesapeake Bay region.

Biologists differ on the ecological value of Phragmites as a food source. For decades the environmentalists' view of Phragmites was that it was a cancer on the landscape, driving out native plants while supplying little nutritive value to wetland ecosystems. Recent research on the impact of Phragmites provides a more balanced view, showing that Phragmites does contribute useful primary productivity and biomass to coastal and wetland ecosystems, albeit not to the same degree that such displaced native plants as the Narrow-Leaved Cattail formerly provided.

Salt marsh conservation

Thanks mainly to progress through the modern

environmental movement, there is now a broader societal understanding of the ecological importance of wetlands and the economic and practical value of natural coastal habitats. However, there isn't a square inch of the Atlantic Coast that hasn't been heavily influenced or thoroughly modified by human activity. Over the past 300 years, more than half of the region's salt marsh habitat has been lost to filling and development. The story in our region is not unique—of the approximately 220 million acres of salt marsh present throughout North America in precontact times, only about 104 million acres are intact today.

Much of the open water at Blackwater National Wildlife Refuge in Maryland was salt marsh 30–40 years ago. Since that time, sea level rise and storm erosion have claimed almost 8,000 acres of wetlands in the refuge. As areas of brackish and fresh marshes become flooded with salt water from the Chesapeake Bay, the unique plants of those ecosystems are lost. The situation is similar at many other Chesapeake Bay and Delaware Bay marshes. The combination of damage from populations of nonnative Nutria, sea level rise, and erosion from storms has done terrible damage to Mid-Atlantic coastal marshes.

In the past 40 years, the realization of the importance of protecting both inland and coastal wetlands has driven state and federal legal protections for wetland areas. But tidal salt marshes continue to face a host of threats beyond potential burial under new shoreline construction projects. Owing to both long-term climate change and the more recent acceleration of global warming and sea level rise, salt marshes are now in a critical period. The accelerating rise in sea level may be too fast for our existing marshes to adapt.

In many locations, you can see the remains of former salt marshes along what are now becoming shallow tidal flats or shallow open water. Large, dark chunks of salt marsh peat, the remains of former marshes, lie surrounded by mud and water. The peat gradually washes away in storms, and all traces of the former marsh vanish.

On the Mid-Atlantic Coast, the sea level has risen about 18 inches over the past three centuries. In recent years Hurricanes Irene, Florence, and Dorian have torn away large chunks of salt marsh in many areas of the East Coast. The extratropical Superstorm Sandy did massive damage to salt marshes in New Jersey and on the Delmarva coast, but those same marshes saved many coastal communities from further destruction by absorbing the brunt of storm surge waves. Most smaller salt marshes are situated in more protected bays and inlets and suffered less damage in recent storms. But all of these salt marshes face the same ultimate challenge—today the marshes are ringed by roads and houses, and as the sea rises, there is no room for the marshes to retreat from the higher water.

Change comes slowly in salt marshes. Mosquito control ditches that were cut into many of the region's larger salt marshes in the mid-1930s still remain open after many decades. The ditches accomplished little to control mosquitos. Yet they exist to this day as reminders of how even such a productive ecosystem as the salt marsh may not be able to repair itself and adapt within human time scales.

Among all the grim news for wildlife there are also success stories. Since the US banning of DDT in 1972, populations of Bald Eagles and Ospreys, which had

Salt marshes and a bit of maritime woods along the shore of Sinepuxent Bay at Assateague Island National Seashore, Maryland. Assateague is an excellent place to see coastal Bald Eagles,Ospreys, and, in the fall, migrating hawks and Peregrine Falcons.

been decimated, have made a spectacular recovery, and these magnificent birds are now common sights along the Mid-Atlantic Coast.

A young (fourth year) Bald Eagle. It takes four to five years for Bald Eagles to acquire the solid brown plumage with bright white head and tail. *Eagle photo courtesy of Janis Blanton.*

The Blackwater National Wildlife Refuge contains about one-third of Maryland's wetlands, with about 28,000 acres of salt and brackish marshes and coastal forest areas.

Estuaries and Brackish Marshes

The Edwin B. Forsythe National Wildlife Refuge on the shores of Manahawkin Bay in southern New Jersey is a gorgeous complex of salt and brackish marshes, managed for migrating waterfowl. About 78 percent of Forsythe is salt marsh. The marsh pictured above is a brackish marsh with both freshwater and saltwater plant species. Forsythe is famed for its excellent birding, particularly in the spring and fall migration seasons.

An estuary is a semi-enclosed body of water where freshwater from rivers mixes with salt water from the ocean. Estuaries are extraordinarily productive environments and are the nurseries and feeding grounds for most of our coastal wildlife.

The large estuaries of the Mid-Atlantic Coast originated as deep river valleys when the sea level was much lower than today. At the peak of the Wisconsinan Glaciation (the Ice Age) 25,000 years ago, so much of the earth's water was bound up in ice that the sea level was 400 feet lower than today (see map, pp. 20–21). The Hudson, Delaware, Susquehanna, Potomac, James, and other rivers cut deep channels through the Mid-Atlantic Coastal Plain and the continental shelf beyond. As the Wisconsinan Glaciation ended, the planet warmed. Sea levels rose and flooded the river valleys, creating the Delaware and Chesapeake Bays, as well as the Albemarle and Pamlico Sounds behind the Outer Banks of North Carolina (see map, p. xiii). Geologists call these flooded river channels drowned river valleys, and most of the large estuaries of the US East Coast originated in this way.

Some 80–90 percent of the Mid-Atlantic Coast consists of estuaries, along with the lagoon and sound shorelines associated with the barrier islands and peninsulas. The sounds and bays behind the barrier

Salt and brackish marshes have an enormous capacity to filter and trap sediments—and pollutants—in coastal waters. The combination of marsh grass stems, Ribbed Mussels (*Geukensia demissa*, shown), and the bacteria, algae, and diatoms on the marsh surface all combine to make a perfect natural filtration system for coastal waters. In this time of climate change and intensifying storms, marshes also act as a protective buffer against waves and storm surges.

islands are called bar-built estuaries, particularly where rivers meet the coast and mix with ocean water to form brackish waters.

Salinity in estuaries

Ocean water has a salinity of about 32–35 parts of salt per thousand parts of water, or 32–35 ppt. The freshwater flowing into estuaries has almost no salt, about 0.5 ppt or less. Everything between salt water and freshwater is defined as brackish water. The central bodies of estuaries like the Delaware and Chesapeake Bays have brackish salinities ranging from 10–25 ppt, but near the ocean mouths, salinities can range as high as 30 ppt.

The salt content of estuaries can vary dramatically over short periods, as well as by the season of the year. Heavy storm rainfalls resulting in river flooding push large volumes of freshwater into estuaries and can quickly lower the salinity of even a large estuary such as the Chesapeake Bay. Estuary plants and animals must be able to adapt to significant swings in salinity, particularly in spring and fall and after storms, including hurricanes and nor'easters.

Environmental filtration in estuaries

The interaction of freshwater and salt water is chemically much more complicated than just varying salinities. Although river water has little or no salt, rivers carry large volumes of silt and organic particles from the land into estuary waters. Large river-borne particles such as sand grains settle out of the water through gravity alone. Still, the biochemical interactions of tiny silt particles, salt water, and freshwater also act to aggregate the fine silt particles and cause them to settle to the bottom. This chemical process is vital in helping estuaries capture silt and sediments so that they eventually become integrated into mudflats and tidal wetlands rather than washing out to sea with each tide. Unfortunately, the vast oyster beds that used to filter estuary waters are now gone due to overharvesting and diseases introduced by humans. Without filtering by oysters, many estuary waters have become too murky to support seagrass beds, an essential component of estuary health. Although rivers in flood can

Opposite: True freshwater marshes sometimes exist near brackish marshes and even ocean beaches. Often the only way to distinguish marsh types is to examine the plant species. This freshwater marsh on New Jersey's Cape May Point is only a short walk from the ocean beach. Even though this marsh is fresh, it is not free from the influence of salt aerosols (salt spray), which can damage plants and stunt nearby forests.

Small coastal freshwater wetlands also benefit from some salt spray: the salt introduces vital mineral nutrients to sandy areas that are naturally poor in minerals.

The beautiful freshwater marshes of Cape May Point State Park, New Jersey, exist entirely on a base of sand less than a quarter mile from an ocean beach.

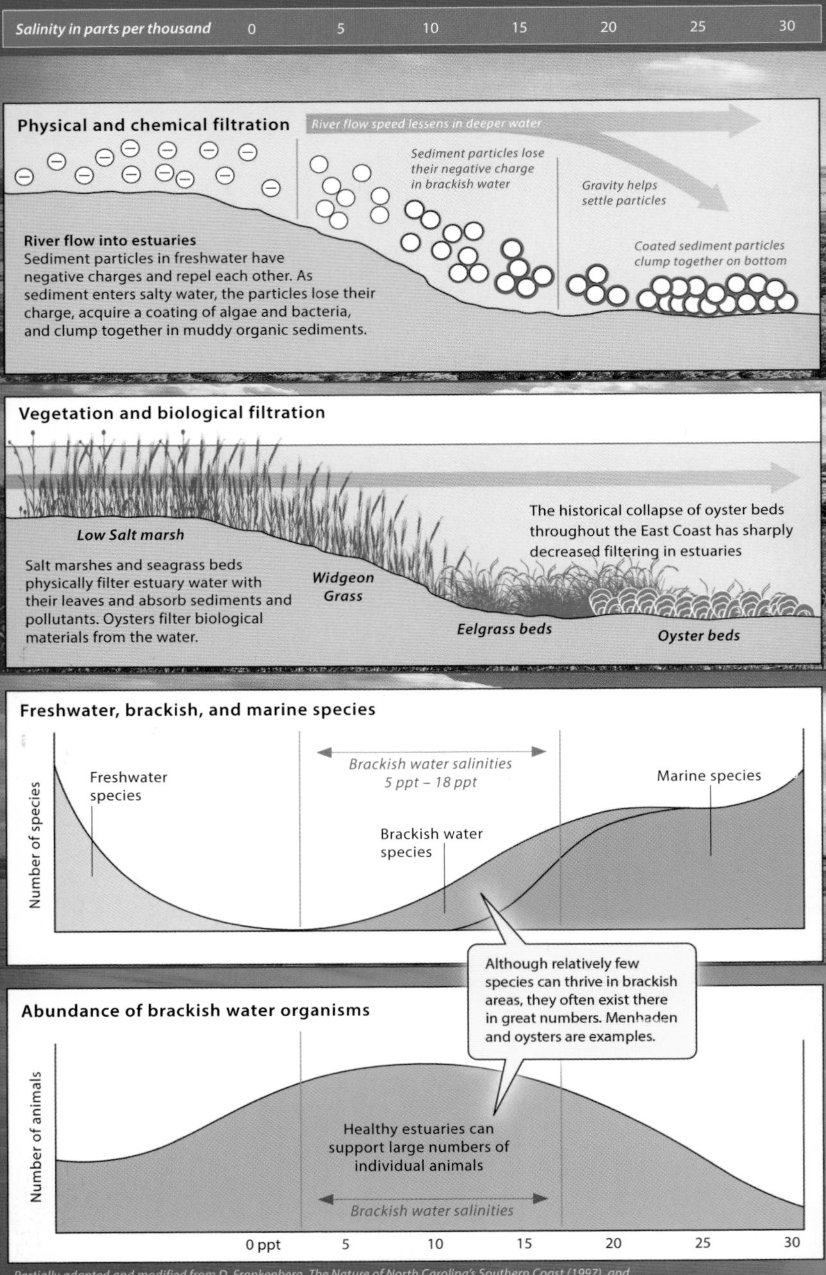

Salinity in parts per thousand
0
5
10
15
20
25
30
Physical and chemical filtration
River flow speed lessens in deeper water
Sediment particles lose their negative charge in brackish water
Gravity helps settle particles
Coated sediment particles clump together on bottom
River flow into estuaries
Sediment particles in freshwater have negative charges and repel each other. As sediment enters salty water, the particles lose their charge, acquire a coating of algae and bacteria, and clump together in muddy organic sediments.
Vegetation and biological filtration
The historical collapse of oyster beds throughout the East Coast has sharply decreased filtering in estuaries
Low Salt marsh
Salt marshes and seagrass beds physically filter estuary water with their leaves and absorb sediments and pollutants. Oysters filter biological materials from the water.
Widgeon Grass
Eelgrass beds
Oyster beds
Freshwater, brackish, and marine species
Brackish water salinities 5 ppt – 18 ppt
Freshwater species
Marine species
Brackish water species
Number of species
Although relatively few species can thrive in brackish areas, they often exist there in great numbers. Menhaden and oysters are examples.
Abundance of brackish water organisms
Number of animals
Healthy estuaries can support large numbers of individual animals
Brackish water salinities
0 ppt
5
10
15
20
25
30

Partially adapted and modified from D. Frankenberg, The Nature of North Carolina's Southern Coast (1997), and P. Webb, Introduction to Oceanography (2019), https://rwu.pressbooks.pub/webboceanography

Physical, chemical, and biological properties of estuaries

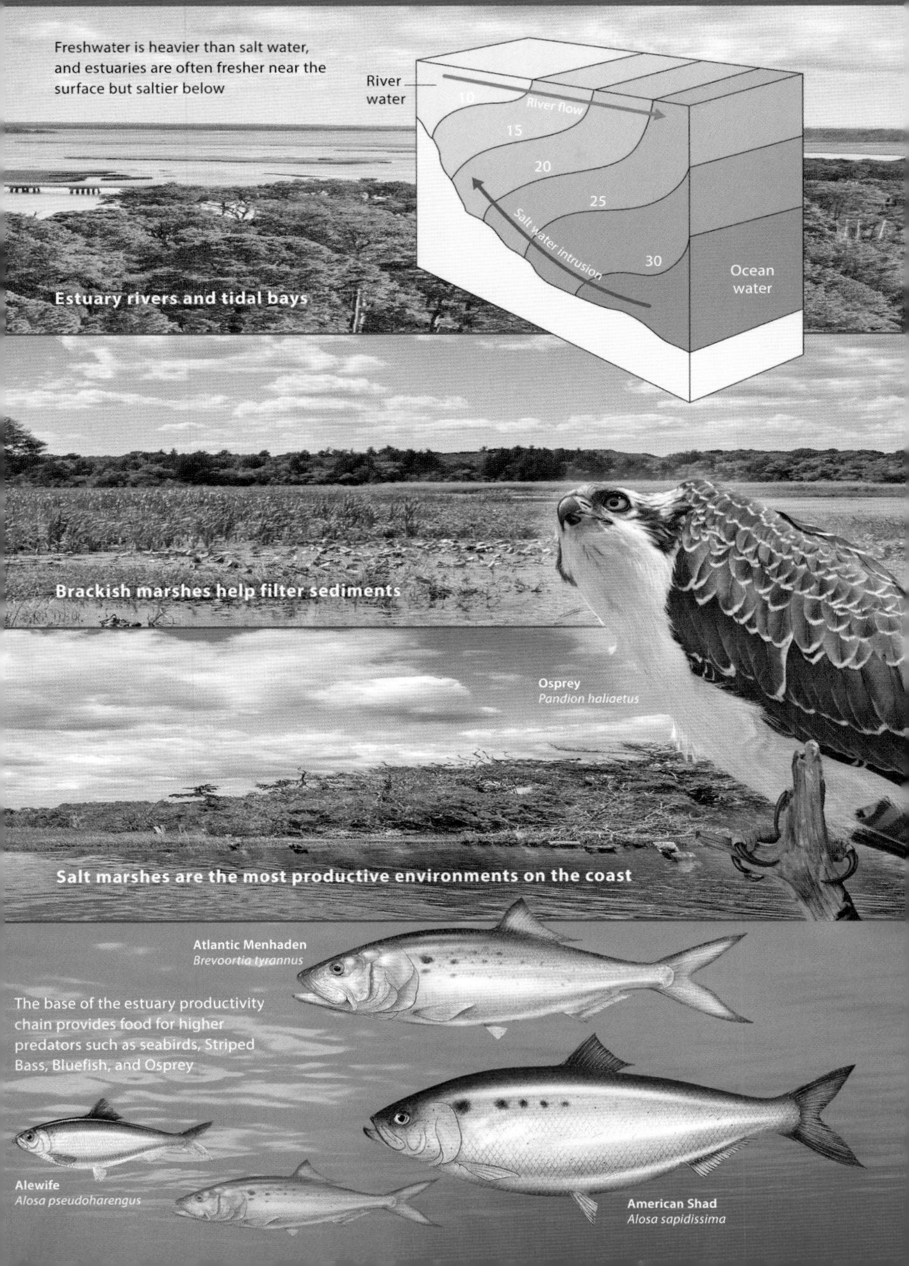
Freshwater is heavier than salt water, and estuaries are often fresher near the surface but saltier below
River water
River flow
10
15
20
25
30
Salt water intrusion
Ocean water
Estuary rivers and tidal bays
Brackish marshes help filter sediments
Osprey
Pandion haliaetus
Salt marshes are the most productive environments on the coast
Atlantic Menhaden
Brevoortia tyrannus
The base of the estuary productivity chain provides food for higher predators such as seabirds, Striped Bass, Bluefish, and Osprey
Alewife
Alosa pseudoharengus
American Shad
Alosa sapidissima

Thongdumhyu

Clam Worm
Nereis succinea

carry huge volumes of silt and sand into estuary bays, the geochemical actions within estuary waters capture most sand and silt particles within the bottoms, tidal flats, and coastal marshes. Little river sediment on the East Coast now reaches the Atlantic Ocean.

Biological diversity (the number of species) in estuaries may be lower than either freshwater or ocean environments. Few organisms can tolerate the mixed estuary water, which is too fresh for ocean species and too salty for freshwater species. However, animals and plants that are adapted to estuary conditions can be very numerous, and this accounts for the high overall biological productivity of estuaries.

Tidal flats

Subtidal areas with sandy or muddy bottoms have a rich infauna of animals that burrow into the bottom sediments for shelter. Most clams and marine worms, some crabs, and even some fish bury themselves at least partially as protection in flat bottom areas that often lack rock or plant shelter. Animals that live primarily on or just above the bottom surface are called epifauna. These include most of the familiar shoreline crabs, which welcome rock crevices or Eelgrass patches as a shelter but don't usually dig burrows in the warmer months.

geraldmarella

Seemingly lifeless, tidal flats are in fact loaded with animal life below the mud surface and form a crucial habitat for migrating shorebirds. Here a Black-Bellied Plover (*Pluvialis squatarola*) in nonbreeding plumage pulls a Bloodworm (*Glycera* sp.) from the mud.

Segmented worms and other bottom infauna

Along with the familiar clams, soft sand and mud bottoms contain a complex community of segmented worms known as the bristle worms or polychaetes. Clam Worms and Bloodworms are two of the most common types of larger worms and are familiar as bait for sport fishers. Both move freely through the bottom sediments in search of small animal prey, including clams and other worms. Some marine worms are sessile (fixed in place), building permanent or semipermanent tubes in the mud from which they project their feeding appendages. Ice cream cone worms, bamboo worms, amphitrite worms, and feather duster worms are filter feeders, using their tentacles to grab plankton or small bits of organic material from the flowing water. Bottom worms are very sensitive to any vibration or unusual water movement near them and will quickly disappear into their tubes under the surface. The best tactic to observe bottom life is to find a likely spot in shallow, clear water, approach the area with care, stand stock-still, and wait patiently until the bottom dwellers cautiously resume their normal feeding behavior.

Subtidal zone

The subtidal zone lies from the lowest tide line down to about 20 feet. At this level, life is truly aquatic, although many crabs visit lower intertidal zones in search of food, particularly at night. Because these permanently submerged shallows receive enough sunlight for plant growth, most seaweeds (macroalgae) live in this zone, as do Eelgrass and Widgeon Grass. Wave action shapes this environment both physically, through the continually churning waves and their resulting shore currents, and chemically, through supplying oxygen and nutrients. For sessile filter feeders such as barnacles and mussels, the constant water movement is critical to life, ensuring a steady supply of food. Beyond 10 feet of water depth, the algae and seagrass populations drop sharply owing to the low

Using its unmistakable orange bill, the American Oystercatcher (*Haematopus palliatus*) specializes in slicing open bivalves such as oysters, clams, and mussels, which are abundant in healthy tidal flats and the shallow subtidal zone.

Invertebrates in and near the bottom sediments of the subtidal zone.

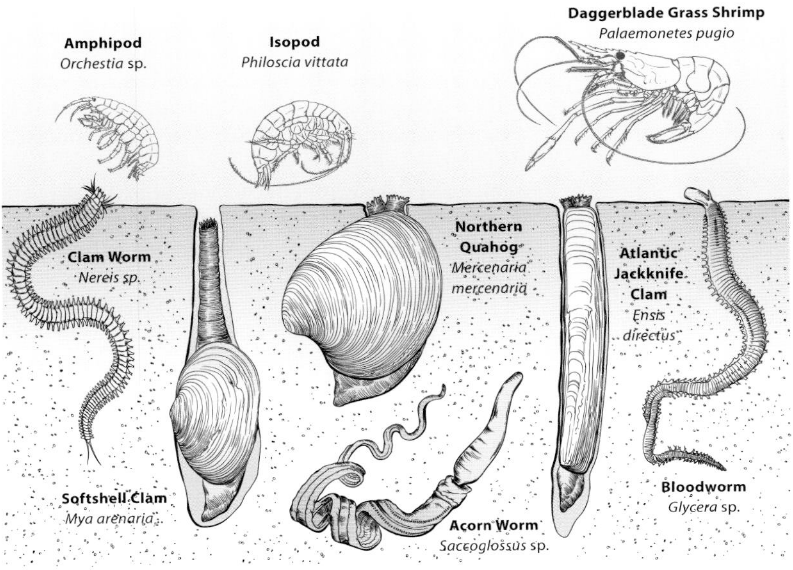
Amphipod
Orchestia sp.
Isopod
Philoscia vittata
Daggerblade Grass Shrimp
Palaemonetes pugio
Clam Worm
Nereis sp.
Northern Quahog
Mercenaria mercenaria
Atlantic Jackknife Clam
Ensis directus
Softshell Clam
Mya arenaria
Acorn Worm
Saccoglossus sp.
Bloodworm
Glycera sp.

Northern Quahog
Mercenaria mercenaria

Softshell Clam
Mya arenaria

Atlantic Jackknife Clam
Ensis directus

light levels. At about 20 feet, the properties of wave action, superheating in summer, supercooling in winter, and intertidal species' depth limits quickly make the environment more like deeper bottom conditions.

Border zones between one environment and another, or ecotones, are the most productive environments. As a transition zone between tidal areas and deeper waters, the subtidal zone is one of the most productive zones of estuaries. Many open-water fish spend early life in the relative safety of shallows, particularly where Eelgrass beds and rocky bottoms with crevices offer hiding places. Larger predators such as Bluefish and Striped Bass sweep through the shallows for prey, and many wading and diving birds specialize in picking off unwary crabs, fish, and shrimp that live in a few feet of water. Ospreys glide high above, looking for the slightest movements from such favored prey as small flounders and Atlantic Menhaden.

Clams

Soft sediment bottoms and tidal flats such as those that line the shores of estuaries can look deceptively lifeless unless you look for the single or paired siphons of clams buried within them. Northern Quahogs have short, paired siphons, and the top edge of their shells is rarely buried more than an inch below the surface. In smooth sand or mud bottoms, look for a figure eight of the twin open siphon holes. Quahogs are called by a variety of names based on their size, but littlenecks, cherrystones, chowder clams, and quahogs are all the same species: the Northern Quahog. Softshell Clams, or steamers, have an extremely long, sturdy pair of siphons encased in a thick black membrane. The long siphons allow the Softshell Clams to bury themselves far below other clams, sometimes 10 inches deep. The Atlantic Jackknife Clam, or razor clam, has a very short siphon that looks keyhole-shaped at the surface. These clams bury themselves vertically with a short but strong foot on the lower end opposite the siphon. Atlantic Jackknife Clams sometimes pop up above the surface, often when disturbed by mud worms probing their burrows from below. If a Jackknife Clam senses movement, it disappears in a flash into its burrow.

Island Beach State Park, New Jersey, on a barrier island just north of Barnegat Inlet. The marshes here along the Barnegat Bay shore of the park are healthy but warn of trouble ahead. The trees on the former high ground of this marsh island are dying as salt water rises to infiltrate the soil. The high salt meadows surrounding the island are now barely above the normal high-tide line, indicating that they will soon become low salt marsh.

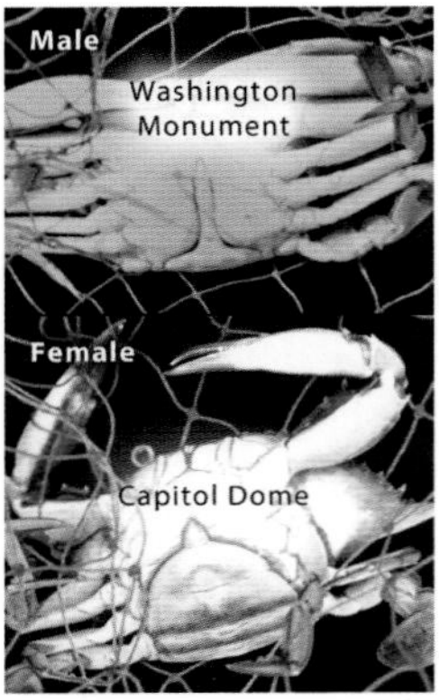
Male
Washington Monument
Female
Capitol Dome

Sexing Blue Crabs: The male abdominal apron has the thin outline of the Washington Monument; the female abdomen shows a thick outline of the Capitol Dome.

significant instances of a European animal that made the jump across the Atlantic, probably by riding on the mossy bottoms of sailing ships or in wet ballast stones dumped overboard in a Massachusetts port. Since 1817, the Green Crab has spread along the Atlantic Coast from Nova Scotia down to Cape May, New Jersey. Green Crabs are voracious omnivores, favoring small crabs, mussels, and Softshell Clams. Still, there may be a hidden positive side to Green Crabs: researchers at Brown University have discovered that salt marshes with Green Crabs are healthier because the Green Crabs prey on abundant Purple Marsh Crabs, which eat marsh grasses.

The shells of these common subtidal crab species are often found along the wrack line of beaches and marshes, but that does not always mean that crabs have died or been killed by predators. Hard-shelled animals like crabs must molt their old shells to grow, and most crab species molt several times during the warm months. Molted carapace and claw shells that wash up on the shoreline are clean, with no organic matter inside, and are generally whole and in good condition. Crabs killed by gulls or herons are smashed and thoroughly dismembered, often on a rock or other hard surface, and you usually don't find the remains along the wrack line.

In spite of its intimidating looks, the Common Spider Crab is a sluggish and inoffensive member of the deeper subtidal community, where it largely scavenges the remains of other bottom invertebrates. Spider Crabs prefer the deeper waters of the bays and harbors but are also common in shallow seagrass communities.

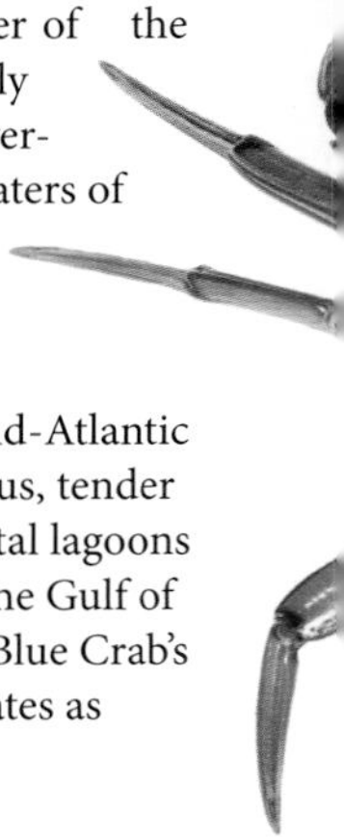

Blue Crabs

Blue Crabs are a foundation species for Mid-Atlantic Coastal estuaries. Famous for their delicious, tender meat, the crabs are found in brackish coastal lagoons and estuaries from Nova Scotia, through the Gulf of Mexico, and as far south as Uruguay. The Blue Crab's scientific name, *Callinectes sapidus*, translates as "beautiful savory swimmer."

Today Blue Crabs are the most valuable fishery in the Chesapeake Bay. Still, Blue Crab populations in the Chesapeake go through cycles of boom and bust, and that makes it challenging to manage the commercial harvest. Blue Crab populations naturally fluctuate with annual changes in environmental conditions, mainly due to habitat loss or degradation in water clarity. The hurricanes of 2018 caused significant inundations of muddy freshwater into the Chesapeake Bay, and this damaged the seagrass meadows that are crucial to young Blue Crabs. In 2018 approximately 147 million mature female crabs were estimated to be in the bay; that number was significantly down from a population peak of around 455 million crabs in prior decades.

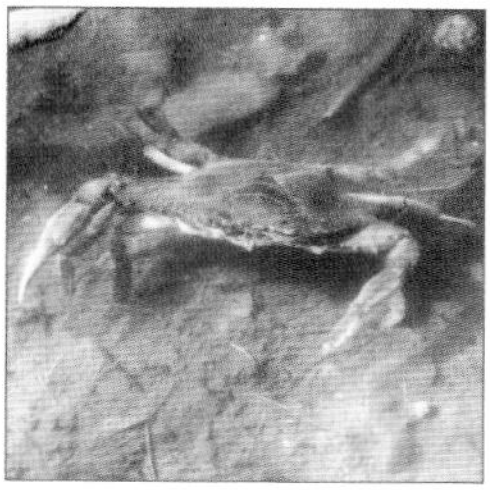

A Blue Crab quietly patrols a salt marsh creek, drifting a few inches above the creek bottom, seeking whatever small animal life it can capture. Blue Crabs are excellent swimmers and navigate the creeks easily.

Blue Crabs are aggressive predators wherever they live, and they take many kinds of bottom-dwelling invertebrates, small clams, and fish, as well as scavenging for dead items. Young Blue Crabs fall prey to Striped Bass, Bluefish, Cownose Rays, and other predatory fish, but

Blue Crab
Callinectes sapidus

Female Blue Crabs have particularly colorful claws, tipped in red "fingernail polish." The greenish rear legs are for swimming and allow the Blue Crab to move rapidly through the water to catch prey or avoid predators like herons and gulls.

Photo: Igor Dudchak

For a more detailed look at the complex relationship of Horseshoe Crabs and Red Knot shorebirds, see this modern natural history classic:

The Narrow Edge: A Tiny Bird, an Ancient Crab, and an Epic Journey, by Deborah Cramer. New Haven: Yale University Press, 2015.

most adult Blue Crabs are large enough to drive off or escape from all but the largest predators. In New Jersey waters Blue Crabs overlap with populations of the similarly sized Green Crab, where they compete with (and occasionally eat) each other.

Male and female Blue Crabs don't look alike, and thus can be sexed easily (see illustration, p. 370). Males have blue-tipped claws and a narrow abdominal apron that is shaped like the Washington Monument. Females have red-tipped claws, and mature females have an abdominal apron shaped like the US Capitol Dome in Washington.

Blue Crabs are highly mobile within the Chesapeake Bay. More females are caught in the southern part of the Chesapeake because females migrate to areas of higher salinity near the mouth of the bay to lay their eggs, whereas males tend to stay in the central part of the bay in less saline waters.

Horseshoe Crabs

The Atlantic Horseshoe Crab is an unmistakable member of the tidal and subtidal communities, with its distinct shape, hard-leather shell, and menacing-looking (but harmless) long tail. Horseshoe Crabs are not true crabs at all but members of the ancient order Xiphosura, which also contains spiders and mites. They favor sandy or muddy bottoms and normally live at the deeper end of the subtidal zone, where they plow through the bottom, feeding on small invertebrates. In May and June, Horseshoe Crabs travel into the low tidal zone to lay eggs, often during a spring (unusually high) tide. These eggs are very attractive to shorebirds, and a good indication that the crabs are breeding is the sight of flocks of birds avidly picking at the eggs in the surf line. Commercial fishers also harvest Horseshoe Crabs for bait. The Atlantic Coast population of these sea creatures has fallen sharply over the past 40 years owing to overharvesting and the destruction of beach habitat.

Red Knots feeding on Horseshoe Crab eggs on the shores of Delaware Bay.

Atlantic Horseshoe Crab blood is the sole source of an essential medical compound—limulus amebocyte lysate (LAL)—used to test for the presence of harmful bacterial toxins in human blood. Drug manufacturers use LAL to test the safety of pharmaceutical and medical devices that contain blood products. Horseshoe Crabs are not usually killed in harvesting LAL. The animals are caught, their blood is drawn, and they are returned to the wild. About 60 percent of Horseshoe Crabs survive the experience.

At one time, Horseshoe Crabs were so abundant and so prolific in laying eggs in springtime that the migrating population of shorebirds like the Red Knot became dependent upon the eggs as a food source. Each spring, Red Knots undertake a heroic migration north from South America, flying long distances over the Atlantic Ocean before making landfall along the Mid-Atlantic Coast, particularly around Delaware Bay. As the hungry, exhausted Knots landed, they were formerly greeted with an almost limitless supply of freshly laid Horseshoe Crab eggs, which provided more than enough fuel to recover their fat reserves for the long journey north into the Canadian Arctic. Unfortunately, reckless overharvesting has dramatically reduced Atlantic Horseshoe Crab populations from Cape Cod down to the Carolinas, and the Red Knot popula-

Red Knot
Calidris canutus

Atlantic Horseshoe Crab
Limulus polyphemus
Eggs (inset, lower left); baby crabs in early summer; and a tagged crab (inset, upper right). If you spot a tagged crab, please follow the instructions and report it. The research will help protect this species from overharvesting.

Photos courtesy of Frank Gallo

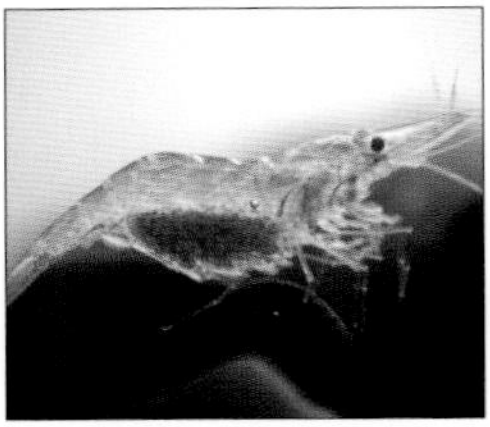
Daggerblade Grass Shrimp
Palaemonetes pugio

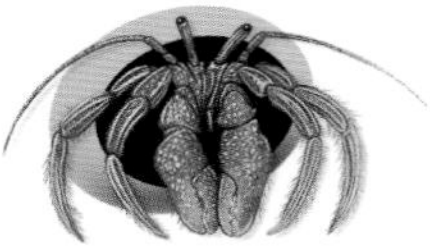
Long-Clawed Hermit Crab
Pagurus longicarpus

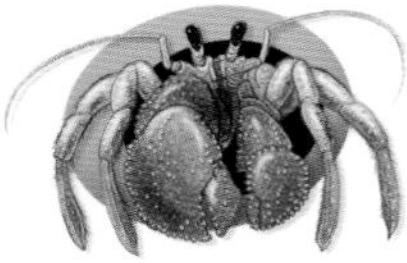
Flat-Clawed Hermit Crab
Pagurus pollicaris

tion has dropped steeply as a result. There is evidence of another problem for Red Knots: as the earth has warmed, Horseshoe Crabs are breeding earlier in the spring. This disrupts the migration of Red Knots, since the birds now arrive after the peak of Horseshoe Crab egg-laying.

Other crustaceans

Two other types of small crustaceans are commonly found in the subtidal zone: hermit crabs and grass shrimp (also called prawns). Colored a pale, translucent gray, grass shrimp are an essential link in the estuary food chain. They feed on detritus—the remains of salt marsh grasses and other plants washed into bays and coastal waters. The nibbling of millions of grass shrimp breaks down plants into particles that become food for small zooplankton and bacteria, which complete the process of turning old marsh grasses into animal biomass. The shrimp are an important food source for larger predators such as crabs, the young of many fish species, and birds. Hermit crabs are important scavengers on the subtidal zone, feeding on detritus and animal remains. Hermit crabs do not grow their shells; instead, they adopt the discarded shells of snails for protection and shelter. The small Long-Clawed Hermit Crab is common in both rocky and sandy or muddy bottoms in the subtidal zone and usually inhabits old snail shells. The larger Flat-Clawed Hermit Crab prefers deeper waters with rocky or shell bottoms and usually picks larger homes such as old Moon Snail shells or small whelk shells.

Striped Bass (Rockfish)
Morone saxatilis

A beautiful brackish marsh at the Currituck Banks Reserve, in Corolla, North Carolina, on the Outer Banks. In the foreground and along the creek edges is Big Cordgrass (Spartina cynosuroides), a sure sign of a brackish marsh.

A single Eelgrass plant (*Zostera marina*), with rhizomes (underground stems) and roots showing.

Brant
Branta bernicla

Subtidal and brackish marsh fish

Small fish, including Atlantic Silverside, Striped Killifish, and Sand Lance, and the young of such larger fish as Bluefish and Striped Bass frequent the subtidal zone, particularly where vegetation can shelter them from larger predatory fish. The subtidal zone and seagrass meadows are the great nursery areas of coastal waters, providing a wealth of food and protection for virtually all the major fish species of the Mid-Atlantic Coast. Striped Bass (Rockfish), Alewife, American Butterfish, American Shad, Atlantic Menhaden (Bunker), Black Sea Bass, Blueback Herring, Fluke, Scup (Northern Porgy), Smooth and Spiny Dogfish sharks, Tautog (Blackfish), and Summer Flounder are just some of the species that depend on the subtidal zones of estuaries for a portion of their lives.

Seagrass communities

Eelgrass and Widgeon Grass beds develop in shallow-water areas with soft bottom sediments. Eelgrass is widespread all along the coasts of the North Atlantic Ocean and is the dominant seagrass species north of Cape Hatteras on the East Coast. A critical component of all our large estuaries, Eelgrass is a flowering grass (family Zosteraceae) that has adapted to life in saltwater. It spreads primarily through underground stems called rhizomes within the bottom sediments. The thick tangle of Eelgrass rhizomes stabilizes soft sediments and keeps the plants from washing away. In estuaries all along the Mid-Atlantic Coast, young Blue Crabs and other crustaceans shelter from predators in seagrass. A single acre of seagrass can support nearly 40,000 fish and 50 million small invertebrates, making seagrass meadows one of the most productive coastal ecosystems.

Healthy Eelgrass and Widgeon Grass beds offer both food and shelter to the young of many fish species, as well as adult fish. Atlantic Silverside, Spot, Tautog (Blackfish), and Summer Flounder all find shelter in seagrass meadows. The many small fish also attract predators: Bluefish and Striped Bass cruise the meadows in search of prey, and many bird species find food in the Eelgrass. Dabbling ducks, geese, and swans eat the grasses directly. Diving ducks such as the Red-

NORTHERN PIPEFISH
Syngnathus fuscus
ATLANTIC SILVERSIDE
Menidia menidia
TAUTOG (BLACKFISH)
Tautoga onitis
BAY SCALLOP
Argopecten irradians
BLUE CRAB
Callinectes sapidus
NORTHERN QUAHOG
Mercenaria mercenaria
COMMON SEA STAR
Asterias rubens
LINED SEAHORSE
Hippocampus erectus
BAY SCALLOP
Argopecten irradians
ATLANTIC
HORSESHOE CRAB
Limulus polyphemus
Blue Crab: Kim Nguyen;
Atlantic Horseshoe Crab: Ethan Daniels.

Forest & Kim Starr

Widgeon Grass
Ruppia maritima

Breasted Merganser and Bufflehead pick off young fish, shrimp, snails, and worms living within the Eelgrass. In shallower seagrass areas, long-legged waders such as the Great Blue Heron and the Great Egret stab for fish and shrimp in the meadows. Historically Eelgrass was the primary food of Brant, a common small goose that winters in Long Island Sound and along ocean coasts of the Jersey Shore. After a population crash of Eelgrass (and Brant) in the 1930s, Brant have gradually shifted to eating Sea Lettuce and other algae, and Brant populations have recovered.

Eelgrass is not the only marine flowering plant species in Mid-Atlantic estuaries. Widgeon Grass also grows in Eelgrass beds and is an important food source for many diving and dabbling duck species (a wigeon—slightly different spelling—is a kind of dabbling duck). The leaves of Widgeon Grass are much more slender than those of Eelgrass, and they are eagerly sought by American Wigeons, American Black Ducks, scaup, teals, and other coastal ducks. Sea Lettuce is usually abundant in Eelgrass beds as well. In the Chesapeake, Eelgrass is the more common grass in the areas of higher salinity in the south of the bay, and Widgeon Grass dominates seagrass beds in the more brackish central bay areas.

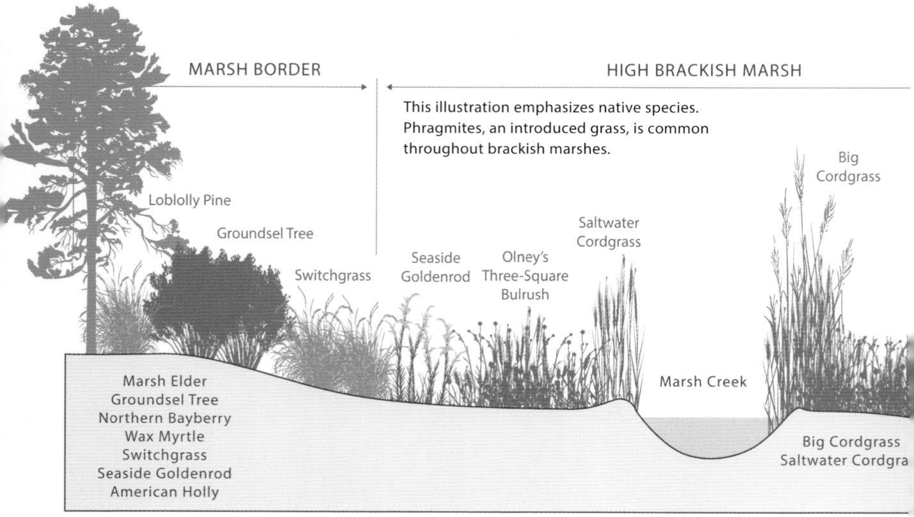
MARSH BORDER
HIGH BRACKISH MARSH
This illustration emphasizes native species. Phragmites, an introduced grass, is common throughout brackish marshes.
Big Cordgrass
Loblolly Pine
Groundsel Tree
Saltwater Cordgrass
Switchgrass
Seaside Goldenrod
Olney's Three-Square Bulrush
Marsh Creek
Marsh Elder
Groundsel Tree
Northern Bayberry
Wax Myrtle
Switchgrass
Seaside Goldenrod
American Holly
Big Cordgrass
Saltwater Cordgra

Eelgrass beds are a crucial habitat for the Bay Scallop. Young scallops attach themselves to Eelgrass stems well above the bottom, and this protects them from predatory crabs. Eelgrass beds slow the currents of water within and over them. This calming of currents, and the complex structure created by all the grass leaves, provides valuable shelter for many small invertebrates. Daggerblade Grass Shrimp are common in Eelgrass beds, where they form an essential food resource for the many species of young fish that shelter in Eelgrass meadows. The beds also shelter bivalves such as the Northern Quahog, which are present in large numbers in healthy seagrass communities.

Unfortunately, the invasive Common Reed or Phragmites (*Phragmites australis australis*) is common in all brackish marshes along the US East Coast, displacing native grasses that are much more valuable to wildlife.

Brackish marshes

Brackish marshes occur in areas of lower salinity (10–18 ppt) in large estuaries such as the Delaware and Chesapeake Bays and the Albemarle and Pamlico Sounds behind the Outer Banks of North Carolina. Smaller areas of brackish marsh also occur near many river mouths where ocean waters mix with river waters. In Chesapeake Bay, brackish marshes line the shores near Annapolis south to the Maryland-Virginia line across the bay.

This book emphasizes marine coastal environments, so the marshes covered here are salt marshes that

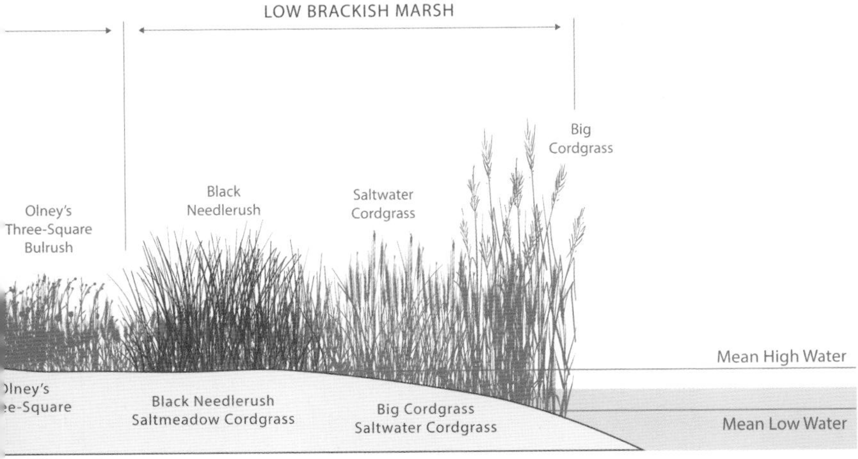
LOW BRACKISH MARSH
Big Cordgrass
Olney's Three-Square Bulrush
Black Needlerush
Saltwater Cordgrass
Mean High Water
Black Needlerush
Saltmeadow Cordgrass
Big Cordgrass
Saltwater Cordgrass
Mean Low Water

The staff of Chincoteague National Wildlife Refuge in coastal Virginia maintain brackish marsh areas to support migrating waterfowl. Here the vegetation along the banks of Swans Cove Pool shows characteristics of both brackish and salt marshes.

SALTWATER CORDGRASS *Spartina alterniflora*

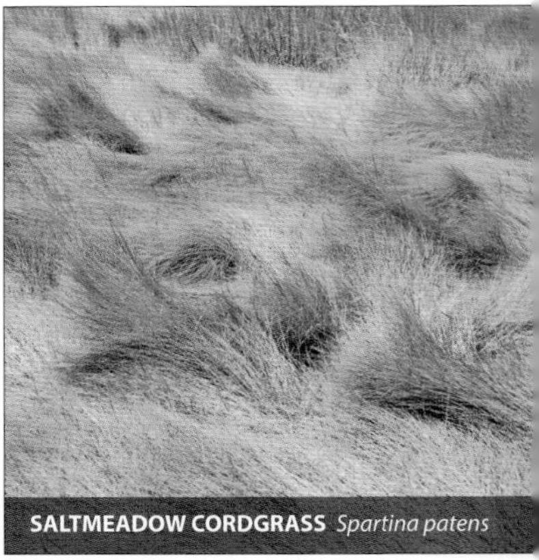

SALTMEADOW CORDGRASS *Spartina patens*

SPIKE GRASS *Distichlis spicata*

BLACK NEEDLERUSH *Juncus roemerianus*

OLNEY'S THREE-SQUARE BULRUSH *Schoenoplectus americanus*

BIG CORDGRASS *Spartina cynosuroides*

OMMON REED *Phragmites australis*

NARROW-LEAVED CATTAIL *Typha angustifolia*

ICKEREL WEED *Pontederia cordata*

WILD RICE *Zizania palustris*

EASIDE GOLDENROD *Solidago sempervirens*

PERENNIAL SALTMARSH ASTER *Symphyotrichum tenuifolium*

Simona Pavan

Olney's Three-Square Bulrush, or Chairmaker's Rush
Schoenoplectus americanus

show some features of the true brackish marshes you might see in the northern reaches of Delaware and Chesapeake Bays, or near river mouths along the ocean coastline. The primary differences between salt marshes and brackish marshes near the ocean lie in the mix of marsh grasses. In true salt marshes, Saltwater Cordgrass and Saltmeadow Cordgrass dominate both the higher and lower parts of the marsh, along with Black Needlerush in many southern salt marshes. In true brackish marshes, you'll still see Saltwater and Saltmeadow Cordgrass. Still, the dominant brackish marsh plant is Olney's Three-Square Bulrush (*Schoenoplectus americanus*), also known as Chairmaker's Rush. Big Cordgrass is another diagnostic plant for marshes with brackish characteristics. Big Cordgrass lives up to its name by growing six to eight feet tall, usually near the open-water edges of brackish marshes, so it's easy to spot. If you see Big Cordgrass, you'll know the marsh is brackish. Along the upper edges of brackish marshes, you'll see Narrow-Leaved Cattails, a cattail species that tolerates some salt in the water. In brackish marshes south of Delaware Bay, Black Needlerush occupies the drier areas of salt marshes and marsh edges, and it dominates many brackish marshes south of Chesapeake Bay.

Most of the herbs, wildflowers, and marsh border plants that you'll see in coastal salt marshes also occur in estuary brackish marshes. Seaside Goldenrod, Sea Lavender, Switchgrass, and Glassworts are found in both salt and brackish marshes. Along the marsh edges, you'll see Marsh Elder, Northern Bayberry (in northern areas), Wax Myrtle (southern regions), and the invasive Common Reed, or Phragmites.

Forests and the health of estuaries

The transformation of the lands around Mid-Atlantic Coast estuaries, from mature forests to mostly open farmland and suburban landscapes, has also transformed the aquatic environment. The bottoms of Delaware Bay and Chesapeake Bay once teemed with life. Vast oyster reefs and seagrass meadows dominated the shallow areas. In the past century, the heavy runoff of sediment from farms, overharvesting of oysters, excess nutrients from fertilizers, and hypoxia in the bottom waters have all combined to produce estuaries dominated by floating and swimming creatures like fish and jellyfish. The excessive runoff of farm and suburban fertilizers has caused free-floating algae populations to explode, and the excess algae decrease water clarity and the amount of sunlight that reaches seagrass beds. In the precolonial Chesapeake Bay, the dominant filter feeders were oysters and other shellfish. Today that filtering role is filled largely by the Sea Nettle jelly, which drifts throughout the water column—and annoys countless swimmers and boaters with its painful stings. Although efforts to restore some of the oyster reefs of the Chesapeake are widespread, those efforts also depend on keeping modern sediment and fertilizer from killing off the newly established reefs and seagrass beds. Similar problems affect every estuary on the East Coast, particularly in smaller bodies of water such as the narrow sounds and bays behind the barrier islands.

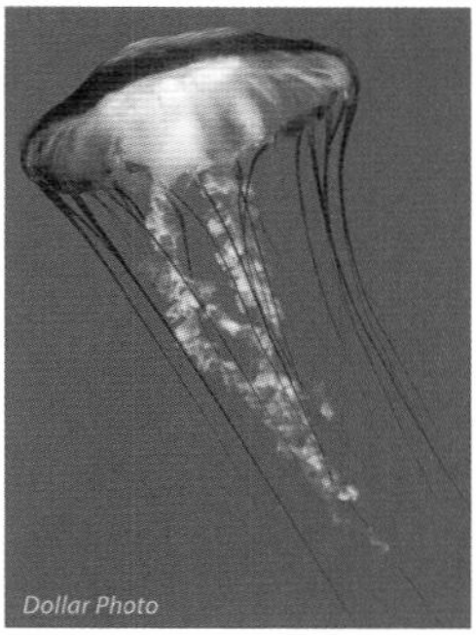
Dollar Photo

Atlantic Sea Nettle
Chrysaora quinquecirrha

When looking at environmental problems, it's always important to keep things in perspective. For all of its environmental challenges, Chesapeake Bay remains an enormously beautiful and productive ecosystem and supports an abundance of wildlife and seafood harvests. Today the Chesapeake produces more than 500 million pounds of seafood harvests every year, as well as hundreds of millions of dollars of revenue in the boating, general recreation, sport fishing, hunting, and wildlife-viewing industries. The health of the bay and our other estuaries is well worth fighting to protect.

Estuary birds

Long-legged waders, including Great Blue Herons, Great Egrets, Snowy Egrets, Greater and Lesser Yellowlegs, and Glossy Ibis all stalk the shallows, picking off crabs, small fish, and other animals. In winter, feeding Brant geese are most often seen floating over the subtidal zone, occasionally dipping down to browse Eelgrass or Sea Lettuce.

Snowy Egret
Egretta thula

Loons and grebes are diving birds that feed mainly on small fish in the subtidal zone but also take small clams and other bottom invertebrates. Common and Red-Throated Loons and Horned Grebes are frequent

© Pat Lynch 2018

Osprey
Pandion haliaetus

The return of the Osprey

These days the most emblematic bird of estuaries and salt marshes is the Osprey, which both nests and hunts over wetlands throughout the Mid-Atlantic region. The return of the Osprey as a common coastal bird is a wonderful environmental success story.

Following World War II, the widespread use of the insecticide DDT devastated American populations of Ospreys, because DDT and its organochlorine breakdown products readily entered the coastal food chain and became concentrated in top-level predators such as the Osprey. The DDT-based chemicals made the eggshells of birds of prey like the Osprey too thin to hatch successfully, and in the postwar decades Osprey populations plunged.

After the use of DDT was banned in the United States in 1972, the Osprey population began a long, slow recovery. Today the Osprey is once again one of our most visible wetland hawks, and Osprey nests are a common sight above salt marshes.

spring and fall migrants in coastal waters. The tiny Pied-Billed Grebe is a common migrant along the shore and major rivers in fall. It is less common in spring migration and is rare in the region for the rest of the year.

One of the most abundant birds of the subtidal zone is the Double-Crested Cormorant (see illustration, p. 220). These angular black birds are often seen sunning their outspread wings on docks, pilings, breakwaters, channel markers, and any other suitable perch along the shoreline. Cormorants are powerful underwater swimmers that feed primarily on small fish but will also take crabs when they can find them. In winter, the larger and much less common Great Cormorant may be seen, particularly on coastal piers and harbor breakwaters on the Jersey Shore and around the ocean coasts just south of Delaware Bay.

The classic feeding tilt of a dabbling duck, in this instance a female Mallard (*Anas platyrhynchos*). Dabbling ducks like the Mallard and the American Black Duck (*Anas rubripes*) feed in water shallow enough that they can reach down to find aquatic vegetation and other foods without submerging their whole bodies.

Diving and dabbling ducks

In fall and winter, the bird life of the Mid-Atlantic Coast is primarily defined by large rafts of duck species that all dive partially or fully underwater to feed. Dabbling ducks such as the Mallard and the closely related American Black Duck feed by tilting themselves down from the surface, rarely fully submerging

Buffleheads are small sea ducks that are common on both freshwater and saltwater ponds and bays. Buffleheads are powerful underwater swimmers that eat insects and plants in freshwater and crustaceans and mollusks in salt water.

their buoyant bodies. Blue-Winged and Green-Winged Teals and American Wigeons are also common dabbling ducks along the coast in spring and fall and, to a lesser extent, in winter. As dabblers, these ducks are limited to feeding on the immediate shoreline and to shallow, sheltered subtidal areas like harbors and bays. But when not actively feeding, dabblers often drift well away from the shore for safety.

Diving ducks like the Greater Scaup (*Aythya marila*) frequent the bays and sounds of the Mid-Atlantic Coast in winter. Diving ducks are strong underwater swimmers that feed on submerged vegetation and bottom invertebrates.

The true diving ducks, which fully submerge and swim well underwater, are the most numerous ducks along the Mid-Atlantic Coast in fall, winter, and early spring. Greater and Lesser Scaup, White-Winged and Surf Scoters, Common Goldeneyes, and Buffleheads are the most common diving ducks. All these species eat small bottom invertebrates and aquatic plants such as Sea Lettuce, Eelgrass, and Widgeon Grass.

Bufflehead
Bucephala albeola

WOOD DUCKS
Aix sponsa
Female
Male

WOOD DUCK FAMILY

Wood Ducks are our most spectacularly colored duck species and one of the few types of North American ducks to nest in tree cavities. Thus for much of the year Wood Ducks frequent smaller bodies of fresh and brackish water near coastal forests and swamps. Wood Ducks prefer to nest in trees next to or over water.

While most abundant in freshwater swamps, Wood Ducks in eastern North America tend to migrate closer to the East Coast in winter, and thus they appear regularly in wooded marshes and the coastal marshes of large estuaries like the Chesapeake and Delaware Bays. As dabbling ducks, Wood Ducks do not dive for their mixed diets of seeds, berries, snails, aquatic vegetation, and various insects, and they are most common in shallow water near trees.

Wood Duck family at Blackwater National Wildlife Refuge, Dorchester County, Maryland.

Pat Lynch ©12

BRANT *Branta bernicla*

CANADA GOOSE *Branta canadensis*

Paul Reeves

Straight, erect neck, found south of Barnegat Inlet, NJ

TUNDRA SWAN *Cygnus columbianus*

Curved neck posture — Mostly found north of Delaware Ba

MUTE SWAN *Cygnus olor*

MALLARD *Anas platyrhynchos*

Elliotte Harold

AMERICAN BLACK DUCK *Anas rubripes*

Erik Tofft

NORTHERN SHOVELER *Spatula clypeata*

Paul

GADWALL *Mareca strepera*

AMERICAN WIGEON *Mareca americana*

Erni

GREEN-WINGED TEAL *Anas carolinensis*

Paul

BLUE-WINGED TEAL *Anas discors*

Bernie Duhamel

CANVASBACK *Aythya valisineria*

Mirko Rosenau

REDHEAD *Aythya americana*

Tim Zurowski.

RING-NECKED DUCK *Aythya collaris*

jnjhuz

BUFFLEHEAD *Bucephala albeola*

HOODED MERGANSER *Lophodytes cucullatus*

Tim Zurowski

COMMON GOLDENEYE *Bucephala clangula*

andreanita

COMMON MERGANSER *Mergus merganser*

Ian Maton

RED-BREASTED MERGANSER *Mergus serrator*

Martha Marks

COMMON COOT *Fulica americana*

Mircea Costina

PIED-BILLED GREBE *Podilymbus podiceps*

Joseph Scott

BALD EAGLE *Haliaeetus leucocephalus*

See p. 301 for more on vultures

TURKEY VULTURE *Cathartes aura*

BLACK VULTURE *Coragyps atratus*

Alewife
Alosa pseudoharengus

NOAA

Mummichog
Fundulus heteroclitus

Mergansers are diving ducks with long, thin bills that are edged with toothlike serrations to help them seize their specialty: small fish and slippery aquatic invertebrates. Red-Breasted, Common, and Hooded Mergansers are widespread in the cold months but leave the coast to breed in freshwater lakes and ponds in more northern areas of the United States and Canada.

Open water

The deeper waters of large estuaries like Delaware Bay and the Chesapeake Bay are not much different from the open ocean waters just beyond them. Salinities at the mouth of the Chesapeake and Delaware Bays range from 25 ppt to 30 ppt, hardly different from the ocean salinity of about 32–35 ppt. The deep central basins of the lower Chesapeake and Delaware Bays are home to a wide variety of estuary and ocean fish, including virtually all of our major saltwater sport fish and commercial food fish. Just as important, deep estuary waters are home to huge schools of smaller fish that form the foundation of both estuary and coastal food chains. These smaller fish species, often collectively called forage fish, may be less familiar because few forage fish species are caught for direct human consumption. Atlantic Menhaden, Alewife, Atlantic Silversides, various herring species, and Bay Anchovy are the foundational species in open estuary waters, but smaller salt marsh fish like the Mummichog are also critical forage species in shallower, more brackish areas of estuaries.

Most large gamefish and commercial food fish are the top predators in coastal and estuary systems, and these predators need abundant forage fish stocks. Striped Bass (Rockfish), Bluefish, Weakfish, Cobia, Tautog (Blackfish), and other species feed on forage fish, as do Ospreys, Bald Eagles, various herons, Double-Crested Cormorants, and mergansers. Sightings of marine mammals such as the Bottlenose Dolphin and the Humpback Whale have become more frequent in recent years because forage fish stocks in the larger estuaries have been abundant. Unfortunately, the abundance of Atlantic Menhaden (Bunker) schools have caused commercial Menhaden fishing operations to call for increased harvest quotas. This increased commercial fishing pressure comes when the importance

The ubiquitous Great Blue Heron (Ardea herodias), a top predator in all wetlands and present in all seasons on the Mid-Atlantic Coast.

MENHADEN AND OTHER FORAGE FISH

"The most valuable fish in the sea"

Forage fish are smaller species of fish and squid that directly convert the energy and nutrients of plankton into high-protein, fat-rich food sources for sport fish, food fish, marine mammals, and seabirds of coastal waters. In healthy marine ecosystems these abundant species are present in great schools that are a critical link in the ocean food chain. From Ospreys and Bald Eagles to Striped Bass, Bluefish, tuna, and mackerel to our four major dolphin species and to Pilot and Humpback Whales—all depend heavily or exclusively on Atlantic Menhaden. Virtually all sport fish longer than 12 inches prey on Menhaden. Thus Menhaden and other forage fish are a critical resource for maintaining a healthy coastal ecosystem. The flow of nutrients goes both ways: small animals feed larger animals, and as the larger animals die and decay, their nutrients reenter the food cycle.

TOP PREDATORS: Marine mammals, seabirds, sport fish

Without an abundant population of Atlantic Menhaden, the sport fisheries for species such as Bluefish, Striped Bass, Weakfish, major tuna and mackerel species, Cobia, and Blue and White Marlin would all quickly collapse. Marine mammals at the top of the food chain, including Humpback Whales, Fin Whales, Pilot Whales, and our five major seal species, would all starve and disappear from our waters.

FORAGE FISH SPECIES—The critical link in the ocean food chain

The filter-feeding forage fish, such as the Atlantic Menhaden and various herring species, convert the energy and nutrients of plankton into usable food for the rest of the marine food chain. Small but enormously abundant coastal fish such as Atlantic Silversides and Sand Lance are critical to seabird populations.

- Atlantic Menhaden
- Atlantic Herring
- Blueback Herring
- Sand Lance
- Atlantic Silversides
- American Butterfish
- Alewife

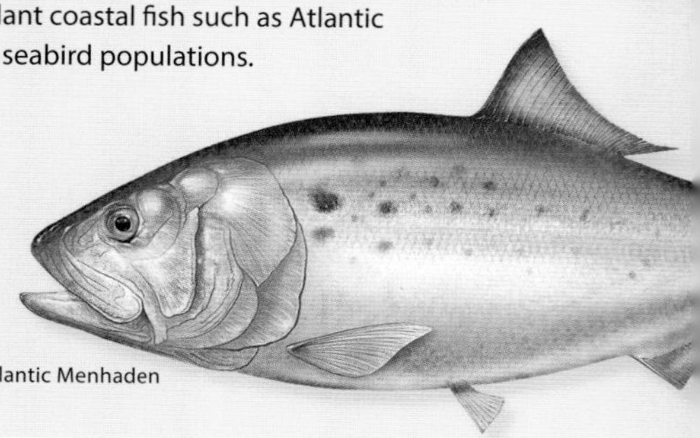

Atlantic Menhaden

ZOOPLANKTON AND PHYTOPLANKTON SPECIES

The trillions of microscopic or tiny free-floating plants (phytoplankton) or animals (zooplankton) form the base of the ocean food chain, but this wealth of nutrients and energy is not directly available to most larger animals.

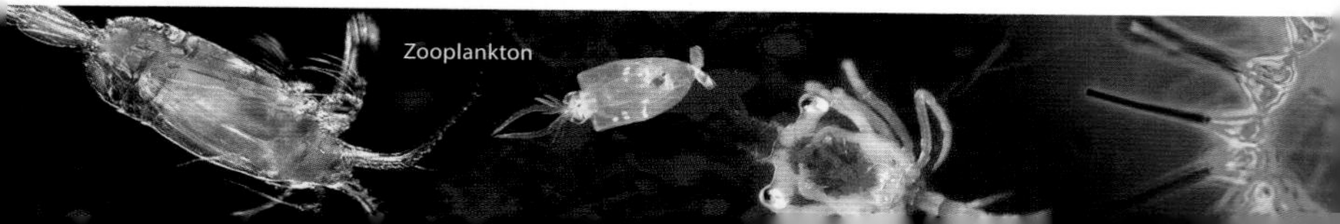

Zooplankton

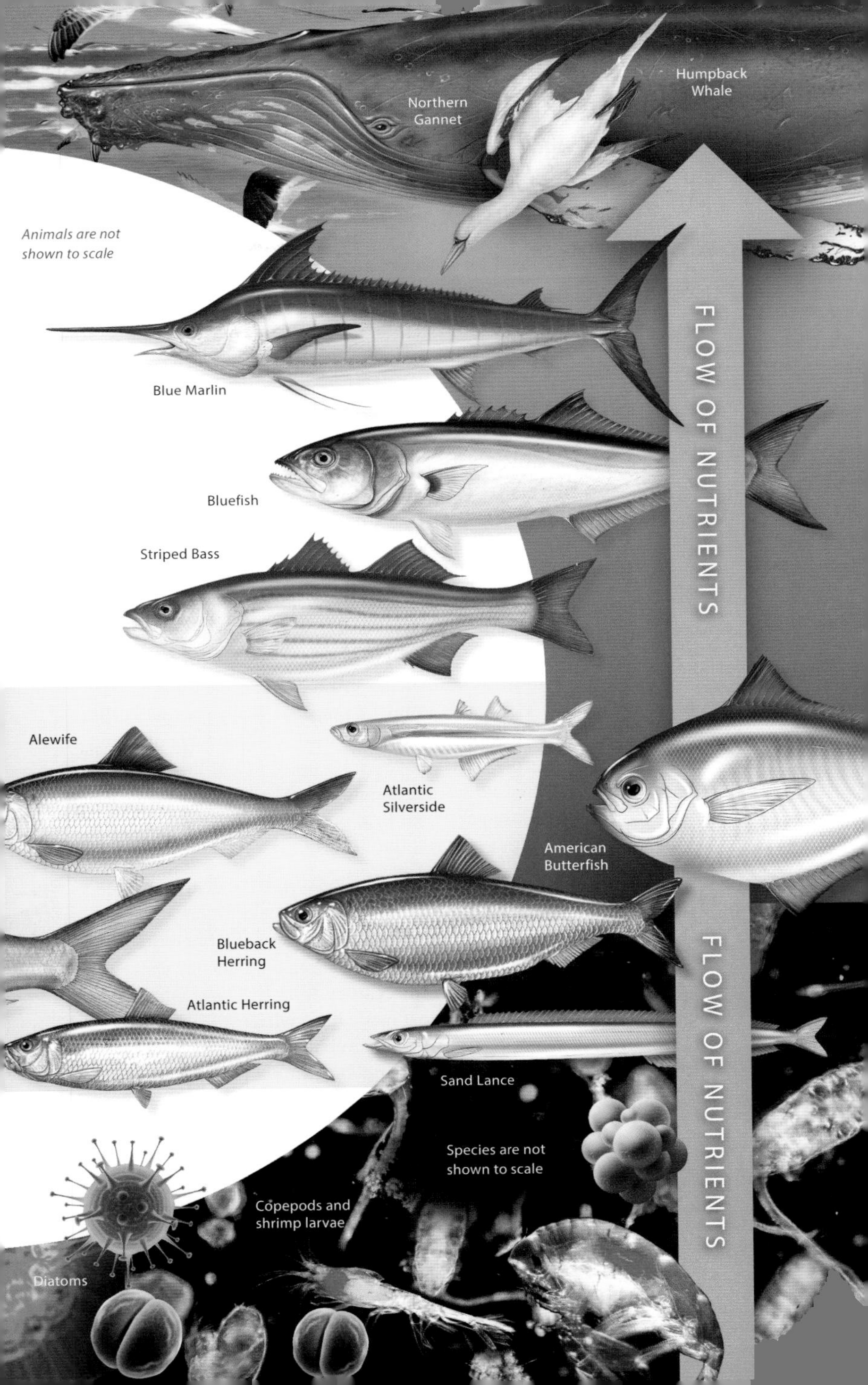
Humpback Whale
Northern Gannet
Animals are not shown to scale
Blue Marlin
Bluefish
Striped Bass
Alewife
Atlantic Silverside
American Butterfish
Blueback Herring
Atlantic Herring
Sand Lance
Species are not shown to scale
Copepods and shrimp larvae
Diatoms
FLOW OF NUTRIENTS
FLOW OF NUTRIENTS

A feeding Humpback Whale (*Megaptera novaeangliae*) can gulp hundreds gallons of water and fish at a time. The whale then closes its mouth and strains the water out through the baleen plates you can see lining the roof of its mouth.

of forage fish species has captured the attention of bay conservation, sport fishing, whale-watching, birding, and wildlife advocacy groups. The greater harvesting of Menhaden in the Chesapeake Bay comes at a critical time for Striped Bass stocks, which have dropped sharply in recent years. It's not yet clear how directly increased fishing pressure on Menhaden has affected the falling Striped Bass population, but conservation groups point out that it certainly isn't helpful.

Humpback Whales regularly visit the deeper, more oceanic waters of large estuaries like Delaware Bay and the Chesapeake Bay. Occasionally the much rarer North Atlantic Right Whale also enters bay waters. Before nineteenth-century Atlantic Coast whaling operations almost made both whale species extinct, Humpbacks and Right Whales were regular visitors to the Chesapeake and Delaware Bays. Humpback Whales feed on forage fish species like Menhaden. Many people have noted that the recent increase in Humpback sightings in the New York Bight and along the Mid-Atlantic Coast directly corresponds to increases in Menhaden populations in the region.

Hypoxia and estuaries

Nitrogen is a naturally occurring element and, along with carbon, hydrogen, and oxygen, is a fundamental building block of life. In natural environments, nitrogen is in high demand and is usually in limited supply and carefully conserved, particularly in plant physiology. This growth-limiting role of scarce nitrogen is especially important in marine and estuary ecosystems. When a large artificial amount of nitrogen—such as sewage or lawn and farm fertilizer runoff—is introduced into an aquatic environment, the nitrogen accelerates the growth of simple, fast-reproducing algae, cyanobacteria, and diatoms, collectively called phytoplankton. Like all green plants, phytoplankton release oxygen as they photosynthesize. However, at night or in low-light conditions, phytoplankton use more oxygen than they release, and in their overabundance, the phytoplankton can rapidly deplete the dissolved oxygen in polluted waters.

Excess nitrogen in coastal waters produces an unnaturally heavy growth of algae. When algae die, their cells bind up oxygen as they decay, creating a downward spiral of falling dissolved oxygen levels called hypoxia.

This condition of low dissolved oxygen is called hypoxia, and hypoxia usually follows large phytoplankton blooms in late summer, when water temperatures are

Common Mergansers
Mergus merganser

HUMPBACK WHALE (*Megaptera novaeangliae*)

This highly inquisitive whale readily approaches boats. The Humpback Whale exhibits a wide range of sometimes spectacular social and feeding behaviors at the surface, including breaching, lob-tailing, and flipper-slapping. Humpbacks often feed in groups, where the whales cooperate to surround schools of small fish with nets or clouds of bubbles blown from their blowholes while underwater (bubble-netting). The blow is low and bushy. The Humpback often rolls its tail high out of the water at the beginning of a dive. Humpbacks sometimes enter large, deep estuaries.

Typical adult size range: 35–45 feet

Average adult weight: 25–35 tons

Diet: Sand Lance, Atlantic Menhaden, Atlantic Herring, other smaller schooling fish

Approximate life-span: 50 years

A feeding Humpback emerges at the center of a ring of bubbles it has blown (a bubble net) to trap a school of Sand Lance within the ring. The whale then surfaces in the center of the ring and gulps down the trapped fish.

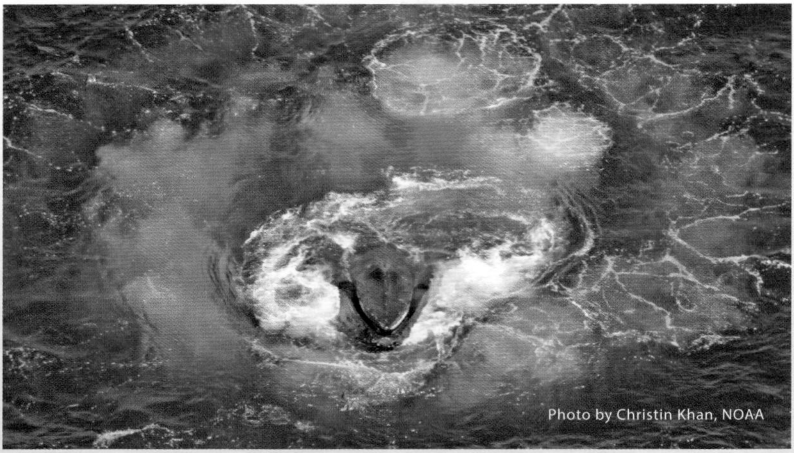
Photo by Christin Khan, NOAA

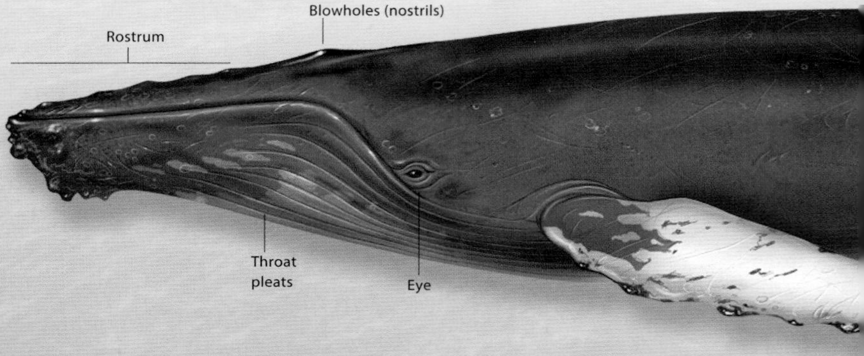
Blowholes (nostrils)
Rostrum
Throat pleats
Eye

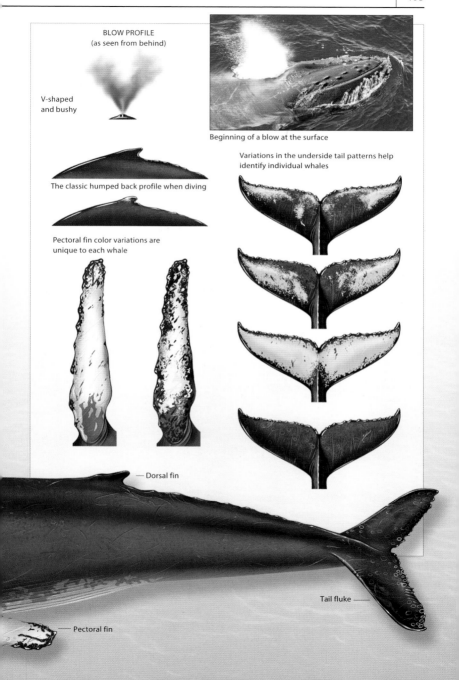

BLOW PROFILE
(as seen from behind)

V-shaped
and bushy

Beginning of a blow at the surface

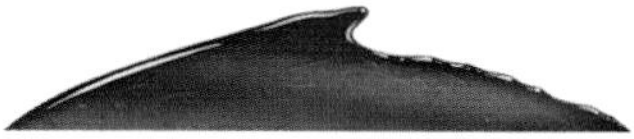

The classic humped back profile when diving

Pectoral fin color variations are
unique to each whale

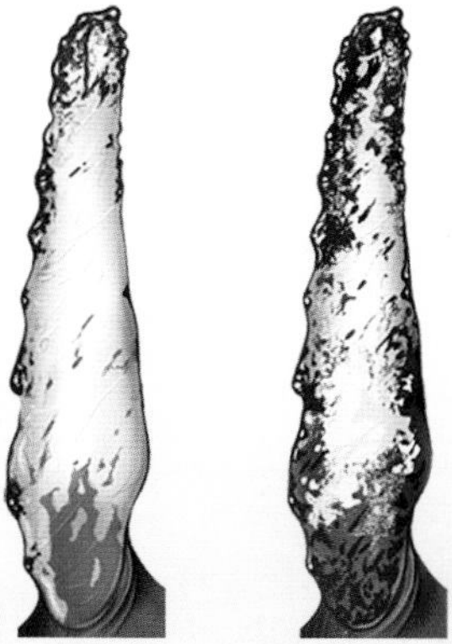

Variations in the underside tail patterns help
identify individual whales

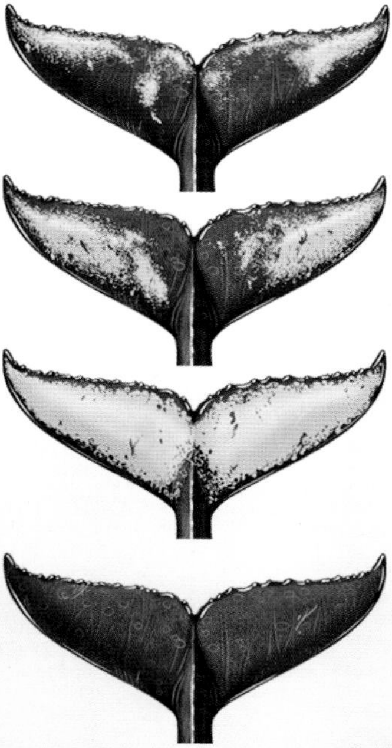

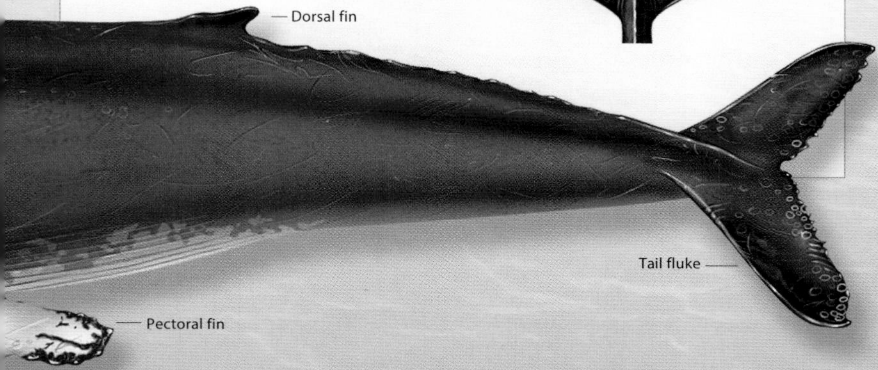
Dorsal fin
Tail fluke
Pectoral fin

Illustrations not to scale; lengths cited are typical ranges

SCUP (NORTHERN PORGY)
Stenotomus chrysops

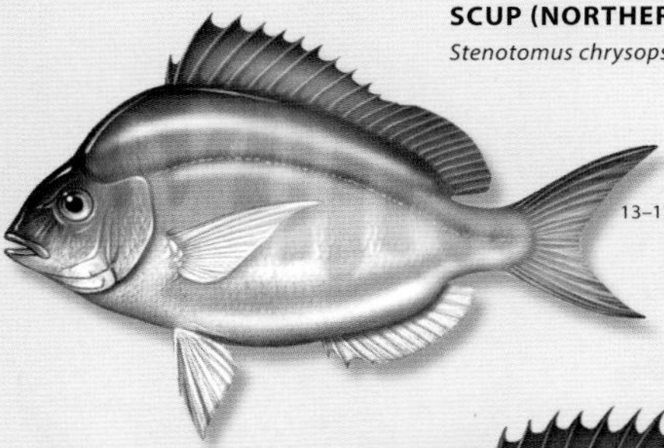

13–17 in.

TAUTOG (BLACKFISH)
Tautoga onitis

12–15 in.

BLACK SEA BASS
Centropristis striata

18–24 in.

CUNNER
Tautogolabrus adspersus

12–15 in.

BLUEFISH
Pomatomus saltatrix

12–30 in.

STRIPED BASS
Morone saxatilis

1–6 ft.

AMERICAN BUTTERFISH
Peprilus triacanthus

6–9 in.

WEAKFISH
Cynoscion regalis

18–36 in.

Illustrations not to scale; lengths cited are typical ranges

SPINY DOGFISH
Squalus acanthias

18–34 in.

SUMMER FLOUNDER
Paralichthys dentatus

15–20 in.

WINDOWPANE FLOUNDER
Scophthalmus aquosus

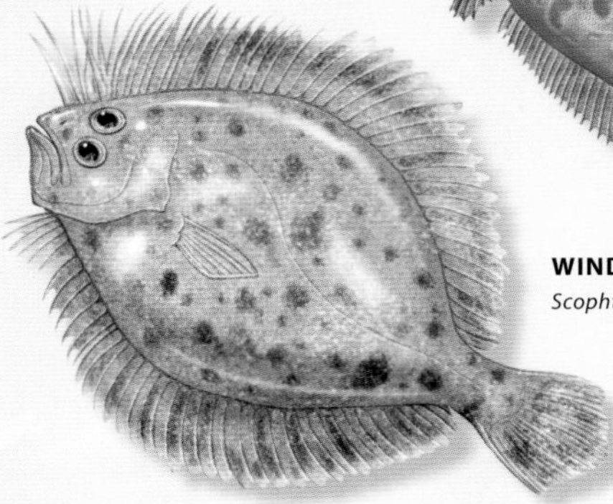
9–10 in.

WINTER FLOUNDER
Pseudopleuronectes americanus

18–24 in.

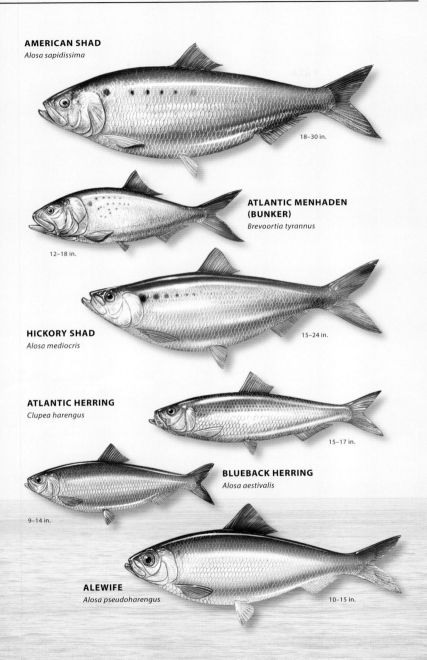

AMERICAN SHAD
Alosa sapidissima

18–30 in.

ATLANTIC MENHADEN (BUNKER)
Brevoortia tyrannus

12–18 in.

HICKORY SHAD
Alosa mediocris

15–24 in.

ATLANTIC HERRING
Clupea harengus

15–17 in.

BLUEBACK HERRING
Alosa aestivalis

9–14 in.

ALEWIFE
Alosa pseudoharengus

10–15 in.

Eutrophication and hypoxia (low dissolved oxygen in the water) can cause massive fish kills, particularly in late summer, when water temperatures are high. Schools of fish like Atlantic Menhaden swim into the hypoxic water and then suffocate before they can locate better water.

highest. As the algae die from lack of oxygen, water conditions worsen because as the dead algae decompose, their tissues absorb what little oxygen remains in the water. Hypoxia is stressful for all aquatic organisms, and if it lasts too long or if dissolved oxygen levels fall too low, hypoxia is lethal to both the phytoplankton and aquatic animals. Overfertilized aquatic environments are said to be eutrophic—fertilized to the point where the system continually cycles through boom-and-bust sequences of rapid algae growth, mass algae death, and lethal hypoxia. Over time, eutrophic systems become aquatic dead zones in which only the simplest phytoplankton can survive. In the Chesapeake and Delaware Bays, hypoxia regularly occurs in the deepest central basins in mid- to late summer.

Runoff from agriculture and waste from industrial hog and chicken farming all contribute to large amounts of nitrogen and phosphorus entering coastal waters, particularly around the Delmarva Peninsula. Septic systems help drive eutrophication as detergents containing phosphorous leak into groundwater and local ponds and streams.

In summer, Mid-Atlantic estuaries tend to form two distinct temperature layers, with warm waters on top and cold waters below. Not much mixing of layers happens in summer, so the cold bottom layer is isolated from atmospheric oxygen, and this makes hypoxia even worse in deep waters. Most of the larger estuaries along the Mid-Atlantic Coast show signs of eutrophication and hypoxia, as do small bays and inlets along the coasts and barrier islands.

Excess nitrogen also destroys essential coastal seagrass communities. Abundant algae in the waters above seagrass beds create murky waters that filter out vital sunlight. Excess nitrogen has also been found to harm the biochemistry of Eelgrass and Widgeon Grass. In the Chesapeake and Delaware Bays, many once-rich Eelgrass and Widgeon Grass beds have vanished. With the loss of these seagrasses, the young of many important food fish, sport fish, and Blue Crabs no longer have the food and shelter they need to survive to adulthood.

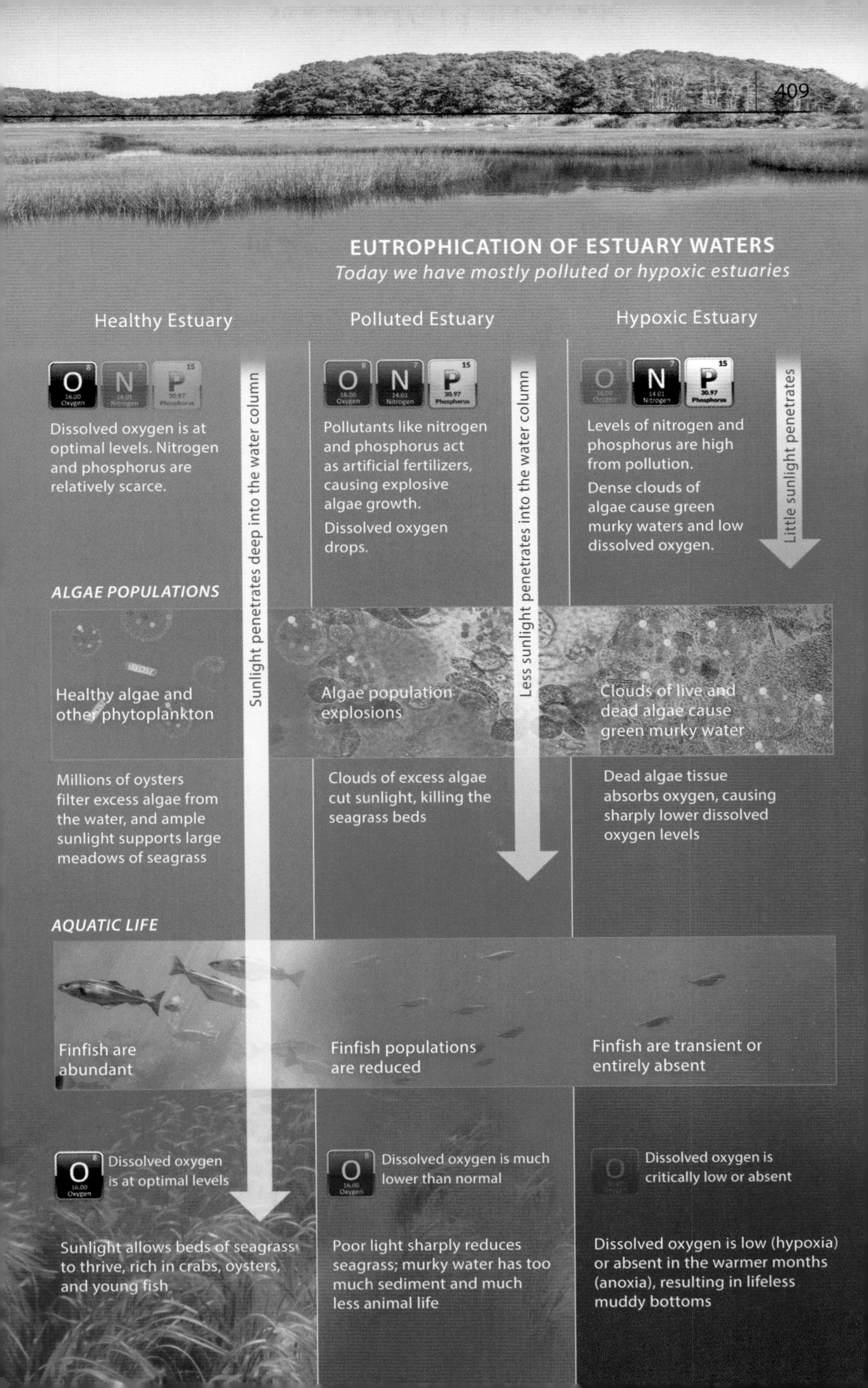
EUTROPHICATION OF ESTUARY WATERS
Today we have mostly polluted or hypoxic estuaries
Healthy Estuary
Polluted Estuary
Hypoxic Estuary
O 16.00 Oxygen
N 14.01 Nitrogen
P 30.97 Phosphorus
Dissolved oxygen is at optimal levels. Nitrogen and phosphorus are relatively scarce.
Sunlight penetrates deep into the water column
Pollutants like nitrogen and phosphorus act as artificial fertilizers, causing explosive algae growth.
Dissolved oxygen drops.
Less sunlight penetrates into the water column
Levels of nitrogen and phosphorus are high from pollution.
Dense clouds of algae cause green murky waters and low dissolved oxygen.
Little sunlight penetrates
ALGAE POPULATIONS
Healthy algae and other phytoplankton
Algae population explosions
Clouds of live and dead algae cause green murky water
Millions of oysters filter excess algae from the water, and ample sunlight supports large meadows of seagrass
Clouds of excess algae cut sunlight, killing the seagrass beds
Dead algae tissue absorbs oxygen, causing sharply lower dissolved oxygen levels
AQUATIC LIFE
Finfish are abundant
Finfish populations are reduced
Finfish are transient or entirely absent
Dissolved oxygen is at optimal levels
Dissolved oxygen is much lower than normal
Dissolved oxygen is critically low or absent
Sunlight allows beds of seagrass to thrive, rich in crabs, oysters, and young fish
Poor light sharply reduces seagrass; murky water has too much sediment and much less animal life
Dissolved oxygen is low (hypoxia) or absent in the warmer months (anoxia), resulting in lifeless muddy bottoms

Willet, Pea Island National Wildlife Refuge, on the Outer Banks of North Carolina.

Further Reading

The Mid-Atlantic Coast

Alexander, J., and J. Lazell. 2000. *Ribbon of Sand: The Amazing Convergence of the Ocean and the Outer Banks*. Chapel Hill: University of North Carolina Press.

Burger, J. 1996. *A Naturalist along the Jersey Shore*. New Brunswick, NJ: Rutgers University Press.

Cronon, W. 2003. *Changes in the Land: Indians, Colonists, and the Ecology of New England*. Rev. ed. New York: Hill and Wang.

Dolan, R., and H. Lins. 1986. *The Outer Banks of North Carolina*. US Geological Survey Professional Paper 1177-B. *Available free online.*

Pelton, T. 2018. *The Chesapeake in Focus: Transforming the Natural World*. Baltimore: Johns Hopkins University Press.

Pilkey, O., et al. 1989. *The North Carolina Shore and Its Barrier Islands: Restless Ribbons of Sand*. Durham, NC: Duke University Press.

Rice, J. 2016. *Nature and History in the Potomac Country: From Hunter-Gatherers to the Age of Jefferson*. Baltimore: Johns Hopkins University Press.

Safina, C. 2011. *The View from Lazy Point: A Natural Year in an Unnatural World*. New York: Henry Holt.

Swift, E. 2018. *Chesapeake Requiem: A Year with the Watermen of Vanishing Tangier Island*. New York: William Morrow.

General coastal and regional environments

Bertness, M. D. 2007. *Atlantic Shorelines: Natural History and Ecology*. Princeton, NJ: Princeton University Press.

Lippson, A., and R. Lippson. 2006. *Life in the Chesapeake Bay: An Illustrated Guide to the Fishes, Invertebrates, Plants, Birds, and Other Inhabitants of the Bays and Inlets from Cape Cod to Cape Hatteras*. 3rd ed. Baltimore: Johns Hopkins University Press.

Lippson, A., and R. Lippson. 2009. *Life along the Inner Coast: A Naturalist's Guide to the Sounds, Inlets, Rivers, and Intracoastal Waterway from Norfolk to Key West*. Chapel Hill: University of North Carolina Press.

Perry, B. 1985. *The Middle Atlantic Coast: A Sierra Club Naturalist's Guide*. San Francisco: Sierra Club Books.

Shumway, S. W. 2008. *A Naturalist's Guide to the Atlantic Seashore: Beach Ecology from the Gulf of Maine to Cape Hatteras*. Guilford, CT: Falcon Guides.

White, C. P. 2009. *Chesapeake Bay, Nature of the Estuary: A Field Guide*. Atglen, PA: Schiffer.

Beaches and dunes

Leatherman, S. P. 2003. *Dr. Beach's Survival Guide: What You Need to Know about Sharks, Rip Currents, and More before Going in the Water*. New Haven: Yale University Press.

Neal, W. J., O. H. Pilkey, and J. T. Kelley. 2007. *Atlantic Coast Beaches: A Guide to Ripples, Dunes, and Other Natural Features of the Seashore*. Missoula, MT: Mountain Press.

Pilkey, C. O., and O. H. Pilkey. 2016. *Lessons from the Sand: Family-Friendly Science Activities You Can Do on a Carolina Beach*. Chapel Hill: University of North Carolina Press.

Pilkey, O. H., T. M. Rice, and W. J. Neal. 2004. *How to Read a North Carolina Beach: Bubble Holes, Barking Sands, and Rippled Runnels*. Chapel Hill: University of North Carolina Press.

Shumway, S. W. 2008. *A Naturalist's Guide to the Atlantic Seashore: Beach Ecology from the Gulf of Maine to Cape Hatteras*. Guilford, CT: Falcon Guides.

Birds

Beehler, Bruce M. 2019. *Birds of Maryland, Delaware, and the District of Columbia*. Batimore: Johns Hopkins University Press.

Boyle, W. J. 2011. *The Birds of New Jersey: Status and Distribution*. Princeton, NJ: Princeton University Press.

Dunn, J., and J. Alderfer. 2011. *National Geographic Field Guide to the Birds of North America*. 6th ed. Washington, DC: National Geographic.

Fussel, J. O. 1994. *A Birder's Guide to Coastal North Carolina*. Chapel Hill: University of North Carolina Press.

Olsen, K. M., and H. Larsson. 2003. *Gulls of North America, Europe, and Asia*. Princeton, NJ: Princeton University Press.

Peterson, R. T. 2010. *Peterson Field Guide to Birds of Eastern and Central North America*. 6th ed. Boston: Houghton Mifflin.

Sibley, D. 2014. *The Sibley Field Guide to Birds of Eastern North America*. 2nd ed. New York: Knopf.

Sutton, C. and P. 2006. *Birds and Birding at Cape May: What to See, When and Where to Go*. Mechanicsburg, PA: Stackpole Books.

Fish

Boschung, H., et al. 1986. *The Audubon Society Field Guide to North American Fishes, Whales, and Dolphins*. New York: Knopf.

Coad, B. 1992. *Guide to the Marine Sport Fishes of Atlantic Canada and New England*. Toronto: University of Toronto Press.

Robbins, C., and C. Ray. 1986. *A Field Guide to Atlantic Coast Fishes of North America*. Boston: Houghton Mifflin.

Geology

Frankenberg, D. 2012. *The Nature of the Outer Banks: Environmental Processes, Field Sites, and Development Issues, Corolla to Ocracoke*. 2nd ed. Chapel Hill: University of North Carolina Press.

Frankenberg, D. 2012. *The Nature of North Carolina's Southern Coast: Barrier Islands, Coastal Waters, and Wetlands*. 2nd ed. Chapel Hill: University of North Carolina Press.

Harper, D. 2013. *Roadside Geology of New Jersey*. Missoula, MT: Mountain Press.

Leatherman, S. P. 1982. *Barrier Island Handbook*. College Park, MD: University of Maryland.

Leatherman, S. P., ed. 1979. *Barrier Islands: From the Gulf of St. Lawrence to the Gulf of Mexico*. New York: Academic Press.

Means, J. 2010. *Roadside Geology of Maryland, Delaware, and Washington, DC*. Missoula, MT: Mountain Press.

Insects

Borror, D., and R. White. 1970. *A Field Guide to the Insects of North America North of Mexico*. Boston: Houghton Mifflin.

Dunkle, S. W. 2000. *Dragonflies through Binoculars: A Field Guide to Dragonflies of North America*. New York: Oxford University Press.

Klots, A. 1951. *A Field Guide to the Butterflies of North America, East of the Great Plains*. Boston: Houghton Mifflin.

Mammals and other land animals

Conant, R. 1958. *A Field Guide to Reptiles and Amphibians of the United States East of the 100th Meridian*. Boston: Houghton Mifflin.

Kays, R. W., and D. E. Wilson. 2009. *Mammals of North America*. 2nd ed. Princeton, NJ: Princeton University Press.

Marine environments

Bertness, M. D. 2007. *Atlantic Shorelines: Natural History and Ecology*. Princeton, NJ: Princeton University Press.

Marine invertebrates and shells

Abbott, R. 1968. *Seashells of North America*. New York: Golden.

Gosner, K. L. 1978. *A Field Guide to the Atlantic Seashore from the Bay of Fundy to Cape Hatteras*. Boston: Houghton Mifflin.

Meinkoth, N. 1981. *The National Audubon Society Field Guide to North American Seashore Creatures*. New York: Knopf.

Marine mammals and turtles

Boschung, H., et al. 1986. *The Audubon Society Field Guide to North American Fishes, Whales, and Dolphins*. New York: Knopf.

Kinze, C. C. 2001. *Marine Mammals of the North Atlantic*. Princeton, NJ: Princeton University Press.

Leatherwood, S., and R. R. Reeves. 1983. *The Sierra Club Handbook of Whales and Dolphins*. San Francisco: Sierra Club Books.

Perrine, D. 2003. *Sea Turtles of the World*. Stillwater, MN: Voyageur.

Salt marshes

Teal, J., and M. Teal. 1969. *Life and Death of the Salt Marsh*. New York: Ballantine Books.

Warren, R. S., J. Barrett, and M. Van Patten. 2009. *Salt Marsh Plants of Long Island Sound*. Bulletin 40. New London: Connecticut Arboretum.

Weis, J. S., and C. A. Butler. 2009. *Salt Marshes: A Natural and Unnatural History*. New Brunswick, NJ: Rutgers University Press.

Trees, plants, and wildflowers

Brown, L. 1979. *Grasses: An Identification Guide*. Boston: Houghton Mifflin.

Hosier, P. E. 2018. *Seacoast Plants of the Carolinas: A New Guide for Plant Identification and Use in the Coastal Landscape*. Chapel Hill: University of North Carolina Press.

Peterson, R. T., and M. McKenny. 1968. *A Field Guide to the Wildflowers of Northeastern and North-Central North America*. Boston: Houghton Mifflin.

Silberhorn, G. M. 1999. *Common Plants of the Mid-Atlantic Coast: A Field Guide*. Baltimore: Johns Hopkins University Press.

Snowy egrets (Egretta thula)

Dawn, Jennette's Pier, Nags Head, North Carolina, on the Outer Banks.

Illustration Credits

All photography, artwork, diagrams, and maps are by the author, unless otherwise noted with a page credit and this listing.

Additional photography credits

6, Saltmarsh Sparrow nest, Jeanna Mielcarek; 23, Core Banks aerial, NOAA; 31, Storm scarp, Ryan Torrance; 35, Mantoloking, NJ, NASA; 37, Storm overwash, NOAA; 44, Barrier island breach, USGS; 45, Hurricane Irene rainfall, National Weather Service (NWS); 51, Tree stumps, Dianna K; 102–3, Humpback Whale, Carl Safina; 58, Nor'easter, NASA; 61, Temperature gradients, NASA; 62, Gulf Stream SST, NOAA; 71, Flooding, US Navy; 80, Hurricane Florence, NWS; 81, Fish kill, NOAA; 89, Benjamin West painting, Wikimedia Commons; 90, Whittredge painting, Metropolitan Museum of Art Open Access; 99, Capture of Blackbeard painting, Wikimedia Commons; 103, Entangled Humpback, NOAA; 105, Shipwreck painting, Metropolitan Museum of Art Open Access; 106–7, Stower paintings, Wikimedia Commons; 122, Seaside painting, Metropolitan Museum of Art Open Access; 141, Ponies, Dianna K; 169, Beach replenishment, US Army Corps of Engineers; 175, Rip currents, National Park Service; 179, Sea surface temps, NOAA; 187, Stumps on beach, Dianna K; 190–91, Moon Jellies, Wikimedia Commons; 208, Horseshoe Crab eggs and baby Horseshoe Crabs, Frank Gallo; 281, Southern Pine Beetle, Erich G. Vallery; 290, Black and White Warbler, Robin Ladouceur; 298, Common Yellowthroat, Robin Ladouceur; 307, Daggerblade Grass Shrimp, Brian Gratwicke; 353, Bald Eagle, Janice Blanton; 373, Red Knots and Horseshoe Crabs, USF&WS; 371, Horseshoe Crabs, Frank Gallo; 396, Mummichog, NOAA.

Images used under license from Adobe Stock

15, Rocky Mountains, Videowokart; 19, Canadian forest, Zlikovec; 21, Nova Scotia forest, Petrov Vadim; 30, Breaking wave, Noradoa; 33, Dunes and wind art, Photosbyjam; 61, School of tuna, Pavel-A; 63, Moon and sea, Alfredo; 73, Smokestacks, AZP Worldwide; 75, Glacier, Alexey Seafarer; 78, Tide gauge, Linjerry; 84, Constant ship, SpiritofAmerica; 85, New York from Sandy Hook, Andrew Kazmierski; 86, Ships, SpiritofAmerica; 95, Potomac rapids, Jonbilious; 99, Pistol, JRB; 100, Ocracoke Island, Jennifer; 112, Discovery ship, Winterbilder; 113, Williamsburg house, Deaton Photos; 114, Feral hog, Jarek106; 115, Red Wolf, Abeselom Zerit; 114–15, Tobacco farm, Antonello; 116, Oysters, Yeko Photo Studio; 117, Blue Crabs, Kelli; 118, Snow Geese, Cherles; 120, Canada Geese, Capic; 126, Wildwood, NJ, CreativeFamily; 168, Beach houses, TravelView; 187, Shark teeth, Gerasimov174; 189, Moon Jelly, Sergzei; 189, Lion's Mane Jelly, OnePony; 189, By-the-Wind-Sailor, The Ocean Agency; 209, Ghost Crab, Arinahabich; 211, Sand Dollar, hereswendy; 228, Oystercatcher, Brian Kushner; 228, Dunlin, Steve Byland; 291, Baltimore Checkerspot, David; 300, Red-Bellied Woodpecker, brm1949; 334, American Bittern, FotoRequest; 335, Short-Eared Owl, Wenona Suydam; 340, Osprey, Abeselom Zerit; 348, Marsh Rabbit, moosehenderson; 360, Black-Bellied Plover, geraldmarella; 364, Oyster shells, weerayut; 371, Blue Crab, Igor Dudchak; 373, Red Knot, Brian Kushner; 388, Mallard, Andrea; 393, Shoveler, Eric Tofft; 393, Blue-Winged Teal, Paul; 393, Canvasback, Bernie Duhamel; 394, Redhead, Mirko Rosenau; 394, Bufflehead, jnihuz; 394, Common Merganser, Andreanita.

Images used under license from Dollar Photo Club (now owned by Adobe Stock)

101, Right Whale, 25749346; 121, Sea Nettle, helgidinson; 164, Piping Plover, Steve Byland; 189, PMOW, DoctorJools; 191, PMOW top, MSNN; 191, Sea Nettle, Helgidinson; 212, Gray Seal, Mark Bridger; 219, Brown Pelicans, Kenneth Keifer; 228, Black-Bellied Plover, 30255061; 229, Semi-palmated Sandpiper, imaton; 229, Greater Yellowlegs, Glenn Young; 257, Robin, Rachelle Vance; 257, Cardinal, Riverwalker; 257, American Goldfinch, Steve Byland; 257, Red Fox, Pim Leijen; 257, Meadow Vole, CreativeNature; 282, Black-Crowned Night-Heron, 59388274; 292, Cooper's Hawk, Chris Hill; 292, Yellow-Rumped Warbler, birdiegal; 292, American Redstart, Michael Hill; 300, Robin, Rachele Vance; 300, Downy Woodpecker, Greg Williams; 302, White-Tailed Deer, Nicolase Lowe; 302, Raccoon, hkuchera; 302, Deer Mouse, DMM Photography; 302, Chipmunk, elharo; 302, Gray Squirrel, Orhan Cam; 302, Red Squirrel, Anterovium; 303, Flying Squirrel, Tony Campbell; 303, Red Fox, dannytax; 303, Coyote, Josef Pittner; 303, Eastern Cottontail, mandritoiu; 303, Woodchuck, Mario Beauregard; 303, Weasel, hakoar; 334, Greater Yellowlegs, Glenn Young; 335, Blue-Winged Teal, Steve Byland; 335, Gadwall, Steve Oehlenschlage; 335, Clapper Rail, pstclair; 335, Wood Duck, wildphoto4; 338, Greenhead Fly, allocricetulus; 341, Northern Harrier, Steve Byland; 348, Eastern Cottontail, mandritiou; 385, Sea Nettle, helgidinson; 392, Brant, marcobarone; 393, Gadwall, Steve Oehlenschlager; 393, Wigeon, photobyjimshane; 394, Hooded Merganser, Steve Oehlenschlager.

Images used under license from Shutterstock

39, Barnegat Inlet, Eileen-10; 40, Oregon Inlet, Mark Van Dyke; 77, Houston flooding, IrinaK; 101, Teach sign, Lee Snider; 123, Garden State Parkway, EQRoy; 124–25, Atlantic City, Jon Bilious; 127, Star Jet rollercoaster, Mike Ver Sprill; 156, Fowler's Toad, Jeff Holcombe; 181, Soft sand, Joanna-V; 187, Shells on beach, Ryan McGurl; 189, Cannonball Jelly, Sherry V. Smith; 190–91, Cannonball Jelly L, Ymgerman; Cannonball Jelly R, Sky2015; 190–91, Lion's Mane L, Greg Amptman; Lion's Mane R, Konstantin Novikov; 191, PMOW bottom, SciencePics; 191, Northern Comb Jelly, John Wollwerth; 210, Octopus, Safakcakir; 210, Moon Snail, Matthew McClure; 210, Moon Snail collar, Matthew McClure; 210, Hermit Crab, Vagabondivan; 212, Harbor Seal, Wim Claes; 214, Loggerhead nest, Thomas Barrat; 217, Beach Flea, Paul Carpenter; 228, Sanderling, Brian Lesenby; 230–31, Piping Plovers, Ray Hennessy, 231, Least Terns, Ray Hennessy; 247, British Soldiers Lichen, Jenny Webber; 254, Lone Star Tick, Melinda Fawver; 254, Black-Legged Tick, Sarah2; 255, Virginia Opossum, Lisa Hagan; 300, Common Yellowthroat, Paul Reeves; 335, Green-Winged Teal, Erni; 338, Lone Star Tick, Melinda Fawver; 338, Black-Legged Tick, sarah2; 338, American Dog Tick, Elliotte Harold; 346, Snow Goose, Anne Richard; 346, Blue Goose, Agami Photo; 350, Nutria, Sonja Guijarro; 360, Clam Worm, Thongdumhyu; 363, Oyster reef, JoMo333; 364, Oyster reef, Alisha Newton; 377, Blue Crab, Kim Nguyen; 377, Horseshoe Crab in Eelgrass, Ethan Daniels; 384, Olney's Three-Square, SimonaPavan; 392, Tundra Swan, Paul Reeves; 392, Black Duck, Elliotte Harold; 393, Green-Winged Teal, Erni; 394, Ring-Necked Duck, Tim Zurowski; 394, Goldeneye, Tim Zurowski; 395, Red-Breasted Merganser, Ian Maton; 395, Common Coot, Martha Marks; 395, Pied-Billed Grebe, Mircea Costina; 408, Fish kill, Jillian Cain.

Saltwater Cordgrass, Assateague Island National Seashore, Maryland.

Great Egret (Ardea alba)

Index

Note: Page numbers in italic indicate illustrations.

Sunset, Sinepuxent Bay, Assateague Island National Seashore, Maryland

And everyone that heareth these sayings of mine, and doeth them not, shall be likened unto a foolish man, which buildeth his house upon the sand:

And the rain descended, and the floods came, and the winds blew and beat upon that house; and it fell: and great was the fall of it.

Matthew 7: 26–27, King James Version

Bird tracks

Tracks are shown at about 60% life size, as they might look in sand or firm mud.

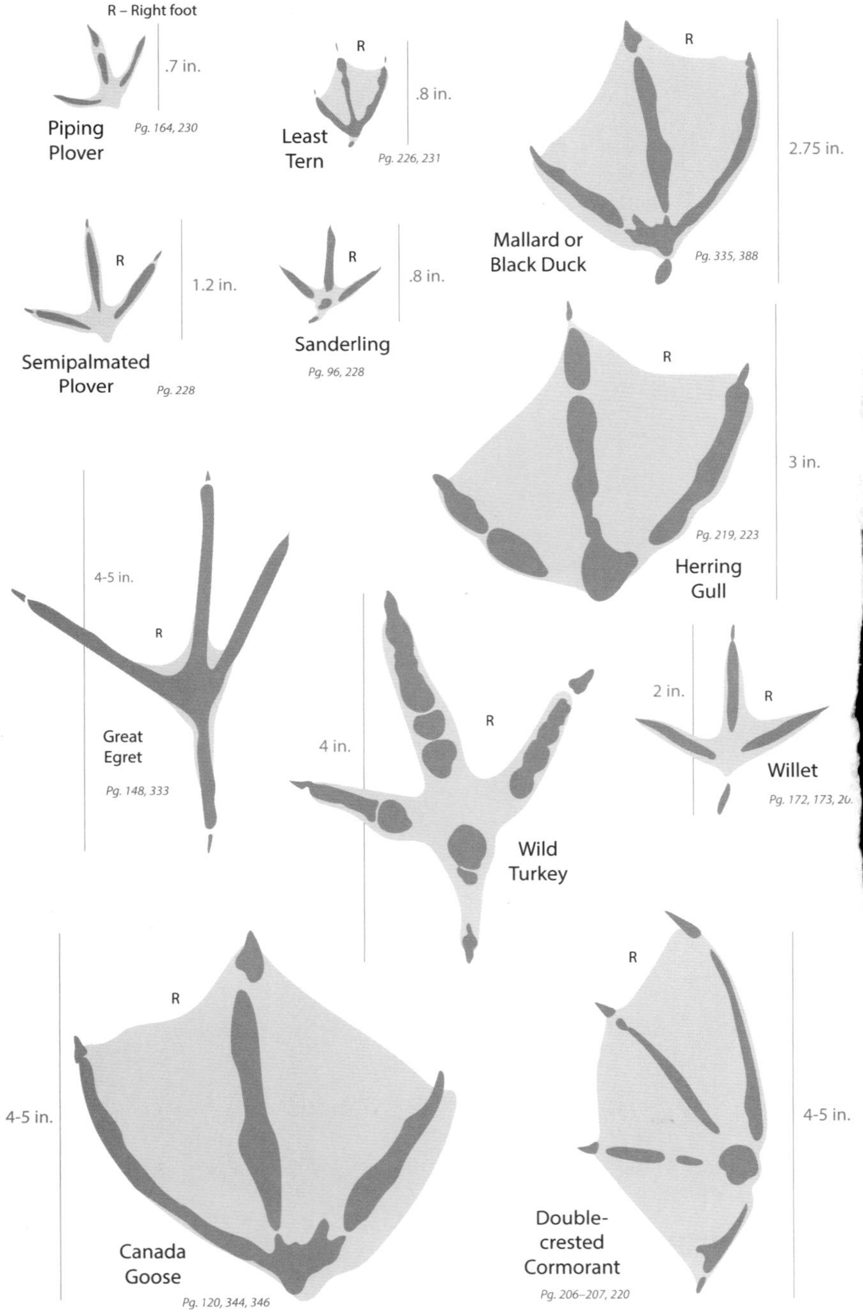

R – Right foot
R
.7 in.
Piping Plover
Pg. 164, 230
R
.8 in.
Least Tern
Pg. 226, 231
R
2.75 in.
Mallard or Black Duck
Pg. 335, 388
R
1.2 in.
Semipalmated Plover
Pg. 228
R
.8 in.
Sanderling
Pg. 96, 228
R
3 in.
Herring Gull
Pg. 219, 223
4-5 in.
R
Great Egret
Pg. 148, 333
4 in.
R
Wild Turkey
2 in.
R
Willet
Pg. 172, 173,
R
4-5 in.
Canada Goose
Pg. 120, 344, 346
R
4-5 in.
Double-crested Cormorant
Pg. 206–207, 220